Plays of To-Day:
First Volume

Plays of To-Day:
First Volume

CHAINS by Elizabeth Baker.
ABRAHAM LINCOLN by John Drinkwater.
JANE CLEGG by St. John Ervine.
THE VOYSEY INHERITANCE by H. Granville-Barker.
HINDLE WAKES by Stanley Houghton.

Play Anthology Reprint Series

BOOKS FOR LIBRARIES PRESS
FREEPORT, NEW YORK

First Published 1925 by Sidgwick & Jackson, Ltd.

Reprinted 1970 by arrangement

NOTICE

ALL these plays are fully protected as regards publication and performance. Possession of this volume confers no right on professional or amateur actors to produce any of these plays, in whole or in part, in public or in private, for charity or otherwise, without written permission from the owners or controllers of the dramatic rights. A notice stating where applications for such permissions should be made is printed on the page facing the opening of each play.

INTERNATIONAL STANDARD BOOK NUMBER:
0-8369-8214-2

LIBRARY OF CONGRESS CATALOG CARD NUMBER:
76-132137

PRINTED IN THE UNITED STATES OF AMERICA

CHAINS

ELIZABETH BAKER

CHAINS

was first produced by the Play Actors at the Court Theatre, London, on April 18, 1909, and revived at the Frohman Repertory Theatre (Duke of York's Theatre), London, on May 17, 1910, with the following cast:

CHARLEY WILSON	Dennis Eadie.
LILY WILSON	Hilda Trevelyan.
FRED TENNANT	Frederick Lloyd.
MAGGIE MASSEY	Sybil Thorndike.
MORTON LESLIE	Arthur Whitby.
SYBIL FROST	Dorothy Minto.
PERCY MASSEY	Donald Calthrop.
ALFRED MASSEY	Edmund Gwenn.
MRS. MASSEY	Florence Haydon.
FENWICK	Lewis Casson.
WALTER FOSTER	Hubert Harben.

Applications for permission to perform this play should be made, for amateur performances, to SAMUEL FRENCH, LTD., Southampton Street, Strand, London, W.C.2; for professional production, to the Author in the care of the Publishers.

CHAINS

ACT I

SCENE : Sitting-room at 55 Acacia Avenue. The principal articles of furniture are the centre table, set for dinner for three, and a sideboard on the right. There are folding doors at the back, leading to the front room, partly hidden by curtains; on the left a low French window leading into the garden. On the right is a fire burning; and above it a door into the kitchen. The furniture of the room is a little mixed in style. A wicker armchair is on one side of the fireplace, a folding carpet-chair on the other. The other chairs, three at the table and two against the walls, are of bent wood. The sideboard is mahogany. The carpet-square over oil-cloth is of an indeterminate pattern in subdued colours, dull crimson predominating. Lace curtains at window. Family photographs, a wedding group and a cricket group, and a big lithograph copy of a Marcus Stone picture, are on the walls. There is a brass alarm clock on the mantelpiece and one or two ornaments. A sewing-machine stands on a small table near the window; and on the edge of this table and on the small table on the other side of the window are pots of cuttings. A couple of bookshelves hang over the machine. A small vase of flowers stands in the centre of the dinner table.

LILY WILSON, *much worried, is laying the centre table. She is a pretty, slight woman, obviously young, wearing a light cotton blouse, dark skirt and big pinafore. The front door is heard to close.* CHARLEY WILSON enters. *He is an ordinary specimen of the city clerk, dressed in correct frock-coat, dark trousers, carefully creased, much cuff and a high collar.*

LILY. Here you are, then. [*She puts up her face and they kiss hurriedly.*] Did I hear Mr. Tennant with you?

CHARLEY. Met on the step.

LILY. How funny! Well, that's nice. We can have dinner almost directly.

CHARLEY. [*putting down his hat carefully on sideboard, and stretching himself slowly, with evident enjoyment.*] Saturday, thank the Lord!

LILY. [*laughing prettily.*] Poor thing!

CHARLEY. [*looking at his silk hat.*] I should like to pitch the beastly thing into the river. [*He shakes his fist at it. Then he stretches his neck as if to lift it out of the collar and shaking down his cuffs till he can get a fine view of them, regards them meditatively.*] Pah!

LILY. [*anxiously.*] What's the matter with them? Are they scorched?

CHARLEY. Scorched! No, they're white enough. Beastly uniform!

LILY. But you must wear cuffs, dear.

CHARLEY. A chap came to the office to-day in a red tie. Old Raffles had him up, and pitched into him. Asked him if he was a Socialist. Chap said he wasn't, but liked red. " So do I," says the Boss, " but I don't wear a golf coat in the city! " Thought he was awfully smart, and it did make Poppy swear.

LILY. Who's Poppy, dear?

CHARLEY. Popperwell. He almost left there and then. Said he should wear whatever tie he liked.

LILY. It would have been rather silly of him, wouldn't it? He's so sure there.

CHARLEY. That's what he said. He thought better of it and swallowed it. Well—dinner ready?

LILY. Waiting.

CHARLEY. [*going out.*] I'll be down in a jiffy.

LILY *goes to the fire.* TENNANT *heard outside whistling a bar of the song* "*Off to Philadelphia*". *He comes in. He is a broad-shouldered young fellow, a little shy in his manner with women.*

TENNANT. Nice day, Mrs. Wilson.

LILY. Beautiful.

TENNANT. I've brought you home the paper, if you'd like it. It's the " Daily Mirror ".

LILY. Oh, thank you. I do like the pictures. Charley is getting so dreadfully serious now in his reading, and won't buy it. He takes the " Daily Telegraph ". He thinks the gardening notes are so good.

TENNANT. He's luxurious. It's a penny.

LILY. Oh, he shares it with somebody. [*Pause.*]

TENNANT. How goes the garden?

LILY. It's rather trying—I should like to give up those peas and things, and have chickens. They would be so useful.

LILY *goes out.* TENNANT *takes a map out of his pocket and stands studying it.* CHARLEY *and* LILY *enter together.* CHARLEY *has made a wonderful change into a loose, rather creased suit of bright brown, flannel shirt with soft collar, flowing tie and old slippers. A pipe is sticking out of one pocket, and a newspaper out of the other. They sit down, and* LILY *tries not to look worried as* CHARLEY *laboriously cuts the small joint which she has brought in with her and put before him. He splashes the gravy a little and has to use the sharpener.* LILY *serves vegetables.*

CHARLEY. I think I shall get one of Robertson's pups.

LILY. It would be lovely.

CHARLEY. He's got one he'll let me have cheap.

TENNANT. I saw them last night. They're a good breed. Make fine house-dogs.

CHARLEY. That's what you want round here. A quiet neighbourhood like this is A1 for burglars.

LILY. You don't think we shall have any, do you?

CHARLEY. No. 24 had 'em the other night.

TENNANT. What were they after?

LILY. 24? That's the new people. What a shame!

CHARLEY. Wanted the wedding presents.

LILY. And Mrs. Thompson told me they had real silver at 24.

CHARLEY. Trust the burglars for knowing that. They won't risk their skins for electro. So we shan't have 'em.

LILY. Charley! You forget the biscuit barrel and the tray.

TENNANT. Where's the bobby?

LILY. There's only one about here.

CHARLEY. They don't have bobbies for burgles in these sort of places, only for rows. And we don't have rows. We're too respectable.

LILY. I think it's so mean of burglars to come to people like us.

CHARLEY. [*with a burst of laughter.*] Let 'em go to Portman Square, you say?

LILY. Well, of course, it's wrong to steal at all; but it doesn't seem quite so bad. [*She stops, a little confused.*]

TENNANT. Of course it isn't.

CHARLEY. [*lying back comfortably in his chair.*] Going away Sunday?

TENNANT. No—the fact is—

LILY. Maggie is coming round this afternoon. Shall we ask the Leslies for whist to-night?

CHARLEY. All right. Don't make it too early, though. [*Looking out of the French windows into the garden.*] I've got to get in my peas.

TENNANT. Green peas?

CHARLEY. Green peas in that patch? My dear chap, don't I wish I could!

LILY. [*to* TENNANT.] Have some more?

TENNANT. No, thanks.

CHARLEY. For one thing, there's the soil! It's rotten. Then there're the sparrows..

LILY. Some of them are so tame, dear, and they don't seem to care a bit for the cat next door.

CHARLEY. [*bitterly.*] They don't care for anything. I wish they'd take a fancy to a few snails.

LILY. They don't eat snails.

CHARLEY. You spoil 'em. She gives 'em soaked bread all through the winter, and then expects me to grow things. Lord!

> LILY *collects plates.* TENNANT *goes out.* CHARLEY *lights pipe.* CHARLEY *goes to window, where he stands leaning against the post and smoking.*

LILY. The baby across the road is such a darling, Charley.

CHARLEY. Is it?

LILY. The girl was out with it this morning, and I called her over.

CHARLEY. What is it?

LILY. It's a boy.

> CHARLEY'S *replies are without interest and he continues to gaze out into garden.*

They're going to call him Theodore Clement Freeman. It's rather a lot, isn't it?

CHARLEY. What's he got it all for?

LILY. After her father and his father, and Freeman is a family name.

CHARLEY. What did they want to give 'em all to him for? They should keep some for the next.

LILY. Charley!

CHARLEY. It's silly. Still, it's their business.

LILY. It might be a girl.

CHARLEY. Well—there's the others.

LILY. Charley!

CHARLEY. My dear girl, why not?
LILY. I don't like you to speak like that.
CHARLEY. I— [*Stops suddenly, looks at her, and comes over. He takes her face between his hands.*] You silly! [*Kisses her.*]

LILY *goes out with a tray of things singing.* CHARLEY *rolls up his sleeves and goes into the garden.*

TENNANT *comes in and looks round.* CHARLEY *comes to the window with a spade.*

TENNANT. You—er—busy?
CHARLEY. [*lighting his pipe.*] Um! Want a job? There's a nice little lot of squirming devils under that flower-pot that want killing. Take your time over it.
TENNANT. Thanks. My fancy doesn't lie in gardening.
CHARLEY. Filthy soil, this.
TENNANT. Mrs. Wilson would like to keep chickens.
CHARLEY. Not if I know it! I'd rather go into a flat. [*Leaning against the door and smoking thoughtfully.*] I could chuck the lot sometimes. These twopenny-halfpenny back-yards make me sick.

Pause.

I'd give something for a piece of good land. Something to pay you for your labour. [*Rousing.*] Well—going out?
TENNANT. [*uneasily.*] Yes—presently.
CHARLEY. [*turning to look at him*]. What's up?
TENNANT. I've—er—got some news for you.
CHARLEY. Anything wrong?
TENNANT. No—no! The fact is—I'm going to hook it.
CHARLEY. [*astonished.*] Hook it? Where to?
TENNANT. I'm sick of the whole show. I can't stand it any longer.
CHARLEY. [*trying to realise the situation.*] Do you mean you've left Molesey's?
TENNANT. Yes. I'm going to leave England—and so, you see, I've got to leave here—your place.

CHARLEY. Leave England? Got a crib?
TENNANT. No, nothing.
CHARLEY. What are you going for, then?
TENNANT. Because I'm sick of it.
CHARLEY. So am I, and so are others. Do you mean you are just going out because you want a change?
TENNANT. That's about it. I've had enough of grind.
CHARLEY. Well, perhaps you'll get grind somewhere else.
TENNANT. It'll be a change of grind, then. That's something.
CHARLEY. Canada?
TENNANT. No, Australia.
CHARLEY. Phew! That's a long shot. Got any friends there?
TENNANT. No.
CHARLEY. It's a bit risky, isn't it?
TENNANT. Of course it's risky. But who wouldn't have a little risk instead of that beastly hole every day for years? Scratch, scratch, scratch, and nothing in the end, mind you?
CHARLEY. [*ironically.*] You might become a junior partner.
TENNANT. [*ignoring the remark.*] Suppose I stay there. They'll raise the screw every year till I get what they think is enough for me. Then you just stick. I suppose I should marry and have a little house somewhere, and grind on.
CHARLEY. [*looking round.*] Like me.
LILY *heard singing*.
TENNANT. No offence, old chap. It's all right for some. It suits you. You're used to it. I want to see things a bit before I settle.
CHARLEY *is silent. His pipe has gone out and he is staring at the floor.*

So I thought I'd go the whole plunge. I've got a little cash, of course, so I shan't starve at first, anyhow.

    CHARLEY *makes no remark.* TENNANT *becomes apologetic.*

I'm—I feel a bit of a beast—but the fact is—I—it was decided in a hurry—I—er—

    CHARLEY *looks up.*

I'm going on Monday.

    CHARLEY. On Monday! Why, that's the day after to-morrow.

    TENNANT. Yes, I know. It was like this. I heard of a man who's going Monday—a man I know—and it came over me all at once, why shouldn't I go too? I went to see him Friday—kept it dark here till I'd seen the guv'nor, and now it's all fixed. I'm awfully sorry to have played you like this—

    CHARLEY. Oh, rot! That's nothing. But I say, it's the rummest go I ever heard of. What did Molesey say?

    TENNANT. Slapped me on the back! What d'ye think of that? I thought he'd call me a fool. He pointed out that I could stay there for ever, if I liked—which was jolly decent of him—but when I said I'd rather not, thanks muchly, he banged me on the back, and said he wished he could do the same and cut the office. He didn't even stop the money for notice.

    CHARLEY. Did he give you a £5 note?

    TENNANT. [*laughing.*] You don't want much. The old chap was quite excited, asked me to write—how's that?

    Pause.

[*Rising.*] The thing is—I can't see why I didn't go before. Why did I ever go into the beastly office? There was nobody to stop me going to Timbuctoo, if I liked. I say, will you tell Mrs. Wilson?

    CHARLEY. She's only in the kitchen. Lil!—Lil! [*Shouting.*]

    LILY. [*from outside.*] Yes, dear.

CHARLEY. Come here! Here's news.
LILY *enters, wiping her hands on her pinafore and smiling.*
LILY. Yes?
CHARLEY. [*waving his pipe towards* TENNANT.] What d'ye think he's going to do?
LILY. [*studying* TENNANT *seriously.*] Do? How—
TENNANT. [*nervously.*] I—I'm going to leave you, Mrs. Wilson.
LILY. To leave us? [*With enlightenment.*] You're going to be married!
TENNANT. Good Heavens, no! Not that!
CHARLEY. Whatever made you think of that?
LILY. What else could he do?
TENNANT. I'm going abroad.
Going over to the garden door.
CHARLEY. He's going to seek his fortune. Lucky dog!
LILY. Have you got a good appointment, Mr. Tennant?
TENNANT. No, nothing. I'm going on the chance.
LILY. Whatever for? Didn't you like Molesey's?
TENNANT. Oh, they were good enough and all that, but I got sick of the desk. I'm going farming.
LILY. And throwing up a good situation?
TENNANT. I suppose you'd call it good.
LILY. It was so sure. You'd have been head clerk in time. I'm sure you would. It does seem such a pity.
TENNANT. Sounds a bit foolish, I expect.
LILY. Of course you must get tired of it sometimes. But to throw it up altogether! I do hope you won't be sorry for it. Charley gets tired of it sometimes—don't you, dear?
CHARLEY. [*from the garden door.*] Just a bit—now and then.
LILY. Everybody does, I expect. It would be very

nice, of course, to see other places and all that—but you can always travel in your holidays.

CHARLEY. How far on the Continong can you go in a fortnight, Lil?

TENNANT. I don't think you quite understand. It isn't so much that I want to see things—though that'd be jolly—but I want a change of work.

LILY. [*sympathetically.*] It is trying to do the same thing over and over again. But then the hours are not so very long, are they?

CHARLEY. Nine to six, with an hour for lunch and tea thrown in. Count your many blessings, Freddy.

LILY. [*reproachfully, and crossing to him.*] You know, Charley, we've often talked it over, and you've said how regular the hours were.

CHARLEY. So they are.

CHARLEY *disappears for a moment into garden, but is now and again to be seen outside the door with a flower-pot or some other thing for the garden.*

LILY. And you have the evenings, and they give you Saturday morning at Molesey's as you get on, don't they?

TENNANT. Yes, it's all true, Mrs. Wilson—but I can't stand it. Anybody can have the job.

CHARLEY. It's the spring, Freddy. That's the matter with you.

LILY. I do hope you won't be sorry for it. It would be so dreadful if you failed, after giving up such a good situation. Of course we are very sorry to lose you, Mr. Tennant—you have been so kind.

TENNANT. [*hastily and with much embarrassment.*] Oh, please don't.

LILY. And we have always got on so very well together. I'm sure it will be very difficult to get any one to suit us so well again. But you won't forget us, and if we have your address, we can write sometimes—

CHARLEY. And if anything striking occurs, I'll send a

cable. The novelty will be worth it. [*Coming just inside the door with the spade in his hand.*] For the rest, I'll describe one day and you can tick it off for the whole lot of the others. Rise at 7, breakfast; catch the 8.30, City—
The door-bell is heard.
Who on earth—!
He goes into the garden.
LILY. Maggie, I expect.
She goes out.
TENNANT, *after making a step towards the garden, turns to the door, only to meet* MAGGIE MASSEY *and* LILY. MAGGIE *is of medium height, well-proportioned, good-looking without being pretty.*
MAGGIE. [*shaking hands with* TENNANT.] How do you do?
LILY. What do you think, Maggie? Mr. Tennant is going to leave us. Guess what for!
MAGGIE. He's going to be married?
CHARLEY. Good Lord! There's another.
MAGGIE. Hullo, Charles, you there!
LILY. He's going to leave England.
MAGGIE. How nice for him!
LILY. [*emphatically.*] Nice! But he's got nothing to do there!
MAGGIE. [*to* TENNANT.] Are you going to emigrate?
TENNANT. Yes; I'm going to Australia to try my luck.
CHARLEY. Isn't he an idiot?
MAGGIE. Do you think so?
CHARLEY. Throwing up a nice snug little place at Molesey's and rushing himself on to the already overstocked labour market of the Colonies.
MAGGIE. You are really going on your luck?
TENNANT. Yes.
MAGGIE. How fine!
LILY. Maggie! Think of the risk!

MAGGIE. He's a man. It doesn't matter.

LILY. If he'd been out of work, it would have been so very different.

MAGGIE. That would have spoilt the whole thing. I admire his pluck.

LILY. Well, he's got no one depending on him, so he will suffer alone.

MAGGIE. You're not very encouraging, Lil. I have heard of a married man doing the same.

CHARLEY. [*quickly.*] Who was that?

LILY. How very foolish!

MAGGIE. Oh, he was already out of work.

LILY. That is different—although even then—

MAGGIE. His wife went to live with her people again and he went out to the Colonies and made a home for her.

LILY. [*sceptically.*] How did he do that?

MAGGIE. I don't know. You are quite free to do as you like, aren't you, Mr. Tennant? How does that feel?

TENNANT. I have only just started to think about it. Directly the idea came into my head, off I had to go.

CHARLEY, *who has stood listening, turns slowly and walks away.*

MAGGIE. You are lucky to have found it out in time.

TENNANT. In time?

MAGGIE. Before you got too old to do anything.
Pause.

CHARLEY. [*near the garden window, but outside.*] Climb on to the dustbin, only mind the lid's on tight.

TENNANT. That's Leslie coming over. I'll go. [*Goes.*]

Enter from the garden MORTON LESLIE, *a big fair man, clean-shaven, lazy and good-natured.* CHARLEY *follows.*

LESLIE. I nearly smashed your husband, Mrs. Wilson . . Good day, Miss Maggie—and I'm sure I've absolutely killed Mr. Wilson's beans.

CHARLEY. If you don't the birds will—and if they don't

the worms will—and—how can you expect anything to grow in that garden?

LESLIE. I thought it was such an excellent Small Holding! What about the carrots?

CHARLEY. Pah! Carrots! Why not peaches? Come on, Leslie! I've got the papers in the other room.

CHARLEY *lifts the curtain and they go into the front room.*

LILY. I'm afraid Charley must be tired. He seems quite irritable.

MAGGIE. So am I when I get home from business. [*Throwing out her arms and smiling at* LILY.] No more shop for me in a month or two, Lil.

LILY. [*excitedly.*] You're going to marry Mr. Foster?

MAGGIE *nods.*

Oh, how lovely! How nice for you, dear! I am so glad. What did mother say?

MAGGIE. [*with a little laugh.*] Mother is charmed.

LILY. Everybody is, of course. He is such a nice man. He will spoil you, Maggie. You lucky girl!

MAGGIE. Yes, I suppose I am.

LILY. You don't like to show it, of course, dear.

MAGGIE. Don't I? You should have seen me last night! I took off my shop collar and apron and put them on the floor and danced on them—till mother came to see what was the matter.

LILY. You must be fond of him, dear.

MAGGIE. No, I'm not, particularly.

LILY. Maggie!

MAGGIE. [*walking up and down.*] That's funny now. I didn't mean to say that. It just came. [*A pause.*] How queer! [*A pause.*] Well, it's the truth, anyway. At least, it's not quite true. When I came here to-day I was awfully happy about it—I am fond of him at least—I—well —he's very nice—you know. [*Irritably.*] What did you want to start this for, Lil?

VOL. I   C

LILY. [*aggrieved.*] I start it? I did nothing.

MAGGIE. I was so satisfied when I came.

LILY. [*soothingly and taking her sister's hat and coat from her.*] You're a little tired, dear. We'll have an early cup of tea. Have you got your ring, dear?

MAGGIE *holds out her left hand.*

How sweet! Sapphires! He must be rich, Maggie.

Pause.

MAGGIE. I wish I was a good housekeeper, Lil.

LILY. [*reassuring.*] Oh, you'll soon learn, dear; and his other housekeeper wasn't very good.

MAGGIE. I wasn't thinking of that.

LILY. But you talked of housekeeping, dear.

MAGGIE. Yes, but that's quite different from being married. If I could cook decently, I would have left the shop before.

LILY. But you are going to leave the shop!

MAGGIE. [*unheeding.*] Or if I understood anything about the house properly, but I couldn't be even a mother's help unless I could wash.

LILY. I don't know what you mean, Maggie. You haven't got to wash. You know Mr. Foster can afford to send it all out. [*Sighing enviously.*] That must be nice.

MAGGIE. I heard of a girl the other day, Fanny White—you know her—she's gone to Canada.

LILY. Canada! Who's talking about Canada? What's that to do—?

MAGGIE. I was envious. She used to be with us at the shop.

LILY. [*impatiently.*] Yes, I know. Well, you've done better than she, anyway, Maggie, if she is going to Canada. She'll only be a servant, after all. What else can she do? And then in the end she'll marry some farmer man and have to work fearfully hard—I've heard about the women over there—and wish she had never left

England. While here are you, going to marry a rich man who's devoted to you, with plenty of money and long holidays, and your own servant to begin with! Really, Maggie—!

MAGGIE. [*stretching a little and smiling.*] Isn't it gorgeous? [*Shaking herself.*] Well—it must be Mr. Tennant's fault. He shouldn't get mad ideas into his head—

LILY. And he really is mad. Throwing up a most excellent situation. My dear, I call him just stupid!

CHARLEY. [*lifting the curtain and coming forward with* LESLIE.] There's no hurry.

LESLIE. Oh, I'll start on it to-night. My wife's gone away and left me for the day, and I'm a forsaken grass widower.

LILY. [*laughing.*] Poor Mr. Leslie! Won't you come in here to-night? Don't you think it would be very nice, Charley, as Mr. Tennant is going so soon—

LESLIE. Tennant? Where's he going?

MAGGIE. You'll never guess.

LESLIE. He's leaving you? He's going to get married?

CHARLEY. [*impatiently.*] You're as bad as a woman!

MAGGIE. I thought you more brilliant, Mr. Leslie.

LESLIE. I thought of the happiest thing that could happen to a man, Miss Maggie.

LILY. No, it's not marrying. He's going abroad.

LESLIE. Got a fortune?

MAGGIE. He's just going to try his luck. He's emigrating.

LESLIE. What a fool! He's got the sack, I suppose?

MAGGIE. No. He's thrown it up.

LESLIE. Thrown up a safe job? Oh, he's an ass, a stupid ass! You surely don't ask me to come and wish good luck to an ass?

MAGGIE. You can help with a dirge then.

LESLIE. Much more like it. But, I say, is it really true? He must have got something to go to?

CHARLEY. He hasn't. He's got a little cash, of course. He's always been a careful beast.

LESLIE. And he's going to throw it away! And then I suppose he'll be out of work over there, and we shall be hearing of the unemployment in the Colonies! It's just this sort of thing that makes a man a Conservative. It's what I call getting off the ladder and deliberately kicking it down.

CHARLEY. Well, I don't, then. I think he's a lucky chap to be able to do something he likes. He's got some pluck.

LILY. Why, dear, you know you think it's very silly of him!

LESLIE. [*laughing*.] You must look after your husband, Mrs. Wilson, I can see. He'll be running away. Well, so long, old chap! I'll come back later. Just give me a hitch over the wall. You'll be sorry about those beans next week. [*Pause*.]

They go out. A crash is heard.

CHARLEY. Hullo! What's up?

LESLIE. [*in the distance*.] Smashed a box of tomato plants. Phew!

LILY, *laughing, goes out with* MAGGIE.

*A long whistle—*CHARLEY *comes back into the room and stands looking into the fire. Pause.*

Enter TENNANT.

TENNANT. I'm just going round to Carter's. Anything you want? [*Pause*.] I suppose Leslie had something to say about me?

CHARLEY. He doesn't want to come with you.

TENNANT *laughs*.

You don't seem to know much about it, but I suppose you've fixed on a town. Sydney?

TENNANT. No, Brisbane. [*Pulling out a map*.] The chap I know is cattle-raising. Look!

He opens the map on the table: they both lean over it, CHARLEY'S *burnt-out pipe still in his hand.*

We're going to Brisbane, then this way [*moving his finger*] across Queensland. He knows something at Merivale—here—see—in the Darling district. Then we shall push on to Maronoa—that's the county—we're going to a tiny place—Terramoa—but of course I mayn't get anything—

CHARLEY. [*who is practically lying over the map.*] Not fruit-farming then? That's more my line.

TENNANT. No. If ever you thought of that—see—this is a good district—I heard of a man there once—see—this way—Ship to Sydney—Vineyards and all sorts—suit you.

CHARLEY. U-m! Or one could go this way. [*Pointing with his pipe.*]

LILY'S *voice heard calling " Charley "—*TENNANT *stands upright.*

LILY. [*enters—laughing.*] Charley! What are you doing?

CHARLEY *jumps up and* TENNANT *folds up the map.* Looking at the plans?

TENNANT. I'm off.

Goes out.

LILY. Finished gardening already, dear?

CHARLEY. [*putting on his coat.*] Don't feel like it.

LILY. [*holding out a newspaper.*] Look here, dear, this will do for us, I think.

CHARLEY. [*glancing round.*] What is it?

LILY. An advertisement. [*Reading.*] " Wanted, by Young Man, board-residence in quiet family within easy reach of city. Western suburb preferred." I must answer it.

CHARLEY. I say—give Tennant a chance to get out first.

LILY. But he is going, dear, so there's no risk. And it's such a good chance. Besides, we can ask Mr Tennant for a reference.

CHARLEY. [*sharply.*] No, don't. Surely we can exist a week without anybody.

LILY. Oh yes! Only I thought—it's a pity to miss— You don't want Mr. Tennant to go, do you, dear? He is nice company for you.

CHARLEY. He's a nice chap. But you needn't get lodgers to keep me company.

LILY. [*laughs.*] What an idea! Of course not.

CHARLEY. [*going to her and turning her face towards him.*] I say, Lil, aren't you ever dull here?

LILY. No—well—hardly ever. There's always something to do. What a question!

CHARLEY. Don't you ever get sick of it? It's jolly hard work sometimes. [*He takes her hands and looks at them, stroking them as if unconsciously.*] Why, they're getting quite rough. [*She pulls them away.*]

LILY. It's the washing, dear. It does roughen your hands.

CHARLEY. [*taking them again and kissing them.*] They weren't rough when we married.

LILY. [*she turns away.*] You silly boy, of course they weren't. I never did washing at home. What do you think, dear? Maggie is going to be married.

CHARLEY. [*with little interest.*] To Foster?

LILY. Yes. Isn't she lucky? He's quite well off.

CHARLEY. So she won't do the washing. I shall never be rich.

LILY. You'll be head clerk one of these days.

CHARLEY. One of these days!

LILY. And then we'll have a servant.

CHARLEY. Perhaps I shall never be head clerk.

LILY. Oh yes, you will!

CHARLEY. I don't know that I'm excited at the idea —a sort of policeman over the other chaps. I'd rather be as I am.

LILY. But think of the position—and the money!

CHARLEY *nods gloomily—he walks to garden door.* Where's your ambition, dear?

CHARLEY. Perfectly safe. No fear of that getting lost. The man who built that road [*pointing out of the window*] ought to be hanged.

LILY. They're not very pretty, those houses. Mrs. Freeman told me this morning that they're going to raise our rents a little.

CHARLEY. [*turning round sharply.*] What? That's because they've brought the fares down. Just like 'em.

LILY. I was thinking this morning, dear, that perhaps we could take two boarders. It would help a little. That little room at the back, over the scullery, would do nicely with a single bed.

CHARLEY. That's where I keep my cuttings and things.

LILY. Yes, dear, but you could have half the coal shed. We never fill it.

CHARLEY. I don't want the coal shed. I say—must we have two?

LILY. It would make things better, dear.

CHARLEY. But it's beastly, choking up your house with a lot of fellers. You don't like it, do you?

LILY. No, dear, of course not.

CHARLEY. You don't seem much put out.

LILY. It's no good being cross about it, dear, is it? If it's got to be done, we may as well make the best of it.

CHARLEY. Oh, make the best of it. [*Fretfully.*] You might at least seem vexed.

LILY. [*patiently.*] Of course I don't like it, dear, and of course I'd much rather be alone with you and have all my house to myself—though really the boarders don't worry much, you know. They are always home late and only have meals with us.

CHARLEY. Who wants 'em at meals? I don't, if you do!

LILY. [*pathetically.*] You are very unkind. I never said I wanted them. I'm only doing my best to make things smooth. You might help me, Charley. [*She turns away.*]

CHARLEY. [*crossing to* LILY *and patting her on her hand.*] I'll be all right later. But I say it is a bit thick. An Englishman's home is his castle. I like that! Why, the only place where you can be alone is the bedroom. We'll be letting that next. [*He laughs sarcastically.*]

LILY. [*shocked.*] Charley! What are you saying?

CHARLEY. Ha, ha, what a joke! The—well, never mind. The day we let the bathroom, Lil—I'm off to the Colonies. [*He stops, suddenly struck with a thought.*]

LILY. You silly boy.

CHARLEY. Supposing I did, eh?

LILY. We're not going to let the bathroom, so you needn't suppose anything.

CHARLEY. [*abstractedly—sitting on a corner of the table.*] Why not?

LILY. Did you speak, dear?

CHARLEY. [*starting.*] Eh?—No, no!—nothing.

LILY *goes, closing door.*

CURTAIN

ACT II

SCENE: *Sitting-room at 55 Acacia Avenue. The folding doors between front and back parlour are opened, with red curtains looped up. The front parlour, a glimpse of which is visible between curtains, is in full light and a corner of the piano can be seen. The furniture in this room is of the imitation Sheraton variety. There is an ornamental overmantel with photographs and vases, and a marble clock in the middle of the mantelpiece.*
Some one is playing the piano, and LILY, *standing beside it, is singing in a sweet but rather weak voice, "Sing me to sleep". No one is in the back parlour, but through the curtains can be seen* MORTON LESLIE, *lolling on mantelpiece;* SYBIL FROST, *a pretty fair-haired girl, much given to laughing at everything;* PERCY MASSEY, *a good-looking, somewhat weak youth of perhaps twenty-one or twenty-two, sitting very close to* SYBIL, *and* TENNANT, *standing in the bay window.*
CHARLEY *comes in quietly through the side door into the back parlour during the singing. When* LILY *comes to the refrain of the song, every one except* CHARLEY *joins in. He stays in the back parlour, and sitting down in the shadow, lights a cigarette.* LILY *sits down amid a good deal of clapping and words of admiration.*

SYBIL. I do love that song.
PERCY. Now, you sing something.
SYBIL. [*with a giggle.*] I couldn't really—you know I couldn't.

PERCY. Oh yes, you can—that nice little coon thing you sang at the Richards'.

SYBIL. I've got a cold.

MAGGIE. [*crossing from piano.*] Of course you have.

SYBIL. [*laughing.*] But it's quite true. Really. And I couldn't really sing after Mrs. Wilson.

LILY. Sybil! Do sing, please.

LESLIE. We're all waiting, Miss Frost.

SYBIL. Oh, please—I can't. Let some one else sing first.

> MAGGIE *comes to the doorway and catches sight of* CHARLEY. *She comes in. In the front parlour* SYBIL *can be seen still resisting, while* LILY, LESLIE, *and* PERCY MASSEY *beseech her.*

MAGGIE. You here—all alone?

CHARLEY. 'Um.

MAGGIE. What's the matter?

CHARLEY. Nothing.

MAGGIE. Why didn't you come into the front room?

CHARLEY. I can hear quite as well here.

MAGGIE. Got the hump?

CHARLEY. What for? Head's a bit nasty, so I'm smoking it off.

MAGGIE. It isn't that—it's all this about Tennant.

CHARLEY. [*irritably.*] I'm not grieving over him, if that's what you mean.

MAGGIE. As if I did! and as if you'd confess if you were. Are you sick of everything?

CHARLEY. Sick! I'd cut the whole beastly show to-morrow if— [*He stops suddenly.*]

> LILY'S *voice can be heard distinctly from the front room.*

LILY. Well, we'll ask Mr. Tennant to sing first.

SYBIL. Oh, I can't sing, really—

CHARLEY. Why doesn't the girl sing when she's asked?

MAGGIE. She says she has a cold. [*She laughs a little.*]

CHARLEY. Rot! Affectation I call it.

MAGGIE. Percy's awfully smitten, isn't he?

CHARLEY. [*surprised.*] With her?

MAGGIE. Of course. But you haven't noticed that. Lily's been arranging it.

CHARLEY. But he's such a kid.

MAGGIE. He's twenty-two.

CHARLEY. What's that?

MAGGIE. Lots of men marry at twenty-two.

CHARLEY. More fools they! Getting tied up before they've seen anything.

MAGGIE. [*thoughtfully.*] I can never understand why a man gets married. He's got so many chances to see the world and do things—and then he goes and marries and settles down and is a family man before he's twenty-four.

CHARLEY. It's a habit.

MAGGIE. If I were a man I wouldn't stay in England another week. I wouldn't be a quill-driver all my life.

    CHARLEY *gets up and walks restlessly up and down the room.*

If I were a man—

CHARLEY. Men can't do everything.

MAGGIE. I say, don't you think it's fine of Mr. Tennant to throw up everything and take the risk?

CHARLEY. I'd do the same if . .

LILY. [*coming forward a little.*] Where's Charley? Oh, never mind, I daresay he's got a lantern and is looking for worms or something. Are you ready, Mr. Tennant?

MAGGIE. I wonder what Lil would say if you did!

    CHARLEY *stops dead and looks at* MAGGIE.

CHARLEY. If I did? What are you talking about?

MAGGIE. Why shouldn't you?

CHARLEY. Why shouldn't I? Aren't there a thousand reasons?

MAGGIE. There's Lily, certainly—but . .

CHARLEY. She wouldn't understand. She'd think I was deserting her.

A pause.

But that's not all. I might manage her—I don't know—but—you see, I've got a berth I can stay in all my life . .

TENNANT *starts singing the first verse of " Off to Philadelphia ".*

It's like throwing up a dead cert. And then . .

MAGGIE. It would be a splash.

CHARLEY. Yes — and think of all your people! What'd they say? They'd say I was running away from Lil—of course, it would seem like it. . .

Another pause.

It's impossible. I might never get anything to do—and then—

His voice is suddenly drowned as the front room party sing the chorus " With my Knapsack ". etc. Knock at front door.

I—

MAGGIE. I believe I heard a knock.

She goes out in corridor as TENNANT *commences the second verse.*

CHARLEY *sits on the edge of the table watching and listening. The door opens and* MAGGIE *enters, followed by* FENWICK. FENWICK *is a man of middle age, short and slight, with a quiet, rather crushed manner.*

MAGGIE. Mr. Fenwick didn't want to come in when he heard all the singing. He thought we had a party.

She goes through curtains.

CHARLEY. Oh, it's nothing—a sort of family sing-song.

FENWICK. Miss Massey would have me come in—but really I'd rather come some other—

CHARLEY. Stuff! Sit down. I'll pull the curtains if it's anything special you've come about. I thought it was perhaps over those geranium cuttings. Afterwards, if you feel like it, we'll go and join them. [*Draws curtains and turns up light.*] Freddy Tennant—you know him, don't you—he's going to seek his fortune in the Colonies.

FENWICK. Is he?

CHARLEY. Yes, and we'll drink his health. What's up?

FENWICK. I didn't see you at the train to-day.

CHARLEY. No, you were late. I came on with Malcolm.

FENWICK. The chief sent for me.

CHARLEY. Wasn't a rise, I suppose?

FENWICK. Do I look like it? It's the other thing.

CHARLEY. Docking?

FENWICK. [*nodding first and then speaking slowly.*] He said he'd sent for me as senior of my department. The company has had a bad year and they can't give the usual rises.

CHARLEY. None?

FENWICK. None. Haven't you had a letter?

CHARLEY. No. I say, have I got the sack?

FENWICK. No, you haven't. But they're offering you the same alternative they offered me—stay on at less—or go.

CHARLEY. [*walking up and down.*] What are you going to do?

FENWICK. What can I do? Stay, of course—what else is there?

CHARLEY. Sit down under it?

FENWICK. What else?

Postman's knock.

CHARLEY. There's the postman. Wait a bit.

He goes out R. and the voices in the other room can be distinctly heard laughing, while some one is playing a waltz tune very brilliantly.

CHARLEY *comes back with a letter in his hand, closes door, and music dies down.*

CHARLEY. Here it is. [*He opens and reads it, then throws it on the table.*]

FENWICK. A bit of a blow, isn't it?

CHARLEY. I didn't expect it. Did you?

FENWICK. Not until last week when Morgan started making inquiries as to salaries, et cetera. Then I guessed.

CHARLEY. We can't do anything.

FENWICK. Of course not.

CHARLEY. But I say, you know, it's all rot about a bad year. Don't expect we've been exactly piling it up, but it's nothing to grumble about.

FENWICK. That doesn't affect us, anyway. We've got to do as we're told. I fancy old Morgan is hit, too. He was sugary, but of course he had to obey the instructions of the directors, and so on.

CHARLEY. It's no good swearing at him.

FENWICK. It's no good swearing at anybody. What's a Board? Where is it?

The curtains part and LILY *appears in the opening.*

LILY. Charley—are you there? Are you never coming back? Oh, Mr. Fenwick!

FENWICK *rises; shake hands.*

FENWICK. Good evening. I'm afraid I'm an awful nuisance, but I just called to see your husband about a little business.

LILY. You'll stay to supper, won't you? You and Charley can sit and talk business the whole time. I'm afraid Charley doesn't like music very much—do you, dear?

CHARLEY. Oh, sometimes.

LILY. [*big laugh from behind curtains.*] You should hear Mr. Leslie. He's so funny, he's been giving Mr. Tennant advice what to do when he's a lonely bachelor in Australia. He made us roar with laughter.

Goes back laughing.

CHARLEY. Silly ass!

FENWICK. [*startled.*] What?

CHARLEY. That chap Leslie! It'd do him good to go to Australia for a bit. He'd stick to his berth if they docked his screw to ten bob. He's got no pride in him.

FENWICK. Well, we—at least, I—can't say much—I'm going to stay on. You, too, I suppose.

CHARLEY. [*with a sort of defiance.*] Why should I? What's to hinder me leaving? Why shouldn't I go to Morgan and say, " Look here—just tell those directors that I won't stand it! I'm not going to be put up or down—take this or that—at their will and pleasure "?

There is a burst of laughter from the inner room.

FENWICK. That's all very well—and if you've got something else—

CHARLEY. [*fiercely.*] I haven't—not an idea of one —but why should that hinder? Look at Tennant, he's chucked his job and no one wanted to take off anything.

FENWICK. [*quite undisturbed.*] Tennant? Oh, he's going to the Colonies? Very risky. I nearly went there myself once.

CHARLEY. Why didn't you quite?

FENWICK. Various things. All my people were against it. Oh, well, what was the good of going? It was only a passing fancy, I daresay. Once you leave a place the chances are you won't get another. There are so many of us . .

CHARLEY. Of course, it's safe and it's wise and it's sensible and all that—but it's damnable.

FENWICK. It's come suddenly to you—I've almost got used to the idea. [*With a little laugh.*] You do, you know, after a little. You're young . . [*With sigh.*] Well, there it is. [*A pause.*] But I'd looked for that rise. It'll make a difference. [*Pulling himself together.*] However, it can't be helped. We've got something left and I'm safe, and that's more than a good many people can say. I'm sorry I came to-night, Wilson.

LESLIE'S *voice can be heard, shouting out a comic song.* [*Smiling.*] Life doesn't seem to worry him.

CHARLEY. Won't you stay and have supper?

FENWICK. Thanks, no. I don't feel exactly sociable.

CHARLEY. [*with a short laugh.*] Neither do I, old chap. Fact is, I was feeling a bit off when you came.

FENWICK. You're a little restless, but it'll work off. Look at me. I felt like that once.

They go out.

The curtains are pulled wide and LESLIE *and* PERCY MASSEY *enter.* TENNANT *can be seen in the front parlour.*

LESLIE. May we interrupt? [*Looking around.*] Empty was the cradle.

Re-enter CHARLEY.

Where's the business?

CHARLEY. Fenwick's been, but he's just gone.

LESLIE. Fenwick? Wasn't cheerful company, was he?

CHARLEY. [*crossly.*] What's the matter with him?

LESLIE. He never is, that's all.

CHARLEY. He isn't exactly boisterous. He nearly emigrated once, he tells me.

TENNANT. [*coming forward.*] Why didn't he quite?

LESLIE. Not enough devil in him. Hundreds of 'em almost go.

CHARLEY. Did you?

LESLIE. [*with energy.*] I'm comfortable enough where I am. I've been telling this chap here he's a fool, but he won't believe me. He says he'd rather be a fool in the Colonies than a wise man here. Don't know what he means quite, but it sounds rather smart. [*Waving his pipe oracularly as he faces the three men.*] I've known lots of chaps who've wanted to go. The guv'nor is unpleasant or there's too much overtime or they get jealous of their girl or something of that sort and off they must go. I've known a few who went—and sorry they were, too. You can't do anything out there. Read the emigration books, read your papers. Failure all along the line. Market overcrowded. Only capitalists need apply—the Colonies don't want you—

CHARLEY. Neither does England—

LESLIE. Of course not, but [*waving his arm impressively*]—but you're here and got something. That's the whole point. My advice is—stick where you are. Tennant's a stupid ass to give up a decent berth; he deserves to fail. Of course, we should all like to see the world. I should—

TENNANT. It's more than that.

CHARLEY. Yes, yes, you don't understand. It isn't the idea of travelling—it's because you want to feel—oh! [*He stretches out his arms.*] I don't suppose you ever feel so—

LESLIE. Can't say I did.

TENNANT. Aren't you ever sick of the thing, Leslie?

CHARLEY And don't you ever want to pitch all the ledgers into the dustbin and burn the stools?

LESLIE. Never—though I've met many that have. I tell you, it's a good thing to have a safe berth nowadays. Many fellows would only be too glad to pick up Tennant's berth—or yours, Wilson. Think of the crowds that will answer the advertisement at Molesey's— Last week our firm wanted a man to do overtime work, and they don't pay too high a rate—I can tell you. They had five hundred and fifteen applications—five hundred and fifteen! Think of that! And that's what would happen to you if you went, Wilson, and that'll be the end of Tennant. Sorry to be unpleasant—but truth—

TENNANT. But there's room on the land—

LESLIE. Land! What on earth can a bally clerk do with a spade? He'd be trying to stick it behind his ear— *Shout of laughter from* PERCY MASSEY.

He's got no muscle—he's got a back that would break if he stooped—he'd always have a cold in his nose—

CHARLEY. Shut it, Leslie. You can't call Tennant exactly anæmic. And look at this. [*He strips off his coat and turns back his shirt sleeves to display his arms.*] How's that?

TENNANT *looks on with interest.* LESLIE *comes near and pinches* CHARLEY'S *arm, while* PERCY MASSEY *looks on smilingly.*

LESLIE. All right for a back garden. I suppose you think you're an authority on the land question 'cause you grow sweet peas?

CHARLEY. [*digging his hands into his pockets without turning down his sleeves again.*] I don't think anything of the kind. What I do know is that if I had a chance I could farm land with anybody. Do you think I chose this beastly business of quill-driving because it's the best work I know? Do you?

LESLIE. I don't suppose you chose it at all. Your father chose it for you.

PERCY. [*to* CHARLEY.] Well, I say, what's the matter with it?

CHARLEY. You wait till you're a few years older.

LESLIE. Wilson's caught the land fever. Take up an allotment—that'll cure you. Your garden isn't big enough. Have you got that map, Tennant?

TENNANT. It's in my room. Shall we go up?

LESLIE. Is there a fire?

TENNANT. No.

LESLIE. Bring it down, there's a good chap. I like take things comfortable. I'll wait down here.

TENNANT *goes out.*
LESLIE *rises ; goes back to the front room.*
PERCY. I say, Charley—
CHARLEY. Well?
PERCY. I've got a rise.
CHARLEY. Congratulations—wish I had.
PERCY. Foster's given me Beckett's job.
CHARLEY. And Beckett?
PERCY. Well, he's got the sack, you know. It's a bit rough on him, but I couldn't help it, could I?
CHARLEY. I suppose you're doing it cheaper?
PERCY. That's about the line. I'm awfully sorry for Beckett. He's not young, and it's awfully hard to get anything when you're middle-aged.
CHARLEY. So I believe. Well, anyhow, you're in luck—aren't you?
PERCY. Yes, it's sooner than I thought.
They sit in silence.
TENNANT *re-enters, and goes into inner room.*
I say, Charley, what did you start on?
CHARLEY. Eh? What d'ye mean?
PERCY. You—and—and Lily—you know.
CHARLEY *looks at him steadily.*
CHARLEY. Oh, that's it, is it?
PERCY. You didn't begin with a house, of course.
CHARLEY. You know as well as I do that we had three rooms—and jolly small ones.
PERCY. Still you were comfortable.
CHARLEY. It was warm—winter and summer.
PERCY. It wasn't very expensive?
CHARLEY. You have to choose your housekeeper carefully.
PERCY. If you're going to chaff—
CHARLEY. Don't be an idiot. You've now got ninety, I suppose. You can manage on that.
PERCY. You really think so?

CHARLEY. I know from experience.
PERCY. You don't ask who the lady is?
CHARLEY. Sybil is a pretty little girl.
PERCY. Well, I suppose you did guess a bit.
CHARLEY. Not me! Maggie and Lil did it between them.
PERCY. Did it?
CHARLEY. Made the match—Maggie told me.
PERCY. [*indignantly.*] They did nothing of the kind. I met Sybil here and . .
CHARLEY. 'Um—um!
PERCY. We just came together—it was bound to be.

There is a sound of laughter outside and LILY *and* SYBIL *are seen carrying in cakes and lemonade.*

CHARLEY. She is pretty—
PERCY. Yes, in rather an unusual—
CHARLEY. But so are others.
PERCY. I say, old man.
CHARLEY. Well, aren't they? I suppose you won't listen to advice.
PERCY. What about?
CHARLEY. You're too young to marry.
PERCY. I'm twenty-three. So were you when you married.
CHARLEY. I was too young.
PERCY. Do you mean . .
CHARLEY. [*impatiently.*] Oh, don't look so scandalised. No, I'm not tired of Lily. It's not that at all—but, are you satisfied to be a clerk all your life?
PERCY. I say, Tennant's upset you. Of course I'm satisfied to be a clerk.
CHARLEY. But are you?
PERCY. [*impatiently.*] Don't I say so?
CHARLEY. Have you ever felt a desire to kick your hat into the fire? Have you?
PERCY. No! Not yet!

CHARLEY. Not yet. There you are—but you will. Don't you ever want to see anything more of the world —did you ever have that feeling ?

PERCY. [*a little thoughtfully*.] Well, I did once. I wanted to go out with Robinson. But the dad wouldn't consent. It was a bit risky, you know, and this job came along—and so I wouldn't go.

CHARLEY. Did Robinson come back ?

PERCY. No, he's got a decent little place out there.

CHARLEY. They don't all fail, then ?

PERCY. Of course not—but lots do. I might be one of those.

CHARLEY. Well, the thing is if you ever thought of doing anything now's your time. You can't do it afterwards. Take my tip and don't get engaged yet. You're too young to decide such an important question.

PERCY. No younger than you were—and I must say . .

CHARLEY. Don't be so touchy—can't you see I'm talking to you for your good ?

PERCY. I think you're crazed.

CHARLEY. [*sharply*.] Why am I crazed, as you call it ? Isn't it because I know a little what your life is going to be ? Haven't I gone backwards and forwards to the city every day of my life since I was sixteen and am I crazed because I suggest it's a bit monotonous ? [*Going close to* PERCY *and putting his hand on his shoulder solemnly.*] I'm not saying she isn't the right girl for you—I'm only suggesting that perhaps she isn't ! She's pretty and she's handy . .

PERCY. I say ! I won't have that.

CHARLEY. Don't. Pass it over. It's just this — think—and don't marry the first pretty girl and live in three rooms because your brother-in-law did it.

PERCY. She wasn't—the first pretty girl . .

SYBIL. [*appearing at opening and smiling demurely.*]

Mrs. Wilson says— Oh, Mr. Wilson, have you been fighting?

CHARLEY. [*suddenly remembering that he has his coat off.*] I beg your pardon. [*He pulls it on hastily.*] [*To* PERCY.] Remember!

PERCY. [*with his eyes on* SYBIL.] Rot! [*Goes back with* SYBIL.]

LILY. [*coming towards him.*] Who said anything about fighting? Now I suppose you've been arguing with everybody and shouted at them. You do get so cross when you argue—don't you, dear? Supper is quite ready. I sent Sybil to tell you . .

CHARLEY. Sybil's feeding Percy. She's got all her work cut out.

LILY. How rude you are! Do you know, I'm quite angry with you. You've hardly been in the whole evening.

CHARLEY. Fenwick . .

LILY. Yes, I saw him. He looks so lifeless, don't you think?

CHARLEY. He says I shall grow like him.

LILY. What an idea! Why, how could you?

The COMPANY *move about the two rooms, the* MEN *handing refreshments to the* WOMEN—*they* ALL *come more forward.*

LESLIE. What do you think—? I lost the 8.15 this morning!

CHARLEY. Should have thought it would have waited for you.

LESLIE. I left the house at the usual time and there was a confounded woman at the station with about five trunks and a paper parcel, who took up the whole doorway.

Much laughing from SYBIL *and an encouraging smile from* LILY.

By the time I got over the train was gone. Never did such a thing in my life before.

LILY. You haven't sung to us, Charley, dear.

MAGGIE. He's tired.
LILY. Not too tired for that, are you?
SYBIL. Oh, do, Mr. Wilson, I know you sing splendidly. Per— Mr. Massey told me so.
PERCY. S'sh! don't give me away—he's my brother-in-law.
CHARLEY. Not to-night, Lil—I—I'm a little hoarse.
LILY. That's being out in the garden at all hours.
LESLIE. Don't say that, Mrs. Wilson. Your husband wants to go as a farmer in the Colonies—and you'll discourage him.
LILY. You silly man, Mr. Leslie. [*To* CHARLEY.] You must have something hot when you go to bed, dear.
LESLIE. I love being a little ill. My wife's an awfully good nurse.
SYBIL. I believe you put it on sometimes, Mr. Leslie.
LESLIE. Well, do you know—I believe I do. Ladies won't put their pretty fingers round your neck for nothing. But if you have a little hoarseness—not too much to be really unpleasant—or a headache is a very good thing—it is delightful—I always say to myself:

" O woman! in our hours of ease
Uncertain, coy, and hard to please;
When pain and anguish wring the brow,
A ministering angel thou! "

LILY. We ought to have " Auld Lang Syne "—
TENNANT. Please don't.
LILY. It would be so nice for you to remember. [*Going up.*] Yes, we must. Come. [*She puts out her hands and makes them* ALL *form a ring, with hands crossed and all round table.*]

  TENNANT *and* CHARLEY *join most reluctantly and are not seen to sing a note.*

There! That's better.
SYBIL. Now I must go, Mrs. Wilson.
LILY. Must you really? Come and get your things.

They go out.

A tapping is heard at the window in the near room— MAGGIE *runs and opens it.*

VOICE. Is my husband there, Mrs. Wilson?

LESLIE. Y—es. I'm here. Coming, darling.

SYBIL *and* LILY *re-enter R.*

LESLIE. My wife has sent for me home, Mrs. Wilson.

MAGGIE. Are you going over the wall?

SYBIL. Oh, do, Mr. Leslie—I should love to see you.

LESLIE. If it will give you any pleasure it shall be done, though I am not at my best on the fence.

They all crowd round—he shakes hands, smiling profusely, and disappears through the window.

VOICE. Mind the flower-pot. No—not there—that's the dustbin. Not the steps.

There is a great shout to announce his safe arrival.

LESLIE. Safe!

SYBIL. I do think he is so funny!

LILY. Yes, isn't he? Are you going by 'bus?

PERCY. I'm going Miss Frost's way.

SYBIL. [*much surprised.*] Are you really?

MAGGIE. How extraordinary!

Much kissing between SYBIL, LILY, *and* MAGGIE. SYBIL *and* PERCY *go out.*

LILY. She's so sweet, isn't she? And Percy's so awfully gone.

MAGGIE. [*as they start clearing away the dishes.*] Very. So he was over Daisy Mallock and Ruby Denis —and who's the other girl with the hair?

LILY. The hair? What do you mean?

MAGGIE. The one with the hair all over her eyes—nice hair, too.

LILY. Gladys Vancouver? Poor Percy—I'm afraid he is a little bit of a flirt.

MAGGIE. He's got nothing else to do with his evenings.

LILY. And then people like Mr. Tennant think it's a dull life.

MAGGIE. Well, good night all. No, don't come out, Mr. Tennant—I'm quite a capable person.

TENNANT. Oh, but I shall—if you'll allow me.

MAGGIE. I'd rather you didn't—still, if you will.

[*They go out with* LILY.]

 CHARLEY *looks round and sighs with relief—he walks round, looks out of the window, then at the garden—he takes up the paper, but after trying in vain to settle to it, throws it on the floor—he re-fills his pipe and lights it. Re-enter* TENNANT.

TENNANT. Well. [*He pauses, but* CHARLEY *does not stir.*] I say, Wilson, I never thought you'd take it like this.

 CHARLEY *does not answer, but only shifts restlessly.*

I thought you'd think I was a fool too. In fact I was half ashamed to say anything about it. It wouldn't do for most people, you know. I'm in an exceptional position, and even in spite of that they call me an ass. I've got a little cash, too.

CHARLEY. [*quickly.*] So have I.

TENNANT. Yes, but the cases are different. I can rough it.

CHARLEY. Let me have the chance to rough it.

TENNANT. You're married.

 CHARLEY *does not reply.*

You're settled. Your friends are here. I've got nothing and nobody to worry about.

 They both smoke in silence.

I say, don't sit up and think. Go to bed.

CHARLEY. I'm going soon. Don't stay up, old chap.

TENNANT. You'll get over it.

 He goes out.

 Enter LILY—*she pulls down blind and fastens catch of window.*

LILY. I'm going up now. Don't be long. You look so tired.

CHARLEY. [*irritably*.] Oh, don't fret about me. I'm a little worried, that's all.

LILY. [*timidly*.] Did Mr. Fenwick bring bad news? He looked miserable enough.

CHARLEY. [*looking at her steadily*.] Yes, I'm not going to have that rise.

LILY. Oh, dear—what a shame! Why?

CHARLEY. Lots of reasons—but that's all.

LILY. Of course, you're worried. Still—it might have been worse. You might have been sent away.

CHARLEY. Yes.

LILY. It's very disheartening—after all we'd planned to do with it. You won't be able to have the greenhouse, now, will you, dear?

CHARLEY. [*with a short laugh*.] What's the good of a greenhouse in that yard? It isn't that.

LILY. [*a little timidly*.] But we can manage very well, dear. We—you remember what I said this morning—about the other lodger.

CHARLEY. Oh, don't, for heaven's sake. It isn't losing the cash I mind; it's having to give in like this. I want to go to them and tell them to do their worst and get somebody else.

LILY. But, dear, you might lose your place.

CHARLEY. I should.

LILY. But that—we couldn't afford that, could we? Why, we can manage quite well as we are. I can be very careful still—

CHARLEY. I'm tired of going on as we've been going.

LILY. What do you want to do?

CHARLEY. I—I want to go away. [*Pause*.]

LILY. And leave me?

CHARLEY. [*suddenly remembering*.] Oh—er—

LILY. It's just that horrid Mr. Tennant—

CHARLEY. It's nothing to do with him—at least . .

LILY. I said it was. He wants you to go with him—and you want to go—you're tired of me—

CHARLEY. [*going up to her and trying to speak gently, but being very irritated—his voice is sharp.*] Oh, don't cry . . you don't understand. Look, Lil, supposing I went and you came out afterwards.

LILY. You want to go without me.

CHARLEY. I couldn't take you, dear, but I would soon send for you; it wouldn't be long.

LILY. You want to go without me. You're tired of me.

CHARLEY. Oh, don't cry, Lil. I didn't say I was going. Of course I don't want to leave you, dear. You mustn't take any notice. [*Attempting to take her in his arms.*]

LILY. [*turning away from him, sobs.*] But you do . .

CHARLEY. I don't want to go because I want to leave you . .

LILY. But you said . .

CHARLEY. Never mind what I said. [*He kisses her and pets her like a child.*] Come, go to bed. It's the news—and the excitement about Tennant—and all that. Come, go to bed and I'll be up in a few minutes.

[*CHARLEY leads her to the door and coaxes her outside and stands at the door a few seconds, then he comes back into the room, stands still, looking round. He goes to the front parlour and hunts over the chairs and the piano as if in search of something. Finally he picks up a paper off the floor and brings it to table—it is the map of Australia. He opens it on the table and leans over it, his pipe unnoticed burning out in his left hand.*]

CURTAIN

ACT III

SCENE: *The sitting-room at "Sunnybank", Hammersmith. There is no centre table, but there are various small ones against the wall and in the window. There is a piano, a tall palm in the window, and one or two wicker chairs that creak. The rest of the furniture is upholstered in saddlebags with antimacassars over the sofa head and armchairs. Gramophone in the corner. Big mirror over mantelpiece. Gilt clock in glass case and lustres.*

MRS. MASSEY *is sleeping in one armchair.* MR. MASSEY *is asleep on sofa, pulled across centre.* MAGGIE *sits reading at small table.* MAGGIE *softly rises and goes to fire. She pokes it and a piece of coal falls out.* MRS. MASSEY *turns her head.*

MAGGIE. I'm so sorry, mother, I tried to poke it gently.

MRS. MASSEY. I was hardly asleep, my dear.

MAGGIE. Mother!—you've been sleeping for half an hour!

MRS. MASSEY. It didn't seem like it, dear. Why, your father's asleep.

MAGGIE. Isn't that extraordinary!

MRS. MASSEY. [*admiringly.*] How soundly he sleeps! What's the time?

MAGGIE. Four o'clock.

MRS. MASSEY. I should have thought they'd have been here now.

MAGGIE. Not Percy and Sybil, I hope. You don't expect them until the last minute, do you?

MRS. MASSEY. No, dear—of course not.

MAGGIE. I wouldn't walk the streets this afternoon for any man.

MRS. MASSEY. I don't suppose they find it cold.

MAGGIE. Oh, I daresay they're sitting in the Park.

MRS. MASSEY. I hope they won't be late for tea. I shall want mine soon.

MAGGIE. I'll put on the kettle now, and when Lil and Charley come we will have tea and not wait for the others. We'll have it cosily in here. [*She goes out, returning with kettle, which she puts on fire. Sits close to* MRS. MASSEY.]

MAGGIE. Mother!

MRS. MASSEY. Yes.

MAGGIE. Mother, did you love father when you married him—very much, I mean, very, very much?

MRS. MASSEY. [*much astonished.*] What a question! Of course.

MAGGIE. More than any other man you'd ever seen?

MRS. MASSEY. Of course!

MAGGIE. More than everything and everybody?

MRS. MASSEY. Of course!

MAGGIE. Well, there's something wrong with me, then—or else with Walter. I don't feel a bit like that. There's no " of course " with me. I wouldn't go and sit in the Park with him this afternoon for anything.

MRS. MASSEY. I suppose you've quarrelled?

MAGGIE. No, we haven't. I wish we had.

MRS. MASSEY. Maggie! Don't talk like that.

MAGGIE. But I do. He wants me to marry him next month.

MRS. MASSEY. And a very good thing too.

MAGGIE. He says he's found a house, and wants me to go and look at it. I don't want to see it.

MRS. MASSEY. What's come over you lately? You used to be satisfied. Walter is very nice and attentive—in fact, quite devoted.

MAGGIE. Yes, I know. Just like he was to his first wife, I expect.

MRS. MASSEY. You've such an absurd prejudice against widowers, Maggie. You're jealous.

MAGGIE. I'm not. Not a bit. But I do wish he would do something, and not worry about getting married.

MRS. MASSEY. The poor man is doing something, I should think, running after you every spare minute, and house hunting.

MAGGIE. I would much rather he went to Australia —or somewhere.

MRS. MASSEY. That's that absurd Tennant man again. You're not in love with him, I hope?

MAGGIE. [*promptly.*] Not a scrap! I find him rather dull.

MRS. MASSEY. Then what is it?

MAGGIE. I should like Walter to go out and seek his fortune instead of getting it in a coal merchant's office.

MRS. MASSEY. He mightn't come back.

MAGGIE. [*thoughtfully.*] Perhaps he wouldn't.
Click of gate.

MRS. MASSEY. There's the gate, Maggie.

MAGGIE *goes out* R. *She comes back in a moment, followed by* LILY. LILY *goes to her mother and kisses her. She looks at her father.*

LILY. Father asleep?

MAGGIE. What a question. Shall I take your hat and coat?

LILY *takes them off and hands them to* MAGGIE. You're shivering! Sit close to the fire. Aren't you well?

LILY. [*in a pathetic voice.*] Yes, I'm well, thank you.

MRS. MASSEY. Are you alone?

LILY. Charley is coming on. He's gone to the station with Mr. Tennant.

MRS. MASSEY. To see him off?

LILY. No—Mr. Tennant goes to-morrow.

MAGGIE *goes out with hat and coat. She brings back with her a tray, with cloth, etc., and prepares for tea on a small table.*

MRS. MASSEY. Have you got another lodger?

LILY. No. We—we've got to have two.

MRS. MASSEY. Two? What for?

MAGGIE *stops to listen.*

LILY. They've reduced Charley's salary.

MRS. MASSEY. [*sitting up energetically.*] Reduced it? What for?

LILY. I don't know—I .. oh, I'm so miserable. [*She suddenly covers her face with her hands and sobs.*]

MAGGIE. [*stooping over her.*] Lil, dear, you're not crying over that, are you?

LILY. [*sobbing.*] Oh, no, no! It doesn't matter. We can make room for two lodgers quite well. I don't mind the work.

MAGGIE. Then what is it?

MRS. MASSEY. I suppose you and Charley have quarrelled?

MAGGIE. Tell us, dear.

LILY. Charley—wants—to go away—and leave me.

MRS. MASSEY. What? What's this?

LILY. [*looking apprehensively round at the sleeping figure.*] Hush! don't wake father!

MAGGIE. He won't wake till the tea-cups rattle. Charley wants to leave you!

MRS. MASSEY. I knew they'd quarrelled.

LILY. We haven't—not exactly—but he's been so funny ever since Mr. Tennant said he was going to Australia. He wants to go too.

MRS. MASSEY. What next? Charley ought to be ashamed of himself. Go to Australia indeed! He forgets he is married.

LILY. I don't want him to stay just because he's married, if he wants to leave me.

MAGGIE. You are quite wrong, I'm sure, Lil. He doesn't want to leave you at all. He wants to leave his work.

MRS. MASSEY. Perhaps he does. So do other people very often. Suppose we all stopped work when we didn't like it? A pretty muddle the world would be in. Charley is forgetting there is such a thing as duty.

LILY. He's very unhappy—and I—I can't make him happy.

MRS. MASSEY. So he ought to be miserable with such ideas in his head. I never heard of such a thing! The sooner Mr. Tennant goes the better. He's been putting Charley up to this, I suppose?

MAGGIE. You don't know Mr. Tennant, mother. He's not that sort.

MRS. MASSEY. Then what made Charley think of it at all?

MAGGIE. It's just a feeling you get sometimes, mother. You can't help it. Office work is awf'lly monotonous.

MRS. MASSEY. Of course it is. So is all work. Do you expect work to be pleasant? Does anybody ever like work? The idea is absurd. Any one would think work was to be pleasant. You don't come into the world to have pleasure. We've got to do our duty, and the more cheerfully we can do it, the better for ourselves and everybody else.

LILY. I—I didn't mean to tell you.

MRS. MASSEY. He ought to be talked to.

LILY. Don't say anything, please—not yet. Perhaps after tea we can all talk about it, and it may do him good.

MAGGIE *goes out.* LILY *starts to arrange the tea-cups.* MR. MASSEY *rouses.* *Re-enter* MAGGIE *with tea-pot.*

MASSEY. Tea?

MAGGIE. Yes, Daddy.

MASSEY. In here? There's no room.

MAGGIE. It's cosy. I'll bring yours to the sofa.

MASSEY. Where am I to put it?—on the floor?

MAGGIE. I'll bring up a table for you if you must have

one. You wouldn't do for a Society gentleman. Can't you balance a cup on your knee?

MASSEY. I don't mean to try. Hope you haven't got out those finicky little cups. I want my own.

MAGGIE. I've got your own—here. [*She holds up a very big breakfast cup, plain white with gilt band.*]

MASSEY. I didn't hear you come in, Lil. Where's Charley?

LILY. Coming on.

MASSEY. What've you done with Foster, Mag?

MAGGIE. He's not coming.

MAGGIE *takes tea round.*

MASSEY. Gone away for the week-end?

MAGGIE. [*taking a cup for herself and sitting down beside* LILY.] Oh, no! He's not coming. That's all. Lily and I are grass widows. It's a very nice feeling.

MASSEY. It's all right about you, but Lil looks a bit off. You've got a cold. Your eyes are red.

LILY. Yes, father.

MRS. MASSEY. You've dropped some bread and butter on the carpet, Alfred.

MASSEY. [*irritably.*] Of course I have! I knew I should.

MAGGIE. [*running to pick it up.*] Percy hasn't come back with Sybil yet, Dad. We expect they're sitting in the Park.

MASSEY. [*his attention taken from his grievance.*] What, in this weather?

MAGGIE. The seats will be dry and they sit close together, you know. I've often seen them do it.

MASSEY. [*chuckling.*] You have, have you? And what about yourself? What about yourself? You! Lord! what a nest of turtle doves it is—nothing but billing and cooing!

MAGGIE. Especially Percy.

MASSEY. P'raps so. He's young at it. Well, he'll be the next, I suppose. And you, too, Mag?

MAGGIE. I'm in no hurry.

MRS. MASSEY. [*a little impatiently to Maggie.*] Don't talk like that, my dear.

MASSEY. Of course she says she isn't. She's a modest young woman—I never heard you say you were in a hurry, my dear.

MRS. MASSEY. Of course I shouldn't—to you.

MASSEY. Ha, ha! You put on the shy business then. Lord! these women. [MAGGIE *moves towards table.*] Come, now, Mag, confess! You think of it sometimes.

MAGGIE. I think of it a lot.

MASSEY. There you are! There you are! What did I say!

MAGGIE. And what do you think I think about it?

MASSEY. How should I know? Wedding, I suppose. I bet you never think of anything else after the wedding day.

MAGGIE. [*slowly.*] I think of the wedding dress, and the bridesmaids, and the pages. Shall I have pages, Mum?

MRS. MASSEY. Maggie!

MAGGIE. I suppose I shan't. I think of the house I'm going to have, Daddy—and the furniture, and I'm going to have a cat and a dog—

MASSEY. [*slyly.*] Nothing else, of course. Just a cat and a dog. Ha, ha!

MRS. MASSEY. Alfred, don't suggest. It isn't nice.

MASSEY. A cat and dog—ha, ha, ha!

MAGGIE. Don't laugh, Daddy. I'm telling you the solemn truth—I think most of all that I shall never, never, never have to go into a shop again.

MASSEY. I wish old Foster could hear you.

MAGGIE. Why?

MASSEY. He'd say—" And where do I come in?"

MAGGIE. Well, of course he'll be there. I wish—

MRS. MASSEY. Maggie, my dear—I should like a little more tea! Have you got some more hot water?

MAGGIE. I'll get some. [*Goes out.*]

MASSEY. It's all very well for her to chaff, but she ain't quite natural about this affair of hers. She ought to be more pleased—excited like.

MRS. MASSEY. I think they've had a little quarrel. People often do. She's a little bit down about it. We've had a talk about it.

MASSEY. Well, she can't have any quarrel about him himself. He's all right, and got a jolly soft job, too. He'll make her a good husband. He's insured for £500.

MRS. MASSEY. Is he? That's very nice. If anything happened to him she'd be all right.

MASSEY. He's a thoughtful sort of chap. Of course he's not exactly young, but he's steady.

MRS. MASSEY. The poor child is jealous of his first wife.

MASSEY. You don't say so? Jealous, is she? That's all right—that's a healthy feeling. I'm glad she's jealous, but she'll get over it once she's married. Jealous! Lord! Fancy, Mag, too—I wouldn't have thought it. He'll be head clerk one of these days—he can stay at Whitakers all his life. He told me.

LILY. Do you think he'll ever get tired of it?

MRS. MASSEY. What an idea!

MASSEY. [*roaring.*] Tired! Tired of what? A good job? Why ever should he be? He couldn't have anything better—Ten to half-past five every day of his life, except Saturdays, and then it's one—and three weeks' holiday. Think of that!

LILY. But, I—

Enter MAGGIE *with hot water. The door-bell is heard.*

MRS. MASSEY. Let them in, Lily, my dear—it's Percy and Syb.

LILY *goes out R.*

Re-enter LILY *a moment after, followed by* PERCY *and* SYBIL.

SYBIL *kisses* MRS. MASSEY *and* MAGGIE.

SYBIL. Aren't we dreadfully late, Mrs. Massey? I'm so sorry!

PERCY. Awfully sorry, but my watch is—

MAGGIE. Don't blame the poor thing—it's all right.

MASSEY. The watch, was it? Come here, my girl!

SYBIL *goes to him with giggling shyness. He takes her face between his hands.* Was it the watch? Not a bit of it! It was this—[*He pats her cheek*] these roses. Lucky young dog! Percy! [*He kisses her.*]

MAGGIE. Rather cold in the Park, isn't it?

PERCY. Not very.

MAGGIE. There's a north-east wind. Still, you can find a sheltered seat.

PERCY. Just beyond the glass house thing.

MAGGIE. What did I tell you? [*Looking triumphantly round.*]

SYBIL. [*covering her cheeks.*] What a tease you are, Maggie!

MASSEY. Don't listen to her!

PERCY. You're only giving yourself away, Mag. What do you know about sheltered seats and glass houses?

MAGGIE. It wasn't exactly guess work. [*Click of gate.*]

MRS. MASSEY. There's Walter.

MAGGIE. What?

MASSEY. Isn't she surprised? Now isn't she surprised? Fancy! Walter!

MAGGIE. He said he wasn't coming. [*She looks out of the window.*] Charley is with him.

LILY. Will you open the door, Maggie?

MAGGIE. [*almost at the same moment.*] Go to the door, Percy.

PERCY. Well, you're two dutifully loving young women, I must say.

MAGGIE. You forget—we're used to it. [PERCY *goes out.*] Come, Sybil, and take off your things.
Exeunt SYBIL *and* MAGGIE.
Enter WALTER FOSTER, *a man of about* 35, *prosperous looking, rather stout of build, and fair.* CHARLEY *also enters, and* PERCY.
FOSTER. [*looking round for* MAGGIE.] Good afternoon. [*Shakes hands with* MRS. MASSEY *and* MASSEY.]
MRS. MASSEY. She's gone up with Sybil, Walter
FOSTER. Oh! I was afraid she was out, perhaps.
MASSEY. Well, Charles, you're not looking spry.
CHARLEY. I'm a bit seedy—nothing much.
MASSEY. And when's that madman lodger of yours going, eh?
CHARLEY. To-morrow.
MASSEY. Of all the fools he's the biggest I know.
The door opens, and SYBIL *and* MAGGIE *come back.*
MAGGIE. I was just telling Sybil, Percy, that tea is laid in the sitting-room. We didn't know when you'd be in.
She crosses up to FOSTER *and lifts her face to be kissed.*
SYBIL. Isn't she dreadful?
MASSEY. Well, you won't be alone, don't you worry. Charley here wants some tea, and Lil will have to see he gets it, won't you, Lil?
LILY. Yes, Dad.
MAGGIE. [*to* FOSTER.] Have you had tea?
FOSTER. Yes, thanks.
Exeunt all, except MASSEY, MAGGIE, *and* FOSTER.
MASSEY. [*finally he looks at the two, then at the clock; poking the fire, then humming a little.*] Have you seen the " Argus ", Mag?
MAGGIE. In the kitchen. I'll get it. [*Makes a move to the door.*]
MASSEY. No, no, I'm going out.
Goes.

MAGGIE. Father calls that tact.

FOSTER. [*coming over to her.*] What?

MAGGIE. Didn't you notice? He doesn't want the "Argus", really.

FOSTER. [*just understanding.*] You mean he's left us together?

MAGGIE. Yes.

FOSTER. Awfully kind of him! I say, Maggie, you don't mind my coming, do you? I really had to. We—hadn't made arrangements about Tuesday.

MAGGIE *laughs a little sadly.*

MAGGIE. And you couldn't write them? You are very good to me, Walter.

FOSTER. Don't talk like that.

A pause.

Maggie, I—you haven't kissed me yet.

MAGGIE. I did—when you came in.

FOSTER. No—I kissed you.

MAGGIE. I'm sorry—I—I don't care for kissing in front of people.

FOSTER. [*getting bolder.*] There's no one here now.

MAGGIE *rises, turns, and looks at him very straight; then lifts her face—pause—and going to him, kisses him on the lips. He keeps her close to him till she gently moves herself away.*

I've got something here—you said the other day you wanted—you would like one of those Dutch brooches.

He puts his hand in his coat pocket and brings out a little parcel.

Here it is!

MAGGIE. [*unfastens it.*] It is good of you! You are so thoughtful!

She looks at him.

I suppose— [*She kisses him again.*]

Delighted, he keeps hold of her hand. She looks

at him, and then at her hand imprisoned in his, and then away at the fire.

FOSTER. What's the matter, dear?

MAGGIE. [*impatiently drawing her hand away.*] It's still the mood. I can't help it. I don't feel like love-making.

FOSTER. All right, dear—I won't bother you.

MAGGIE. Perhaps if you did bother—no, never mind. You know I asked you not to come to-day.

FOSTER. Yes.

MAGGIE. Well, I had no reason, except that I didn't feel like it. But I ought to feel like you always, didn't I?

FOSTER. You're different from me. I always feel like you.

MAGGIE. Walter, I don't want to settle down. I want to go and—and do things.

FOSTER. What things, dear?

MAGGIE. Oh, I don't know. [*A pause.*] Did you ever go abroad?

FOSTER. Yes, to Paris, once at Easter.

MAGGIE. Oh! just for a holiday. Wouldn't you just love to go out and try your luck? Have a change? Do something with your hands? Aren't you ever tired of what you are doing?

FOSTER. I can't say I am, really. Why should I? The work is not too hard. But you like change. I have a good salary, you know, dear. When we are married you can go about a lot, you'll be quite free.

MAGGIE. No, I shan't.

FOSTER. But you can have a servant and all that, you know.

MAGGIE. Oh, yes—yes—I understand.

FOSTER. If I went abroad—suppose it, for instance— I shouldn't have you, should I?

MAGGIE. No, and a good thing for you. You deserve

something better. You know—you know, Walter, that I don't love you half or a quarter as you love me.

FOSTER. Yes, I know that. But you don't love anybody else.

MAGGIE. No. Have you ever thought that I'm really marrying you to get out of the shop?

FOSTER. Of course not. Of course you are glad to leave the shop because you don't like it. You are so tied.

MAGGIE. I should love to be absolutely independent, quite—altogether free for a whole year. Oh!

FOSTER. [*a little hurt.*] You will be free when you are married to me, Maggie. You can do anything you like.

MAGGIE. [*looking at him despairingly for a moment, then suddenly going up to him.*] You are a dear!—you are, really! Marry me quick, Walter!

He takes her in his arms delightedly.

Quick—or—or—

FOSTER. Or what? [*Very tenderly.*]

MAGGIE. Or I shall run away.

FOSTER. And where would you run to?

MAGGIE. Perhaps if I'd known where to run to—I should have gone before.

FOSTER. Dearest, don't talk like that!

MAGGIE. [*turning away a little.*] But I don't! I'm safe!

MASSEY *is heard outside the door, coughing and making a noise. Enters.*

I'm afraid you've caught a cold in the kitchen, Daddy. I thought you went for the " Argus "?

MASSEY. So I did. [*He looks down at it.*]

MAGGIE. And you've brought the " Family Herald ". [*She takes it from him.*]

Enter MRS. MASSEY, CHARLEY, LILY, PERCY, *and* SYBIL.

MRS. MASSEY. Play something, Lily.

LILY *goes to piano and picks out some music.* SYBIL

and PERCY *occupy one big chair between them.* CHARLEY *stands idly at window, turning over an album.*

PERCY. Going to church, mother?

MRS. MASSEY. No, dear, it's a very nasty night. Such a cold wind.

PERCY. Last Sunday it was the rain—and the week before it was foggy, and the week before—

SYBIL. Don't be such a very rude boy!

She puts her hand over his mouth and he takes it and holds it.

MRS. MASSEY. [*complacently.*] You're a bad boy to make fun of your old mother. I went to church this morning.

PERCY. You're getting a oncer, mother.

MRS. MASSEY. Well, I should only go to sleep if I went.

PERCY. Think of the example you set if you put in an appearance.

MRS. MASSEY. Yes, dear; I have thought of that, but it wouldn't do for them to see me asleep.

FOSTER. [*who always has the effect of trying to smooth things over.*] I'm sure it is better for you to rest, Mrs. Massey, than walk such a distance twice a day!

MRS. MASSEY. Yes, it is rather a long way. It's quite a quarter of an hour's walk, and I don't care to ride on Sundays.

LILY *plays, choosing the mournful hymn " Abide with me ".* CHARLEY *fidgets, goes to the piano and then back again to the window.*

MASSEY. Can't you find a seat, Charles? You look uncomfortable.

CHARLEY. Plenty, thanks. Sybil only has half a one.

SYBIL. Oh, Mr. Wilson. [*She fidgets away from* PERCY, *who pulls her back again.*]

LILY *has played the tune through. She stops.*

MRS. MASSEY. That's such a nice tune, don't you think, Walter?

FOSTER. Very!—rather plaintive, but soothing.

LILY *starts another—this time " Sun of my Soul "*.

CHARLEY. For heaven's sake, Lil, play something cheerful.

LILY *stops, turns undecidedly on the stool, looks round imploringly at* CHARLEY, *turns a few pages and then rises and goes out of the room hurriedly.*

SYBIL. She's crying!

MASSEY. What?

MRS. MASSEY. You've hurt her, Charley, speaking like that. There was nothing to get cross about. She came this afternoon crying.

CHARLEY. I've done nothing! I—

Exit MRS. MASSEY *in much indignation.*

MASSEY. Had a tiff?

CHARLEY. A tiff—we don't tiff.

MASSEY. Well, then, don't shout at her like that. [*To* SYBIL.] Here—are you sure she was crying?

SYBIL. Yes, quite.

MASSEY. That's queer. She didn't use to.

CHARLEY. She's been worrying, I expect. Women worry so quick.

MASSEY. What's she got to worry about? A bit hysterical, perhaps.

Re-enter MRS. MASSEY.

MASSEY. Is she better?

MRS. MASSEY. She's got a headache, she says. But it isn't that; I know what's the matter. When she came to-day she could hardly speak—

CHARLEY. [*interrupting.*] Is she worrying over me?

MASSEY. What's she got to worry over you about?

CHARLEY. I happened to say—I got the hump, I think . . I feel a bit restless . .

MRS. MASSEY. [*hotly.*] You know what it is well enough. You want to go away with that Tennant man and leave your wife—

MASSEY. [*shouting.*] What!

SYBIL *looks shocked*, PERCY *astonished, while* FOSTER *tries to pretend he didn't hear.*

MRS. MASSEY. The poor child's breaking her heart because she says he wants to leave her.

CHARLEY. I never said anything of the kind—I never thought of such a thing, I—

MRS. MASSEY. Do you want to go away with that man?

MASSEY. I should think you're mad, both of you, to talk about it. Go with who? What for? What're you talking about?

MRS. MASSEY. Lily told me distinctly this afternoon that Charley wanted to go to Australia. She nearly cried her eyes out. Of course that means he wants to leave her. What else could it mean? She said he'd been funny and she was miserable. I said Charley ought to be ashamed of himself to want to go away like that, and so I think so.

MASSEY. [*sitting up very straight and looking angry.*] What's all this, Charley? What . .

FOSTER *on tip-toe slowly goes to door.*

CHARLEY. Don't go, Foster. Let's have all the family in. You're going to be part of it some day.

FOSTER. [*sitting down again.*] I'm quite ready to go.

CHARLEY. No, don't. Let's have it out. You may as well know, all of you.

MRS. MASSEY. [*with a resignation of despair.*] Then you do want—to go and leave her? It's disgraceful!

CHARLEY. [*angrily.*] What stuff you all talk! I—

MRS. MASSEY. Do you or do you not want to go?

CHARLEY. Yes, I do!

General consternation.

MRS. MASSEY. There! I said so.

Enter MAGGIE.

How's the poor dear?

MAGGIE. She says her head is better and she will come down in a minute. What's the matter?

MRS. MASSEY. Charley wants to go to Australia and leave his wife. He's told us so.

CHARLEY. Well, suppose it was true, wouldn't it be better than going without telling you? But it isn't true.

MASSEY. Do you want to take Lil with you?

CHARLEY. How could I?

Enter LILY—*all mutter words of encouragement. General movement towards her. Everybody offers chairs in sympathy. She sits by her father.*

CHARLEY. Look here now, just listen! It's quite true I want to go. I want to do as Tennant's done, chuck everything and try my luck in the Colonies. As soon as I had a fair start Lil would come out.

MASSEY. [*interrupting.*] Yes, and suppose you failed? You should have thought of that before you married. You can't run off when you like when you've a wife.

CHARLEY. [*excitedly.*] But why not?

MRS. MASSEY. [*interrupting.*] Why not?—just hear him.

CHARLEY. It's that I'm just sick of the office and the grind every week and no change!—nothing new, nothing happening. Why, I haven't seen anything of the world. I just settled down to it—why?—just because other chaps do, because it's the right thing. I only live for Saturday—

PERCY. So do I!—so does everybody!

CHARLEY. But they shouldn't—

PERCY. You don't mean to suggest, I hope, that we ought to like our work, do you?

MASSEY. Do you suppose I like plumbing? Do you think I ever did? No, but I stuck to it, and now look at me, got a nice little bit in the bank and bought my own house. [*Looks proudly round.*] Of course I hated it, just as you do.

MAGGIE. Then why didn't you try something else, Daddy?

MASSEY. I like that! What could I do? I was

taught plumbing. We don't have choice. Your grandfather put me to it, and of course I stuck to it.

MAGGIE. But why didn't you ask for a choice?

MASSEY. Me! Why should I do such a thing? Father was a plumber, and if it was good enough for him, it was good enough for me. Suppose I had thrown it up and gone to Canada for a lark? A nice thing for my family. [*To* MAGGIE.] You wouldn't have had the education you've had, my girl. We've got to live somehow, and if you get a good job stick to it, say I—none of your highty flighty notions. Live 'em down!

FOSTER. [*gently.*] We all have moments of discontent, I fancy, but we get over them.

MAGGIE. [*turns to* FOSTER.] Did you ever have any?

FOSTER. A long time ago, but I'm quite safe now, dear.

MAGGIE *shrugs her shoulders and turns half away impatiently.*

CHARLEY. I never said you couldn't live them down. I never said, did I, that I was going away? I only said I should like to. Did I ever say more, Lil?

LILY. [*meekly.*] No, dear.

MRS. MASSEY. But you shouldn't want to. It's ridiculous.

CHARLEY. It wasn't till Tennant started about his going—

MRS. MASSEY. I knew it was that man Tennant—

CHARLEY. . . that I thought of it. But if he threw up his job, I thought, why shouldn't I?

MASSEY. Because he's a fool, you needn't be another.

MAGGIE. He's not a fool, and I wish Charley could go too.

LILY. Maggie, how can you?

MAGGIE. [*crossing to fireplace.*] Why should a young man be bound down to one trade all his life? I wish I were a man—I'd—

MRS. MASSEY. Well, you're not, so it doesn't matter.

CHARLEY. Of course it must make a difference my being married.

MASSEY. Remember your wife's here and don't talk as if you were sorry about it.

CHARLEY. [*turning on them fiercely.*] For heaven's sake, can't you listen fair? My wife needn't go to her father for protection from me. I'm not a scoundrel just because I've got an idea, am I?

A pause—nobody answers.

But I'll tell you what, marriage shouldn't tie a man up as if he was a slave. I don't want to desert Lily—she's my wife and I'm proud of it—but because I married, am I never to strike out in anything? People like us are just cowards. We seize on the first soft job—and there we stick, like whipped dogs. We're afraid to ask for anything, afraid to ask for a rise even—we wait till it comes. And when the boss says he won't give you one—do we up and say, "Then I'll go somewhere where I can get more"? Not a bit of it! What's the good of sticking on here all our lives? Why shouldn't somebody risk something sometimes? We're all so jolly frightened—we've got no spunk —that's where the others get the hold over us—we slog on day after day, and when they cut our wages down we take it as meek as Moses. We're not men, we're machines. Next week I've got my choice—either to take less money to keep my job or to chuck it and try something else. You say—everybody says—keep the job. I expect I shall—I'm a coward like all of you—but what I want to know is, why can't a man have a fit of restlessness and all that without being thought a villain?

FOSTER. But, after all, we undertake responsibilities when we marry, Mr. Wilson. We can't overlook them.

CHARLEY. I don't want to. But I don't think we ought to talk as if when a man gets married he must always bring in just the same money.

FOSTER. If you have the misfortune to have your salary reduced, nobody would blame you.

CHARLEY. I don't know. I felt a bit of a beast when I had to tell Lil about that.

MAGGIE. [*suddenly.*] If you went away, Lily could come and live with us.

MRS. MASSEY. [*scandalised.*] How could she? Everybody would think she was divorced or something.

FOSTER. Live with us, dear?

MAGGIE. [*impatiently.*] No, here, I meant.

CHARLEY. I've got a little cash put by that she could live on. Don't cry, Lil, for heaven's sake! Can't any of you see my point—or won't you?

MASSEY. I suppose you're a Socialist.

CHARLEY. Doesn't anybody but a Socialist ever have an idea?

MASSEY. They're mostly mad, if that's what you mean. And they're always talking about the wickedness of the boss and the sweetness of the working man.

CHARLEY. I never said anything about either, and I'm not a Socialist.

PERCY. You'll be better when Tennant's gone.

CHARLEY. [*viciously.*] Just you wait till you're two years older, my boy.

FOSTER. You see it isn't as if you had any prospects in the Colonies. Has Mr. Tennant?

CHARLEY. He's got an introduction to a firm.

MASSEY. What's the good of that?

LILY. [*tearfully.*] Perhaps I could go with Charley. I'm quite willing to—rough it a little.

MAGGIE. You'd help him more by staying here.

MRS. MASSEY. He doesn't want her. He said so.

LILY. [*still tearfully.*] If Charley really means it—I think—I—

MRS. MASSEY. My dear, don't think anything about it. It's worrying you and making you ill—you want nursing, not frightening. [*This with a glare of indignation at* CHARLEY.]

LILY. I'm all right.

CHARLEY. [*suddenly dropping his defiance.*] Oh, let's go home, Lil. You're tired.

MRS. MASSEY. Have you just noticed that?

MAGGIE. Mother!

MRS. MASSEY. She's my child, and if her husband won't think of her, I must.

LILY. Mother, dear, Charley means all right. I'm sure he does. Yes, dear—I'm quite ready to go.

FOSTER. [*with the air of pouring oil on troubled waters.*] Well, at any rate, it needn't be settled to-night. Perhaps after a night's rest—

MAGGIE. [*vehemently.*] I like impulse.

MASSEY. I expect you do. You don't know what's good for you.

MAGGIE. Well, at any rate, Daddy, you can't say I have much. There's not much chance at Jones & Freeman's.

PERCY. So you've caught it too, Mag.

SYBIL. Don't tease.

Enter LILY, *dressed for going out, also* MRS. MASSEY. LILY *goes round, kissing and shaking hands, with a watery smile and a forced tearful cheerfulness.*

CHARLEY. [*without going all round and calling from the door.*] Good night, all!

Exeunt LILY *and* CHARLEY.

MRS. MASSEY. Well, I must say—

PERCY. Oh, let's drop it, mother. Play something, Maggie.

MAGGIE. I don't want to.

MRS. MASSEY. Walter would like to hear something, wouldn't you, Walter?

FOSTER. If Maggie feels like it.

MAGGIE. She doesn't feel like it.

MASSEY. Be as pleasant as you can, my girl—Charley's enough for one evening.

MAGGIE *goes to the piano and sitting down plays noisily with both pedals on, the chorus, "Off to Philadelphia".*

MRS. MASSEY. Maggie, it's Sunday!

MAGGIE. I forgot!

MRS. MASSEY. You shouldn't forget such things—Sybil, my dear—

SYBIL. I don't play.

MASSEY. Rubbish! Come on!

SYBIL *goes to the piano and* PERCY *follows her.*

PERCY. [*very near to* SYBIL *and helping to find the music.*] Charley is a rotter! What d'ye think he was telling me the other day?

SYBIL. I don't know.

PERCY. Told me to be sure I'd got the right girl.

SYBIL. Brute!

PERCY. What do you think I said? Darling!

Kisses her behind music.

MASSEY. [*looking round.*] Take a bigger sheet.

SYBIL *sits at piano quickly and plays the chorus to " Count your many Blessings". To which they all sing*:

"Count your blessings, count them one by one,
Count your blessings, see what God has done.
Count your blessings, count them one by one,
And it will surprise you what the Lord has done."

CURTAIN

VOL. I   F

ACT IV

SCENE: Sitting-room at 55 Acacia Avenue. Early morning.

LILY *discovered, cutting sandwiches. Ring at door.*
LILY *admits* MAGGIE, *who is dressed for the shop.*

LILY. [*rather nervously.*] You, Maggie! How early. What is it?

MAGGIE. I've come to help Mr. Tennant off, Lil. Where's Charley? Is he up?

LILY. Oh, yes. [MAGGIE *goes to the garden door and stands looking out.*] He's been up a long while.

MAGGIE. So the great day has come. [*Turning.*] Is Charley going, or isn't he, Lil?

LILY. [*nervously and avoiding* MAGGIE'S *eyes.*] No, of course not.

MAGGIE. Why not?

LILY. Because—why, how can he? [*Tearfully.*] Don't speak in that tone, Maggie.

MAGGIE. He would have decided to go, if you had encouraged him.

LILY. I did encourage him. You heard me last night. I told him—and I told him again after we got home—" If you want to go, I'll never stand in your way ".

MAGGIE. Yes, I heard. Is that how you told him last night?

LILY. It doesn't matter how I said it. He'll get over it. Everybody says he will—except you. And how could he go? It's just an idea he's got over Mr. Tennant.

MAGGIE. [*angrily.*] Of course it's Mr. Tennant. Everybody speaks as if Mr. Tennant was a wicked person going round tempting poor husbands to desert their wives. "It's all that Mr. Tennant." "What a blessing when that man goes", etc., etc., as if he had a bad character. The truth is, that he's done a jolly good thing. He's stirred us all up. He's made us dissatisfied.

LILY. What's the good of that? Nobody can make things different if they wanted to.

MAGGIE. Don't talk nonsense. Hasn't he made things different himself? [*Getting a little heroic.*] Heaps of fellows in London go on doing the same old thing, in the same old way, only too glad if it's safe. Look how everybody runs for the Civil Service. Why? Because it's safe, of course, and because they'll get a pension. Look at the post office clerks and Somerset House and lawyer's clerks and bank clerks—

LILY. Bank clerks don't get pensions—

MAGGIE. I know they don't, but once in a bank, always in a bank. Is there anything to look forward to —and aren't they all just—exactly alike? I once went past a lot of offices in the city—I don't know what sort of offices they were. But the windows had dingy drab blinds, and inside there were rows and rows of clerks, sitting on high stools, bending over great books on desks. And over each there was an electric light under a green shade. There they were scribbling away—and outside there was a most beautiful sunset. I shall never, never, forget those men.

LILY. They don't have long hours.

MAGGIE. [*promptly.*] Nine to six.

LILY. I always thought it was ten to four.

MAGGIE. Don't you believe it. That's what I thought once. You're thinking of the bank clerks, of course. My dear, the doors close at half-past three or four—but the clerks—why, they never see the daylight.

LILY. In the summer they do.

MAGGIE. [*impressively.*] I don't care what you say,

or what anybody says, it's not right. And if the men have got used to it, it's all the worse. They want stirring up—and it's the women who've got to do the stirring.

LILY. Whatever can they do?

MAGGIE. Lots. It's the women who make the men afraid. In the old days the women used to help the men on with their armour and give them favours to wear, and send them forth to fight. That's the spirit we want now. Instead of that we say to the men :—" I shouldn't trouble, my dear, if I were you. You're safe here. Do be careful."

LILY. You're very unjust. Look at the Boer War, and how brave the women were then.

MAGGIE. That isn't the only kind of war. Is a soldier to be the only kind of man that a woman's going to encourage? Can't she help the man who wants to make a better thing of life? Oh, what a lovely chance you had and didn't take it, Lil!

LILY. How can you talk like that! What a fuss you're making over a little thing.

MAGGIE. It wasn't a little thing. Here is Charley, with all sorts of " go " in him and fire and energy. Why couldn't you go to him and say, " I'm proud of you. Throw up the horrid business and go and seek your fortune." It was all he wanted, I do believe. Instead of which, he's got every blessed person against him—wife, mother-in-law, father-in-law, and all his friends and relations, and everything he can have. Everybody thinks him mad.

LILY. You ought to have married him, I should think!

MAGGIE. Don't get spiteful, Lil!

LILY. Wait till you're married yourself to Walter—

MAGGIE. I'm not going to marry Walter.

LILY. [*struck with astonishment.*] You're not going to marry Walter? Maggie!

MAGGIE. I've broken it off. I did it last night.

LILY. Whatever for? Did you quarrel? You were a

little touchy last night, I thought—but Walter is so good-tempered.

MAGGIE. I'm sure it's very good of him, but I don't wish to be forgiven and taken back. It was all through Mr. Tennant.

LILY. [*anxiously.*] You don't love him?

MAGGIE. [*exasperated.*] No, I'm not in love with anybody; but all last week I was thinking and thinking, and it wasn't till last night that I found I was just marrying—to get away from the shop!

LILY. But he was devoted to you and so kind.

MAGGIE. I don't want kindness. My shopwalker is very kind where I am, and I don't see any need to change.

LILY. How extraordinary you talk!

MAGGIE. Well, when I heard Charley talking last night, I thought what a fool I was to throw up one sort of —cage—for another.

LILY. But you are free when you're married—

MAGGIE. Nobody is — more especially the woman. But the thing is, I shouldn't want to be, if I loved the man. But I don't love Walter, only his house. Now, I can leave the shop any day, when I've saved enough—and run away. But I couldn't run away from Walter.

LILY. [*horrified.*] Run away—

MAGGIE. [*suddenly beginning to laugh.*] Can you see me? Running away from Walter? Walter! Oh! [*She laughs, but* LILY *looks very grave.*]

LILY. You don't take the matter seriously.

MAGGIE. It shows how seriously I do take it. Have you ever heard of any girl throwing up a good match, who wasn't dead serious?

TENNANT *enters.*

TENNANT. Good morning. Oh, good morning, Miss Massey.

LILY. You're ready for breakfast, aren't you?
Goes out.

MAGGIE. Aren't you surprised to see me here? I wanted to give you a send off.

TENNANT. Awfully good of you.

MAGGIE. You're quite a hero in my eyes, you know, and I feel I must cheer or do something extra. [LILY *comes in with porridge.*]

LILY. You'll have some, won't you, Maggie?

MAGGIE. Thanks. Here, I'll pour out the tea.

LILY *goes out.*

[*To* TENNANT.] Aren't you just frightfully excited?

TENNANT. Can't say I am.

MAGGIE. [*sighing and looking admiringly at him.*] I should be wild, absolutely wild, if I were going.

TENNANT. I'm going to chance it, you know. There's no fortune waiting for me.

MAGGIE. That's the point of it. You know it's awfully unsettling, all this talk about Australia. You've made me so dissatisfied. I don't feel I can go back to the shop.

TENNANT. [*easily.*] You'll get over that.

MAGGIE. Oh, I suppose so.

LILY *enters with toast and puts it down beside him.*

TENNANT. [*turning.*] Please don't bring anything else, Mrs. Wilson. I can't eat it.

LILY. But it's such a journey to the boat.

TENNANT. Oh, that's nothing—besides, I've got these sandwiches. [*Laying his hand on the package near him.*]

LILY. Are you sure there are enough? I can soon cut some more.

TENNANT. Heaps, thanks. [*Earnestly.*] Really, I shan't know what to do with them.

LILY. I'll put you an apple or two in.

TENNANT. No, don't—

LILY. Oh, but they won't take up much room.

TENNANT. [*resignedly.*] Thanks very much.

CHARLEY *enters.*

LILY. Oh, there you are. You'll have breakfast now, dear, won't you?

CHARLEY. I'll have it later. You here, Mag?

MAGGIE. Of course. Do you think this great event could go off without me?

LILY *and* MAGGIE *go out.*

TENNANT. [*smilingly.*] Miss Massey seems to think it's a sort of picnic.

CHARLEY. [*absently.*] Does she?

TENNANT. She'd marry well out there, I daresay.

CHARLEY. Would she?

TENNANT. She looks strong and healthy. Her sort get snapped up in no time.

CHARLEY. You're catching the 10.15, aren't you?

TENNANT. [*surprised.*] Yes. Why? Coming to the station?

CHARLEY. There's another just after twelve—

TENNANT, *who has been swinging his chair backwards, comes to a pause as* CHARLEY *comes up to him.*

TENNANT. Is there? I don't know. But what—

CHARLEY. [*lowering his voice.*] Look here, old chap, suppose I come too?

TENNANT. What!

CHARLEY. [*who keeps his voice rather low the whole time, though visibly excited.*] Don't shout! I haven't told anybody—but I mean it. I want you to look out for me at Plymouth.

TENNANT. But, Wilson—I say—you—

CHARLEY. Don't! It's all settled. There's no use arguing. I've made up my mind. I'm going to leave here as usual and coming on by the second train and pick you up at Plymouth. Don't stare like that—I've thought it all out—

TENNANT. But your wife—your people here—you can't do it. When I've gone, you'll get over it.

CHARLEY. Get over it? I'm not going to get over anything. I've been a coward, see?—and now I'm going to cut and run. It's no good telling Lil—she wouldn't understand—but when I'm out there and get something and making a tidy little place for her, she'll be all right. She's nervous—the women are like that, you know—they can't help it—and her people, too—well, they're old, and when you're old, you're afraid.

TENNANT. [*interrupting.*] You mean to go! to-day?

CHARLEY. Why not? Why not? If I put it off, I'll never go. It wants a bit of doing, and if you don't do these things at the time, well, you give in. I've packed a bag with some things—I did it this morning.

TENNANT. That's why you were up so early—

CHARLEY. I have written a note to Lil. [*Argumentatively.*] It's the only thing to do—there's no other way—I say, Freddy, you'll stand by me? It's easy for chaps like you—

LESLIE MORTON *crosses behind sitting-room window.*

TENNANT. [*uneasily.*] Well—you know best—

CHARLEY. Of course—it's the only thing—

The door opens and voices can be heard outside, laughing.

Who's this coming? It's that ass . .

He rises as MAGGIE, LILY, *and* MORTON LESLIE *enter.*

LESLIE. [*a little short of breath.*] Where's that fool? Thought I'd come and give you a good-bye kiss, old fellow. I would cry, but I've only brought one handkerchief.

MAGGIE. Lily will lend you one of Charley's. But won't you miss the 8.15? Do be careful.

LESLIE. Miss Maggie, I'll tell you a great, an awful secret. [*He goes to her and says in a loud whisper.*] I mean to miss it.

MAGGIE. I don't believe it—you couldn't do such a thing.

LESLIE. [*to* CHARLEY.] Well, Wilson, how is it? You look—

CHARLEY. [*curtly.*] I'm all right. You don't expect me to laugh all the time, do you?

LESLIE. Certainly not. I'm afraid you're still pining for the flesh pots—or is it cocoanuts—

CHARLEY. No, it's gourds—

TENNANT. Tin mugs, you mean.

LESLIE. Take my word for it, before a week's out, you'll be thankful you're sitting opposite your own best tea service, on a Sunday afternoon.

CHARLEY. I say, it's about time you were off, Freddy.

TENNANT. [*looking at his watch.*] So it is.

LILY. You're sure you've got everything. [*To* TENNANT.]

LESLIE. Don't forget to write, please—and do let us know what boat you're coming back by.

TENNANT. [*laughing.*] Shut up! Where did I put my cap?

They ALL *make a rush for the cap, and* MAGGIE *brings it from the hall.*

CHARLEY. [*picking up a paper off the table.*] Here, is this yours?

TENNANT. Another map—it doesn't matter. Burn it.

CHARLEY. Australia!

TENNANT. [*looking at* CHARLEY.] Put it in the fire.

CHARLEY. [*defiantly.*] It might be useful. [*He opens it and fixes it with a pin against the wall.*]

LILY. Now we shall be able to follow your travels, shan't we?

LESLIE. The time has come! Well, good-bye, old man. Allow me to prophesy you'll soon be back—remember what I said—

MAGGIE. [*from the door.*] It's a most glorious morning! The sun is shining for you, Mr. Tennant—and there's not a cloud in the sky.

LESLIE. I hope you won't lose all your money—

MAGGIE. The sea will be all beautiful with the dearest little ripples.

LESLIE. And if by any wonderful stroke of luck you do make anything, let us know. Good-bye.

MAGGIE. All the men are running off to the city—but you're going to Australia.

TENNANT *is rushed out.*

LILY *and* CHARLEY *follow him.*

MAGGIE *runs in quickly and opens the sitting-room window, through which* TENNANT *can be seen shaking hands again and again with* CHARLEY *and* LILY.

MAGGIE. Good luck!

LESLIE. [*shouting through window.*] Give my love to What's-his-name, the Prime Minister!

MAGGIE. [*singing.*] " For I've lately got a notion for to cross the briny ocean."

LESLIE. [*joining.*] " And I'm off to Philadelphia in the morning."

LESLIE *drawls out the last word, bursts out laughing and turns away.*

MAGGIE. Anybody would think you were excited.

LESLIE. If a man will be a fool, Miss Maggie, he may as well go away a happy fool. A cheer costs nothing. So much for him. Now it's me.

MAGGIE. How many trains have you missed?

LESLIE. [*seriously.*] Quite two, I should think. But I promise you it shan't happen again.

Goes out.

CHARLEY *and* LILY *enter.*

LILY. [*wiping her eyes.*] So he's gone. Poor man, I do hope he'll get on all right.

CHARLEY. [*easily and in a brighter tone.*] He'll be all right. He can stand a little roughing.

LILY. It was such a pity you couldn't get the time to go and see him off, dear.

CHARLEY. Oh, that's nothing.
LILY. I'll have breakfast ready for you soon.
Goes out.
CHARLEY. There's no hurry.
MAGGIE *is looking at the map.*
MAGGIE. It's a big place.
CHARLEY. Um. A chance to get some fresh air there.
MAGGIE. [*turning.*] So you're not going after all?
CHARLEY. Oh—er—how can I, Mag?
MAGGIE. It means such a lot, of course.
CHARLEY. Courage or cheek—I don't know which. Of course, it's quite a mad idea—any fool can see that.
MAGGIE. You're not a fool. It's the others who're fools. If only you could hold out a little longer. Lil would be all right. She might fret a little at first—but she's the clinging sort—
CHARLEY. But think what everybody would say!
MAGGIE. You're getting over it already!
CHARLEY. What else can I do? I—I—shall settle down.
MAGGIE. Settle down! Charley—why should you? I've refused to settle down. Why can't you?
CHARLEY. What do you mean? What's it got to do with you?
MAGGIE. [*triumphantly.*] I've refused to marry Walter.
CHARLEY. [*surprised, but not particularly interested.*] What on earth for?
MAGGIE. It was all through Mr. Tennant—
CHARLEY. Tennant? You're—
MAGGIE. [*impatiently.*] Oh, dear, NO. I'm not pining for him. But I found out, when there was all this talk about Mr. Tennant, that I was marrying Walter because I wanted to be safe and was afraid of risk. Then I made up my mind I wouldn't do that. I tell you because —if a girl can risk things—surely a man—

CHARLEY. There wasn't any risk for you with Walter. I can't see it.
MAGGIE. A woman isn't tested in the same way as a man. It's the only way I have—
CHARLEY. Well, you know best, and if you don't like him—but everybody thought you did. I must say you've been rather hard on Foster. You led him on. I should have thought it was rather a good thing for you. Still . .
MAGGIE. [*sighing.*] So it's no good, then, saying anything?
CHARLEY. [*uneasily.*] No—er—[*Turning to her.*] Mag! What would you really think of me if I did?
MAGGIE. What? [*Looks at him for a second.*] Charley—will you—after all?
CHARLEY. Supposing I don't give in—supposing I did go—
MAGGIE. Do you mean it?
CHARLEY. Are you sure about Lil—I'm ready to throw up everything—
MAGGIE. I would look after her—she would be all right in a week—I would do anything—
CHARLEY. But if I go it must be at once—at once, you understand.
MAGGIE. Yes, yes . .
CHARLEY. And if Lil thinks me a brute beast for leaving her like this—in this way—you'll explain—you'll stick up for me—
MAGGIE. This way? I don't—
CHARLEY. I'm going to-day, Mag. I've arranged everything. I couldn't stand it. I had to go. I've written to Lil. She'll be all right for money—I've thought of that and I shall soon send for her. I know I shall, and then she'll be glad I did it. I look a brute, but, Mag, it's got to be. [*Postman's knock on front door.*] Hush! Here comes Lil—don't breathe a word—
MAGGIE. To-day!

LILY *enters with letters.*

LILY. Here's the post. Two for you, dear. [*Gives letters to* CHARLEY, *who, however, doesn't look at them, but goes up to map.*]

MAGGIE. [*quickly.*] I'll call back for you, to go to the station.

CHARLEY. All right.

MAGGIE *goes out hurriedly.*

LILY. I'm sure you're ready for breakfast now, dear—and you won't have very much time.

CHARLEY. I'm not very hungry.

LILY. It was so nice of Mr. Leslie to come in like that, wasn't it?

CHARLEY. Yes. He means all right.

LILY. [*as he eats.*] They're very nice neighbours. I think we're very lucky to have them.

CHARLEY. Um. You were up very early. You'll be tired to-night.

LILY. These things don't often happen, do they, and I can keep better hours in future. We generally go along so regularly, don't we?

CHARLEY. [*suddenly turning from his breakfast.*] Yes.

LILY. I've been thinking, dear, that we shall feel a little dull to-night without Mr. Tennant. Shall we go to the theatre?—something light—

CHARLEY. Oh—no—I don't think so—

LILY. Shall we ask the Leslies for whist?

CHARLEY. [*rising.*] No—not them—it doesn't matter, Lil—unless you'd rather.

LILY. Oh, I shall be quite happy at home, by ourselves. I am so glad you would prefer that, dear. [*She goes up to him.*]

CHARLEY. I haven't been up to much in the company line lately, have I?

LILY. You'll be better now, dear. What time shall you be home?

CHARLEY. Oh—er—you know my usual—

LILY. Yes, dear. Don't be late. I've got something to tell you—which will please you, I think.

CHARLEY. Have you?

LILY. Would you like to hear it now?

CHARLEY. Is it important?

LILY. Is it important? You'll have to be such a good man soon, dear—you'll have to set a good example.

CHARLEY. [*uneasily.*] What do you mean?

LILY. Can't you guess? How dull you are! Bend down and let me tell you. [*She pulls down his face and whispers.*]

CHARLEY. [*pulling himself away.*] What! God! [*Taking her by the arms; then turning away a second, and then turning back.*] Is that true?

LILY. Yes, dear.

CHARLEY. Lil—I . .

LILY. You are pleased! But of course you are.

CHARLEY. Of course, dear.

LILY. Isn't it lovely to think of! And can't you imagine mother as grandmamma! Won't she be a fuss! Why, you're quite overcome. There! Go away and get ready. You didn't open your letters. There's the door. I suppose it's Maggie back.

> LILY *goes out, and re-enters a moment after with* MAGGIE.
>
> *They meet* CHARLEY *going out, and* MAGGIE, *looking at him, almost stops him.*

MAGGIE. What have you been saying to Charley, Lil?

LILY. Why?

MAGGIE. I thought he looked a little—upset . .

LILY. He is rather. He's quite overcome, in fact. But then he would be, of course.

> MAGGIE *closes door, still looking at* LILY.

MAGGIE. What about?

LILY. What could I tell him that would make him more pleased than anything else?

MAGGIE. I'm sure I don't know.

LILY. What generally happens when people are married?

MAGGIE. That! [*Pause.*] Lily!

LILY. Charley is delighted.

MAGGIE. [*unconsciously speaking her thought.*] So you've got him after all.

LILY. [*indignant.*] Maggie!!

MAGGIE. Why did you tell him now?

LILY *goes out, a little indignant.*

CHARLEY *enters from kitchen, dressed for the office.*

MAGGIE. Charley!

CHARLEY. What's up? Don't rot, Mag!

MAGGIE. And now—

CHARLEY. Oh, let's drop it. I was a fool all along—a bit of a beast, too—it's done with . .

MAGGIE. But—

CHARLEY. What's the good of talking? Don't make me out more of a brute than I am! No, the thing was meant to be! I was mad. After all, a man can't do just what he likes! It's better as it is. If this hadn't happened I should have done it—and a pretty mess, I daresay, I'd have been in—and dragged her in, too—

MAGGIE. If—

LILY *enters.*

. . I don't think I can wait for you, after all, Charley.

CHARLEY. Don't trouble.

MAGGIE. Good-bye.

She goes.

LILY. You didn't open your letters, dear.

CHARLEY. What are they?

LILY. [*tearing one open.*] About the new lodger—very quick replies . .

CHARLEY. [*hastily.*] Oh, leave them over.

LILY. Ready?

CHARLEY. [*moving his neck uneasily in the high collar.*] Yes—this beastly collar.

LILY. It's a pity they make you wear such things.

CHARLEY. I've got a short neck. I suppose you shouldn't be a clerk if you've got a short neck. It doesn't fit the collars.

LILY. What an idea!

CHARLEY *stands looking at the map a moment. Suddenly he tears it down and throws it into the fire.*

CHARLEY. Good-bye, Lil. [*He kisses her.*]

LILY. Good-bye, dear.

He picks up his silk hat and gloves and puts the hat on as he reaches the door.

LILY. [*runs to the door.*] Good-bye.

CHARLEY. Good-bye. [*From outside.*]

There is a sound of the front door slamming. LILY *starts chorus of hymn:*

"Count your blessings, count them one by one.
Count your blessings, see what God has done, etc."

CURTAIN

# ABRAHAM LINCOLN

JOHN DRINKWATER

ABRAHAM LINCOLN

was first produced at the Birmingham Repertory Theatre on Saturday October 12, 1918, under the direction of the Author, with the following cast :

First Chronicler	Margaret Chatwin.
Second Chronicler	Dorothy Massingham.
MR. STONE	Joseph A. Dodd.
MR. CUFFNEY	J. Adrian Byrne.
SUSAN DEDDINGTON	Cathleen Orford.
MRS. LINCOLN	Mary Raby.
ABRAHAM LINCOLN	William J. Rea.
WILLIAM TUCKER	Scott Sunderland.
HENRY HIND	Christian Morrow.
ELIAS PRICE	Reginald Gatty.
JAMES MACINTOSH	Eric Ross.
WILLIAM SEWARD	Noel Shammon.
JOHNSON WHITE	William Grant.
CALEB JENNINGS	Arthur Claremont.
HAWKINS	H. V. Edwards.
Second Clerk	Leslie Harcourt.
Third Clerk	Percy Rowe.
MR. SLANEY	A. E. Filmer.
A Messenger	H. Victor Tandy.
SALMON CHASE	Samuel Caswell.
MONTGOMERY BLAIR	J. Adrian Byrne.
SIMON CAMERON	Horace Wentworth.
CALEB SMITH	Arnold Ridley.
BURNET HOOK	Eric Ross.
GIDEON WELLES	William Bache.
MRS. GOLIATH BLOW	Isabel Thornton.
MRS. OTHERLY	Maud Gill.
FREDERICK DOUGLASS	Joseph A. Dodd.
EDWIN STANTON	Christian Morrow.
GENERAL GRANT	Scott Sunderland.

CAPTAIN MALINS	Arthur Claremont.
DENNIS	H. Victor Tandy.
An Officer	Arnold Ridley.
WILLIAM SCOTT	William Grant.
First Soldier	H. V. Edwards.
Second Soldier	Percy Rowe.
GENERAL MEADE	J. Adrian Byrne.
CAPTAIN SONE	Horace Wentworth.
GENERAL LEE	Reginald Gatty.
An Officer of his Staff	C. Vernon.
JOHN WILKES BOOTH	Noel Shammon.
A Doctor	Joseph A. Dodd.

Ladies and Gentlemen—
Alma Broadbridge, Nancy Byrne, Hilda Cheshire, Gladys Hampton, Dorothy Jones, Sydney Leon, Nancy Staples, Dorothy Taylor, and others.

The settings were designed by BARRY V. JACKSON, and the stage management was in the hands of A. E. FILMER.

All applications for permission to perform this play by amateurs in the United Kingdom must be addressed to SAMUEL FRENCH, LTD., 26 Southampton Street, Strand, London, W.C.2, or their authorised representatives.

The fee for a single representation or for the first of a series of performances is Five Guineas. In the event of further performances being given the fee for each and every representation subsequent to the first is Four Guineas. This reduction applies only in the case of the performances being consecutive and at the same theatre or hall.

Owing to the play not being available for performance by amateurs in certain towns, it is essential that applications for permission should be made to Messrs. SAMUEL FRENCH, LTD., before making arrangements.

ABRAHAM LINCOLN

TWO CHRONICLERS.

THE TWO SPEAKING TOGETHER. Kinsmen, you shall
   behold
Our stage, in mimic action, mould
A man's character.

This is the wonder, always, everywhere—
Not that vast mutability which is event,
The pits and pinnacles of change,
But man's desire and valiance that range
All circumstance, and come to port unspent.

Agents are these events, these ecstasies,
And tribulations, to prove the purities
Or poor oblivions that are our being. When
Beauty and peace possess us, they are none
But as they touch the beauty and peace of men,
Nor, when our days are done,
And the last utterance of doom must fall,
Is the doom anything
Memorable for its apparelling;
The bearing of man facing it is all.

So, kinsmen, we present,
This for no loud event
That is but fugitive,
But that you may behold
Our mimic action mould
The spirit of man immortally to live.

FIRST CHRONICLER. Once when a peril touched the days
Of freedom in our English ways,
And none renowned in government
Was equal found,
Came to the steadfast heart of one,
Who watched in lonely Huntingdon,
A summons, and he went,
And tyranny was bound,
And Cromwell was the lord of his event.

SECOND CHRONICLER. And in that land where voyaging
The pilgrim Mayflower came to rest,
Among the chosen, counselling,
Once, when bewilderment possessed
A people, none there was might draw
To fold the wandering thoughts of men,
And make as one the names again
Of liberty and law.

And then, from fifty fameless years
In quiet Illinois was sent
A word that still the Atlantic hears,
And Lincoln was the lord of his event.

THE TWO SPEAKING TOGETHER. So the uncounted spirit wakes
To the birth
Of uncounted circumstance.
And time in a generation makes
Portents majestic a little story of earth
To be remembered by chance
At a fire-side;
But the ardours that they bear,
The proud and invincible motions of character—
These—these abide.

Scene I

The parlour of Abraham Lincoln's House at Springfield, Illinois, early in 1860. MR. STONE, *a farmer, and* MR. CUFFNEY, *a store-keeper, both men of between 50 and 60, are sitting before an early spring fire. It is dusk, but the curtains are not drawn. The men are smoking silently.*

MR. STONE. [*after a pause.*] Abraham. It's a good name for a man to bear, anyway.

MR. CUFFNEY. Yes. That's right.

MR. STONE. [*after another pause.*] Abraham Lincoln. I've known him forty years. Never crooked once. Well.

He taps his pipe reflectively on the grate. There is another pause. SUSAN, *a servant-maid, comes in, and busies herself lighting candles and drawing the curtains to.*

SUSAN. Mrs. Lincoln has just come in. She says she'll be here directly.

MR. CUFFNEY. Thank you.

MR. STONE. Mr. Lincoln isn't home yet, I daresay?

SUSAN. No, Mr. Stone. He won't be long, with all the gentlemen coming.

MR. STONE. How would you like your master to be President of the United States, Susan?

SUSAN. I'm sure he'd do it very nicely, sir.

MR. CUFFNEY. He would have to leave Springfield, Susan, and go to live in Washington.

SUSAN. I daresay we should take to Washington very well, sir.

MR. CUFFNEY. Ah! I'm glad to hear that.

SUSAN. Mrs. Lincoln's rather particular about the tobacco smoke.

MR. STONE. To be sure, yes, thank you, Susan.

SUSAN. The master doesn't smoke, you know. And Mrs. Lincoln's specially particular about this room.

MR. CUFFNEY. Quite so. That's very considerate of you, Susan.

They knock out their pipes.

SUSAN. Though some people might not hold with a gentleman not doing as he'd a mind in his own house, as you might say.

She goes out.

MR. CUFFNEY. [*after a further pause, stroking his pipe.*] I suppose there's no doubt about the message they'll bring?

MR. STONE. No, that's settled right enough. It'll be an invitation. That's as sure as John Brown's dead.

MR. CUFFNEY. I could never make Abraham out rightly about old John. One couldn't stomach slaving more than the other, yet Abraham didn't hold with the old chap standing up against it with the sword. Bad philosophy, or something, he called it. Talked about fanatics who do nothing but get themselves at a rope's end.

MR. STONE. Abraham's all for the constitution. He wants the constitution to be an honest master. There's nothing he wants like that, and he'll stand for that, firm as a Sampson of the spirit, if he goes to Washington. He'd give his life to persuade the state against slaving, but until it is persuaded and makes its laws against it, he'll have nothing to do with violence in the name of laws that aren't made. That's why old John's raiding affair stuck in his gullet.

MR. CUFFNEY. He was a brave man, going like that, with a few zealous like himself, and a handful of niggers, to free thousands.

MR. STONE. He was. And those were brave words when they took him out to hang him. " I think, my friends, you are guilty of a great wrong against God and humanity. You may dispose of me very easily. I am nearly disposed of now. But this question is still to be settled—this negro question, I mean. The end of that is not yet." I was there that day. Stonewall Jackson was there. He turned away. There was a colonel there giving orders. When it was over, " So perish all foes of the human race " he called out. But only those that were afraid of losing their slaves believed it.

MR. CUFFNEY. [*a pause.*] It was a bad thing to hang a man like that . . There's a song that they've made about him.

He sings quietly :
" John Brown's body lies a mould'ring in the grave,
But his soul goes marching on . . "

MR. STONE. I know.

THE TWO TOGETHER. [*singing quietly.*]
" The stars of heaven are looking kindly down
On the grave of old John Brown . . "

After a moment MRS. LINCOLN *comes in. The men rise.*

MRS. LINCOLN. Good evening, Mr. Stone. Good evening, Mr. Cuffney.

MR. STONE AND MR. CUFFNEY. Good evening, ma'am.

MRS. LINCOLN. Sit down, if you please.

They all sit.

MR. STONE. This is a great evening for you, ma'am.

MRS. LINCOLN. It is.

MR. CUFFNEY. What time do you expect the deputation, ma'am ?

MRS. LINCOLN. They should be here at seven o'clock. [*With an inquisitive nose.*] Surely, Abraham hasn't been smoking.

MR. STONE. [*rising.*] Shall I open the window, ma'am ? It gets close of an evening.

MRS. LINCOLN. Naturally, in March. You may leave the window, Samuel Stone. We do not smoke in the parlour.

MR. STONE. [*resuming his seat.*] By no means, ma'am.

MRS. LINCOLN. I shall be obliged to you.

MR. CUFFNEY. Has Abraham decided what he will say to the invitation?

MRS. LINCOLN. He will accept it.

MR. STONE. A very right decision, if I may say so.

MRS. LINCOLN. It is.

MR. CUFFNEY. And you, ma'am, have advised him that way, I'll be bound.

MRS. LINCOLN. You said this was a great evening for me. It is, and I'll say more than I mostly do, because it is. I'm likely to go into history now with a great man. For I know better than any how great he is. I'm plain-looking and I've a sharp tongue, and I've a mind that doesn't always go in his easy, high way. And that's what history will see, and it will laugh a little, and say, "Poor Abraham Lincoln". That's all right, but it's not all. I've always known when he should go forward, and when he should hold back. I've watched, and watched, and what I've learnt America will profit by. There are women like that, lots of them. But I'm lucky. My work's going farther than Illinois—it's going farther than any of us can tell. I made things easy for him to think and think when we were poor, and now his thinking has brought him to this. They wanted to make him Governor of Oregon, and he would have gone and have come to nothing there. I stopped him. Now they're coming to ask him to be President, and I've told him to go.

MR. STONE. If you please, ma'am, I should like to apologise for smoking in here.

MRS. LINCOLN. That's no matter, Samuel Stone. Only, don't do it again.

MR. CUFFNEY. It's a great place for a man to fill. Do you know how Seward takes Abraham's nomination by the Republicans?

MRS. LINCOLN. Seward is ambitious. He expected the nomination. Abraham will know how to use him.

MR. STONE. The split among the Democrats makes the election of the Republican choice a certainty, I suppose?

MRS. LINCOLN. Abraham says so.

MR. CUFFNEY. You know, it's hard to believe. When I think of the times I've sat in this room of an evening, and seen your husband come in, ma'am, with his battered hat nigh falling off the back of his head, and stuffed with papers that won't go into his pockets, and god-darning some rascal who'd done him about an assignment or a trespass, I can't think he's going up there into the eyes of the world.

MRS. LINCOLN. I've tried for years to make him buy a new hat.

MR. CUFFNEY. I have a very large selection just in from New York. Perhaps Abraham might allow me to offer him one for his departure.

MRS. LINCOLN. He might. But he'll wear the old one.

MR. STONE. Slavery and the South. They're big things he'll have to deal with. " The end of that is not yet." That's what old John Brown said, " The end of that is not yet ".

ABRAHAM LINCOLN *comes in, a greenish and crumpled top hat leaving his forehead well uncovered, his wide pockets brimming over with documents. He is 50, and he still preserves his clean-shaven state. He kisses his wife and shakes hands with his friends.*

LINCOLN. Well, Mary. How d'ye do, Samuel. How d'ye do, Timothy.

MR. STONE AND MR. CUFFNEY. Good evening, Abraham.

LINCOLN. [*while he takes off his hat and shakes out sundry papers from the lining into a drawer.*] John Brown, did you say? Ay, John Brown. But that's not the way it's to be done. And you can't do the right thing the wrong way. That's as bad as the wrong thing, if you're going to keep the state together.

MR. CUFFNEY. Well, we'll be going. We only came in to give you good-faring, so to say, in the great word you've got to speak this evening.

MR. STONE. It makes a humble body almost afraid of himself, Abraham, to know his friend is to be one of the great ones of the earth, with his yes and no law for these many, many thousands of folk.

LINCOLN. It makes a man humble to be chosen so, Samuel. So humble that no man but would say "No" to such bidding if he dare. To be President of this people, and trouble gathering everywhere in men's hearts. That's a searching thing. Bitterness, and scorn, and wrestling often with men I shall despise, and perhaps nothing truly done at the end. But I must go. Yes. Thank you, Samuel; thank you, Timothy. Just a glass of that cordial, Mary, before they leave.

He goes to a cupboard.
May the devil smudge that girl!
Calling at the door.
Susan! Susan Deddington! Where's that darnation cordial?

MRS. LINCOLN. It's all right, Abraham. I told the girl to keep it out. The cupboard's choked with papers.

SUSAN. [*coming in with bottle and glasses.*] I'm sure I'm sorry. I was told—

LINCOLN. All right, all right, Susan. Get along with you.

SUSAN. Thank you, sir.
She goes.

LINCOLN. [*pouring out drink.*] Poor hospitality for whiskey-drinking rascals like yourselves. But the thought's good.

MR. STONE. Don't mention it, Abraham.

MR. CUFFNEY. We wish you well, Abraham. Our compliments, ma'am. And God bless America. Samuel, I give you the United States, and Abraham Lincoln.

MR. CUFFNEY *and* MR. STONE *drink.*

MRS. LINCOLN. Thank you.

LINCOLN. Samuel, Timothy—I drink to the hope of honest friends. Mary, to friendship. I'll need that always, for I've a queer, anxious heart. And, God bless America.

He and MRS. LINCOLN *drink.*

MR. STONE. Well, good night, Abraham. Good night, ma'am.

MR. CUFFNEY. Good night, good night.

MRS. LINCOLN. Good night, Mr. Stone. Good night, Mr. Cuffney.

LINCOLN. Good night, Samuel. Good night, Timothy. And thank you for coming.

MR. STONE *and* MR. CUFFNEY *go out.*

MRS. LINCOLN. You'd better see them in here.

LINCOLN. Good. Five minutes to seven. You're sure about it, Mary?

MRS. LINCOLN. Yes. Aren't you?

LINCOLN. We mean to set bounds to slavery. The South will resist. They may try to break away from the Union. That cannot be allowed. If the Union is set aside America will crumble. The saving of it may mean blood.

MRS. LINCOLN. Who is to shape it all if you don't?

LINCOLN. There's nobody. I know it.

MRS. LINCOLN. Then go.

LINCOLN. Go.

MRS. LINCOLN. [*after a moment.*] This hat is a disgrace to you, Abraham. You pay no heed to what I say, and you think it doesn't matter. A man like you ought to think a little about gentility.

LINCOLN. To be sure: I forget.

MRS. LINCOLN. You don't. You just don't heed. Samuel Stone's been smoking in here.

LINCOLN. He's a careless, poor fellow.

MRS. LINCOLN. He is, and a fine example you set him. You don't care whether he makes my parlour smell poison or not.

LINCOLN. Of course I do—

MRS. LINCOLN. You don't. Your head is too stuffed with things to think about my ways. I've got neighbours if you haven't.

LINCOLN. Well, now, your neighbours are mine, I suppose.

MRS. LINCOLN. Then why won't you consider appearances a little?

LINCOLN. Certainly. I must.

MRS. LINCOLN. Will you get a new hat?

LINCOLN. Yes, I must see about it.

MRS. LINCOLN. When?

LINCOLN. In a day or two. Before long.

MRS. LINCOLN. Abraham, I've got a better temper than anybody will ever guess.

LINCOLN. You have, my dear. And you need it, I confess.

SUSAN *comes in.*

SUSAN. The gentlemen have come.

MRS. LINCOLN. I'll come to them.

SUSAN. Does the master want a handkerchief, ma'am? He didn't take one this morning.

LINCOLN. It's no matter now, Susan.

SUSAN. If you please, I've brought you one, sir.

She gives it to him, and goes.

MRS. LINCOLN. I'll send them in. Abraham, I believe in you.

LINCOLN. I know, I know.

MRS. LINCOLN *goes out.* LINCOLN *moves to a map of the United States that is hanging on the wall, and stands silently looking at it. After a few moments* SUSAN *comes to the door.*

SUSAN. This way, please.

She shows in WILLIAM TUCKER, *a florid, prosperous merchant;* HENRY HIND, *an alert little attorney;* ELIAS PRICE, *a lean lay-preacher; and* JAMES MACINTOSH, *the editor of a Republican journal.* SUSAN *goes.*

TUCKER. Mr. Lincoln. Tucker my name is—William Tucker.

He presents his companions.

Mr. Henry Hind—follows your profession, Mr. Lincoln. Leader of the bar in Ohio. Mr. Elias Price, of Pennsylvania. You've heard him preach, maybe. James Macintosh you know. I come from Chicago.

LINCOLN. Gentlemen, at your service. How d'ye do, James. Will you be seated?

They sit round the table.

TUCKER. I have the honour to be chairman of this delegation. We are sent from Chicago by the Republican Convention, to inquire whether you will accept their invitation to become the Republican candidate for the office of President of the United States.

PRICE. The Convention is aware, Mr. Lincoln, that under the circumstances, seeing that the Democrats have split, this is more than an invitation to candidature. Their nominee is almost certain to be elected.

LINCOLN. Gentlemen, I am known to one of you only. Do you know my many disqualifications for this work?

HIND. It's only fair to say that they have been discussed freely.

LINCOLN. There are some, shall we say graces, that I lack. Washington does not altogether neglect these.

TUCKER. They have been spoken of. But these are days, Mr. Lincoln, if I may say so, too difficult, too dangerous, for these to weigh at the expense of other qualities that you were considered to possess.

LINCOLN. Seward and Hook have both had great experience.

MACINTOSH. Hook had no strong support. For Seward, there are doubts as to his discretion.

LINCOLN. Do not be under any misunderstanding, I beg you. I aim at moderation so far as it is honest. But I am a very stubborn man, gentlemen. If the South insists upon the extension of slavery, and claims the right to secede, as you know it very well may do, and the decision lies with me, it will mean resistance, inexorable, with blood if needs be. I would have everybody's mind clear as to that.

PRICE. It will be for you to decide, and we believe you to be an upright man, Mr. Lincoln.

LINCOLN. Seward and Hook would be difficult to carry as subordinates.

TUCKER. But they will have to be carried so, and there's none likelier for the job than you.

LINCOLN. Will your Republican Press stand by me for a principle, James, whatever comes?

MACINTOSH. There's no other man we would follow so readily.

LINCOLN. If you send me, the South will have little but derision for your choice.

HIND. We believe that you'll last out their laughter.

LINCOLN. I can take any man's ridicule—I'm trained to it by a . . somewhat odd figure that it pleased God to give me, if I may so far be pleasant with you. But this slavery business will be long, and deep, and bitter. I know it. If you do me this honour, gentlemen, you must look to me for no compromise in this matter. If abolition comes in due time by constitutional means, good. I want it. But, while we will not force abolition, we will give slavery no approval, and we will not allow it to extend its boundaries by one yard. The determination is in my blood. When I was a boy I made a trip to New Orleans, and there I saw them, chained, beaten, kicked as a man would be ashamed to kick a thieving dog. And I saw a young girl driven up and down the room that the bidders might satisfy themselves. And I said then, " If ever I get a chance to hit that thing, I'll hit it hard."

A pause.

You have no conditions to make?

TUCKER. None.

LINCOLN. (*rising*.) Mrs. Lincoln and I would wish you to take supper with us.

TUCKER. That's very kind, I'm sure. And your answer, Mr. Lincoln?

LINCOLN. When you came, you did not know me, Mr. Tucker. You may have something to say now not for my ears.

TUCKER. Nothing in the world, I assure—

LINCOLN. I will prepare Mrs. Lincoln. You will excuse me for no more than a minute.

He goes out.

TUCKER. Well, we might have chosen a handsomer article, but I doubt whether we could have chosen a better.

HIND. He would make a great judge—if you weren't prosecuting.

PRICE. I'd tell most people, but I'd ask that man.

TUCKER. He hasn't given us yes or no yet. Why should he leave us like that, as though plain wasn't plain?

HIND. Perhaps he wanted a thought by himself first.

MACINTOSH. It wasn't that. But he was right. Abraham Lincoln sees deeper into men's hearts than most. He knows this day will be a memory to us all our lives. Under his eye, which of you could have given play to any untoward thought that had started in you against him since you came into this room? But, leaving you, he knew you could test yourselves to your own ease, and speak the more confident for it, and, if you found yourselves clean of doubt, carry it all the happier in your minds after. Is there a doubt among us?

TUCKER.
HIND. } No, none.
PRICE.

MACINTOSH. Then, Mr. Tucker, ask him again when he comes back.

TUCKER. I will.

They sit in silence for a moment, and LINCOLN *comes in again, back to his place at the table.*

LINCOLN. I wouldn't have you think it graceless of me to be slow in my answer. But once given, it's for the deep good or the deep ill of all this country. In the face of that a man may well ask himself twenty times, when he's twenty times sure. You make no qualification, any one among you?

TUCKER. None. The invitation is as I put it when we sat down. And I would add that we are, all of us, proud to bear it to a man as whom we feel there is none so fitted to receive it.

LINCOLN. I thank you. I accept.

He rises, the others with him. He goes to the door and calls.

Susan.

There is silence. SUSAN *comes in.*

SUSAN. Yes, Mr. Lincoln.

LINCOLN. Take these gentlemen to Mrs. Lincoln. I will follow at once.

The four men go with SUSAN. LINCOLN *stands silently for a moment. He goes again to the map and looks at it. He then turns to the table again, and kneels beside it, possessed and deliberate, burying his face in his hands.*

THE CURTAIN FALLS

THE TWO CHRONICLERS. Lonely is the man who understands.
Lonely is vision that leads a man away
From the pasture-lands,
From the furrows of corn and the brown loads of hay,
To the mountain-side,
To the high places where contemplation brings
All his adventurings
Among the sowers and the tillers in the wide
Valleys to one fused experience,
That shall control
The courses of his soul,
And give his hand
Courage and continence.

THE FIRST CHRONICLER. Shall a man understand,
He shall know bitterness because his kind,
Being perplexed of mind,
Hold issues even that are nothing mated.
And he shall give
Counsel out of his wisdom that none shall hear;
And steadfast in vain persuasion must he live,
And unabated
Shall his temptation be.

SECOND CHRONICLER. Coveting the little, the instant gain,
The brief security,
And easy-tongued renown,
Many will mock the vision that his brain
Builds to a far, unmeasured monument,
And many bid his resolutions down
To the wages of content.

FIRST CHRONICLER. A year goes by.

THE TWO TOGETHER.   Here contemplate
A heart, undaunted to possess

Itself among the glooms of fate,
In vision and in loneliness.

Scene II

A year later. Seward's room at Washington. WILLIAM SEWARD, *Secretary of State, is seated at his table with* JOHNSON WHITE *and* CALEB JENNINGS, *representing the Commissioners of the Confederate States.*

WHITE. It's the common feeling in the South, Mr. Seward, that you're the one man at Washington to see this thing with large imagination. I say this with no disrespect to the President.

SEWARD. I appreciate your kindness, Mr. White. But the Union is the Union—you can't get over that. We are faced with a plain fact. Six of the Southern States have already declared for secession. The President feels, and I may say that I and my colleagues are with him, that to break up the country like that means the decline of America.

JENNINGS. But everything might be done by compromise, Mr. Seward. Withdraw your garrison from Fort Sumter, Beauregard will be instructed to take no further action, South Carolina will be satisfied with the recognition of her authority, and, as likely as not, be willing to give the lead to the other states in reconsidering secession.

SEWARD. It is certainly a very attractive and, I conceive, a humane proposal.

WHITE. By furthering it you might be the saviour of the country from civil war, Mr. Seward.

SEWARD. The President dwelt on his resolution to hold Fort Sumter in his inaugural address. It will be difficult to persuade him to go back on that. He's firm in his decisions.

WHITE. There are people who would call him stubborn. Surely if it were put to him tactfully that so simple a course might avert incalculable disaster, no man would nurse his dignity to the point of not yielding. I speak plainly, but it's a time for plain speaking. Mr. Lincoln is doubtless a man of remarkable qualities : on the two occasions when I have spoken to him I have not been unimpressed. That is so, Mr. Jennings?

JENNINGS. Certainly.

WHITE. But what does his experience of great affairs of state amount to beside yours, Mr. Seward? He must know how much he depends on certain members of his Cabinet, I might say upon a certain member, for advice.

SEWARD. We have to move warily.

JENNINGS. Naturally. A man is sensitive, doubtless, in his first taste of office.

SEWARD. My support of the President is, of course, unquestionable.

WHITE. Oh, entirely. But how can your support be more valuable than in lending him your unequalled understanding?

SEWARD. The whole thing is coloured in his mind by the question of slavery.

JENNINGS. Disabuse his mind. Slavery is nothing. Persuade him to withdraw from Fort Sumter, and slavery can be settled round a table. You know there's a considerable support even for abolition in the South itself. If the trade has to be allowed in some districts, what is that compared to the disaster of civil war?

WHITE. We do not believe that the Southern States wish with any enthusiasm to secede. They merely wish to establish their right to do so. Acknowledge that by evacuating Fort Sumter, and nothing will come of it but a perfectly proper concession to an independence of spirit that is not disloyal to the Union at heart.

SEWARD. You understand, of course, that I can say nothing officially.

JENNINGS. These are nothing but informal suggestions.

SEWARD. But I may tell you that I am not unsympathetic.

WHITE. We were sure that that would be so.

SEWARD. And my word is not without influence.

JENNINGS. It can be used to bring you very great credit, Mr. Seward.

SEWARD. In the meantime, you will say nothing of this interview, beyond making your reports, which should be confidential.

WHITE. You may rely upon us.

SEWARD. [*rising with the others.*] Then I will bid you good morning.

WHITE. We are profoundly sensible of the magnanimous temper in which we are convinced you will conduct this grave business. Good morning, Mr. Seward.

JENNINGS. And I—

There is a knock at the door.

SEWARD. Yes—come in.

A CLERK *comes in.*

CLERK. The President is coming up the stairs, sir.

SEWARD. Thank you.

The CLERK *goes.*

This is unfortunate. Say nothing, and go at once.

LINCOLN *comes in, now whiskered and bearded.*

LINCOLN. Good morning, Mr. Seward. Good morning, gentlemen.

SEWARD. Good morning, Mr. President. And I am obliged to you for calling, gentlemen. Good morning.

He moves towards the door.

LINCOLN. Perhaps these gentlemen could spare me ten minutes.

WHITE. It might not—

LINCOLN. Say five minutes.

JENNINGS. Perhaps you would—

LINCOLN. I am anxious always for any opportunity to exchange views with our friends of the South. Much enlightenment may be gained in five minutes. Be seated, I beg you—if Mr. Seward will allow us.

SEWARD. By all means. Shall I leave you?

LINCOLN. Leave us—but why? I may want your support, Mr. Secretary, if we should not wholly agree. Be seated, gentlemen.

SEWARD *places a chair for* LINCOLN, *and they sit at the table.*

LINCOLN. You have messages for us?

WHITE. Well, no, we can't say that.

LINCOLN. No messages? Perhaps I am inquisitive?

SEWARD. These gentlemen are anxious to sound any moderating influences.

LINCOLN. I trust they bring moderating influences with them. You will find me a ready listener, gentlemen.

JENNINGS. It's a delicate matter, Mr. Lincoln. Ours is just an informal visit.

LINCOLN. Quite, quite. But we shall lose nothing by knowing each other's minds.

WHITE. Shall we tell the President what we came to say, Mr. Seward?

LINCOLN. I shall be grateful. If I should fail to understand, Mr. Seward, no doubt, will enlighten me.

JENNINGS. We thought it hardly worth while to trouble you at so early a stage.

LINCOLN. So early a stage of what?

JENNINGS. I mean—

SEWARD. These gentlemen, in a common anxiety for peace, were merely seeking the best channel through which suggestions could be made.

LINCOLN. To whom?

SEWARD. To the Government.

LINCOLN. The head of the Government is here.

WHITE. But—

LINCOLN. Come, gentlemen. What is it?

JENNINGS. It's this matter of Fort Sumter, Mr.

President. If you withdraw your garrison from Fort Sumter it won't be looked upon as weakness in you. It will merely be looked upon as a concession to a natural privilege. We believe that the South at heart does not want secession. It wants to establish the right to decide for itself.

LINCOLN. The South wants the stamp of national approval upon slavery. It can't have it.

WHITE. Surely that's not the point. There's no law in the South against slavery.

LINCOLN. Laws come from opinion, Mr. White. The South knows it.

JENNINGS. Mr. President, if I may say so, you don't quite understand.

LINCOLN. Does Mr. Seward understand?

WHITE. We believe so.

LINCOLN. You are wrong. He doesn't understand, because you didn't mean him to. I don't blame you. You think you are acting for the best. You think you've got an honest case. But I'll put your case for you, and I'll put it naked. Many people in this country want abolition; many don't. I'll say nothing for the moment as to the rights and wrongs of it. But every man, whether he wants it or not, knows it may come. Why does the South propose secession? Because it knows abolition may come, and it wants to avoid it. It wants more: it wants the right to extend the slave foundation. We've all been to blame for slavery, but we in the North have been willing to mend our ways. You have not. So you'll secede, and make your own laws. But you weren't prepared for resistance; you don't want resistance. And you hope that if you can tide over the first crisis and make us give way, opinion will prevent us from opposing you with force again, and you'll be able to get your own way about the slave business by threats. That's your case. You didn't say so to Mr. Seward, but it is. Now, I'll give you my answer.

Gentlemen, it's no good hiding this thing in a corner. It's got to be settled. I said the other day that Fort Sumter would be held as long as we could hold it. I said it because I know exactly what it means. Why are you investing it? Say, if you like, it's to establish your right of secession with no purpose of exercising it. Why do you want to establish that right? Because now we will allow no extension of slavery, and because some day we may abolish it. You can't deny it; there's no other answer.

JENNINGS. I see how it is. You may force freedom as much as you like, but we are to beware how we force slavery.

LINCOLN. It couldn't be put better, Mr. Jennings. That's what the Union means. It is a Union that stands for common right. That is its foundation—that is why it is for every honest man to preserve it. Be clear about this issue. If there is war, it will not be on the slave question. If the South is loyal to the Union, it can fight slave legislation by constitutional means, and win its way if it can. If it claims the right to secede, then to preserve this country from disruption, to maintain that right to which every state pledged itself when the Union was won for us by our fathers, war may be the only way. We won't break up the Union, and you shan't. In your hands, and not in mine, is the momentous issue of civil war. You can have no conflict without yourselves being the aggressors. I am loath to close. We are not enemies, but friends. We must not be enemies. Though passion may have strained, do not allow it to break our bonds of affection. That is our answer. Tell them that. Will you tell them that?

WHITE. You are determined?

LINCOLN. I beg you to tell them.

JENNINGS. It shall be as you wish.

LINCOLN. Implore them to order Beauregard's return. You can telegraph it now, from here. Will you do that?

WHITE. If you wish it.

LINCOLN. *Earnestly.* Mr. Seward, will you please place a clerk at their service. Ask for an answer.

SEWARD *rings a bell. A* CLERK *comes in.*

SEWARD. Give these gentlemen a private wire. Place yourself at their disposal.

CLERK. Yes, sir.

WHITE *and* JENNINGS *go out with the* CLERK. *For a moment* LINCOLN *and* SEWARD *are silent.* LINCOLN *pacing the room,* SEWARD *standing at the table.*

LINCOLN. Seward, this won't do.

SEWARD. You don't suspect—

LINCOLN. I do not. But let us be plain. No man can say how wisely, but providence has brought me to the leadership of this country, with a task before me greater than that which rested on Washington himself. When I made my Cabinet, you were the first man I chose. I do not regret it; I think I never shall. But remember, faith earns faith. What is it? Why didn't those men come to see me?

SEWARD. They thought my word might bear more weight with you than theirs.

LINCOLN. Your word for what?

SEWARD. Discretion about Fort Sumter.

LINCOLN. Discretion?

SEWARD. It's devastating, this thought of war.

LINCOLN. It is. Do you think I'm less sensible of that than you? War should be impossible. But you can only make it impossible by destroying its causes. Don't you see that to withdraw from Fort Sumter is to do nothing of the kind? If one half of this country claims the right to disown the Union, the claim in the eyes of every true guardian among us must be a cause for war, unless we hold the Union to be a false thing instead of the public consent to decent principles of life that it is. If we withdraw from Fort Sumter, we do nothing to destroy that cause.

We can only destroy it by convincing them that secession is a betrayal of their trust. Please God we may do so.

SEWARD. Has there, perhaps, been some timidity in making all this clear to the country?

LINCOLN. Timidity? And you were talking of discretion.

SEWARD. I mean that perhaps our policy has not been sufficiently defined.

LINCOLN. And have you not concurred in all our decisions? Do not deceive yourself. You urge me to discretion in one breath and tax me with timidity in the next. While there was hope that they might call Beauregard back out of their own good sense, I was determined to say nothing to inflame them. Do you call that timidity? Now their intention is clear, and you've heard me speak this morning clearly also. And now you talk about discretion—you, who call what was discretion at the right time timidity, now counsel timidity at the wrong time, and call it discretion. Seward, you may think I'm simple, but I can see your mind working as plainly as you might see the innards of a clock. You can bring great gifts to this Government, with your zeal, and your administrative experience, and your love of men. Don't spoil it by thinking I've got a dull brain.

SEWARD. [*slowly.*] Yes, I see. I've not been thinking quite clearly about it all.

LINCOLN. [*taking a paper from his pocket.*] Here's the paper you sent me. " Some Thoughts for the President's Consideration. Great Britain . . Russia . . Mexico . . policy. Either the President must control this himself, or devolve it on some member of his Cabinet. It is not my especial province. But I neither seek to evade nor assume responsibility."

There is a pause, the two men looking at each other without speaking. LINCOLN *hands the paper to*

SEWARD, *who holds it for a moment, tears it up, and throws it into his basket.*

SEWARD. I beg your pardon.

LINCOLN. [*taking his hand.*] That's brave of you.

MR. SLANEY, *a Secretary, comes in.*

SLANEY. There's a messenger from Major Anderson, sir. He's ridden straight from Fort Sumter.

LINCOLN. Take him to my room. No, bring him here.

SLANEY *goes.*

SEWARD. What does it mean?

LINCOLN. I don't like the sound of it.

He rings a bell. A CLERK *comes in.*

Are there any gentlemen of the Cabinet in the house?

CLERK. Mr. Chase and Mr. Blair, I believe, sir.

LINCOLN. My compliments to them, and will they be prepared to see me here at once if necessary. Send the same message to any other Ministers you can find.

CLERK. Yes, sir.

He goes.

LINCOLN. We may have to decide now—now.

SLANEY *shows in a perspiring and dust-covered* MESSENGER, *and retires.*

LINCOLN. From Major Anderson?

THE MESSENGER. Yes, sir. Word of mouth, sir.

LINCOLN. Your credentials?

THE MESSENGER. [*giving* LINCOLN *a paper.*] Here, sir.

LINCOLN. [*glancing at it.*] Well?

THE MESSENGER. Major Anderson presents his duty to the Government. He can hold the Fort three days more without provisions and reinforcements.

LINCOLN *rings the bell, and waits until a third* CLERK *comes in.*

LINCOLN. See if Mr. White and Mr. Jennings have had any answer yet. Mr. —— what's his name?

SEWARD. Hawkins.
LINCOLN. Mr. Hawkins is attending to them. And ask Mr. Slaney to come here.
CLERK. Yes, sir.
He goes. LINCOLN *sits at the table and writes.*
SLANEY *comes in.*
LINCOLN. [*writing.*] Mr. Slaney, do you know where General Scott is?
SLANEY. At headquarters, I think, sir.
LINCOLN. Take this to him yourself and bring an answer back.
SLANEY. Yes, sir.
He takes the note, and goes.
LINCOLN. Are things very bad at the fort?
THE MESSENGER. The Major says three days, sir. Most of us would have said twenty-four hours.
A knock at the door.
SEWARD. Yes.
HAWKINS *comes in.*
HAWKINS. Mr. White is just receiving a message across the wire, sir.
LINCOLN. Ask him to come here directly he's finished.
HAWKINS. Yes, sir.
He goes. LINCOLN *goes to a far door and opens it. He speaks to the* MESSENGER.
LINCOLN. Will you wait in here?
The MESSENGER *goes through.*
SEWARD. Do you mind if I smoke?
LINCOLN. Not at all, not at all.
SEWARD *lights a cigar.*
Three days. If White's message doesn't help us—three days.
SEWARD. But surely we must withdraw as a matter of military necessity now.
LINCOLN. Why doesn't White come?
SEWARD *goes to the window and throws it up. He*

stands looking down into the street. LINCOLN *stands at the table looking fixedly at the door. After a moment or two there is a knock.*

LINCOLN. Come in.

HAWKINS *shows in* WHITE *and* JENNINGS, *and goes out.* SEWARD *closes the window.*

LINCOLN. Well?

WHITE. I'm sorry. They won't give way.

LINCOLN. You told them all I said?

JENNINGS. Everything.

LINCOLN. It's critical.

WHITE. They are definite.

LINCOLN *paces once or twice up and down the room, standing again at his place at the table.*

LINCOLN. They leave no opening?

WHITE. I regret to say, none.

LINCOLN. It's a grave decision. Terribly grave. Thank you, gentlemen. Good morning.

WHITE *and* JENNINGS. Good morning, gentlemen.

They go out.

LINCOLN. My God. Seward, we need great courage, great faith.

He rings the bell. The SECOND CLERK *comes in.*

LINCOLN. Did you take my messages?

THE CLERK. Yes, sir. Mr. Chase and Mr. Blair are here. The other Ministers are coming immediately.

LINCOLN. Ask them to come here at once. And send Mr. Slaney in directly he returns.

THE CLERK. Yes, sir.

He goes.

LINCOLN. [*after a pause.*] "There is a tide in the affairs of men . ." Do you read Shakespeare, Seward?

SEWARD. Shakespeare? No.

LINCOLN. Ah!

SALMON CHASE, *Secretary of the Treasury, and* MONTGOMERY BLAIR, *Postmaster-General, come in.*

LINCOLN. Good morning, Mr. Chase, Mr. Blair.

SEWARD. Good morning, gentlemen.

BLAIR. Good morning, Mr. President. How d'ye do, Mr. Seward.

CHASE. Good morning, Mr. President. Something urgent?

LINCOLN. Let us be seated.

As they draw chairs up to the table, the other members of the Cabinet, SIMON CAMERON, CALEB SMITH, BURNET HOOK, *and* GIDEON WELLES, *come in. There is an exchange of greetings, while they arrange themselves round the table.*

LINCOLN. Gentlemen, we meet in a crisis, the most fateful, perhaps, that has ever faced any Government in this country. It can be stated briefly. A message has just come from Anderson. He can hold Fort Sumter three days at most unless we send men and provisions.

CAMERON. How many men?

LINCOLN. I shall know from Scott in a few minutes how many are necessary.

WELLES. Suppose we haven't as many.

LINCOLN. Then it's a question of provisioning. We may not be able to do enough to be effective. The question is whether we shall do as much as we can.

HOOK. If we withdrew altogether, wouldn't it give the South a lead towards compromise, as being an acknowledgement of their authority, while leaving us free to plead military necessity if we found public opinion dangerous?

LINCOLN. My mind is clear. To do less than we can do, whatever that may be, will be fundamentally to allow the South's claim to right of secession. That is my opinion. If you evade the question now, you will have to answer it to-morrow.

BLAIR. I agree with the President.

HOOK. We ought to defer action as long as possible. I consider that we should withdraw.

LINCOLN. Don't you see that to withdraw may postpone war, but that it will make it inevitable in the end.

SMITH. It is inevitable if we resist.

LINCOLN. I fear it will be so. But in that case we shall enter it with uncompromised principles. Mr. Chase?

CHASE. It is difficult. But, on the whole, my opinion is with yours, Mr. President.

LINCOLN. And you, Seward?

SEWARD. I respect your opinion, but I must differ.

A knock at the door.

LINCOLN. Come in.

SLANEY *comes in. He gives a letter to* LINCOLN *and goes.*

LINCOLN. [*reading.*] Scott says twenty thousand men.

SEWARD. We haven't ten thousand ready.

LINCOLN. It remains a question of sending provisions. I charge you, all of you, to weigh this thing with all your understanding. To temporise now cannot, in my opinion, avert war. To speak plainly to the world in standing by our resolution to hold Fort Sumter with all our means, and in a plain declaration that the Union must be preserved, will leave us with a clean cause, simply and loyally supported. I tremble at the thought of war. But we have in our hands a sacred trust. It is threatened. We have had no thought of aggression. We have been the aggressed. Persuasion has failed, and I conceive it to be our duty to resist. To withhold supplies from Anderson would be to deny that duty. Gentlemen, the matter is before you.

A pause.

For provisioning the fort?

LINCOLN, CHASE, *and* BLAIR *hold up their hands.*

LINCOLN. For immediate withdrawal?

SEWARD, CAMERON, SMITH, HOOK, *and* WELLES *hold up their hands. There is a pause of some moments.*

LINCOLN. Gentlemen, I may have to take upon myself

the responsibility of overriding your vote. It will be for me to satisfy Congress and public opinion. Should I receive any resignations?

There is silence.

LINCOLN. I thank you for your consideration, gentlemen. That is all.

They rise, and the Ministers, with the exception of SEWARD, *go out, talking as they pass beyond the door.*

LINCOLN. You are wrong, Seward, wrong.

SEWARD. I believe you. I respect your judgement even as far as that. But I must speak as I feel.

LINCOLN. May I speak to this man alone?

SEWARD. Certainly.

He goes out. LINCOLN *stands motionless for a moment. Then he moves to a map of the United States, much larger than the one in his Illinois home, and looks at it as he did there. He goes to the far door and opens it.*

LINCOLN. Will you come in?

The MESSENGER *comes.*

LINCOLN. Can you ride back to Major Anderson at once?

THE MESSENGER. Yes, sir.

LINCOLN. Tell him that we cannot reinforce him immediately. We haven't the men.

THE MESSENGER. Yes, sir.

LINCOLN. And say that the first convoy of supplies will leave Washington this evening.

THE MESSENGER. Yes, sir.

LINCOLN. Thank you.

The MESSENGER *goes.* LINCOLN *stands at the table for a moment; he rings the bell.* HAWKINS *comes in.*

LINCOLN. Mr. Slaney, please.

HAWKINS. Yes, sir.

He goes, and a moment later SLANEY *comes in.*

LINCOLN. Go to General Scott. Ask him to come to me at once.

SLANEY. Yes, sir.

He goes.

THE CURTAIN FALLS

THE TWO CHRONICLERS.   You who have gone gathering
    Cornflowers and meadowsweet,
  Heard the hazels glancing down
    On September eves,
  Seen the homeward rooks on wing
    Over fields of golden wheat,
  And the silver cups that crown
    Water-lily leaves ;

  You who know the tenderness
    Of old men at eve-tide,
  Coming from the hedgerows,
    Coming from the plough,
  And the wandering caress
    Of winds upon the woodside,
  When the crying yaffle goes
    Underneath the bough ;

FIRST CHRONICLER.   You who mark the flowing
    Of sap upon the May-time,
  And the waters welling
    From the watershed,
  You who count the growing
    Of harvest and hay-time,
  Knowing these the telling
    Of your daily bread ;

SECOND CHRONICLER.   You who cherish courtesy
    With your fellows at your gate,

And about your hearthstone sit
  Under love's decrees,
You who know that death will be
  Speaking with you soon or late,

THE TWO TOGETHER. Kinsmen, what is mother-wit
  But the light of these?

Knowing these, what is there more
  For learning in your little years?
Are not these all gospels bright
  Shining on your day?
How then shall your hearts be sore
  With envy and her brood of fears,
How forget the words of light
  From the mountain-way . .

Blessed are the merciful. . .
  Does not every threshold seek
Meadows and the flight of birds
  For compassion still?
Blessed are the merciful. . .
  Are we pilgrims yet to speak
Out of Olivet the words
  Of knowledge and good-will?

FIRST CHRONICLER. Two years of darkness, and this
  man but grows
Greater in resolution, more constant in compassion.
He goes
The way of dominion in pitiful, high-hearted fashion.

SCENE III

Nearly two years later.
A small reception room at the White House. MRS.
  LINCOLN, *dressed in a fashion perhaps a little too
  considered, despairing as she now does of any sartorial*

grace in her husband, and acutely conscious that she must meet this necessity of office alone, is writing. She rings the bell, and SUSAN, *who has taken her promotion more philosophically, comes in.*

MRS. LINCOLN. Admit any one who calls, Susan. And inquire whether the President will be in to tea.

SUSAN. Mr. Lincoln has just sent word that he will be in.

MRS. LINCOLN. Very well.

SUSAN *is going.*

Susan.

SUSAN. Yes, ma'am.

MRS. LINCOLN. You still say Mr. Lincoln. You should say the President.

SUSAN. Yes, ma'am. But you see, ma'am, it's difficult after calling him Mr. Lincoln for fifteen years.

MRS. LINCOLN. But you must remember. Everybody calls him the President now.

SUSAN. No, ma'am. There's a good many people call him Father Abraham now. And there's some that like him even better than that. Only to-day Mr. Coldpenny, at the stores, said, " Well, Susan, and how's old Abe this morning ? "

MRS. LINCOLN. I hope you don't encourage them.

SUSAN. Oh no, ma'am. I always refer to him as Mr. Lincoln.

MRS. LINCOLN. Yes, but you must say the President.

SUSAN. I'm afraid I shan't ever learn, ma'am.

MRS. LINCOLN. You must try.

SUSAN. Yes, of course, ma'am.

MRS. LINCOLN. And bring any visitors up.

SUSAN. Yes, ma'am. There's a lady waiting now.

MRS. LINCOLN. Then why didn't you say so ?

SUSAN. That's what I was going to, ma'am, when you began to talk about Mr.—I mean the President, ma'am.

MRS. LINCOLN. Well, show her up.

SUSAN *goes.* MRS. LINCOLN *closes her writing desk.*
SUSAN *returns, showing in* MRS. GOLIATH BLOW.
SUSAN. Mrs. Goliath Blow.
She goes.
MRS. BLOW. Good afternoon, Mrs. Lincoln.
MRS. LINCOLN. Good afternoon, Mrs. Blow. Sit down, please.
They sit.
MRS. BLOW. And is the dear President well?
MRS. LINCOLN. Yes. He's rather tired.
MRS. BLOW. Of course, to be sure. This dreadful war. But I hope he's not getting tired of the war.
MRS. LINCOLN. It's a constant anxiety for him. He feels his responsibility very deeply.
MRS. BLOW. To be sure. But you mustn't let him get war-weary. These monsters in the South have got to be stamped out.
MRS. LINCOLN. I don't think you need be afraid of the President's firmness.
MRS. BLOW. Oh, of course not. I was only saying to Goliath yesterday, " The President will never give way till he has the South squealing," and Goliath agreed.
SUSAN *comes in.*
SUSAN. Mrs. Otherly, ma'am.
MRS. LINCOLN. Show Mrs. Otherly in.
SUSAN *goes.*
MRS. BLOW. Oh, that dreadful woman. I believe she wants the war to stop.
SUSAN. [*at the door.*] Mrs. Otherly.
MRS. OTHERLY *comes in and* SUSAN *goes.*
MRS. LINCOLN. Good afternoon, Mrs. Otherly. You know Mrs. Goliath Blow?
MRS. OTHERLY. Yes. Good afternoon.
She sits.
MRS. BLOW. Goliath says the war will go on for another three years at least.

MRS. OTHERLY. Three years? That would be terrible, wouldn't it?

MRS. BLOW. We must be prepared to make sacrifices.

MRS. OTHERLY. Yes.

MRS. BLOW. It makes my blood boil to think of those people.

MRS. OTHERLY. I used to know a lot of them. Some of them were very kind and nice.

MRS. BLOW. That was just their cunning, depend on it. I'm afraid there's a good deal of disloyalty among us. Shall we see the dear President this afternoon, Mrs. Lincoln?

MRS. LINCOLN. He will be here directly, I think.

MRS. BLOW. You're looking wonderfully well, with all the hard work that you have to do. I've really had to drop some of mine. And with expenses going up, it's all very lowering, don't you think? Goliath and I have had to reduce several of our subscriptions. But, of course, we all have to deny ourselves something. Ah, good afternoon, dear Mr. President.

LINCOLN *comes in.* THE LADIES *rise and shake hands with him.*

LINCOLN. Good afternoon, ladies.

MRS. OTHERLY. Good afternoon, Mr. President.

They all sit.

MRS. BLOW. And is there any startling news, Mr. President?

LINCOLN. Madam, every morning when I wake up, and say to myself, a hundred, or two hundred, or a thousand of my countrymen will be killed to-day, I find it startling.

MRS. BLOW. Oh yes, of course, to be sure. But I mean, is there any good news.

LINCOLN. Yes. There is news of a victory. They lost twenty-seven hundred men—we lost eight hundred.

MRS. BLOW. How splendid.

LINCOLN. Thirty-five hundred.

MRS. BLOW. Oh, but you mustn't talk like that, Mr. President. There were only eight hundred that mattered.

LINCOLN. The world is larger than your heart, madam.

MRS. BLOW. Now the dear President is becoming whimsical, Mrs. Lincoln.

SUSAN *brings in tea-tray, and hands tea round.* LINCOLN *takes none.* SUSAN *goes.*

MRS. OTHERLY. Mr. President.

LINCOLN. Yes, ma'am.

MRS. OTHERLY. I don't like to impose upon your hospitality. I know how difficult everything is for you. But one has to take one's opportunities. May I ask you a question?

LINCOLN. Certainly, ma'am.

MRS. OTHERLY. Isn't it possible for you to stop this war? In the name of a suffering country, I ask you that.

MRS. BLOW. I'm sure such a question would never have entered my head.

LINCOLN. It is a perfectly right question. Ma'am, I have but one thought always—how can this thing be stopped? But we must ensure the integrity of the Union. In two years war has become an hourly bitterness to me. I believe I suffer no less than any man. But it must be endured. The cause was a right one two years ago. It is unchanged.

MRS. OTHERLY. I know you are noble and generous. But I believe that war must be wrong under any circumstances, for any cause.

MRS. BLOW. I'm afraid the President would have but little encouragement if he listened often to this kind of talk.

LINCOLN. I beg you not to harass yourself, madam. Ma'am, I too believe war to be wrong. It is the weakness and the jealousy and the folly of men that make a thing so wrong possible. But we are all weak, and jealous, and foolish. That's how the world is ma'am, and we cannot outstrip the world. Some of the worst of us are sullen, aggressive still—just clumsy, greedy pirates. Some of us have grown out of that. But the best of us have an instinct to resist aggression if it won't listen to persuasion. You may say it's a wrong instinct. I don't know. But it's there, and it's there in millions of good men. I don't believe it's a wrong instinct. I believe that the world must come to wisdom slowly. It is for us who hate aggression to persuade men always and earnestly against it, and hope that, little by little, they will hear us. But in the meantime there will come moments when the aggressors will force the instinct to resistance to act. Then we must act earnestly, praying always in our courage that never again will this thing happen. And then we must turn again, and again, and again to persuasion. This appeal to force is the misdeed of an imperfect world. But we are imperfect. We must strive to purify the world, but we must not think ourselves pure above the world. When I had this thing to decide, it would have been easy to say, "No, I will have none of it; it is evil, and I will not touch it." But that would have decided nothing, and I saw what I believed to be the truth as I now put it to you, ma'am. It's a forlorn thing for any man to have this responsibility in his heart. I may see wrongly, but that's how I see.

MRS BLOW. I quite agree with you, Mr. President. These brutes in the South must be taught, though I doubt whether you can teach them anything except by destroying them. That's what Goliath says.

LINCOLN. Goliath must be getting quite an old man.

MRS. BLOW. Indeed, he's not, Mr. President. Goliath is only thirty-eight.

LINCOLN. Really, now? Perhaps I might be able to get him a commission.

MRS. BLOW. Oh, no. Goliath couldn't be spared. He's doing contracts for the Government, you know.

Goliath couldn't possibly go. I'm sure he will be very pleased when I tell him what you say about these people who want to stop the war, Mr. President. I hope Mrs. Otherly is satisfied. Of course, we could all complain. We all have to make sacrifices, as I told Mrs. Otherly.

MRS. OTHERLY. Thank you, Mr. President, for what you've said. I must try to think about it. But I always believed war to be wrong. I didn't want my boy to go, because I believed it to be wrong. But he would. That came to me last week

She hands a paper to LINCOLN.

LINCOLN. [*looks at it, rises, and hands it back to her.*] Ma'am, there are times when no man may speak. I grieve for you, I grieve for you.

MRS. OTHERLY [*rising.*] I think I will go. You don't mind my saying what I did?

LINCOLN. We are all poor creatures, ma'am. Think kindly of me. [*He takes her hand.*] Mary.

MRS LINCOLN *goes out with* MRS. OTHERLY.

MRS. BLOW. Of course it's very sad for her, poor woman. But she makes her trouble worse by these perverted views, doesn't she? And, I hope you will show no signs of weakening, Mr. President, till it has been made impossible for those shameful rebels to hold up their heads again. Goliath says you ought to make a proclamation that no mercy will be shown to them afterwards. I'm sure I shall never speak to one of them again.

Rising.

Well, I must be going. I'll see Mrs. Lincoln as I go out. Good afternoon, Mr. President.

She turns at the door, and offers LINCOLN *her hand, which he does not take.*

LINCOLN. Good afternoon, madam. And I'ld like to offer ye a word of advice. That poor mother told me what she thought. I don't agree with her, but I honour her. She's wrong, but she is noble. You've told me what you think. I don't agree with you, and I'm ashamed of you and your like. You, who have sacrificed nothing, babble about destroying the South while other people conquer it. I accepted this war with a sick heart, and I've a heart that's near to breaking every day. I accepted it in the name of humanity, and just and merciful dealing, and the hope of love and charity on earth. And you come to me, talking of revenge and destruction, and malice, and enduring hate. These gentle people are mistaken, but they are mistaken cleanly, and in a great name. It is you that dishonour the cause for which we stand—it is you who would make it a mean and little thing. Good afternoon.

He opens the door and MRS. GOLIATH, *finding words inadequate, goes.* LINCOLN *moves across the room and rings a bell. After a moment,* SUSAN *comes in.*

LINCOLN. Susan, if that lady comes here again she may meet with an accident.

SUSAN. Yes, sir. Is that all, sir?

LINCOLN. No, sir, it is not all, sir. I don't like this coat. I am going to change it. I shall be back in a minute or two, and if a gentleman named Mr. Frederick Douglass calls, ask him to wait in here.

He goes out. SUSAN *collects the tea-cups. As she is going to the door a quiet, grave, white-haired negro appears facing her.* SUSAN *starts violently.*

THE NEGRO. [*he talks slowly and very quietly.*] It is all right.

SUSAN. And who in the name of night might you be?

THE NEGRO. Mista Frederick Douglass. Mista Lincoln tell me to come here. Nobody stop me, so I come to look for him.

SUSAN. Are you Mr. Frederick Douglass?

DOUGLASS. Yes.

SUSAN. Mr. Lincoln will be here directly. He's gone to change his coat. You'd better sit down.

DOUGLASS. Yes.

He does so, looking about him with a certain pathetic inquisitiveness.

Mista Lincoln live here. You his servant? A very fine thing for young girl to be servant to Mista Lincoln.

SUSAN. Well, we get on very well together.

DOUGLASS. A very bad thing to be slave in South.

SUSAN. Look here, you Mr. Douglass, don't you go mixing me up with slaves.

DOUGLASS. No, you not slave. You servant, but you free body. That very mighty thing. A poor servant, born free.

SUSAN. Yes, but look here, are you pitying me, with your poor servant?

DOUGLASS. Pity? No. I think you very mighty.

SUSAN. Well, I don't know so much about mighty. But I expect you're right. It isn't every one that rises to the White House.

DOUGLASS. It not every one that is free body. That is why you mighty.

SUSAN. I've never thought much about it.

DOUGLASS. I think always about it.

SUSAN. I suppose you're free, aren't you?

DOUGLASS. Yes. Not born free. I was beaten when I a little nigger. I saw my mother— I will not remember what I saw.

SUSAN. I'm sorry, Mr. Douglass. That was wrong.

DOUGLASS. Yes. Wrong.

SUSAN. Are all nig—I mean are all black gentlemen like you?

DOUGLASS. No. I have advantages. They not many have advantages.

SUSAN. No, I suppose not. Here's Mr. Lincoln coming.

LINCOLN, *coated after his heart's desire, comes to the door.* DOUGLASS *rises.*

SUSAN. This is the gentleman you said, sir.
She goes out with the tray.
LINCOLN. Mr. Douglass, I'm very glad to see you.
He offers his hand. DOUGLASS *takes it, and is about to kiss it.* LINCOLN *stops him gently.*
LINCOLN. [*sitting.*] Sit down, will you?
DOUGLASS. [*still standing, keeping his hat in his hand.*] It very kind of Mista Lincoln ask me to come to see him.
LINCOLN. I was afraid you might refuse.
DOUGLASS. A little shy? Yes. But so much to ask. Glad to come.
LINCOLN. Please sit down.
DOUGLASS. Polite?
LINCOLN. Please. I can't sit myself, you see, if you don't.
DOUGLASS. Black, black. White, white.
LINCOLN. Nonsense. Just two old men, sitting together [DOUGLASS *sits to* LINCOLN'S *gesture*]—and talking.
DOUGLASS. I think I older man than Mista Lincoln.
LINCOLN. Yes, I expect you are. I'm fifty-four.
DOUGLASS. I seventy-two.
LINCOLN. I hope I shall look as young when I'm seventy-two.
DOUGLASS. Cold water. Much walk. Believe in Lord Jesus Christ. Have always little herbs learnt when a little nigger. Mista Lincoln try. Very good.
He hands a small twist of paper to LINCOLN.
LINCOLN. Now, that's uncommon kind of you. Thank you. I've heard much about your preaching, Mr. Douglass.
DOUGLASS. Yes.
LINCOLN. I should like to hear you.
DOUGLASS. Mista Lincoln great friend of my people.
LINCOLN. I have come at length to a decision.
DOUGLASS. A decision?

LINCOLN. Slavery is going. We have been resolved always to confine it. Now it shall be abolished.
DOUGLASS. You sure?
LINCOLN. Sure.
DOUGLASS *slowly stands up, bows his head, and sits again.*
DOUGLASS. My people much to learn. Years, and years, and years. Ignorant, frightened, suspicious people. It will be difficult, very slow. [*With growing passion.*] But born free bodies. Free. I born slave, Mista Lincoln. No man understand who not born slave.
LINCOLN. Yes, yes. I understand.
DOUGLASS. [*with his normal regularity.*] I think so. Yes.
LINCOLN. I should like you to ask me any question you wish.
DOUGLASS. I have some complaint. Perhaps I not understand.
LINCOLN. Tell me.
DOUGLASS. Southern soldiers take some black men prisoner. Black men in your uniform. Take them prisoner. Then murder them.
LINCOLN. I know.
DOUGLASS. What you do?
LINCOLN. We have sent a protest.
DOUGLASS. No good. Must do more.
LINCOLN. What more can we do?
DOUGLASS. You know.
LINCOLN. Yes, but don't ask me for reprisals.
DOUGLASS. [*gleaming.*] Eye for an eye, tooth for a tooth.
LINCOLN. No, no. You must think. Think what you are saying.
DOUGLASS. I think of murdered black men.
LINCOLN. You would not ask me to murder?
DOUGLASS. Punish—not murder.

LINCOLN. Yes, murder. How can I kill men in cold blood for what has been done by others? Think what would follow. It is for us to set a great example, not to follow a wicked one. You do believe that, don't you?

DOUGLASS. [*after a pause.*] I know. Yes. Let your light so shine before men. I trust Mista Lincoln. Will trust. I was wrong. I was too sorry for my people.

LINCOLN. Will you remember this? For more than two years I have thought of you every day. I have grown a weary man with thinking. But I shall not forget. I promise that.

DOUGLASS. You great, kind friend. I will love you.

A knock at the door.

LINCOLN. Yes.

SUSAN *comes in.*

SUSAN. An officer gentleman. He says it's very important.

LINCOLN. I'll come.

He and DOUGLASS *rise.*

Wait, will you, Mr. Douglass? I want to ask you some questions.

He goes out. It is getting dark, and SUSAN *lights a lamp and draws the curtains.* DOUGLASS *stands by the door looking after* LINCOLN.

DOUGLASS. He very good man.

SUSAN. You've found that out, have you?

DOUGLASS. Do you love him, you white girl?

SUSAN. Of course I do.

DOUGLASS. Yes, you must.

SUSAN. He's a real white man. No offence, of course.

DOUGLASS. Not offend. He talk to me as if black no difference.

SUSAN. But I tell you what, Mr. Douglass. He'll kill himself over this war, his heart's that kind—like a shorn lamb, as they say.

DOUGLASS. Very unhappy war.

SUSAN. But I suppose he's right. It's got to go on till it's settled.

In the street below a body of people is heard approaching, singing "John Brown's Body". DOUGLASS *and* SUSAN *stand listening,* SUSAN *joining in the song as it passes and fades away.*

THE CURTAIN FALLS

FIRST CHRONICLER. Unchanged our time. And further yet
In loneliness must be the way,
And difficult and deep the debt
Of constancy to pay.

SECOND CHRONICLER. And one denies, and one forsakes.
And still unquestioning he goes,
Who has his lonely thoughts, and makes
A world of those.

THE TWO TOGETHER. When the high heart we magnify,
And the sure vision celebrate,
And worship greatness passing by,
Ourselves are great.

SCENE IV

About the same date. A meeting of the Cabinet at Washington. SMITH *has gone and* CAMERON *has been replaced by* EDWIN STANTON, *Secretary of War. Otherwise the Ministry, completed by* SEWARD, CHASE, HOOK, BLAIR, *and* WELLES, *is as before. They are now arranging themselves at the table, leaving* LINCOLN'S *place empty.*

SEWARD. [*coming in.*] I've just had my summons. Is there some special news?

STANTON. Yes. McClellan has defeated Lee at Antietam. It's our greatest success. They ought not to recover from it. The tide is turning.

BLAIR. Have you seen the President?

STANTON. I've just been with him.

WELLES. What does he say?

STANTON. He only said "at last". He's coming directly.

HOOK. He will bring up his proclamation again. In my opinion it is inopportune.

SEWARD. Well, we've learnt by now that the President is the best man among us.

HOOK. There's a good deal of feeling against him everywhere, I find.

BLAIR. He's the one man with character enough for this business.

HOOK. There are other opinions.

SEWARD. Yes, but not here, surely.

HOOK. It's not for me to say. But I ask you, what does he mean about emancipation? I've always understood that it was the Union we were fighting for, and that abolition was to be kept in our minds for legislation at the right moment. And now one day he talks as though emancipation were his only concern, and the next as though he would throw up the whole idea, if by doing it he could secure peace with the establishment of the Union. Where are we?

SEWARD. No, you're wrong. It's the Union first now with him, but there's no question about his views on slavery. You know that perfectly well. But he has always kept his policy about slavery free in his mind, to be directed as he thought best for the sake of the Union. You remember his words: "If I could save the Union without freeing any slaves, I would do it; and if I could save it by freeing all the slaves I would do it; and if I could save it by freeing some and leaving others alone, I would also do that. My paramount object in this struggle is to save the Union." Nothing could be plainer than that, just as nothing could be plainer than his determination to free the slaves when he can.

HOOK. Well, there are some who would have acted differently.

BLAIR. And you may depend upon it they would not have acted so wisely.

STANTON. I don't altogether agree with the President. But he's the only man I should agree with at all.

HOOK. To issue the proclamation now, and that's what he will propose, mark my word, will be to confuse the public mind just when we want to keep it clear.

WELLES. Are you sure he will propose to issue it now?

HOOK. You see if he doesn't.

WELLES. If he does I shall support him.

SEWARD. Is Lee's army broken?

STANTON. Not yet—but it is in grave danger.

HOOK. Why doesn't the President come? One would think this news was nothing.

CHASE. I must say I'm anxious to know what he has to say about it all.

A CLERK *comes in.*

CLERK. The President's compliments, and he will be here in a moment.

He goes.

HOOK. I shall oppose it if it comes up.

CHASE. He may say nothing about it.

SEWARD. I think he will.

STANTON. Anyhow, it's the critical moment.

BLAIR. Here he comes.

LINCOLN *comes in carrying a small book.*

LINCOLN. Good morning, gentlemen.

He takes his place.

THE MINISTERS. Good morning, Mr. President.

SEWARD. Great news, we hear.

HOOK. If we leave things with the army to take their course for a little now, we ought to see through our difficulties.

LINCOLN. It's an exciting morning, gentlemen. I feel rather excited myself. I find my mind not at its best in excitement. Will you allow me?

Opening his book.
It may compose us all. It is Mr. Artemus Ward's latest.

> THE MINISTERS, *with the exception of* HOOK, *who makes no attempt to hide his irritation, and* STANTON, *who would do the same but for his disapproval of* HOOK, *listen with good-humoured patience and amusement while he reads the following passage from Artemus Ward.*

" High-Handed Outrage at Utica."

" In the Faul of 1856, I showed my show in Utiky, a trooly grate sitty in the State of New York. The people gave me a cordual recepshun. The press was loud in her prases. 1 day as I was givin a descripshun of my Beests and Snaiks in my usual flowry stile what was my skorn & disgust to see a big burly feller walk up to the cage containin my wax figgers of the Lord's Last Supper, and cease Judas Iscarrot by the feet and drag him out on the ground. He then commenced fur to pound him as hard as he cood.

" ' What under the son are you abowt?' cried I.

" Sez he, ' What did you bring this pussylanermus cuss here fur?' and he hit the wax figger another tremenjis blow on the hed.

" Sez I, 'You egrejus ass, that air's a wax figger—a representashun of the false 'Postle.'

" Sez he, ' That's all very well fur you to say; but I tell you, old man, that Judas Iscarrot can't show himself in Utiky with impunerty by a darn site,' with which observashun he kaved in Judassis hed. The young man belonged to 1 of the first famerlies in Utiky. I sood him, and the Joory brawt in a verdick of Arson in the 3d degree."

STANTON. May we now consider affairs of state?

HOOK. Yes, we may.

LINCOLN. Mr. Hook says, yes, we may

STANTON. Thank you.

LINCOLN. Oh, no. Thank Mr. Hook.

SEWARD. McClellan is in pursuit of Lee, I suppose.

LINCOLN. You suppose a good deal. But for the first time McClellan has the chance of being in pursuit of Lee, and that's the first sign of their end. If McClellan doesn't take his chance, we'll move Grant down to the job. That will mean delay, but no matter. The mastery has changed hands.

BLAIR. Grant drinks.

LINCOLN. Then tell me the name of his brand. I'll send some barrels to the others. He wins victories.

HOOK. Is there other business?

LINCOLN. There is. Some weeks ago I showed you a draft I made proclaiming freedom for all slaves.

HOOK. [*aside to Welles.*] I told you so.

LINCOLN. You thought then it was not the time to issue it. I agreed. I think the moment has come. May I read it to you again. " It is proclaimed that on the first day of January in the year of our Lord one thousand eight hundred and sixty-three, all persons held as slaves within any state, the people whereof shall then be in rebellion against the United States, shall be then, thenceforward, and forever free." That allows three months from to-day. There are clauses dealing with compensation in a separate draft.

HOOK. I must oppose the issue of such a proclamation at this moment in the most unqualified terms. This question should be left until our victory is complete. To thrust it forward now would be to invite dissension when we most need unity.

WELLES. I do not quite understand, Mr. President, why you think this the precise moment.

LINCOLN. Believe me, gentlemen, I have considered this matter with all the earnestness and understanding of which I am capable.

HOOK. But when the "New York Tribune" urged you to come forward with a clear declaration six months ago, you rebuked them.

LINCOLN. Because I thought the occasion not the right one. It was useless to issue a proclamation that might be as inoperative as the Pope's bull against the comet. My duty, it has seemed to me, has been to be loyal to a principle, and not to betray it by expressing it in action at the wrong time. That is what I conceive statesmanship to be. For long now I have had two fixed resolves. To preserve the Union, and to abolish slavery. How to preserve the Union I was always clear, and more than two years of bitterness have not dulled my vision. We have fought for the Union, and we are now winning for the Union. When and how to proclaim abolition I have all this time been uncertain. I am uncertain no longer. A few weeks ago I saw that, too, clearly. So soon, I said to myself, as the rebel army shall be driven out of Maryland, and it becomes plain to the world that victory is assured to us in the end, the time will have come to announce that with that victory, and a vindicated Union, will come abolition. I made the promise to myself—and to my Maker. The rebel army is now driven out, and I am going to fulfil that promise. I do not wish your advice about the main matter, for that I have determined for myself. This I say without intending anything but respect for any one of you. But I beg you to stand with me in this thing.

HOOK. In my opinion, it's altogether too impetuous.

LINCOLN. One other observation I will make. I know very well that others might in this matter, as in others, do better than I can; and if I was satisfied that the public confidence was more fully possessed by any one of them than by me, and knew of any constitutional way in which he could be put in my place, he should have it. I would gladly yield it to him. But, though I cannot claim undivided confidence, I do not know that, all things considered, any other person has more; and, however this may be, there is no way in which I can have any other man put where I am. I am here; I must do the best I can, and bear the responsibility of taking the course which I feel I ought to take.

STANTON. Could this be left over a short time for consideration?

CHASE. I feel that we should remember that our only public cause at the moment is the preservation of the Union.

HOOK. I entirely agree.

LINCOLN. Gentlemen, we cannot escape history. We of this administration will be remembered in spite of ourselves. No personal significance or insignificance can spare one or another of us. In giving freedom to the slave we assure freedom to the free. We shall nobly save or meanly lose the last, best hope on earth.

He places the proclamation in front of him.

" Shall be thenceforward and forever free." Gentlemen, I pray for your support.

He signs it.

THE MINISTERS *rise.* SEWARD, WELLES, *and* BLAIR *shake* LINCOLN'S *hand and go out.* STANTON *and* CHASE *bow to him, and follow.* HOOK, *the last to rise, moves away, making no sign.*

LINCOLN. Hook.

HOOK. Yes, Mr. President.

LINCOLN. Hook, one cannot help hearing things.

HOOK. I beg your pardon?

LINCOLN. Hook, there's a way some people have, when a man says a disagreeable thing, of asking him to repeat it, hoping to embarrass him. It's often effective. But I'm not easily embarrassed. I said one cannot help hearing things.

HOOK. And I do not understand what you mean, Mr. President.

LINCOLN. Come, Hook, we're alone. Lincoln is a good enough name. And I think you understand.

HOOK. How should I?

LINCOLN. Then, plainly, there are intrigues going on.

HOOK. Against the government?

LINCOLN. No. In it. Against me.

HOOK. Criticism, perhaps.

LINCOLN. To what end? To better my ways?

HOOK. I presume that might be the purpose.

LINCOLN. Then, why am I not told what it is?

HOOK. I imagine it's a natural compunction.

LINCOLN. Or ambition?

HOOK. What do you mean?

LINCOLN. You think you ought to be in my place.

HOOK. You are well informed.

LINCOLN. You cannot imagine why every one does not see that you ought to be in my place.

HOOK. By what right do you say that?

LINCOLN. Is it not true?

HOOK. You take me unprepared. You have me at a disadvantage.

LINCOLN. You speak as a very scrupulous man, Hook.

HOOK. Do you question my honour?

LINCOLN. As you will.

HOOK. Then I resign.

LINCOLN. As a protest against . . ?

HOOK. Your suspicion.

LINCOLN. It is false?

HOOK. Very well, I will be frank. I mistrust your judgment.

LINCOLN. In what?

HOOK. Generally. You over-emphasise abolition.

LINCOLN. You don't mean that. You mean that you fear possible public feeling against abolition.

HOOK. It must be persuaded, not forced.

LINCOLN. All the most worthy elements in it are persuaded. But the ungenerous elements make the most noise, and you hear them only. You will run from the terrible name of Abolitionist even when it is pronounced by worthless creatures whom you know you have every reason to despise.

HOOK. You have, in my opinion, failed in necessary firmness in saying what will be the individual penalties of rebellion.

LINCOLN. This is a war. I will not allow it to become a blood-feud.

HOOK. We are fighting treason. We must meet it with severity.

LINCOLN. We will defeat treason. And I will meet it with conciliation.

HOOK. It is a policy of weakness.

LINCOLN. It is a policy of faith—it is a policy of compassion. [*Warmly.*] Hook, why do you plague me with these jealousies? Once before I found a member of my Cabinet working behind my back. But he was disinterested, and he made amends nobly. But, Hook, you have allowed the burden of these days to sour you. I know it all. I've watched you plotting and plotting for authority. And I, who am a lonely man, have been sick at heart. So great is the task God has given to my hand, and so few are my days, and my deepest hunger is always for loyalty in my own house. You have withheld it from me. You have done great service in your office, but you have grown envious. Now you resign, as you did once before when I came openly to you in friendship. And you think that again I shall flatter you and coax you to stay. I don't think I ought to do it. I will not do it. I must take you at your word.

HOOK. I am content.
He turns to go.
LINCOLN. Will you shake hands?
HOOK. I beg you will excuse me.
He goes. LINCOLN *stands silently for a moment, a travelled, lonely captain. He rings a bell, and a* CLERK *comes in.*
LINCOLN. Ask Mr. Slaney to come in.
CLERK. Yes, sir.
He goes. LINCOLN, *from the folds of his pockets, produces another book, and holds it unopened.* SLANEY *comes in.*
LINCOLN. I'm rather tired to-day, Slaney. Read to me a little. [*He hands him the book.*] "The Tempest"—you know the passage.
SLANEY. [*reading.*] Our revels now are ended; these our actors,
As I foretold you, were all spirits, and
Are melted into air, into thin air;
And like the baseless fabric of this vision,
The cloud-capped towers, the gorgeous palaces,
The solemn temples, the great globe itself,
Yea, all which it inherit, shall dissolve
And, like this insubstantial pageant faded,
Leave not a rack behind. We are such stuff
As dreams are made on, and our little life
Is rounded with a sleep.
LINCOLN.   We are such stuff
As dreams are made on, and our little life . .

THE CURTAIN FALLS

FIRST CHRONICLER. Two years again.
Desolation of battle, and long debate,
Counsels and prayers of men,
And bitterness of destruction and witless hate

And the shame of lie contending with lie,
Are spending themselves, and the brain
That set its lonely chart four years gone by,
Knowing the word fulfilled,
Comes with charity and communion to bring
To reckoning,
To reconcile and build.

THE TWO TOGETHER. What victor coming from the
    field
    Leaving the victim desolate,
But has a vulnerable shield
    Against the substances of fate?
That battle's won that leads in chains
    But retribution and despite,
And bids misfortune count her gains
    Not stricken in a penal night.

His triumph is but bitterness
    Who looks not to the starry doom
When proud and humble but possess
    The little kingdom of the tomb.
Who, striking home, shall not forgive,
    Strikes with a weak returning rod,
Claiming a fond prerogative
    Against the armoury of God.

Who knows, and for his knowledge stands
    Against the darkness in dispute,
And dedicates industrious hands,
    And keeps a spirit resolute,
Prevailing in the battle, then
    A steward of his word is made,
To bring it honour among men,
    Or know his captaincy betrayed.

Scene V

An April evening in 1865. A farmhouse near Appomatox.
GENERAL GRANT, *Commander-in-chief, under Lincoln, of the Northern armies, is seated at a table with* CAPTAIN MALINS, *an aide-de-camp. He is smoking a cigar, and at intervals he replenishes his glass of whisky.* DENNIS, *an orderly, sits at a table in the corner, writing.*

GRANT. [*consulting a large watch lying in front of him.*] An hour and a half. There ought to be something more from Meade by now. Dennis.

DENNIS. [*coming to the table.*] Yes, sir.

GRANT. Take these papers to Captain Templeman, and ask Colonel West if the twenty-third are in action yet. Tell the cook to send some soup at ten o'clock. Say it was cold yesterday.

DENNIS. Yes, sir.

He goes.

GRANT. Give me that map, Malins.

MALINS *hands him the map at which he is working.*

GRANT. [*after studying it in silence.*] Yes. There's no doubt about it. Unless Meade goes to sleep it can only be a question of hours. Lee's a great man, but he can't get out of that.

Making a ring on the map with his finger.

MALINS. [*taking the map again.*] This ought to be the end, sir.

GRANT. Yes. If Lee surrenders, we can all pack up for home.

MALINS. By God, sir, it will be splendid, won't it, to be back again?

GRANT. By God, sir, it will.

MALINS. I beg your pardon, sir.

GRANT. You're quite right, Malins. My boy goes

to school next week. My word, I may be able to go down with him and see him settled in.

DENNIS *comes back.*

DENNIS. Colonel West says, yes, sir, for the last half hour. The cook says he's sorry, sir. It was a mistake.

GRANT. Tell him to keep his mistakes in the kitchen.

DENNIS. I will, sir.

He goes back to his place.

GRANT. [*at his papers.*] Those rifles went up this afternoon?

MALINS. Yes, sir.

Another ORDERLY *comes in.*

ORDERLY. Mr. Lincoln has just arrived, sir. He's in the yard now.

GRANT. All right, I'll come.

THE ORDERLY *goes.* GRANT *rises and crosses to the door, but is met there by* LINCOLN *and* SLANEY. LINCOLN, *in top boots and tall hat that has seen many campaigns, shakes hands with* GRANT *and takes* MALINS' *salute.*

GRANT. I wasn't expecting you, sir.

LINCOLN. No; but I couldn't keep away. How's it going?

They sit.

GRANT. Meade sent word an hour and a half ago that Lee was surrounded all but two miles, which was closing in.

LINCOLN. That ought about to settle it, eh?

GRANT. Unless anything goes wrong in those two miles, sir. I'm expecting a further report from Meade every minute.

LINCOLN. Would there be more fighting?

GRANT. It will probably mean fighting through the night, more or less. But Lee must realise it's hopeless by the morning.

AN ORDERLY. [*entering.*] A despatch, sir.

GRANT. Yes.

THE ORDERLY *goes, and a* YOUNG OFFICER *comes in from the field. He salutes and hands a despatch to* GRANT.

OFFICER. From General Meade, sir.

GRANT. [*taking it.*] Thank you.

He opens it and reads.

You needn't wait.

THE OFFICER *salutes and goes.*

Yes, they've closed the ring. Meade gives them ten hours. It's timed at eight. That's six o'clock in the morning.

He hands the despatch to LINCOLN.

LINCOLN. We must be merciful. Bob Lee has been a gallant fellow.

GRANT. [*taking a paper.*] Perhaps you'll look through this list, sir. I hope it's the last we shall have.

LINCOLN. [*taking the paper.*] It's a horrible part of the business, Grant. Any shootings?

GRANT. One.

LINCOLN. Damn it, Grant, why can't you do without it? No, no, of course not? Who is it?

GRANT. Malins.

MALINS. [*opening a book.*] William Scott, sir. It's rather a hard case.

LINCOLN. What is it?

MALINS. He had just done a heavy march, sir, and volunteered for double guard duty to relieve a sick friend. He was found asleep at his post.

He shuts the book.

GRANT. I was anxious to spare him. But it couldn't be done. It was a critical place, at a gravely critical time.

LINCOLN. When is it to be?

MALINS. To-morrow, at daybreak, sir.

LINCOLN. I don't see that it will do him any good to be shot. Where is he?

MALINS. Here, sir.
LINCOLN. Can I go and see him?
GRANT. Where is he?
MALINS. In the barn, I believe, sir.
GRANT. Dennis.
DENNIS. [*coming from his table.*] Yes, sir.
GRANT. Ask them to bring Scott in here.
DENNIS *goes.*
I want to see Colonel West. Malins, ask Templeman if those figures are ready yet.
He goes, and MALINS *follows.*
LINCOLN. Will you, Slaney?
SLANEY *goes. After a moment, during which* LINCOLN *takes the book that* MALINS *has been reading from, and looks into it,* WILLIAM SCOTT *is brought in under guard. He is a boy of twenty.*
LINCOLN. [*to the* GUARD.] Thank you. Wait outside, will you?
THE MEN *salute and withdraw.*
Are you William Scott?
SCOTT. Yes, sir.
LINCOLN. You know who I am?
SCOTT. Yes, sir.
LINCOLN. The General tells me you've been court-martialled.
SCOTT. Yes, sir.
LINCOLN. Asleep on guard?
SCOTT. Yes, sir.
LINCOLN. It's a very serious offence.
SCOTT. I know, sir.
LINCOLN. What was it?
SCOTT. [*a pause.*] I couldn't keep awake, sir.
LINCOLN. You'd had a long march?
SCOTT. Twenty-three miles, sir.
LINCOLN. You were doing double guard?
SCOTT. Yes, sir.

LINCOLN. Who ordered you?
SCOTT. Well, sir, I offered.
LINCOLN. Why?
SCOTT. Enoch White—he was sick, sir. We come from the same place.
LINCOLN. Where's that?
SCOTT. Vermont, sir.
LINCOLN. You live there?
SCOTT. Yes, sir. My . . we've got a farm down there, sir.
LINCOLN. Who has?
SCOTT. My mother, sir. I've got her photograph, sir.

He takes it from his pocket.

LINCOLN. [*taking it.*] Does she know about this?
SCOTT. For God's sake, don't, sir.
LINCOLN. There, there, my boy. You're not going to be shot.
SCOTT. [*after a pause.*] Not going to be shot, sir.
LINCOLN. No, no.
SCOTT. Not—going—to—be—shot.

He breaks down, sobbing.

LINCOLN. [*rising and going to him.*] There, there. I believe you when you tell me that you couldn't keep awake. I'm going to trust you, and send you back to your regiment.

He goes back to his seat.

SCOTT. When may I go back, sir?
LINCOLN. You can go back to-morrow. I expect the fighting will be over, though.
SCOTT. Is it over yet, sir?
LINCOLN. Not quite.
SCOTT. Please, sir, let me go back to-night—let me go back to-night.
LINCOLN. Very well.

He writes.

Do you know where General Meade is?

SCOTT. No, sir.

LINCOLN. Ask one of those men to come here.

SCOTT *calls one of his guards in.*

LINCOLN. Your prisoner is discharged. Take him at once to General Meade with this.

He hands a note to the man.

THE SOLDIER. Yes, sir.

SCOTT. Thank you, sir.

He salutes and goes out with the SOLDIER.

LINCOLN. Slaney.

SLANEY. [*outside.*] Yes, sir.

He comes in.

LINCOLN. What's the time?

SLANEY. [*looking at the watch on the table.*] Just on half-past nine, sir.

LINCOLN. I shall sleep here for a little. You'd better shake down too. They'll wake us if there's any news.

LINCOLN *wraps himself up on two chairs.* SLANEY *follows suit on a bench. After a few moments* GRANT *comes to the door, sees what has happened, blows out the candles quietly, and goes away.*

THE CURTAIN FALLS

THE FIRST CHRONICLER. Under the stars an end is made,
And on the field the southern blade
Lies broken,
And, where strife was, shall union be,
And, where was bondage, liberty.
The word is spoken . .
Night passes.

The Curtain rises on the same scene, LINCOLN *and* SLANEY *still lying asleep. The light of dawn fills the room.* THE ORDERLY *comes in with two smoking cups of coffee and some biscuits.* LINCOLN *wakes.*

LINCOLN. Good morning.

ORDERLY. Good morning, sir.

LINCOLN. [*taking coffee and biscuits.*] Thank you.

THE ORDERLY *turns to* SLANEY, *who sleeps on, and he hesitates.*

LINCOLN. Slaney. [*Shouting.*] Slaney.

SLANEY. [*starting up.*] Hullo! What the devil is it? I beg your pardon, sir.

LINCOLN. Not at all. Take a little coffee.

SLANEY. Thank you, sir.

He takes coffee and biscuits. THE ORDERLY *goes.*

LINCOLN. Slept well, Slaney?

SLANEY. I feel a little crumpled, sir. I think I fell off once.

LINCOLN. What's the time?

SLANEY. [*looking at the watch.*] Six o'clock, sir.

GRANT *comes in.*

GRANT. Good morning, sir; good morning, Slaney.

LINCOLN. Good morning, general.

SLANEY. Good morning, sir.

GRANT. I didn't disturb you last night. A message has just come from Meade. Lee asked for an armistice at four o'clock.

LINCOLN. [*after a silence.*] For four years life has been but the hope of this moment. It is strange how simple it is when it comes. Grant, you've served the country very truly. And you've made my work possible.

He takes his hand.

Thank you.

GRANT. Had I failed, the fault would not have been yours, sir. I succeeded because you believed in me.

LINCOLN. Where is Lee?

GRANT. He's coming here. Meade should arrive directly.

LINCOLN. Where will Lee wait?

GRANT. There's a room ready for him. Will you receive him, sir?

LINCOLN. No, no, Grant. That's your affair. You are to mention no political matters. Be generous. But I needn't say that.

GRANT. [*taking a paper from his pocket.*] Those are the terms I suggest.

LINCOLN. [*reading.*] Yes, yes. They do you honour.

He places the paper on the table. An ORDERLY *comes in.*

ORDERLY. General Meade is here, sir.

GRANT. Ask him to come here.

ORDERLY. Yes, sir.

He goes.

GRANT. I learnt a good deal from Robert Lee in early days. He's a better man than most of us. This business will go pretty near the heart, sir.

LINCOLN. I'm glad it's to be done by a brave gentleman, Grant.

GENERAL MEADE *and* CAPTAIN SONE, *his aide-de-camp, come in.* MEADE *salutes.*

LINCOLN. Congratulations, Meade. You've done well.

MEADE. Thank you, sir.

GRANT. Was there much more fighting?

MEADE. Pretty hot for an hour or two.

GRANT. How long will Lee be?

MEADE. Only a few minutes, I should say, sir.

GRANT. You said nothing about terms?

MEADE. No, sir.

LINCOLN. Did a boy Scott come to you?

MEADE. Yes, sir. He went into action at once. He was killed, wasn't he, Sone?

SONE. Yes, sir.

VOL. I   L

LINCOLN. Killed? It's a queer world, Grant.

MEADE. Is there any proclamation to be made, sir, about the rebels?

GRANT. I—

LINCOLN. No, no. I'll have nothing of hanging or shooting these men, even the worst of them. Frighten them out of the country, open the gates, let down the bars, scare them off. Shoo!

He flings out his arms.

Good-bye, Grant. Report at Washington as soon as you can.

He shakes hands with him.

Good-bye, gentlemen. Come along, Slaney.

MEADE *salutes and* LINCOLN *goes, followed by* SLANEY.

GRANT. Who is with Lee?

MEADE. Only one of his staff, sir.

GRANT. You might see Malins will you, Sone, and let us know directly General Lee comes.

SONE. Yes, sir.

He goes out.

GRANT. Well, Meade, it's been a big job.

MEADE. Yes, sir.

GRANT. We've had courage and determination. And we've had wits, to beat a great soldier. I'd say that to any man. But it's Abraham Lincoln, Meade, who has kept us a great cause clean to fight for. It does a man's heart good to know he's given victory to such a man to handle. A glass, Meade? [*Pouring out whisky.*] No? [*Drinking.*]

Do you know, Meade, there were fools who wanted me to oppose Lincoln for the next Presidency. I've got my vanities, but I know better than that.

MALINS *comes in.*

MALINS. General Lee is here, sir.

GRANT. Meade, will General Lee do me the honour of meeting me here.

MEADE *salutes and goes.*

GRANT. Where the deuce is my hat, Malins? And sword.

MALINS. Here, sir.

MALINS *gets them for him.* MEADE *and* SONE *come in, and stand by the door at attention.* ROBERT LEE, *General-in-Chief of the Confederate forces, comes in, followed by one of his staff. The days of critical anxiety through which he has just lived have marked themselves on* LEE'S *face, but his groomed and punctilious toilet contrasts pointedly with* GRANT'S *unconsidered appearance. The two commanders face each other.* GRANT *salutes, and* LEE *replies.*

GRANT. Sir, you have given me occasion to be proud of my opponent.

LEE. I have not spared my strength. I acknowledge its defeat.

GRANT. You have come—

LEE. To ask upon what terms you will accept surrender. Yes.

GRANT. [*taking the paper from the table and handing it to* LEE.] They are simple. I hope you will not find them ungenerous.

LEE. [*having read the terms.*] You are magnanimous, sir. May I make one submission?

GRANT. It would be a privilege if I could consider it.

LEE. You allow our officers to keep their horses. That is gracious. Our cavalry troopers' horses also are their own.

GRANT. I understand. They will be needed on the farms. It shall be done.

LEE. I thank you. It will do much towards conciliating our people. I accept your terms.

LEE *unbuckles his sword, and offers it to* GRANT.

GRANT. No, no. I should have included that. It has but one rightful place. I beg you.

LEE *replaces his sword.* GRANT *offers his hand and* LEE *takes it. They salute, and* LEE *turns to go.*

THE CURTAIN FALLS

THE TWO CHRONICLERS. A wind blows in the night,
And the pride of the rose is gone,
It laboured, and was delight,
And rains fell, and shone
Suns of the summer days,
And dews washed the bud,
And thanksgiving and praise
Was the rose in our blood.

And out of the night it came,
A wind, and the rose fell,
Shattered its heart of flame,
And how shall June tell
The glory that went with May,
How shall the full year keep
The beauty that ere its day
Was blasted into sleep?

Roses. Oh, heart of man:
Courage, that in the prime
Looked on truth, and began
Conspiracies with time
To flower upon the pain
Of dark and envious earth.
A wind blows, and the brain
Is the dust that was its birth.

What shall the witness cry,
He who has seen alone
With imagination's eye
The darkness overthrown?

Hark: from the long eclipse
The wise words come—
A wind blows, and the lips
Of prophecy are dumb.

Scene VI

The evening of April 14th, 1865. The small lounge of a theatre. On the far side are the doors of three private boxes. There is silence for a few moments. Then the sound of applause comes from the auditorium beyond. The box doors are opened. In the centre box can be seen LINCOLN *and* STANTON, MRS. LINCOLN, *another lady, and an officer, talking together.*

The occupants come out from the other boxes into the lounge, where small knots of people have gathered from different directions, and stand or sit talking busily.

A LADY. Very amusing, don't you think?

HER COMPANION. Oh, yes. But it's hardly true to life, is it?

ANOTHER LADY. Isn't that dark girl clever? What's her name?

A GENTLEMAN. [*consulting his programme.*] Eleanor Crowne.

ANOTHER GENTLEMAN. There's a terrible draught, isn't there? I shall have a stiff neck.

HIS WIFE. You should keep your scarf on.

THE GENTLEMAN. It looks so odd.

ANOTHER LADY. The President looks very happy this evening, doesn't he?

ANOTHER. No wonder, is it? He must be a proud man.

A young man, dressed in black, passes among the people, glancing furtively into LINCOLN'S *box, and disappears. It is* JOHN WILKES BOOTH.

A LADY. [*greeting another.*] Ah, Mrs. Bennington, When do you expect your husband back?

They drift away. SUSAN, *carrying cloaks and wraps, comes in. She goes to the box, and speaks to* MRS. LINCOLN. *Then she comes away, and sits down apart from the crowd to wait.*

A YOUNG MAN. I rather think of going on the stage myself. My friends tell me I'm uncommon good. Only I don't think my health would stand it.

A GIRL. Oh, it must be a very easy life. Just acting —that's easy enough.

A cry of "Lincoln" comes through the auditorium. It is taken up, with shouts of "The President", "Speech", "Abraham Lincoln", "Father Abraham", and so on. The conversation in the lounge stops as the talkers turn to listen. After a few moments, LINCOLN *is seen to rise. There is a burst of cheering. The people in the lounge stand round the box door.* LINCOLN *holds up his hand, and there is a sudden silence.*

LINCOLN. My friends, I am touched, deeply touched, by this mark of your good-will. After four dark and difficult years, we have achieved the great purpose for which we set out. General Lee's surrender to General Grant leaves but one confederate force in the field, and the end is immediate and certain. [*Cheers.*] I have but little to say at this moment. I claim not to have controlled events, but confess plainly that events have controlled me. But as events have come before me, I have seen them always with one faith. We have preserved the American Union, and we have abolished a great wrong. [*Cheers.*] The task of reconciliation, of setting order where there is now confusion, of bringing about a settlement at once just and merciful, and of directing the life of a reunited country into prosperous channels of good-will and generosity, will demand all our wisdom, all our loyalty. It is the proudest hope of my life that I may be of some service in this work. [*Cheers.*] Whatever it may be, it can be but little in return for all the kindness and forbearance that I have received. With malice toward none, with charity for all, it is for us to resolve that this nation, under God, shall have a new birth of freedom ; and that government of the people, by the people, for the people, shall not perish from the earth.

> *There is a great sound of cheering. It dies down, and a boy passes through the lounge and calls out " Last act, ladies and gentlemen ". The people disperse, and the box doors are closed.* SUSAN *is left alone and there is silence.*
> *After a few moments,* BOOTH *appears. He watches* SUSAN *and sees that her gaze is fixed away from him. He creeps along to the centre box and disengages a hand from under his cloak. It holds a revolver. Poising himself, he opens the door with a swift movement, fires, flings the door to again, and rushes away. The door is thrown open again, and the* OFFICER *follows in pursuit. Inside the box,* MRS. LINCOLN *is kneeling by her husband, who is supported by* STANTON. *A* DOCTOR *runs across the lounge and goes into the box. There is complete silence in the theatre. The door closes again.*

SUSAN. [*who has run to the box door, and is kneeling there, sobbing.*] Master, master. No, no, not my master.

> *The other box doors have opened, and the occupants with others have collected in little terror-struck groups in the lounge. Then the centre door opens, and* STANTON *comes out, closing it behind him.*

STANTON. Now he belongs to the ages.

THE CHRONICLERS *speak*.
 FIRST CHRONICLER. Events go by. And upon circumstance
Disaster strikes with the blind sweep of chance,
And this our mimic action was a theme,
Kinsmen, as life is, clouded as a dream.

 SECOND CHRONICLER. But, as we spoke, presiding everywhere
Upon event was one man's character.
And that endures ; it is the token sent
Always to man for man's own government.

THE CURTAIN FALLS

JANE CLEGG

ST. JOHN ERVINE

JANE CLEGG

was first produced at the Gaiety Theatre, Manchester, on April 21, 1913, by Miss Horniman's Company, with the following cast:—

HENRY CLEGG	Bernard Copping.
JANE CLEGG	Sybil Thorndike.
MRS. CLEGG	Clare Greet.
JENNY CLEGG	Mabel Salkeld.
JOHNNIE CLEGG . . .	Tommy Nickson.
MR. MUNCE	Eliot Makeham.
MR. MORRISON . . .	Ernest Haines.

The play was produced by Mr. LEWIS CASSON.

Applications for permission to perform this play, whether amateur or professional, should be made to Messrs. JAMES B. PINKER AND SON, Talbot House, Arundel Street, London, W.C.2.

JANE CLEGG

ACT I

JANE CLEGG, *a tall, dark woman, aged thirty-two years, is seated at a large table, sewing. It is almost nine o'clock, and, as the evening is chilly, a bright fire burns in the grate. The room has a cosy air, although it is furnished in the undistinguished manner characteristic of the homes of lower middle-class people. A corner of the table is reserved for a meal for a latecomer.* JOHNNIE *and* JENNY, *aged ten and eight years respectively, are playing on a rug in front of the fire. The girl is impatient and sometimes knocks over the structures which her brother laboriously builds.* MRS. CLEGG, *the grandmother of the children, is seated in a low rocking-chair, her arms folded across her breast, idly watching them. She is a stout, coarse, and very sentimental woman, and her voice has in it a continual note of querulousness. She glances at the clock and then speaks to her daughter-in-law.*

MRS. CLEGG. I can't think wot's keepin' 'Enry.

JANE CLEGG. [*without looking up from her sewing.*] Busy, I suppose.

MRS. CLEGG. 'E's always busy. I don't believe men are 'alf so busy as they make out they are! Besides I know 'Enry! I 'aven't 'ad the motherin' of 'im for nothink. 'E don't kill 'imself with work, 'Enry don't.

JANE CLEGG. [*in an undertone.*] Oh, hush, mother, before the children.

MRS. CLEGG. Oh, I daresay they know all about 'im.

157

Children knows more about their parents nowadays than their parents knows about them, from wot I can see of it.

JANE CLEGG. Henry's work keeps him out late. It isn't as if he had regular hours like other men. A traveller isn't like ordinary people.

MRS. CLEGG. No, that's true. It isn't a proper life for a man, not travellin' isn't. A married man, any'ow. They see too much. I don't believe in men seein' too much. It unsettles 'em.

JANE CLEGG. Oh, I don't know! Some men are born to be unsettled and some aren't. I suppose that's the way with everything.

MRS. CLEGG. You take things too calm, you do. I 'aven't any patience with you! Look at the way you took it when 'e went after that woman! . .

JANE CLEGG. Oh, please, please!

MRS. CLEGG. I'd 'ave tore 'er 'air off. That was the least you could 'ave done.

JENNY. [*knocking the bricks over.*] Oh, I'm tired of this game.

JOHNNIE. There! You've gone and done it again. Why can't you play properly?

MRS. CLEGG. Wot you playin' at, Johnnie?

JOHNNIE. [*crossly.*] A game, grannie!

MRS. CLEGG. I know you're playin' a game! What kind of a game?

JOHNNIE. [*beginning to build up the bricks again.*] Oh, only a game. I'm pretending to be mother, and Jenny's pretending to be father. We're building a house with these bricks, but it's no good. . . Jenny keeps on knocking it all down.

JANE CLEGG. Jenny, dear, that's very naughty!

JENNY. It takes so long, mother!

JOHNNIE. Well, you can't play this game unless you go slowly. It's awful responsibility building a house.

MRS. CLEGG. Don't use such big words, Johnnie.

It isn't natcherl for a child your age to be talkin' like that.

JENNY, *laughing mischievously, scatters the bricks.*
Oh, oh, you naughty little girl! 'Owever could you!

JOHNNIE. Oh, don't, Jenny! You've spoilt it all.

JENNY. It's such a silly game! Let's play something quick.

JANE CLEGG. Jenny, you must go to bed.

JENNY. [*petulantly.*] Oh, mother!

MRS. CLEGG. You 'aven't no patience, young woman, that's wot you 'aven't.

JOHNNIE. She spoils everything.

JENNY. Well, I like quick games. Building houses takes an awful long time. Let's play something else!

JANE CLEGG. No, Jenny, you must go to bed. You can't play any more games to-night.

JENNY. Mother!

JANE CLEGG. Run along, now!

MRS. CLEGG. See! That's wot you get for bein' naughty.

JENNY. I didn't mean to be naughty, mother.

JOHNNIE. No, but you were.

JENNY. Please, mother, I'm sorry. Let me stay up a little while longer.

She puts her arms about her mother's neck affectionately.

JANE CLEGG. That'll do, dear. Kiss grannie, and go to bed.

JENNY. [*beginning to whimper.*] I didn't mean any harm!

JANE CLEGG. [*kissing her.*] Good night, dear!

The child stands about reluctantly, rubbing her eyes.
Now, run along quickly!

JENNY. I don't want to go yet.

MRS. CLEGG. Let 'er stay up a while longer, 'til 'er father comes 'ome. She didn't mean to be naughty, did you, dear?

She pulls JENNY *to her, and clasps her in her arms.*
JENNY. [*still whimpering.*] No, grannie.
MRS. CLEGG. There, you see, she didn't mean it.
JANE CLEGG. Kiss your grannie good night, Jenny, and go to bed.
JENNY. [*now crying loudly.*] Father'd let me stay up.
MRS. CLEGG. You might as well let 'er stay now. You forgive 'er, don't you, Johnnie?
JANE CLEGG. [*firmly.*] Jenny, go to bed at once, dear.
MRS. CLEGG. [*hurriedly and testily.*] Oh, my dear Jane, don't lose your temper, wotever you do! [*To* JENNY.] 'Ere, my sweet'eart, gimme a kiss and say good night. There, there, now! You know it was your own fault, don't you? You were a naughty girl, weren't you? Now, now, stop cryin', do! I can't bear to 'ear a child cryin'. 'Ere, 'ere's a penny for you!
JENNY. [*putting up her lips to be kissed.*] Good night, grannie.
MRS. CLEGG. [*kissing her warmly.*] Good night, my sweet'eart.
JENNY *goes sulkily towards the door.*
JANE CLEGG. Kiss your brother good night, Jenny!
JENNY. No, I don't want to.
JANE CLEGG. Kiss your brother good night, Jenny!
JENNY *stands irresolutely for a moment, and then goes toward her brother. She kisses him, and then, after a pause, gives him a push which knocks him over.*
JENNY. There, spiteful thing!
MRS. CLEGG. Oh, you wicked little girl!
JANE CLEGG. Jenny!
JENNY. What?
JANE CLEGG. Come here.
JENNY. Yes, mother.
She approaches her mother.
JANE CLEGG. Why did you strike Johnnie like that?
JENNY. I don't know, mother. I just wanted to.

MRS. CLEGG. But you shouldn't just want to do things.

JOHNNIE. She didn't hurt me, mother. You didn't mean to hurt me, did you, Jenny?

JENNY. [*crying again.*] No.

JANE CLEGG. Well, say you're sorry, and go to bed.

JENNY. [*putting her arms round* JOHNNIE'S *neck.*] I'm sorry, Johnnie. I didn't mean to be unkind.

JOHNNIE *kisses her ardently.*

JOHNNIE. I'll come to bed too, Jenny, so's you shan't be lonely.

MRS. CLEGG. There, now! Isn't that just like the Good Samaritan? You are a good boy, Johnnie. 'Ere! 'Ere's a kiss for you.

She kisses him noisily.

JOHNNIE. You gave Jenny a penny.

MRS. CLEGG. Oh, oh, that's wot it is, is it? Well, 'ere you are then. Now run along the two of you, and don't get quarrellin' together, wotever you do.

JOHNNIE. Thank you, grannie.

He kisses her, and then kisses his mother.
Good night, mother. Oh, I forgot the bricks. I must put them away. Jenny, come and help.

JENNY. No, I don't want to.

MRS. CLEGG. Oh, now, that is ungrateful of you.

JENNY. I'm going to bed. Good night!

She goes out.

MRS. CLEGG. That child gets more 'eadstrong every day. Jus' like 'er father was, bless 'er. And yet I can't help likin' 'er for it. It reminds me of 'im w'en 'e was 'er age!

JOHNNIE. [*who has collected his toys and put them away.*] Good night, grannie and mother.

He kisses them again and goes out.

MRS. CLEGG. You was a bit 'ard on 'er, Jane, I must say.

JANE CLEGG. She must do what she is told. I wish

VOL. I M

you wouldn't take her part and give her pennies. It only makes her worse.

MRS. CLEGG. Well, well, I can't 'elp it. She's so like 'er poor father!

JANE CLEGG. I wish Henry would come home. It isn't often he's as late as this.

MRS. CLEGG. [*sniffily.*] Goodness only knows where 'e is! Though 'e is my own son, 'e don't be'ave proper, and it's your fault for lettin' 'im.

JANE CLEGG. I can't prevent him from doing what he likes.

MRS. CLEGG. Yes, you can. Any woman can. Watch 'im, that's wot you got to do. Never take your eyes offa them. That's wot I done with 'is father. 'E was the same, always wanted to be gallivantin' about. Busy, 'e said. I busied 'im. I never 'ardly let 'im out of my sight.

JANE CLEGG. What's the good of talking like that? I can't follow Henry everywhere. Your husband's work was at home. It was easy for you to watch him. Besides, I don't want to watch Henry. I don't see any pleasure in being married to a man who has to be watched.

MRS. CLEGG. Oh, you're unnacherl, you are. I wouldn't 'ave felt 'appy if I didn't know all George was doin' of. It isn't as if you 'adn't no reason to watch 'im.

JANE CLEGG. Well, that's all over now, isn't it?

MRS. CLEGG. I'm sure I 'ope so. It was a perfect scandal the way 'e went on with that . . wot was 'er name?

JANE CLEGG. I don't know. Does it matter?

MRS. CLEGG. No, I suppose it don't. The brazened 'ussy! Wot I can't understand is why you was so calm about it.

JANE CLEGG. You have to make allowances.

MRS. CLEGG. Allowances! There's a limit to allowances. That's wot I think.

JANE CLEGG. [*rising and putting her sewing away.*] Yes, I suppose so.

MRS. CLEGG. I suppose you must be fond of 'im or you wouldn't 'ave married 'im.

JANE CLEGG. I was very fond of him.

MRS. CLEGG. But you're not now, eh?

JANE CLEGG. [*returning to her seat.*] Oh, I don't know about that. I suppose I'm as fond of him as any woman is of her husband after she's been married to him twelve years. It's a long time, isn't it?

MRS. CLEGG. 'Orrible!

JANE CLEGG. Do you know why I didn't leave Henry when that happened? It was simply because I couldn't.

MRS. CLEGG. 'Ow du mean?

JANE CLEGG. Isn't it simple enough? Johnnie was four and Jenny was two. Henry had a good situation. If I had left him, I should not have earned more than a pound a week at the best, and I couldn't have looked after the children and worked as well. I don't suppose I should have got work at all here. A woman who leaves her husband on moral grounds is treated as badly as a woman who runs away with another man.

MRS. CLEGG. Well, of course, it isn't right to leave your 'usband. Till death do you part, that's wot the Bible says. I wasn't 'intin' at anythink of that sort. I only suggested that you should be firm with 'im.

JANE CLEGG. Why shouldn't I leave him, if he isn't loyal?

MRS. CLEGG. Oh, my dear, 'ow can you ask such a question? Wotever would people say?

JANE CLEGG. But why shouldn't I leave him?

MRS. CLEGG. Because it isn't right, that's why.

JANE CLEGG. But why isn't it right?

MRS. CLEGG. You are a one for askin' questions! Nice thing it would be, I'm sure, if women started leavin' their 'usbands like that.

JANE CLEGG. If I'd been able to, I should have left Henry then. I hadn't any money, so I couldn't.

MRS. CLEGG. This is wicked, this is. Doesn't the Bible say you should take 'im for better or worse?

JANE CLEGG. The Prayer Book!

MRS. CLEGG. Well, it's the same thing.

JANE CLEGG. I don't care what it says. It isn't right to ask a woman to take a man for worse. Or a man to take a woman.

MRS. CLEGG. But you promised. You knew wot you was doin' of.

JANE CLEGG. No, I didn't. Do you think I knew that Henry did that sort of thing, or that I would have married him if I had? He married me under false pretences, that's what he did. He knew that woman before he married me. If he told a lie about his samples, he'd be put in jail, but no one thinks anything of his lying to me.

MRS. CLEGG. Well, men is men, and there's an end of it. You just 'ave to put up with them.

JANE CLEGG. I don't believe in putting up with things unless you can't help yourself. I couldn't help myself before, but I can now. Uncle Tom's money makes that possible.

MRS. CLEGG. That made 'im angry, that did. When you wouldn't let 'im 'ave the money to start for 'imself.

JANE CLEGG. You know quite well he'd have lost it all. He's a good traveller, but he couldn't control a business of his own. He's not that sort. I made up my mind when I got the money that I would spend it on Johnnie and Jenny. I want to give them both a good chance. You know how fond Johnnie is of playing with engines and making things. I want to spend the money on making an engineer of him, if that's what he wants to be. I couldn't bear the thought of him becoming one of those little clerks! . . [*She makes a shuddering gesture.*] Oh!

MRS. CLEGG. There's worse than clerks.

JANE CLEGG. I daresay. Why should I give my money to Henry?

MRS. CLEGG. 'E's your 'usband, isn't 'e?

JANE CLEGG. I don't see what that's got to do with it.

MRS. CLEGG. Well, that beats all. I thought you was a Christian, Jane.

JANE CLEGG. [*wearily*.] Oh, I don't know what I am. I only know I'm made to do things that I can't understand for no earthly reason whatever. I must do this and I must do that, and no one tells me why. I wish I'd been well-educated.

MRS. CLEGG. Thank goodness you're not. I don't believe in all this education for women. It unsettles them. I've never been educated, and I'm 'appy enough.

JANE CLEGG. So's a worm, I suppose.

MRS. CLEGG. [*bridling*.] Of course, if you're going to insult me!..

JANE CLEGG. No, I don't want to do that. I only mean that being content isn't everything. I want to know things. I hate being told to do things without knowing why I should do them. It doesn't seem right somehow to have a mind and not use it.

MRS. CLEGG. Well, I don't know wot you mean. I believe in bein' 'appy no matter wot 'appens. That's good enough for me. I don't want to know things. I want to be let alone, an' be 'appy.

JANE CLEGG. Mebbe you're right. [*They are quiet for a moment.*] Oh, isn't it just awful to think that I shall sit here always, mending things and waiting for Henry to come home!

MRS. CLEGG. No, it isn't awful at all. It's nacherl. It's always bin like that, and it always will. It's no good flyin' in the face of Providence.

JANE CLEGG. I never see anything or go anywhere. I have to cook and wash and nurse and mend and teach!

. . And then I'm not certain of Henry. That's what's so hard. I give him everything, and he isn't faithful.

MRS. CLEGG. 'E was always a man for women. There's a lot like that. They don't mean no 'arm, but some'ow they do it. I 'eard tell once of some one that said it was silly of women to complain about things like that, and mebbe 'e was right. They're not made like us, men aren't. I never wanted but one man in my life, but my 'usband, bless 'im, 'e was never satisfied. 'E used to say it near broke 'is 'eart to be a Christian ! 'E 'ad a great respect for Turks an' foreigners. 'Enry takes after 'im. [*She pauses for a moment.*] I dunno ! Men's a funny lot wotever way you take them, an' it's my belief a wise woman shuts 'er eyes to more'n 'alf wot goes on in the world. She'd be un'appy if she didn't, an' it's no good bein' un'appy.

JANE CLEGG. I'm not like that. I demand as much as I give. It isn't fair to take all and give nothing.

MRS. CLEGG. [*impatiently.*] But ! . .

JANE CLEGG. Oh, I know what you're going to say. I don't care what men say or what anybody says ; Henry must give me as much as I give to him. That's only decent.

MRS. CLEGG. Well, I'm sure I 'ope you get it. There's few women does. Men is guilty sinners. You can't get over that. If they ain't sinnin' one way, they're sinnin' another, an' you can't stop 'em. The Lord can't do it, an' it ain't likely you can.

The street door is opened and slammed to.

JANE CLEGG. I suppose this is him !

The door opens and HENRY CLEGG, *a middle-sized man, good-natured, genial, fairly handsome, though a little fleshly and somewhat weak-looking, enters. His manner is brisk. He has a quick way of speaking, and his actions are rapid. He is a man of nervous temperament, to whom repose is impossible. Although he is superficially open and frank, there is about him*

*an air of furtiveness, almost meanness, and he will
turn away quickly from a steady look. He goes to his
wife and kisses her.*

HENRY CLEGG. Well, old girl, feeling anxious, eh?
[*He goes to his mother and kisses her.*]

JANE CLEGG. I thought you were probably working late.

MRS. CLEGG. You didden ought to be so late, 'Enry, you know you oughtn't.

HENRY CLEGG. I had to go into the country this morning about a big order. Hadn't time to look round or do anything. [*He goes to the table.*] Is this my supper?

JANE CLEGG. Yes.

HENRY CLEGG. Any letters?

JANE CLEGG. [*taking a letter off the fireplace and handing it to him.*] Yes, this one was brought round from the office this afternoon by a boy. I've not seen him before.

HENRY CLEGG. [*taking the letter, and opening it.*] Thanks. Oh, yes, they got a new boy in a day or two ago. [*He glances hastily through the letter.*] What'd they send it to me for? [*He looks at a cheque which is enclosed with the letter.*] Now, there's a damn silly thing!

JANE CLEGG. What is?

HENRY CLEGG. Armstrong & Brown have settled their account and the cheque's made payable to me. Someb'dy ought to get the sack for that!

MRS. CLEGG. Why? You're honest, aren't you?

HENRY CLEGG. Yes, mother, but supposing I wasn't, eh?

MRS. CLEGG. 'Ow can you talk like that, 'Enry, an' you brought up the way you was.

HENRY CLEGG. All very fine, mother. If I wasn't honest, and was to hop round to the bank to-morrow morning, and cash this—well, it 'ud be all umpydoodelum with some chap's job, that's all. [*He puts the letter and cheque in his pocket-book, and sitting down, begins to eat his meal.*] I'm done up. Absolutely. Worn-out with work. The chaps at the office are all cursing and swearing at the amount they have to do.

MRS. CLEGG. [*becoming concerned.*] Poor 'Enry! 'E ought to get more 'elp, Mr. 'Arper ought. It ain't right to work people so 'ard.

HENRY CLEGG. He'll never get any more help. He's not that sort. Work the life and soul out of you, he will. It's enough to make a chap turn Socialist.

MRS. CLEGG. Oh, don't you go an' get mixed up with none of them. I've 'eard some 'orrible things about them.

JANE CLEGG. Why don't you and the others refuse to be overworked? He'd have to give in if you stood up to him.

HENRY CLEGG. Stand up to him! Fancy a lot of mouldy clerks standin' up to any one. It's no good me standin' up by myself: the others wouldn't support me, and I'd get the sack. Jolly glad some of 'em would be to get my job.

MRS. CLEGG. If there was a woman or two in your office, I bet you they'd soon show Mr. 'Arper they wouldn't be treated the way 'e treats you men.

HENRY CLEGG. Yes, I daresay. It's all very well for a lot of women to talk. They haven't got any responsibilities. [JANE CLEGG *laughs.*] Oh, you can laugh. These young girls comin' into offices, what responsibility have they got, eh? Live on their fathers they do, and then go and take low salaries and do their fathers out of jobs. It's easy enough to be independent when you've got some one to fall back on. Who could I fall back on if I got the sack, eh?

MRS. CLEGG. Well, you'd be all right. Jane wouldn't see you go short if you was to lose your place, not with all that money of hers.

HENRY CLEGG. Her money! Huh! Fat lot of good it is to me.

JANE CLEGG. Shall I get you some more meat, Henry?

HENRY CLEGG. [*stretching himself in the manner of a replete animal.*] No, thanks. I've had enough!

He rises and crosses to the fire, and sits down beside his mother. He lights a pipe. JANE *removes the remnants of the meal.*

MRS. CLEGG. [*taking a cushion from behind her.*] 'Ere, 'Enry, put that be'ind you. You must be wore out.

She rises and puts the cushion behind his head. He settles himself into it comfortably.

HENRY CLEGG. I could have done well for myself with that money if Jane had let me have it.

MRS. CLEGG. I know you could, 'Enry. I've often told her that. [JANE *re-enters the room.*] 'Aven't I, Jane?

JANE CLEGG. What, mother?

MRS. CLEGG. 'Aven't I often tole you wot good use 'Enry could 'ave made of your money if you'd on'y let 'im 'ave it?

JANE CLEGG. Yes, mother, you have.

MRS. CLEGG. See! But she don't take no interest in wot I say. Says you're not fit to 'ave charge of it!

HENRY CLEGG. [*angrily.*] Who's not fit to have charge of it?

JANE CLEGG. I didn't say that. I said you were not so good at managing a business of your own as you are at being a traveller. That was all.

HENRY CLEGG. How do you know, eh?

JANE CLEGG. I just know.

She brings a chair up to the fire, and sits down between her husband and her mother-in-law.

HENRY CLEGG. [*surlily.*] Blasted fine thing, I must say, when a man's own wife makes little of him.

JANE CLEGG. I don't make little of you, Henry. I just treat you as you are.

HENRY CLEGG. I could have doubled that money three times over. I could still do it. I heard to-day about something! . . Look here, Jane, if you would let me have two hundred of it, I could pull off a good thing in about six months. Straight, I could.

JANE CLEGG. What could you pull off?

HENRY CLEGG. Well, I can't give many particulars about it, because I told the chap I wouldn't say a word to any one, not even to you. He knew you'd come in for a bit of money, and he mentioned it himself. He naturally thought I could get the money easy enough. I didn't like to tell him you'd got it, and wouldn't let me have any of it. Makes a man look such a damned fool, that sort of thing. It's a bit of a spec. at present, of course, and there's one or two's after it. That's why he told me not to tell any one.

MRS. CLEGG. I should think you could tell Jane. That's on'y nacherl, she bein' your wife.

HENRY CLEGG. No, I promised I wouldn't.

JANE CLEGG. Don't bother, Henry. I know you don't like breaking promises. Your friend won't get my money. I've made up my mind that I shall keep it for Johnnie and Jenny.

HENRY CLEGG. [*with great fury.*] There, you hear that, mother! That's the sort of woman she is. Not a spark of love for me in her.

JANE CLEGG. You know, Henry! . .

HENRY CLEGG. Don't talk to me. I don't want to hear what you've got to say.

He begins to stride up and down the room, puffing quickly at his pipe. JANE *sits still,* MRS. CLEGG *weeps.*

MRS. CLEGG. It's no pleasure to me to sit 'ere an' 'ear all this.

HENRY CLEGG. Oh, shut your silly mouth. I've enough on my mind without you adding to it.

MRS. CLEGG. That's not the way to speak to your mother, 'Enry.

HENRY CLEGG. [*snapping at her.*] Isn't it? Well, it's the only way I'm going to speak to her, see! Nice thing when a man's chances in life are spoiled by his wife.

MRS. CLEGG. I'd let you 'ave the money soon enough if it was mine. You know I would, 'Enry. [*She becomes inaudible through weeping.*]

HENRY, *tiring of walking up and down the room, returns to his seat in front of the fire, and sits down moodily.* JANE *continues sewing. There is quiet for a moment, except for* MRS. CLEGG'S *weeping.*

JANE CLEGG. Perhaps you'd better go to bed, mother. You're tired.

MRS. CLEGG. I don't want to go to bed. I'm not tired. I'm 'urt, that's wot I am. 'Urt.

HENRY CLEGG. I should think so too. So'd anybody be. Seven hundred pounds she has, eating its head off in a bank, and won't lend me two hundred of it. Lend it, mind you. I don't want her to give it to me, though I don't see why she shouldn't.

MRS. CLEGG. [*tearfully.*] It says in the Bible wot's 'ers is yours!

JANE CLEGG. [*getting up and moving towards the door.*] Come, mother, it's time you went to bed. You've worn yourself out to-day.

MRS. CLEGG. I'm not goin' to bed yet. I've a right to sit up with my own son, 'aven't I? I'm not goin' to be ordered about.

JANE CLEGG. I'm not ordering you about. I'm going to bed myself. It's no good sitting here talking like this. Henry wants me to give him money which I want to keep for Johnnie and Jenny. He doesn't tell me what he wants it for. He expects me to hand it over to him without any questions! . .

HENRY CLEGG. I can't tell you what it is yet. I promised the chap ! . .

MRS. CLEGG. You wouldn't 'ave 'im break 'is word, would you ?

JANE CLEGG. It wouldn't be the first time he broke his word.

HENRY CLEGG. [*pettishly.*] There ! There she goes again ! Haven't I apologised for that, and said I was sorry ? Haven't I ? And swore I'd never do it again ? Can't you let bygones be bygones ? Unforgiving spirit you have.

MRS. CLEGG. I didden think you'd go an' rake things up like that, Jane. 'E said 'e was sorry, didden 'e ?

JANE CLEGG. Well, it doesn't matter very much about that. I don't care now. You shall not have a farthing until I know what you want it for, and only then if I think it's worth while. Aren't you coming, mother ?

MRS. CLEGG. [*fractiously.*] In a minute, Jane.

JANE CLEGG. I'm going now. Good night.

MRS. CLEGG. [*laboriously getting up from her seat.*] All right, I'll come too.

JANE *is standing in the doorway.* HENRY CLEGG *is seated before the fire.* MRS. CLEGG *moves towards her daughter-in-law. There is a knock at the door.*

'Ooever can that be at this time of night ?

JANE *goes to the door and opens it.* MR. MUNCE *appears. He asks if* HENRY *is at home, and is informed that he is.*

HENRY CLEGG. [*hastily.*] Hilloa, Munce, is that you ?

MUNCE. [*entering the hall.*] Yes, ole man. I want to see you partickler.

HENRY CLEGG. Come on in, will you ?

MUNCE, *a weedy person of the race-course type, enters the room.* JANE, *who has closed the street door, follows him. Introducing* JANE *to* MUNCE.

My wife.

JANE CLEGG. How do you do?
MUNCE. Pleased to meet you.
HENRY CLEGG. My mother.
MRS. CLEGG. Glad to 'ave the pleasure.
MUNCE. Same 'ere. I'm sorry to come in so late, but I wanted to discuss a bit of business with your 'usband, Mrs. Clegg. Very important.
JANE CLEGG. Oh yes. You'd like to be left alone with Henry?
MUNCE. [*very affably*.] If you don't mind.
JANE CLEGG. No, not at all. I was just going to bed.
MUNCE. Ah, I know. Early to bed and early to rise, makes a man 'ealthy, wealthy, an' wise. Quite right, Mrs. Clegg. 'Ear, 'ear.
JANE CLEGG. Good night, Mr. Munce.
MUNCE. Good night, Mrs. Clegg. Pleased to 'ave the pleasure of your acquaintance, I'm sure. [*To* MRS. CLEGG.] Good night, ma'am. Glad to 'ave met you.
MRS. CLEGG. Good night, sir. Good night, 'Enry.
HENRY CLEGG. Good night, mother. [*He kisses her and she goes out.*] I shan't be long, Jane.
JANE *goes out*.
MUNCE. Well, ole chap, 'ow goes it?
HENRY CLEGG. Rotten!
MUNCE. Sorry to 'ear that. Didden expec' to see me roun' 'ere to-night, eih? I bin lookin' for you bes' part the dy!
HENRY CLEGG. I've been busy, old chap! . .
MUNCE. Yes, I know all about that. Thought I'd catch you about now. You know wot I come about, don't you?
HENRY CLEGG. [*desperately*.] I'm sorry, Munce, I can't let you have it just yet.
MUNCE. Wot you mean you can't let me 'ave it? You gotta let me 'ave it, see!
HENRY CLEGG. Don't speak so loudly, old chap. You

see I've had rotten luck lately. Haven't pulled off a single winner. Not one.

MUNCE. That's not my fault, is it?

HENRY CLEGG. No, of course not, only it means I can't pay up just now.

MUNCE. Well, that's a nice thing I must say. 'Ow do you think I'm going to live, eih? I can't afford to lie out of my money like that. I've got bills of my own to meet.

HENRY CLEGG. I know, old chap. Of course, I'm very sorry.

MUNCE. Sorry! What's the good of bein' sorry? That don't 'elp matters. Do you know 'ow much you owe me, eih?

HENRY CLEGG. You haven't given me much chance to forget it, have you?

MUNCE. Twenty-five pounds. That's what it is, and then you 'ave the cheek to tell me you can't pay. That's cool, that is. What've you done with all that money your wife 'ad left to 'er?

HENRY CLEGG. Nothing.

MUNCE. Well, then, why can't you pay up? Look 'ere, Clegg, I'm not jokin'. I'm in a mess. Straight! I must 'ave the money this week. Absolute!

HENRY CLEGG. What's the good of talking like that! If I can't let you have it, I can't, can I?

MUNCE. But you can. You've jus' told me you still got your wife's money.

HENRY CLEGG. Oh, I know! . .

MUNCE. Look 'ere, what you done with it, eih?

HENRY CLEGG. I haven't done anything with it.

MUNCE. You know you're not actin' straight, you aren't. I saw you the other day, you know.

HENRY CLEGG. Oh! Where?

MUNCE. Yes, an' you 'ad a nice bit o' skirt with you, too.

HENRY CLEGG. I say, shut up, you fool.

MUNCE. Oh, it's all right. I know all about it. I never give a pal away. No fear.

HENRY CLEGG. [*airily*.] Oh, there's nothing to give away. I only met her by accident.

MUNCE. Yes, I do not think! Oh, ho, ho, ho! Excuse me laughin', ole chap, won't you? Accident! Oh, ho, ho, ho! . .

HENRY CLEGG. I say, don't make so much noise. They went upstairs to sleep, you know.

MUNCE. Sorry, ole man, but look 'ere, you know, puttin' all jokes aside, when can you let me 'ave the money?

HENRY CLEGG. I don't know!

MUNCE. Don't know! But you oughta know. What am I goin' to do, eih?

HENRY CLEGG. Perhaps it'll be all right next week.

MUNCE. Yes, an' per'aps not. I know. What you done with your ole woman's money?

HENRY CLEGG. I tell you I haven't done anything with it!

MUNCE. Don't you tell me. I know. You bin spendin' it on that bit of skirt I saw you with this afternoon, that's what you bin doin', 'stead o' pyin' your debts.

HENRY CLEGG. [*anxiously*.] Don't shout, old chap.

MUNCE. It's enough to make a chap shout, ain't it? Goin' an' bluein' all your money on a tart, an' you owes me twenty-five poun's. Twenty-five poun's. An' 'ere's me don't know where to turn for money.

HENRY CLEGG. I tell you I haven't spent it on her. Straight, I haven't. Look here, I may as well be honest with you. The girl you saw me with this afternoon, she's a friend of mine, see!

MUNCE. Yes, I thought so. Fine-lookin' bit o' goods, too!

HENRY CLEGG. [*proudly.*] Not bad, is she?

MUNCE. I s'pose your missus don't know about 'er, eih? Ho, ho, ho, ho!

HENRY CLEGG. Don't laugh so loud, old chap. My wife and me don't get on very well. You know!

MUNCE. [*sympathetically.*] I know, old chap. Funny, ain't it, 'ow the one you're married to ain't 'alf so nice as the one you keep.

HENRY CLEGG. And you see, well, things haven't been going right with me lately. Of course, Kitty, that's her name, not my wife, the other one, she's always hard up! . .

MUNCE. Just what I said, didden I? Spendin' all your blinkin' money on a tart 'stead o' pyin' your debts of honour. Debts of honour, mind you! That's wot I call doin' the dirty!

HENRY CLEGG. I'm in a rare old mess, that's wot I am. Kitty's bin to the doctor this mornin'! She's not sure! . .

MUNCE. [*after a prolonged whistle.*] Oh, ho! So's that's 'ow the land lays, is it? So 'elp me!

HENRY CLEGG. I don't know what the devil to do. There's you and Kitty . . she'll want a bit of money to keep her mouth shut. If I could only raise a bit, I'd take her off to Canada or somewhere. I'm damned fond of her, that's what I am. I can't stick my wife. She's hard, Munce, hard as hell.

MUNCE. I 'ope you won't do nothink rash, not afore you've paid me my whack.

HENRY CLEGG. I haven't got the money to be rash. I wish I had.

MUNCE. Well, I dunno. Seems t' me I shall lose what you owe me. I shall 'ave to do somethink. Absolute! [*He gets up, twirls round on his foot, and then sits down again.*] What I can't make out is, what you done with your wife's money.

HENRY CLEGG. [*angrily*.] I tell you I haven't done anything with it.

MUNCE. Well, why can't you pay me then?

HENRY CLEGG. I haven't had it. She's got it!

MUNCE. Well, tell her to give it to you.

HENRY CLEGG. She won't let me have it, not a blasted farthing of it!

MUNCE. What! [*He gapes at* CLEGG *in astonishment, and then goes off into helpless roars of laughter.*] Oh, you bloomin' fool! Ho, ho, ho, ho! Excuse me laughin', won't you? Oh, ho, ho, ho! Won't let you 'ave it? So 'elp me! 'Ere! 'Ere, I say, are you 'er 'usband, or 'er little blue-eyed lad, eih? Oh, ho, ho, ho!

HENRY CLEGG. Shut up, you fool!

MUNCE. 'Ere, not so much o' that, if you please. A man what owes what you owe me, an' runs a tart! . . .

HENRY CLEGG. [*piteously*.] Do keep quiet, old chap. I didn't mean to cut up rough.

MUNCE. I should think not, indeed.

He lies back in his chair, looking a little sulky. Gradually, however, his features relax and he gives way to his sense of the ridiculousness of CLEGG'S *position.*

HENRY CLEGG. They'll hear you, if you don't stop it.

MUNCE. You're a nice one, I must say. Fancy, a man lettin' a woman treat 'im like that. Be a man, old chap; be a man!

HENRY CLEGG. That's all very fine, but you're not married to her.

MUNCE. No, but I'd bloomin' soon make 'er change 'er toon if I was.

HENRY CLEGG. Yes, you'd do a lot.

MUNCE. The idea! Du meana say she ain't let you 'ave some of it?

HENRY CLEGG. Not a sou.

MUNCE. Gawblimey! Seven 'undred quid, wassen it?

HENRY CLEGG. Yes.

MUNCE. You know you didden oughta be a man, you didden. I mean t' say, ole chap, it ain't right. You oughtn't t' let 'er do it, y' know!

HENRY CLEGG. How the hell can I help it? It's her money, isn't it? Her old fool of an uncle left it to her.

MUNCE. But you're 'er 'usband, ole man. You're the 'ead o' the family. You oughta be lookin' after it for 'er.

HENRY CLEGG. Well, she won't let me.

MUNCE. Let you! Make 'er, man. Give 'er a clout aside the 'ead if she gives you any lip. Don't 'ave no 'umbug!

HENRY CLEGG. That wouldn't do any good. I've begged her to let me have a couple of hundred of it, but she won't. I could have cleared you off, and seen Kitty didn't come to any harm!.. Oh, doesn't it make you sick, Munce, to think you've got to go with your cap in your hand to your wife, and be refused?

MUNCE. But why be refused? I wouldn't.

HENRY CLEGG. I don't know what to do. [*He buries his head in his hands for a while, and then sits up again in his chair.*] You see, old chap, I can't pay at present, so it's no good keeping you up any longer.

MUNCE. That's all very fine, Clegg, but it don't 'elp me out of my difficulty, do it? I'm in a nole, an' you're the one that'll 'ave to get me out of it. [*Angrily.*] You don't think I'm goin' to be bust up when you owe me money enough to clear me, an' your wife's got seven 'undred in the bank, do you? You got to get it, my boy, that's what you got to do, an' jolly slippy too.

HENRY CLEGG. [*weakly.*] How can I get it?

MUNCE. I dunno, but you got to get it some'ow. I must 'ave it by nex' Thursday, that's all.

HENRY CLEGG. [*shrugging his shoulders.*] You might as well say you want it in five minutes.

MUNCE. No good talkin' like that. You got to get it,

or there'll be trouble. See! I don't want to be nasty, you know, but I could be nasty if I wanted to, couldn't I?

HENRY CLEGG. Eh?

MUNCE. Your missus would be interested to 'ear about Kitty an' the interestin' event, eih, woulden she?

HENRY CLEGG. You wouldn't give me away, would you? I told you in confidence.

MUNCE. An' 'ow about my twenty-five quid, eih? Mebbe she'd like to 'ear about that. An' ole 'Arper, 'e'd be delighted to 'ear as 'ow 'is traveller owed a bookie twenty-five quid, an' didden know 'ow to pay it, eih?

HENRY CLEGG. You wouldn't do a dirty trick like that, would you?

MUNCE. You pay me me money, an' I won't. 'Ang it all, why should I consider you w'en you don't care a damn about me? I'll be ruined if I don't get the money this week, but you don't think about that. It's all you with you.

HENRY CLEGG. Don't be hard, old chap. I'll do my best, I promise you, I will. Only give me a chance. I'll see if I can get it for you this week. I will, straight. I'll make her give it to me, somehow.

MUNCE. That's right. You stuff 'er up with some yarn or other, an' if she don't give it to you then, make 'er give it to you. [*He rises and prepares to go.*]

HENRY CLEGG. I'll do my best.

MUNCE. [*holding out his hand.*] You'll 'ave to. I'm about desprit, an' that's the God's truth. 'Ere, buck up, ole chap. You'll be all right. She'll pay up right enough. You kiss 'er a bit; that'll put 'er in a good temper. You on'y got to treat 'em reasonable, an' they're all right. Give 'er a bit of a kiss now an' again, an' she'll be like a lamb. You bin runnin' too much after that Kitty, y' know, an' neglectin' your missus, an' o' course that gets their backs up. You got to yoomer 'em. I expec' it'll be all right. I wouden feel so perky about it,

if I didden know she 'ad that money.   Straight, I woulden!
Goo' night, ole chap.   [*He shakes hands with* CLEGG.]
   HENRY CLEGG.   Good night, old chap.
   MUNCE.   You be all right, you see!
They go into the hall together, CLEGG *opens the door, and* MUNCE *passes out.*
Goo' night, ole chap.   Remember me to the missus!
   HENRY CLEGG.   Good night!
He shuts the street door and returns to the sitting-room. He stands in front of the fire for a few moments in an undecided manner. He puts his hand in his pocket and takes out the cheque from Armstrong & Brown. He fingers it for a while, gazing abstractedly at the fire. Then he puts the cheque back into his pocket, turns down the lamps, and goes out of the room, shutting the door behind him.

ACT II

It is two days later, and JANE CLEGG *is seated alone in front of the fire. The table is set for the evening meal. A loud continuous knocking is heard on the street door. She goes to the door and opens it.* JENNY, *who has been lying against the door, stumbles in as it is opened, and collides with her mother.*

JANE CLEGG. My darling, what a noise to make.

JENNY. I wanted to be in first, mother. I couldn't wait for grannie and Johnnie. They're just coming. [*She goes into the street and calls out.*] Come on, grannie! You are a long time.

JANE CLEGG. [*returning to the room.*] It was naughty of you to run away from them like that, Jenny.

MRS. CLEGG *and* JOHNNIE *appear in the doorway.*

MRS. CLEGG. [*out of breath.*] Oh, you young terror, you! Out o' breath, I am!

JENNY. I was first, wasn't I, grannie?

MRS. CLEGG. You was, my chickabiddy.

They all come into the sitting-room.

JENNY. I was the first, mother. I betted Johnnie I would.

JOHNNIE. [*removing his coat.*] Bet, Jenny, not betted.

JENNY. It's all the same.

MRS. CLEGG. Come along, now, and take off your things, there's a dear. You can take off my boots for me [*in a sort of whisper*] and p'raps I'll give you a penny.

JENNY. Oh, thank you, grannie. [*She hugs the old lady, who bends down and kisses her.*]

JANE CLEGG. Run along, dear, and you too, Johnnie. Supper'll be ready very soon.

JOHNNIE. Has daddy come home yet, mother?

JANE CLEGG. No, dear, not yet, but perhaps he'll come in in a minute or two. Now, run along.

[MRS. CLEGG *and* JOHNNIE *go out and are seen climbing the stairs.*]

JENNY. Can I sit next to daddy, mother?

JANE CLEGG. Yes, dear, if he comes.

JENNY. Why doesn't he come? He's always late.

JANE CLEGG. Daddy has a lot to do, dear. [*She sits down, and the child comes to her and rubs her face against her.*]

JENNY. I like when daddy's here.

JANE CLEGG. Do you, darling?

JENNY. Yes, and so does grannie.

JANE CLEGG. That's right, dear.

JENNY. Johnnie likes it too, but he likes being with you best.

JANE CLEGG. You like being with me too, don't you, Jenny?

JENNY. [*emphatically.*] Of course, mother dear. [*She puts her arms about her mother's neck and kisses her.*] I do love you, mother.

JANE CLEGG. [*affectionately.*] My dear!

JOHNNIE. [*from above.*] Jenny!

JENNY. Ye-es!

JOHNNIE. Come on! Grannie's waiting. [*He is seen looking over the banisters.*] She says she gave you a penny to take off her boots, and you haven't done it.

JENNY. Oh, you do it, Johnnie!

JOHNNIE. Shan't!

JENNY. Beast, beast!

JANE CLEGG. Jenny, dear, you mustn't talk like that. [*She kisses* JENNY, *and pats her on the head.*] Now, run along, dear, and help your grannie, and when you're ready we'll have supper.

JOHNNIE. Come on, Jenny.

JENNY. Oh, you!

She runs to the foot of the stairs, and pursues her brother. They are heard scuffling and laughing on the stairs. MRS. CLEGG *is heard saying,* " Oh, you naughty little girl! " *and* " Do give over, do! "

JANE CLEGG. [*calling out to them.*] Johnnie!

JOHNNIE. Yes, mother!

JANE CLEGG. I want you.

JOHNNIE. All right, mother. No, Jenny, don't! Oh! [*He shouts with laughter.*]

JANE CLEGG. Come along, dear!

JOHNNIE. [*running quickly down the stairs.*] Yes, mother.

He enters the room, shutting the door behind him. Yes, mother!

JANE CLEGG. Come and sit here. [*He sits down in front of the fire at her feet.*]

JOHNNIE. Can I read again to-night, mother?

JANE CLEGG. It'll soon be supper-time.

JOHNNIE. Just a little while, please.

The door opens and MRS. CLEGG *and* JENNY *return.* Jenny, you would like me to read again, wouldn't you?

MRS. CLEGG *seats herself on the opposite side of the fire to that at which* JANE CLEGG *is seated.*

JENNY. [*impetuously.*] Oh yes, Johnnie. [*She throws herself down beside him.*]

JOHNNIE. Please, mother!

JANE CLEGG. All right, then. You can read for a little while. I expect your father will be in presently, and then you will have to put the book away!

JOHNNIE. [*rising and going towards the bookshelf.*] Oh, thank you, mother!

MRS. CLEGG. 'E's late again!

JANE CLEGG. [*glancing at the clock.*] Oh, no. He seldom comes in before this time.

MRS. CLEGG. Well, of course, if you call this early! . . [*To* JENNY.] 'Ere, come an' sit on my knee. 'Ave you got your book, Johnnie?

JENNY *climbs on to her grannie's knee.*

JOHNNIE. [*returning to his seat on the floor.*] Yes, grannie!

MRS. CLEGG. Well, now you can read to us, can't you? We'll keep as quiet as quiet, won't we, Jenny, eh? [*She hugs the child to her.*]

JENNY. Yes, grannie. What is the book, Johnnie?

JOHNNIE. "The History of the Steam Engine."

JENNY. [*petulantly.*] Oh, no, I don't want to hear that. I want to hear a story.

JOHNNIE. But it's awfully interesting, Jenny.

JENNY. No, I don't like it. [*She climbs off her grannie's knee and goes to her mother, coaxingly.*] Please, mother, can't I have a story read to me?

JOHNNIE. But, mother, I want to read about steam engines!

MRS. CLEGG. You can't 'ave everythink. You ought to be a little gentleman and read what the lady wants!

JANE CLEGG. What kind of a story do you want, dear?

JENNY. You know, mother, A real story, not about steam engines.

JOHNNIE. But that's real, Jenny. Steam engines is real!

JENNY. Are, silly, are! E-h-h-h! Caught you that time, clever!

A knock on the street door is heard.

JANE CLEGG. There's your father. Johnnie, go and open the door.

JENNY. [*quickly, running to the door.*] No, let me, mother. I'll open it.

JANE CLEGG. All right. Go along.

JENNY *runs down the passage leading to the door, and after fumbling with the handle, opens the door.*
JENNY. Oh, it isn't daddy!
MR. MORRISON. Is Mr. Clegg in?
JENNY. No.
JANE CLEGG. Who is it, dear?
JENNY. It's a gentleman, mother!
JANE CLEGG. All right. [*She rises and goes to the door.*]
MR. MORRISON. Good evening, Mrs. Clegg!
JANE CLEGG. Good evening! Oh, it's you, Mr. Morrison! Come in, will you? We're just going to have supper.
She returns to the room, followed by MORRISON.
JENNY *shuts the street door, and also returns to the room, closing the door leading to the passage after her.*
This is my mother-in-law. [*Introducing them.*] Mr. Morrison.
MR. MORRISON. Pleased to meet you! Hope you're quite well.
MRS. CLEGG. I'm very well, thanks. I hope you are too.
MR. MORRISON. Yes, thanks.
JANE CLEGG. Johnnie, bring a chair for Mr. Morrison!
JOHNNIE. Yes, mother.
MR. MORRISON. Oh, please don't trouble.
JOHNNIE *brings a chair forward.*
JANE CLEGG. Won't you take off your coat? Let me take your hat!
MR. MORRISON. Oh no, thanks.
JANE CLEGG. Perhaps you'll have some supper with us.
MR. MORRISON. No, I won't have anything, thanks. Is Clegg at home?
JANE CLEGG. No, he hasn't come in yet.
MR. MORRISON. Oh! I wanted to see him particularly.

JANE CLEGG. He ought to be here by now. What time did he leave the office?

MR. MORRISON. He hasn't been to-day.

JANE CLEGG. Hasn't been! . .

MRS. CLEGG. Why 'e left 'smornin' same time's usual.

JANE CLEGG. You're sure he hasn't been.

MR. MORRISON. I've only just left, and he hadn't arrived then. The guv'nor sent me round to make inquiries about him.

JANE CLEGG. But how odd!

MRS. CLEGG. I do 'ope nothink 'asn't 'appened to 'im.

MR. MORRISON. [*endeavouring to be consolatory.*] Oh, I don't suppose so. He's probably all right.

JANE CLEGG. He said he'd be at the office the whole of the morning! . . [*To the children.*] You'd better have your supper, now, and go to bed.

JENNY. Oh, please, mother, let me stay up a little longer.

JANE CLEGG. Come along. [*She goes to the table and prepares the children's food.*]

JOHNNIE. Can't I read some of the "History of the Steam Engine", mother?

JENNY. Yes, please, mother.

JANE CLEGG. No, you must have your supper. Sit down, both of you. [*The children begin their meal.*]

MRS. CLEGG. Ah, you're very anxious to hear about the steam engine, now, my lady, but you wasn't so anxious a minute or two ago.

JENNY. [*her mouth full.*] Oh, I was, grannie!

MRS. CLEGG. Now, there's a wicked story for you. [*To MR. MORRISON.*] What do you think of a little girl that doesn't tell the truth, Mr. Morrison?

MR. MORRISON. [*with heavy jocularity.*] Oh, but nice little girls don't tell fibs, do they?

JENNY. I didn't tell fibs, and I only wanted . .

JANE CLEGG. [*sharply*.] Eat your supper, Jenny, quickly.

JENNY. [*reproachfully*.] Mother!

JANE CLEGG. [*to* MR. MORRISON.] Something must have happened to him. Have you made any inquiries? He may have been run over.

MR. MORRISON. No, I shouldn't think that. I expect he's all right.

JANE CLEGG. But why should you think that? You don't know.

MR. MORRISON. No, of course, I don't know, but I should think he's probably all right.

JANE CLEGG. I'll go and inquire at the police station. They may have some information about him there.

MRS. CLEGG. I'm sure I 'ope nothink 'asn't 'appened to 'im. I do 'ate accidents.

MR. MORRISON. I don't think I should go if I were you, Mrs. Clegg.

JANE CLEGG. Why? [*She looks at him for a moment as if she understands what is in his mind.*] Mr. Morrison, you! . . [*She turns to the children.*] Have you finished your supper yet?

JOHNNIE. Oh no, mother, not nearly.

JANE CLEGG. Well, you must go to bed now.

JENNY. Oh, mother!

JANE CLEGG. Yes, run along! You can finish your supper in bed.

JOHNNIE. Can't we have it here?

JANE CLEGG. No, Mr. Morrison has something to say to us, so you must run along. You can pretend you're having a picnic or something.

JENNY. Oh yes, Johnnie, let's!

JOHNNIE. Can I read the "History of the Steam Engine" for a little while in bed?

JANE CLEGG. Yes, but only for a little while. Promise.

JOHNNIE. I promise, mother.

JANE CLEGG. [*bending down and kissing him.*] That's a good boy. Run along now, and take your supper with you. Say good night to grannie and Mr. Morrison. Come along, Jenny.

JOHNNIE. Good night, Mr. Morrison.

MR. MORRISON. [*in a manner of a man unaccustomed to children.*] Oh! Ah! Good night!

JOHNNIE. [*going to his grandmother.*] Good night, grannie.

MRS. CLEGG. Good night, my dear! [*She kisses him.*] *He collects his book and his supper.*

JENNY. [*holding up her face to* MR. MORRISON *to be kissed.*] Good night, Mr. Morrison.

MRS. CLEGG. Oh, oh, oh. There's a forward young woman for you.

MR. MORRISON. [*kissing* JENNY *in some embarrassment.*] Good night, Jenny.

MRS. CLEGG. You're a one, you are. Settin' your cap at the gentleman like that.

JENNY. What's setting your cap, grannie? [*She climbs on to* MRS. CLEGG'S *knee, and hugs her tightly.*]

MRS. CLEGG. You don't need to be told, you young rogue. [*Hugs the child.*] Good night, my dear. Um, um, um, um! Good night, bless you!

JENNY. Good night, dear grannie.

JANE CLEGG. Come and get your supper, dear. Good night, Johnnie. [*She bends down and kisses him.*]

JOHNNIE. Good night, mother! [*He goes into the passage.*]

JENNY. [*carrying her supper.*] Good night, mother!

JANE CLEGG. Good night, my darling. [*Kisses her affectionately.*]

JENNY. Good night, all!

MR. MORRISON. Oh, ah, good night!

MRS. CLEGG. Good night, my sweet'eart!

JENNY. Come to bed soon, grannie.

MRS. CLEGG. All right, my dearie.

JANE CLEGG. Run along now, Jenny.

JENNY. All right, mother! [*She goes into the passage, and then returns to the room.*] Oh, can Johnnie read a story to me, mother, a real story? . .

JOHNNIE. [*from the stairs.*] No, I want to read about the steam engine.

JENNY. You shut up!

JANE CLEGG. Jenny, Jenny! You must go to bed. Johnnie'll read his book to you, and if you don't want to hear it you can go to sleep.

JENNY. Oh, mother! [*She goes slowly to the foot of the stairs.*] 'Night, all!

JANE CLEGG. Good night, dear.

JENNY. [*to* JOHNNIE.] Beast, beast!

She runs up the stairs after him.

JANE CLEGG. Now, now!

There is a scuffle, and then a shout of laughter. JANE CLEGG *listens for a moment, and then shuts the door.*

MRS. CLEGG. She's a caution that child is. Just like 'er father was at 'er age, bless 'er.

MR. MORRISON. She must liven up the house!

MRS. CLEGG. She does indeed.

JANE CLEGG. Mr. Morrison, you know something about my husband!

MR. MORRISON. [*startled.*] Oh no, Mrs. Clegg; that is to say, I've really come to find out! . .

JANE CLEGG. What is it?

MR. MORRISON. Well, the truth of the matter is, I'm afraid—mind you, I don't know! . .

JANE CLEGG. Yes!

MRS. CLEGG. Is there anythink wrong?

MR. MORRISON. I'm afraid Clegg may have made a mistake. Of course, I don't know. That's why I came round, just to find out.

MRS. CLEGG. Mistake! Wot mistake!

JANE CLEGG. What kind of a mistake, Mr. Morrison?
MR. MORRISON. Well, you see, a cheque! . .
JANE CLEGG. Yes?
MR. MORRISON. Of course, it may be a mistake, as I say, only it's odd.
MRS. CLEGG. I dunno wot you're talkin' about.
JANE CLEGG. Go on, Mr. Morrison, explain it all, please.
MR. MORRISON. Well, you see, a firm that owes us some money, rather a big amount, sent the cheque in after a lot of bother, and it appears they made it payable to Clegg and sent it to him at the office two or three days ago.
JANE CLEGG. Yes.
MRS. CLEGG. Yes, that's right. A boy brought the letter 'ere. I saw 'Enry openin' the letter meself. It was a cheque all right. You needn't be alarmed, Mr. Morrison. 'Enry'll 'ave it safe!
MR. MORRISON. That's just the point, Mrs. Clegg. You see he didn't say anything about it. I'm cashier. He ought to have told me. I sent a reminder to the firm, and last night they telephoned through to say they'd sent it, and explained what had happened. Of course, I thought it was odd Clegg hadn't said anything, or given me the cheque, only I thought he'd forgotten it, and I meant to ask him about it this morning. But he never turned up.
MRS. CLEGG. Well?
MR. MORRISON. [*very embarrassed.*] Well! [*Laughing nervously.*] It's funny, isn't it?
MRS. CLEGG. I don't see the joke myself. Of course, 'Enry's forgot about it. It'll be all right. You put yourself to a lot of trouble, sir, for nothink wot I can see of it.
MR. MORRISON. I'm sure I hope so.
MRS. CLEGG. 'Ope so! Of course you 'ave. 'Ere,

Jane, let's 'ave supper. I'm starvin', and I expect 'Enry'll be late again.

JANE CLEGG. You have something, mother. I'll wait for Henry.

MRS. CLEGG. [*Rising and going to the table.*] You look quite upset. Any one 'ud think you believed 'Enry'd took the money.

JANE CLEGG. [*wearily.*] I don't know! . .

MRS. CLEGG. [*angrily.*] Don't know! But you ought to know. 'E's your 'usban'. If the 'ole world believed 'im guilty, you oughtn't. It isn't nice of you. Besides, any one with any sense 'ud know 'Enry wouldn't do such a thing. I know 'e was always one for goin' on, but 'e never done nothink wrong, not really wrong, I mean, like stealing money or anythink. [*She leans over to* JANE *and pats her hands.*] There, there, see! 'E'll explain it all right.

MR. MORRISON. I hope so.

MRS. CLEGG. You seem to 'ave made up your mind already, Mr. Morrison. Jane, why don't you say somethink. 'Owever you can sit there an' 'ear your 'usban's good name took away, I don't know!

JANE CLEGG. How much is it, Mr. Morrison?

MR. MORRISON. I don't know quite. There's this cheque for one hundred and forty pounds, but there may be more.

MRS. CLEGG. 'Ow can you say such things.

JANE CLEGG. Of course, Mr. Morrison, if what you say is true, the money will be repaid.

MRS. CLEGG. Of course, it will. I dessay 'Enry didn't mean to take the money, that is if 'e did take it, which I don't believe, not really take it, I mean, but if 'e did, if mind you, of course it'll be paid. 'E'd be the first to say that 'imself. 'Enry never done nothink under'and, not really under'and.

MR. MORRISON. [*to* JANE CLEGG.] You see, Mrs.

Clegg, all our staff is insured against accidents of this sort, and the difficulty is that the policy contains a clause to the effect that the defaulter must be prosecuted and convicted before the insurance company pays up, otherwise there's no proof of embezzlement.

MRS. CLEGG. I've always 'eard them insurance companies was tricky.

MR. MORRISON. Of course, if the money is paid back, the insurance company won't want to prosecute. In fact, I don't suppose the guv'nor'll say anything about it. As a matter of fact, he doesn't know yet. I'm the only one that knows.

MRS. CLEGG. Well, that's fortunate, any'ow. Isn't it, Jane? It's lucky it 'appened just now, if it 'as 'appened. Jane'll be able to pay it all back as easy as anythink. You see 'er uncle died a little while back an' left 'er seven 'undred poun's. Jus' convenient, I call it.

MR. MORRISON. Very.

JANE CLEGG. If my husband has defaulted, Mr. Morrison, I shall let you have the money immediately.

MR. MORRISON. I'm very glad, Mrs. Clegg. I'm sorry it should have happened. Clegg and I have worked together a good many years now. I shouldn't like to think! . .

JANE CLEGG. I suppose, Mr. Morrison, if the money is repaid instantly, there is no reason why the story should be repeated to any one else.

MR. MORRISON. Well, it's rather hard to decide. The guv'nor ought to know. It's hardly fair to him. Supposing it was to happen again.

MRS. CLEGG. It won't 'appen again. We don't know that it's 'appened at all. We on'y got your word for it, an' you might 'ave made a mistake. You ain't the Lord God Almighty.

MR. MORRISON. [*on his dignity*.] I know that, Mrs. Clegg. You're not treating me with much consideration,

I must say. There was no obligation on my part to come here at all to-night. I only did so because I'm a friend of Clegg's. If I hadn't been, I should have gone straight to the guv'nor and told him what's happened. Seems to me I'm getting very little thanks ! . .

JANE CLEGG. Oh, please, Mr. Morrison, don't say that. You know Mrs. Clegg is an old woman, and Henry's her only son ! . .

MR. MORRISON. Of course, I make allowances.

MRS. CLEGG. 'E's a good son, too. There isn't a cleverer man in this town. I dessay some people's jealous of him.

The noise of a key turning in a lock is heard, and then the street door is opened and shut.

JANE CLEGG. That must be Henry, now. [*She opens the door of the sitting-room, and looks into the hall.*] Is that you, Henry ?

HENRY CLEGG. [*from the hall.*] Yes, dear. I'm sorry I'm late. I've been frightfully rushed at the office to-day.

He appears at the door and is about to kiss her when he observes MORRISON. *He starts violently, then recovers himself a little and smiles feebly.*

Hilloa, Morrison, old chap ! What are you doing here ?

MR. MORRISON. I've just been explaining my visit to Mrs. Clegg.

HENRY CLEGG. [*nervously.*] Oh yes. [*He goes to the table.*] Is this my supper ?

JANE CLEGG. Yes.

HENRY CLEGG. [*sitting down.*] Will you join me, Morrison ?

MR. MORRISON. No, thanks. I've had my meal.

HENRY CLEGG. Have a glass of beer ?

MR. MORRISON. No, thanks.

HENRY CLEGG. I say, what's up with you all ? You look mighty solemn.

VOL. I   O

MRS. CLEGG. 'E says you bin stealin' the firm's money.

HENRY CLEGG. [*starting up.*] What!

JANE CLEGG. Mr. Morrison is worried about that cheque from Armstrong & Brown. He says you haven't given it to him yet.

MR. MORRISON. Of course, it may be a mistake.

HENRY CLEGG. Oh, that! That's all right, old chap, that's all right.

MRS. CLEGG. I tole you 'e could explain it when 'e come 'ome. Nasty minds some people must 'ave.

MR. MORRISON. You've had the cheque three days now, and I ought to have had it the day you received it. It ought not to have been sent to you at all. They telephoned this morning about it.

HENRY CLEGG. Clean forgot all about it.

MR. MORRISON. Funny sort of thing to forget!

MRS. CLEGG. Any one might forget a thing. You don't remember everythink, do you?

MR. MORRISON. I don't know what the guvnor'd say if he knew.

JANE CLEGG. You'd better give the cheque to Mr. Morrison now, Henry.

HENRY CLEGG. Eh?

JANE CLEGG. You said you'd forgotten about it, so I suppose you still have it.

HENRY CLEGG. Oh yes, yes. That'll be all right, Morrison. I'll clear it up to-morrow. I'm a bit tired to-night.

JANE CLEGG. It doesn't require much effort to take a cheque out of your pocket and pass it over to Mr. Morrison.

HENRY CLEGG. Oh, all right, all right. [*He begins to bluster.*] I must say it's a nice thing when a man comes home fagged to find his friend and his wife getting up a tale! . .

MR. MORRISON. [*with asperity.*] I haven't got up

any tale. You haven't accounted for a cheque that ought to have been given to me three days ago, and it's my duty to find out why you haven't accounted for it.

JANE CLEGG. Besides, the whole thing can be cleared up by your passing the cheque over to Mr. Morrison.

MRS. CLEGG. Jane, you 'aven't got no feelin's. 'E's tired, isn't 'e? [*She goes to* CLEGG'S *side, and puts her arms round his neck.*] My poor lad, you're worried to death by 'em.

HENRY CLEGG. [*roughly pushing her away.*] For God's sake leave me alone. As if I hadn't got enough on my mind, without you messing about.

MRS. CLEGG. [*a little tearfully.*] Oh, 'Enry, an' me your own mother, too.

MR. MORRISON. Why didn't you come in to-day?

JANE CLEGG. You told me when you came in that you'd been busy at the office.

HENRY CLEGG. Did I say that? Not at the office. I have been busy, very busy. Fact is, I met a friend of mine in the town to-day and he put me on to a good bit of business. I've been running all over the place after it. Haven't had time to get anything to eat.

MRS. CLEGG [*dolefully.*] Oh, 'Enry, an' you know you 'ave indigestion.

HENRY CLEGG. I think I've pulled it off all right. Fine connection.

MR. MORRISON. Oh yes.

JANE CLEGG. Who was it you met?

HENRY CLEGG. No one you know. [*To* MORRISON.] Sure you won't have something to eat, old chap?

MR. MORRISON. Quite sure, thanks.

HENRY CLEGG. Well, you won't mind if I go on, will you? I'm as hungry as a trooper.

MRS. CLEGG. Jane, look after 'im do. Wot with workin' so hard, an' bein' upset, I wonder 'e's able to eat at all.

JANE CLEGG. Don't you think you'd better let Mr. Morrison have the cheque, Henry. It's hardly fair to keep him here so long. He probably has other things to do.

HENRY CLEGG. I can't let him have it to-night. I left my bag in the cloak-room at the station. I didn't want to be bothered with it when I went after this chap I've just been telling you about, and I was too tired to go and get it again to-night. I'll fetch it with me in the morning. [*Airily.*] It's all right, Morrison, there's no necessity to look as if I'd committed a crime.

JANE CLEGG. [*with cold precision.*] You didn't take your bag with you this morning.

MRS. CLEGG. Jane, 'ow can you doubt your own 'usban'!

JANE CLEGG. You didn't take your bag this morning. It's still upstairs.

MR. MORRISON. I must say I don't like the look of this.

MRS. CLEGG. Well, p'raps 'e thought 'e took it. If the bag's upstairs, the cheque'll be there too. Run up an' get it, Jane, there's a dear, an' then we'll be at peace again.

JANE CLEGG. Shall I go and get it, Henry, or will you?

HENRY CLEGG. Eh? Oh! [*He stops short, and glances sharply about him. There is silence for a few moments.*] I may as well own up. I haven't got the cheque.

MRS. CLEGG. Oh, 'Enry!

HENRY CLEGG. I've cashed it.

There is silence again for a little while.

MR. MORRISON. Of course, you know, this is very serious.

JANE CLEGG. [*quickly.*] Mr. Morrison, you will remember your promise not to say anything about this to Mr. Harper. The money will be paid to-morrow. I'll see to that.

MR. MORRISON. I didn't make any promise, Mrs. Clegg. It's my duty to tell Mr. Harper. This may not be the only sum ! . .

HENRY CLEGG. It is.

MR. MORRISON. And it may happen again. I must tell him, Mrs. Clegg.

MRS. CLEGG. But 'e'll lose 'is situation if you do.

MR. MORRISON. I'm sorry. As I said, we've worked together a good many years, but I must do my duty.

MRS. CLEGG. You wouldn't see 'im disgraced, would you? Oh, Mr. Morrison, don't go an' do it! Think of 'is wife an' children. An' me, too. [*She weeps while she speaks.*] I've lived 'ere all me life, an' no one 'as never bin able to say a word agin me, not no one. I've always kept meself respectable, wotever's 'appened, an' now! [*To her son.*] Oh, 'Enry, tell 'im it ain't true. I'm a nole woman, an' I couldn't bear to die thinkin' you was in prison !

HENRY CLEGG. Prison?

MRS. CLEGG. 'E says you'll be put in prison for this.

MR. MORRISON. Not if the money is repaid.

JANE CLEGG. It will be repaid. [*She goes to* MRS. CLEGG.] It will be all right, mother. The money will be paid. Mr. Morrison, must you tell Mr. Harper?

MR. MORRISON. I'm afraid so, Mrs. Clegg. I can't help it.

MRS. CLEGG. You can 'elp anythink if you want to !

MR. MORRISON. I've got myself to think of, and if the guv'nor found out! . . And there's the future. It might happen again.

JANE CLEGG. Mr. Morrison, will you agree to this? Henry will resign his post with Mr. Harper, and we'll leave the town ! . .

MRS. CLEGG. Oh, no ! . .

JANE CLEGG. We'll go to Canada or somewhere, where we can start afresh. The money shall be paid, and you shan't have any anxiety about the future. Will you agree to say nothing to Mr. Harper if we do that?

MR. MORRISON. I don't want to appear hard!

JANE CLEGG. Please, Mr. Morrison. You see, it isn't only Henry. There's Johnnie and Jenny.

MR. MORRISON. Yes, I see that, of course.

JANE CLEGG. I'd planned things for them, but!.. Oh, well, it can't be helped. You won't speak to Mr. Harper about this, will you?

MR. MORRISON. [*after a short pause.*] All right, Mrs. Clegg, I won't!

JANE CLEGG. You'd better come here to-morrow evening for the money, hadn't you? It might look odd if I were to come to the office with a lot of money.

MR. MORRISON. Perhaps you're right. Very well, I'll come in just before tea. Will that do?

JANE CLEGG. Yes.

MR. MORRISON. Well, I better be going now. I'm glad that's over. [*He holds out his hand to* JANE.] Good night, Mrs. Clegg. I'm sorry to have brought you bad news.

JANE CLEGG. You couldn't help it, and it was better that you should have brought it than any one else.

MR. MORRISON. [*going to* MRS. CLEGG.] That's true. Good night, ma'am!

MRS. CLEGG. [*feebly.*] Good night, sir.

MR. MORRISON. Good night, Clegg.

CLEGG *rises from his chair, and holds out his hand, which* MORRISON *ignores.*

HENRY CLEGG. Oh, good night, old chap.

MR. MORRISON. [*to* JANE.] Don't trouble to come to the door, Mrs. Clegg. I'll let myself out.

JANE CLEGG. It's all right.

MORRISON *and she go out into the passage. She*

opens the door for him and lets him out. MRS. CLEGG *sits at the fire, snivelling.* HENRY CLEGG *moodily eats his supper.* JANE CLEGG *returns to the room, shutting the door after her.*
It's turned colder, I think.
Neither HENRY CLEGG *nor his mother respond.* JANE CLEGG *draws her chair up to the fire. She sits thinking for a few minutes.*

MRS. CLEGG. Aren't you goin' to 'ave your supper, Jane?

JANE CLEGG. I don't feel like eating, thanks!

HENRY CLEGG. [*sullenly.*] No good making a martyr of yourself.

JANE CLEGG. Henry!

HENRY CLEGG. Well?

JANE CLEGG. What did you do with the money?

HENRY CLEGG. I spent it.

MRS. CLEGG. [*horror-stricken.*] You spent it!

HENRY CLEGG. Oh, don't sit there looking like a damned fool. I spent it, that's all.

MRS. CLEGG. Oh, wot disgrace to 'appen. [*She becomes inarticulate.*]

JANE CLEGG. What did you do with it?

HENRY CLEGG. [*blustering.*] God bless my soul, am I not to have any peace? I'm fagged out! . .

JANE CLEGG. I must know what you did with it. I have a right to know. What did you do with it?

HENRY CLEGG. I dunno. One thing and another.

JANE CLEGG. You must know. You've only had it a few days.

MRS. CLEGG. Such a thing's never been known in our family before.

HENRY CLEGG. Oh, shut up, you! Sitting there, snivelling!

JANE CLEGG. What did you do with the money, Henry?

HENRY CLEGG. I tell you I spent it!

JANE CLEGG. You've told so many lies to-night! . .

MRS. CLEGG. [*reproachfully.*] 'E's your 'usban', Jane!

JANE CLEGG. If I'm to repay the money he stole, I must know what he did with it.

HENRY CLEGG. All right. Look here, Jane, you'll see me through this, won't you? They could put me in jail, you know. . . I couldn't stand that! It's Harper's own fault, blast him!

MRS. CLEGG. I knoo it was some one's fault!

HENRY CLEGG. [*to* JANE.] It was like this, you see! You know when they put me on that new round?

JANE CLEGG. Yes.

HENRY CLEGG. Well, it's an expensive round to work. You have to treat these damned shopkeepers like lords before they'll give you an order. And I'm only allowed a pound a week for expenses. I've spent that in a day. Of course, I didn't tell you. I didn't want to upset you, and I thought I should pull round all right. So I should, only for the bad debts. It was that did it. A man went smash and hadn't paid a sou to us, and so old Harper made me responsible for the whole bally lot. He's like that, the old screw. Makes his travellers bear the bad debts. That was how it began. I tried to make it up by horse-racing. You know! Oh, it's a mug's game, I know that, but we're all mugs when we're in a hole. I was in a rotten hole, too. That fellow Munce who came in here the other night, he's a bookie. He was worrying me for money I owed him, and you wouldn't let me have any . .

MRS. CLEGG. I knoo you was doin' wrong in not lettin' 'im 'ave it.

HENRY CLEGG. And then that cheque came. I didn't mean to take it really. It just came into my head. I thought I'd be able to make it up somehow.

JANE CLEGG. Why didn't you tell me about the bad debts?

HENRY CLEGG. What would have been the good? It was before your uncle left you that money.

JANE CLEGG. Why didn't you tell me then?

HENRY CLEGG. I'd started betting then, and I wasn't exactly proud of myself.

MRS. CLEGG. Jus' like 'is poor father was. 'E was proud, too.

HENRY CLEGG. Besides, I thought you'd be sure to let me have the money or some of it. It seemed natural somehow.

MRS. CLEGG. Any nice woman would 'ave let you 'ave it.

JANE CLEGG. It would have been better to have told me than to let Morrison find out. You'll have to leave Mr. Harper now! . .

HENRY CLEGG. I suppose so.

MRS. CLEGG. Oh, what a good job it was your uncle Tom died when 'e did, Jane. It was jus' like the 'and of Providence. You'll be able to make some use of that money, now, 'stead of 'oardin' it up.

JANE CLEGG. Yes, that's true. Only it wasn't the kind of use I wanted to make of it.

MRS. CLEGG. What better use could you make of it than to save your 'usban's good name?

JANE CLEGG. [*beginning to clear away the remnants of the meal.*] Yes, I suppose that's a great privilege.

HENRY CLEGG. [*rising from his seat, and taking the plates from her.*] Here, let me do that. You sit down, and take it easy for a bit. [*He puts the plates down and pushes her into a chair.*] You've had a rotten day of it. [*He puts his arms about her and kisses her.*] You're a jolly good sort, Jane. You are, straight.

JANE CLEGG. [*getting up from her chair, and proceeding with the work of clearing away.*] Yes.

CLEGG *looks for his pipe, which he lights. He takes the chair which his wife has just vacated.*

Don't you think we'd better go to bed. It's getting late.

MRS. CLEGG. Yes, I think so, too. I'm goin' any'ow. [*She rises and goes to her son, whom she fondles.*] Goo' night, my dear, an' don't worry your 'ead about nothink. Jane'll see it's all right.

HENRY CLEGG. Good night, mother.

MRS. CLEGG. [*going to* JANE.] Goo' night, Jane. You've bin a good wife to 'im.

JANE CLEGG. [*indifferently.*] Good night, mother.

The two women kiss, and MRS. CLEGG *goes out of the room. There is quiet for a while.* JANE *takes the dishes out of the room.* CLEGG *stands with his back to the fire, watching her.* JANE *returns to the room, looking dubious.* HENRY *glances up at her quickly.*

HENRY CLEGG. What are you thinking about, Jane?

JANE CLEGG. Oh, I wish I could be sure of you, Henry!

HENRY CLEGG. Well, you are, aren't you?

JANE CLEGG. I don't know. Oh yes, I suppose so. Come on, let's go to bed. [*She gathers up her sewing and moves towards the door.*] Turn out the lamp, will you?

HENRY CLEGG. Yes, dear. [*He turns out the light.* JANE *stands in the doorway.*] Don't be hard on me, Jane. I'm not really a bad chap. I'm only weak. That's all.

JANE CLEGG. I can't help thinking of that woman, Henry.

HENRY CLEGG. [*putting his arms about her.*] You needn't, dear. I swear to God I've not done anything against you. I promised you! . .

JANE CLEGG. Yes, you promised! . .

She goes towards the stairs, and he follows, closing the door after him.

ACT III

It is the next evening. MRS. CLEGG *and* JANE CLEGG *are sitting by the fire. The door leading to the hall is ajar.*

MRS. CLEGG. It's a good job 'Enry was 'ere. Johnnie and Jenny wouldn't 'ave gone to bed so quiet as they did.

JANE CLEGG. [*without looking up.*] No.

MRS. CLEGG. I do 'ope they'll never get to 'ear about this. Such disgrace! Though I must say it serves Mr. 'Arper right. I 'aven't no sympathy for 'im. 'E didden treat 'Enry fair, makin' 'im pay all them bad debts an' all.

JANE CLEGG. It doesn't seem quite fair.

MRS. CLEGG. Poor 'Enry! I expec' 'e felt it, you know. Bound to 'ave. 'E's that sensitive. 'Ighly-strung! I dessay 'e worried about it, on'y 'e wouldn't say nothink.

JANE CLEGG. Perhaps he did.

MRS. CLEGG. You know, I wonder 'e didden give it away in 'is sleep. Talk about it! I've always 'eard that people with things on their mind dreams somethink 'orrible, an' begins talkin' in their sleep, an' their wives gets to 'ear about it.

JANE CLEGG. I don't suppose that always happens. Henry never revealed anything in his sleep.

MRS. CLEGG. P'raps you was asleep an' didden 'ear. 'Is father uset to do it, but I never could make 'ead or tail out o' wot 'e said.

HENRY CLEGG *comes down the stairs as she speaks, and enters the room.*

JANE CLEGG. Are they asleep, Henry?

HENRY CLEGG. [*coming between his mother and wife,*

and sitting down.] Yes. Jenny took a long time to go off. Young beggar! Wanted me to tell stories to her all night.

MRS. CLEGG. Bless 'er!

They sit in silence for a few moments.

MRS. CLEGG. 'Ave you thought of wot you'll do when this . . bother's over, 'Enry?

HENRY CLEGG. Not yet, mother.

JANE CLEGG. We shall leave here, of course. We'll start afresh in Canada.

MRS. CLEGG. It's an awful long way to Canada. I don't know any one there! . .

JANE CLEGG. That's why we shall go. Oh, mother, can't you see, it's bound to come out that Henry took the money. Men don't leave their jobs suddenly without good cause; and how are we to know that Mr. Morrison won't tell people why Henry left Mr. Harper. He might tell without meaning to. Something might be said that would start suspicion in people's minds, and then! . . Oh, it would be awful for Johnnie and Jenny.

HENRY CLEGG. It's all Johnnie and Jenny with you! . .

JANE CLEGG. Yes, it is, Henry. You must get used to that. [*To* MRS. CLEGG.] People are not likely to suspect anything if we go to Canada. Henry can tell his friends that he's tired of England. . . It's easy enough to say that! . .

MRS. CLEGG. I dessay you're right; but it's 'ard at my age to 'ave to go abroad. I'm a nole woman! . .

HENRY CLEGG. Yes, mother, we know that. We can't help it. Do for goodness' sake stop whining about it.

MRS. CLEGG. [*tearfully*.] That isn't the way to speak to your mother, 'Enry!

HENRY CLEGG. No, but you make me talk like it. Nothing but snivelling all day. If we've got to go, we've got to go, and there's an end of it. Jane has all the money, and she's boss here. We've got to do what she tells us.

MRS. CLEGG. It's not right. It's unnatcherl.

HENRY CLEGG. [*getting up and pacing the room.*] All right! You've said that before. If you don't want to go to Canada, damn it, stay behind.

JANE CLEGG. [*gently.*] Henry!

HENRY CLEGG. Well, it's sickening, isn't it. I can't see any sense in crying over spilt milk.

MRS. CLEGG. You didden ought to 'ave spilt no milk! . .

HENRY CLEGG. Oh, for God's sake, shut up! If I'm to have the thing cast up to me for the rest of my life, I might as well go and drown myself.

MRS. CLEGG. Oh, 'Enry! [*She rises from her seat and goes to him.*] I didden mean to cast nothink up at you, 'Enry. I didden reely. [*She puts her arms round him and draws his head down and kisses him.*] You're my son, 'Enry, all I got. . . I love you, 'Enry! . . [*She weeps helplessly and buries her face on his breast.*]

HENRY CLEGG. [*patting her affectionately.*] All right, mother. I'm sorry I was snappy. Here, come and sit down. [*He leads her back to her seat.*] You'll be all right in Canada. [*He makes her sit down.*] We'll have you searching for gold at Klondyke in no time. [*There is a knock at the street door.*] I suppose that's Morrison! Buck up, mother, we can't have him seeing you in tears.

MRS. CLEGG. Awright, 'Enry, dear. I won't cry no more.

JANE CLEGG. You open the door, Henry.

HENRY CLEGG. Right. [*He goes into the hall and opens the street door.* MORRISON *is seen standing in the street.*] Oh, is that you, Morrison! Come in!

MR. MORRISON. [*stepping inside.*] Thanks.

HENRY CLEGG. Leave your hat here, will you?

MR. MORRISON. [*hanging his hat on the hat-stand.*] Thanks. I'm not too soon, am I?

HENRY CLEGG. No, oh no! You're just right. Come in!

They enter the sitting-room. HENRY CLEGG *shuts the door while* MORRISON *greets* MRS. CLEGG *and* JANE CLEGG.

[*Putting a chair for* MORRISON.] Have this chair, will you?

MR. MORRISON. [*sitting down.*] Thanks. It's a nice night, isn't it?

HENRY CLEGG. Yes, I thought we were going to have some rain, but it's kept fine.

MR. MORRISON. Yes. We don't want any more rain just yet, do we?

MRS. CLEGG. There's been a lot of rain lately. I expect it's good for some people, farmers and people like that. I must say I don't like it. I always get the rheumatism that bad.

MR. MORRISON. They do say that a man that's had his leg off can always tell when it's going to rain.

MRS. CLEGG. Indeed!

MR. MORRISON. Yes. He gets a funny feeling in the stump—sort of pins and needles.

HENRY CLEGG. That's funny, that is. You'd wonder why that was.

MRS. CLEGG. I expect it 'as a meaning, if we on'y knoo it. There's nothink without a meanin'. I've always said that, an' I believe it.

JANE CLEGG. Hadn't we better settle Mr. Morrison's business, Henry? I expect he's anxious to get away.

MR. MORRISON. Oh, I'm in no hurry, Mrs. Clegg!..

HENRY CLEGG. Did the guv'nor ask where I was to-day?

MR. MORRISON. Well, you see, I told him the whole facts!..

MRS. CLEGG. You tole Mr. 'Arper! Oh, but you promised you wouldn't.

JANE CLEGG. It doesn't make much difference. It was bound to come out...

HENRY CLEGG. I think you might have kept it to yourself, Morrison.

MR. MORRISON. I daresay you do, but I've got myself to think of. Supposing there'd been a hitch in this affair, where'd I be, eh? The guv'nor was almost sure to find it out, and if he found I'd kept it from him, he might have thought I was in it, too. I've always kept my hands clean! . .

MRS. CLEGG. You better touch wood, Mr. Morrison. You don't know 'ow soon it'll be before you get into trouble.

MR. MORRISON. I'm not that sort. I don't get into trouble. Trouble doesn't come to you; you go to it. That's my belief.

JANE CLEGG. You're a fortunate man, Mr. Morrison. I hope you will always be able to believe that.

MR. MORRISON. I expect I shall.

HENRY CLEGG. What did the guv'nor say?

MR. MORRISON. He was furious at first. Stormed and raged, and threatened to send for the police at once. You know the way he goes on when he's in a temper. I let him go for a while, and then told him of the arrangement I'd made with Mrs. Clegg that the money should be repaid, and that soothed him down. I told him it would be silly to send for the police! . .

MRS. CLEGG. Oh, thank you, Mr. Morrison, thank you!

MR. MORRISON. Because, of course, he might not get the money. That's what I told him. Of course, he'd have got it all right. The insurance company would have paid, if you hadn't, and they'd have been glad enough to get their money back somehow.

MRS. CLEGG. Mr. 'Arper is more to blame than 'Enry. That's wot I think.

MR. MORRISON. Well, of course, that's one way of looking at it.

MRS. CLEGG. It's the only way to look at it. If 'e 'adn't . .

HENRY CLEGG. All right, mother. Morrison doesn't want to hear your views on Mr. Harper. Jane, we'd better settle this, hadn't we? Have you got the money?

JANE CLEGG. Yes. It's upstairs. I'll go and fetch it. It's in notes, Mr. Morrison. I thought that would be more convenient.

MR. MORRISON. Yes, that was the best thing to do, Mrs. Clegg.

JANE CLEGG *goes out and is seen to mount the stairs.*

MRS. CLEGG. I do think Mr. 'Arper ought to 'ave come 'ere 'imself for the money.

MR. MORRISON. Oh!

MRS. CLEGG. 'Ow do we know it'll be all right! . .

MR. MORRISON. Do you mean to suggest that I might steal the money? . .

MRS. CLEGG. I don't mean to suggest anythink, but I believe in bein' on the safe side.

MR. MORRISON. [*hotly.*] Every one isn't like your son, you know.

HENRY CLEGG. [*angrily.*] You needn't put on the virtuous air, Morrison! . .

MR. MORRISON. I'm not putting on any virtuous air. I've tried to make things as pleasant for you as possible, and I get nothing but insults from your mother. You'd think to hear her that I'd stolen the money, not you. . . I've always kept my hands clean. There's nothing in my life I'd be ashamed to let any one know about.

MRS. CLEGG. Well, you ain't yooman, then! I tell you this, Mr. Morrison, I don't believe you. Now!

HENRY CLEGG. Mother, mother!

MRS. CLEGG. No, 'Enry, I won't sit 'ere an' 'ear you made little of. 'Ow do we know 'e's any better'n you. We on'y got 'is word for it.

MR. MORRISON. I must say! . .

MRS. CLEGG. There's things in every one's life they don't want to talk about. If it isn't one thing, it's another.

That's wot I've learned from bein' alive. It's on'y yooman. Wot 'ud be the use of 'avin' a Merciful Father if 'E 'adn't got nothink to be merciful about! That's 'ow I look at it! An' I dessay, Mr. Morrison, for all you're so good an' 'oly, you got somethink you don't want to go braggin' about. There's some people does things they're not ashamed of an' ought to be.

JANE CLEGG *returns to the room while* MRS. CLEGG *is speaking.*

HENRY CLEGG. Don't mind her, Morrison; she's a bit upset.

MRS. CLEGG. Look at Mr. 'Arper!

JANE CLEGG. What's wrong, mother?

MRS. CLEGG. It's that Mr. Morrison with 'is 'oly airs. 'E never done nothink to be ashamed of, 'e says, an' of course 'e's better'n my 'Enry.

JANE CLEGG. Well, well, mother, what's it matter what any one thinks about him, if you're satisfied with him.

MRS. CLEGG. Now, there's ole 'Arper. Look at 'im. Look 'ow 'e treated 'Enry!

MR. MORRISON. If you ask me, Mr. Harper treated him jolly well.

MRS. CLEGG. Oh, indeed! Indeed! Making 'im pay all the bad debts was treatin' 'im well, I suppose!

HENRY CLEGG. [*agitated.*] Mother, for goodness' sake, hold your tongue. [*To* MORRISON.] Don't take any notice of her, old chap. Jane, have you got the money?

MR. MORRISON. What bad debts?

MRS. CLEGG. You know well enough what bad debts. Don't put on the 'oly an' innocent look to me. I know your sort. It wassen 'is fault they didden pay for wot they ordered!

MR. MORRISON. Who didn't pay?

HENRY CLEGG. All right, old chap. Can't you see she's upset.

VOL. I   P

MR. MORRISON. I don't know what she means by bad debts.

MRS. CLEGG. Oh yes, you do. Puttin' 'im on a dear round an' then makin' 'im pay the bad debts!

MR. MORRISON. Look here, Mrs. Clegg, I've had enough of this, see! I don't know what tale he's been telling you! . .

HENRY CLEGG. It doesn't matter, old chap, it doesn't matter. Let's get this business settled. Jane! . .

MR. MORRISON. I'm not going to be shut up. [*To* MRS. CLEGG.] He's had the best and easiest round of the lot, and he hasn't had a single bad debt for a year past, and those he used to have, the guv'nor bore two-thirds. See! I'm not going to stay here and listen to you abusing the guv'nor for nothing!

JANE CLEGG. He hasn't had a single bad debt! . .

HENRY CLEGG. It's all right, dear. I'll explain it all presently. Let's settle this affair first. Morrison doesn't want to hear our quarrels.

JANE CLEGG. I don't understand. You said you had to pay the bad debts, and that you took the money to make them up.

MR. MORRISON. All lies, that's what it is!

MRS. CLEGG. Don't you dare to insult my son, you!

JANE CLEGG. Please keep quiet, mother. Henry, is this true?

MR. MORRISON. Of course it's true!

JANE CLEGG. I'm speaking to my husband, Mr. Morrison. Henry, will you explain? . .

HENRY CLEGG. It's all right, dear. It's quite simple. I can make it clear in a minute or two, but I prefer to do it when we're alone. I object to discussing private matters before strangers.

JANE CLEGG. No, you must tell me now. It's only fair to Mr. Morrison.

MRS. CLEGG. Of course, if you accept 'is word to 'Enry's! . .

HENRY CLEGG. Mother, for the love of God, shut up! You've made enough mess already without making it worse.

MRS. CLEGG. If a mother can't speak up for 'er son! . .

JANE CLEGG. Mother, you'd better reconcile yourself to the fact that Henry has been lying again! . .

HENRY CLEGG. [*blustering.*] This is too much, this is. Look here, Morrison, if you're a gentleman you'll clear out and leave us to settle this matter alone.

MR. MORRISON. I haven't had the money yet.

HENRY CLEGG. That'll be all right. You can come to-morrow.

MR. MORRISON. I won't go till I get it.

HENRY CLEGG. If you don't want to be thrown out, you'll go now! . .

JANE CLEGG. That'll do, Henry. Mr. Morrison will stay until you've explained the position.

HENRY CLEGG. Then he can stay till he's blue in the face. I won't explain. I'm not going to be bullied by him or by you. I'm a man, not a child.

JANE CLEGG. I shall not pay the money until I hear your explanation.

HENRY CLEGG. I don't care. Keep your damn money. They can do what they like.

JANE CLEGG. Very well. I'm sorry, Mr. Morrison. Good night!

MR. MORRISON. This is pretty serious, you know.

JANE CLEGG. I know. Good night!

HENRY CLEGG. [*still blustering.*] I don't care a damn!

MR. MORRISON. I shall go straight to Mr. Harper, and tell him what's happened. I shouldn't be surprised if he applies for a warrant at once.

HENRY CLEGG. [*anxiously.*] What, to-night!

MR. MORRISON. Yes.

JANE CLEGG. I can't help that.

MRS. CLEGG. Oh, Jane, an' 'im your own 'usban'!

MR. MORRISON. [*hesitating*.] I don't understand you, Mrs. Clegg. After all, he is your husband! . .

JANE CLEGG. I wonder. I thought I was marrying a man I could trust. Henry's a liar. I can't trust him.

HENRY CLEGG. Go on. Make me out all that's bad.

JANE CLEGG. Henry, why are you talking as if you were being unjustly treated? You know that you have lied to me from first to last. Even now I don't know how you managed to get into debt as you did.

HENRY CLEGG. I've told you. Gambling.

MR. MORRISON. Good heavens! A gambler, a liar, and a thief!

MRS. CLEGG. It's none of your business.

MR. MORRISON. No, thank God.

JANE CLEGG. You just gambled the money away, Henry? Is that so?

HENRY CLEGG. Yes. I said that about the bad debts to make the thing look a bit better than it was. [*He comes up to her.*] Jane, I'm sorry. I'm really sorry. I ought to have told you the truth. I know that. But I was ashamed, I was really. Get me out of this scrape, Jane, and I swear I won't give you cause to complain again. Morrison, you won't tell old Harper to-night, will you? Good God, man, I might be arrested this evening. Jane, you'll get me out of it, won't you? I couldn't stand it. Look here, I swear I'll be a good husband to you, I will. I'll swear it on the Bible, if you like. I didn't mean what I said just now. It was all talk.

JANE CLEGG. I wonder if you're worth saving, Henry!

MRS. CLEGG *bursts into tears.*

HENRY CLEGG. I'll make myself worth saving, Jane. I will, I swear I will. [*He tries to kiss her, but she turns away from him.*] Morrison, you say something. Mother.

JANE CLEGG. It isn't necessary, Henry. I'll pay the money.

HENRY CLEGG. Oh, God bless you, Jane. [*He collapses into a chair in something like hysterics.*] I couldn't face prison. [*There is a loud persistent knocking on the door. Starting up in agitation.*] Oh, who's that? [JANE *goes towards the door.*] No, no, don't answer. Morrison, it's all right, isn't it? You haven't told the police.

MR. MORRISON. Of course I haven't.

HENRY CLEGG. Oh, my God, I shall go out of my mind! [*The knocking continues.*] Curse it, who can it be? [JANE *goes into the hall, leaving the door open.*] If it's any one for me, Jane, say I'm not in. No, wait a bit! I'll open it.

> JANE *returns to the room, and* CLEGG *goes into the hall, shutting the door behind him. The knocking continues.*

MR. MORRISON. Seems a bit upset, doesn't he?

MRS. CLEGG. [*tearfully.*] You'd be upset if you was 'im. The way you all go for 'im. [*There is the sound of a scuffle at the street door, and a loud shouting.*] 'Ooever is that?

JANE CLEGG. [*opening the door.*] What's the matter, Henry?

> *She opens the door wide, and her husband is seen trying to shut the street door. A voice is heard on the other side of it, shouting,* "*You let me in, or it'll be the worse for you, see!*"

HENRY CLEGG. It's all right, Jane. You go inside, will you?

JANE CLEGG. That's Mr. Munce's voice, isn't it?

MUNCE. I'll show you up, you blasted welsher!

> *He heaves the door open, and stumbles into the hall against* HENRY CLEGG.

Keep me out, would you?

HENRY CLEGG. You've no right ! . .

JANE CLEGG. What is it, Mr. Munce?

MUNCE. I want my money, that's what it is. 'E promised to let me 'ave it ! . .

JANE CLEGG. Come in, won't you?

HENRY CLEGG. No, I can't have you in here to-night. I've got a friend in to see me.

MUNCE. I don't care about your friend. You py me my money !

HENRY CLEGG. I'll settle with you to-morrow.

MUNCE. Yes, I know. I've 'eard that tale before.

JANE CLEGG. What is it, what is it ?

MUNCE. I want my money.

HENRY CLEGG. I tell you, I'll give it to you to-morrow.

JANE CLEGG. Shut the door, Henry. We don't want the neighbours to hear this. Come in, Mr. Munce.

JANE CLEGG *re-enters the room, and is followed by* MUNCE. HENRY CLEGG *stands irresolutely at the door, and then closes it, coming back to the room with the others.*

MUNCE. I don't want to make no fuss. . . [*To* MRS. CLEGG.] Goo-deevnin', ma'am !

HENRY CLEGG. Can't you see we've got a friend here to-night. Nice thing this, I must say, intruding into people's houses like this.

MUNCE. Can't help 'oo you 'ave 'ere, I must 'ave my money, an' I don't go out of 'ere till I get it, see !

JANE CLEGG. What money, Mr. Munce ?

MUNCE. What 'e owes me. This long time, 'e does. You ast 'im. Go on, you ast 'im. I waited patient ! . .

JANE CLEGG. But what's it for ? Henry ! . .

HENRY CLEGG. All right, dear. You'd better leave this to me. [*To* MUNCE.] Look here, Munce, it's no good you going on like this. I'll settle up with you the first thing in the morning, I promise you I will.

MUNCE. Yes, I know all about that, but it won't work, see! I want my money now, see! Look 'ere, I treated you fair, didden I?

HENRY CLEGG. Yes, yes, I know, but I've got a friend here now! . .

MUNCE. Well, you gimme me money an' I'll 'ook it all right!

JANE CLEGG. Mr. Munce, will you please tell me how much my husband owes you, and what it is for?

MUNCE. Bets, that's what it's for. I treated 'im fair I 'ave.

JANE CLEGG. Bets!

MUNCE. Yes, you know! 'Orse-racin'! Twenty-five quid!

JANE CLEGG. But I thought . . Henry, you said you'd taken! . . Oh, what does it all mean?

MUNCE. It means I want my money, that's what it means. Look 'ere, Mrs. Clegg, I'm sorry to upset you or anythink, but I must have it, you know, or I'll be up the pole, straight. Look 'ere, you've got a bit by you now. Let 'im 'ave it, so's 'e can py me!

HENRY CLEGG. It's no good you worrying my wife, Munce. I'll come and see you to-morrow.

MR. MORRISON. Perhaps, Mrs. Clegg, we'd better settle our business first. Then I can leave you with this gentleman.

JANE CLEGG. I'll bring the money in the morning, Mr. Morrison!

MR. MORRISON. If you don't mind, I'd rather take it with me to-night. You know the old proverb: a bird in the hand is worth! . .

JANE CLEGG. Very well, Mr. Morrison.

MR. MORRISON. I'm sorry to appear! . .

JANE CLEGG. You're quite right, Mr. Morrison.

She opens the cash-box and takes out a roll of notes, which she proceeds to count.

MUNCE. No one's more sorry'n I am to make a fuss ! . .

MRS. CLEGG. [*lachrymosely.*] Well, wot you want to come an' make it for ?

MUNCE. You'd make one woulden you if you was me. I never failed to make pyment in my life. That's a fact ! There ain't many bookies can sy that. I always paid up when the money was doo ! An' now your son is puttin' me in Queer Street by not pyin' me what 'e owes me. Ain't that somethink to make a fuss about, eih ? I got my name . .

HENRY CLEGG. All right, old chap ! . .

MUNCE. It ain't all right.

HENRY CLEGG. Oh, shut up ! As soon as my wife has settled with this gentleman, we'll settle your affair too.

MUNCE. An' about time, too.

JANE CLEGG. [*handing the notes to* MR. MORRISON.] I think that's right, Mr. Morrison. Just count them, will you ?

MR. MORRISON. [*taking the notes from her.*] Thank you, Mrs. Clegg. [*He begins to count them.*] I'd better give you a receipt for the amount, hadn't I ?

JANE CLEGG. Yes, please !

MR. MORRISON. [*finishing the counting of the notes.*] Yes, that's quite right. [*He puts the money in his pocket.*] If you can let me have a pen and ink, I'll just write out the receipt.

MUNCE. P'raps you'll let me 'ave my money too, ma'am.

JANE CLEGG. You can wait ! . . [*She puts writing materials before* MORRISON, *who writes the receipt.*]

MUNCE. What you mean " wait " !

JANE CLEGG. Until this gentleman has finished his business. Then we will discuss yours. Please sit down !

MUNCE. Oh, awright ! I don't want to be nasty, on'y I thought when you said " wait " you was plyin' about. I'm sure there ain't a more patienter chap'n me anywhere. Now, is there, Clegg? I ask you fair! . .

MR. MORRISON. [*rising and handing the receipt to* JANE CLEGG.] I think that's right, Mrs. Clegg.

MUNCE. [*to* MR. MORRISON.] You got your whack awright. I wish I'd got mine.

MR. MORRISON. You have the advantage of me, sir.

MUNCE. Eh?

MR. MORRISON. I haven't the pleasure of your acquaintance.

MUNCE. Well, it ain't my fault they ain't interdooced us, is it? O' course, if you want to be nasty! . .

JANE CLEGG. Yes, this will do excellently, Mr. Morrison. [*Holding out her hand to him.*] Good night!

MR. MORRISON. [*shaking her hand warmly.*] Good night, Mrs. Clegg. I'm more than sorry! . .

JANE CLEGG. It was not your fault. Good night.

MR. MORRISON. Good night! [*He glances towards* MRS. CLEGG.] Good night, ma'am. [MRS. CLEGG *makes no response.*] Good night, Clegg!

HENRY CLEGG. [*nervously.*] Shall I come to the door with you?

MR. MORRISON. Oh no, thanks. It doesn't matter. I can let myself out. Good night!

HENRY CLEGG. [*holding out his hand.*] Good night.

MR. MORRISON. [*ignoring* CLEGG's *proffered hand.*] Good night all.

He opens the hall door, closing it after him, and a moment later the noise of the street door being shut is heard.

JANE CLEGG. Now, Mr. Munce! . .

MUNCE. Well, it's like this, Mrs. Clegg, I'm not one to turn nasty for nothink. 'E can bear me aht in that. Can't you, Clegg?

HENRY CLEGG. Oh, you're right enough!

MUNCE. That's true. 'E'll admit it 'isself. But wot

I do say is, I ain't been treated fair. Nah, if it 'adden bin for 'safternoon ! . .

HENRY CLEGG. I say, old man, come to the point. I owe you twenty-five pounds, and you want to be paid. That's the point ! You're only wasting time.

MUNCE. That's right enough, 'o course. Yes, that is the point. 'E owes me twenty-five quid, an' I want it. That's the point right enough.

MRS. CLEGG. People like you don't deserve to get paid anythink. 'Orse-racin' an' gamblin' an' leading people astray.

MUNCE. I don't suppose you'd refuse to tike the money if you mide a bet wi' me an' won, eih ?

MRS. CLEGG. I woulden bet with you or no one, an' I'm sure that 'Enry woulden neither, on'y you persuaded 'im into it.

MUNCE. 'E didden need no persuadin', I give you my word.

HENRY CLEGG. Mother, don't you think you'd better go to bed.

MRS. CLEGG. [*weeping profusely.*] I suppose I 'ad. I don't seem able to do nothink right. I done all I could for you. . . Jane's that 'ard !

HENRY CLEGG. All right, mother.

MRS. CLEGG. [*going to her son and putting her arms about him.*] I love you, 'Enry, dear. You're all I got . . you an' Jenny . . an' Johnnie, o' course. I'm a nole woman, I know, an' . . don't go an' do nothink wrong again, will you, dear. I . . I can't bear to 'ear them sayin' things about you. That Mr. Morrison, 'e said things that 'urt me crool. [*She kisses him affectionately.*] I'm very fond of you, 'Enry. You're so like your poor father.

HENRY CLEGG. All right, mother. Go to bed now. All the bother'll be over in the morning.

MRS. CLEGG. [*wearily.*] Good night, my dear.

HENRY CLEGG. Good night, mother.
He opens the door for her, and she passes out weeping. She stops in the doorway for a moment and says " Good night, Jane ! "
JANE CLEGG. Good night, mother.
MRS. CLEGG. Don't be 'ard on 'im. 'E don't mean nothink.
HENRY CLEGG. Good night, mother.
MRS. CLEGG. Good night, my dear !
She goes into the hall, and HENRY CLEGG *closes the door behind her.*
MUNCE. Ole girl seems a bit upset, eih ?
JANE CLEGG. Yes.
MUNCE. Not surprisin', o' course. [*To* CLEGG.] I s'pose you bin up to somethink or other. You 'ad to py that other chap a tidy bit, eih ?
JANE CLEGG. Mr. Munce, I haven't got the money to pay you ! . .
MUNCE. [*alarmed again.*] Now, look 'ere ! . .
JANE CLEGG. And if I had, I wouldn't pay it.
MUNCE. What you mean you wouldn't py it. 'E owes it, don't 'e ?
JANE CLEGG. I don't know, and I don't care. I've just paid one hundred and forty pounds that he'd taken from his employers ! . .
HENRY CLEGG. Jane, is that fair ?
JANE CLEGG. Fair ! I've almost forgotten what being fair is. You've told lie after lie, and now at the end I find that the money you stole was not used to pay your gambling debts.
MUNCE. Did 'e say 'e took money to py me ?
JANE CLEGG. Yes.
MUNCE. 'E's a liar, then. I on'y wish 'e 'ad.
JANE CLEGG. What did you do with it, Henry ? I've asked you that so many times. . . I wonder I trouble to ask you again. You'll only tell me some fresh lie

MUNCE. I know what 'e done with it!

HENRY CLEGG. Munce!..

MUNCE. You py me my money, then. [*Turning quickly to* JANE.] Look 'ere, Mrs. Clegg, it's 'ard on you, I know, but it's 'ard on me, too. I'll be ruined if I can't py up to-morrow. I will, straight. 'E promised faithfully 'e'd let me 'ave it. I've always acted straight. Look 'ere, now, you'll py me, won't you?

JANE CLEGG. No. He can pay you himself.

MUNCE. 'Ow can 'e py. 'E ain't got no money.

JANE CLEGG. He must have money. He only stole his employer's money three days ago, and if he hasn't paid you, he must have it, unless ..

HENRY CLEGG. I haven't got a ha'penny.

MUNCE. My God, what'll I do. [*Starting up in anger and rushing at* CLEGG.] You py up, you blighter!

JANE CLEGG. Mr. Munce!

MUNCE. [*stopping and beginning to snivel.*] Yes, Mrs. Clegg.

JANE CLEGG. Sit down, please. You'll wake my children.

MUNCE. I'm very sorry. [*He lets his head fall on the table and begins to sob.*] I'm upset, I am, that's what it is.

HENRY CLEGG. It's no good crying like a kid!..

MUNCE. I never failed to py before. I bin straight I 'ave. Oh, Gawd!.. [*Becomes inarticulate.*]

JANE CLEGG. Listen to me, Mr. Munce. [MUNCE *groans loudly.*] Please sit up, Mr. Munce. It's ridiculous to behave like that.

HENRY CLEGG. Of course it is. Anybody'd think you were a woman, the way you're going on!

MUNCE. I don't want to myke no fuss!..

JANE CLEGG. Very well, then, don't make any. Now, listen to me.

MUNCE. Yes, Mrs. Clegg.

JANE CLEGG. I have just paid the gentleman you saw

here a few moments ago, one hundred and forty pounds to replace the money my husband stole from his employer three days ago.

HENRY CLEGG. You needn't advertise the fact.

JANE CLEGG. [*ignoring him.*] My husband told me that he stole the money to pay gambling debts due to you.

MUNCE. 'E never ! . .

JANE CLEGG. One moment, please. It now appears that he has not paid you anything.

MUNCE. Not a 'a'penny, 'e 'asn't.

JANE CLEGG. Well, then, the inference is that he still has the money he stole. You can't dispose of a hundred and forty pounds in a day or two, can you ?

MUNCE. [*to* HENRY CLEGG.] Look 'ere, Clegg, 'ave you got the money or 'ave you not ?

HENRY CLEGG. I tell you I haven't.

JANE CLEGG. Then what did you do with it ?

HENRY CLEGG. I haven't got it. Look here, I'm not going to be cross-examined as if I were a criminal ! . .

JANE CLEGG. You are a criminal. You've robbed your employer.

HENRY CLEGG. [*throwing out his hands.*] There, Munce, that's the sort of thing I have to endure. How'd you like it !

JANE CLEGG. Tell us what you did with the money. Mr. Munce and I have a right to know.

HENRY CLEGG. Well, you shan't know, see. Damn you, I've had enough of your questions. I'm sick of you !

JANE CLEGG. Yes, Henry, I think we've both about reached the end of things ; but that won't help Mr. Munce, will it ?

HENRY CLEGG. I don't care about Munce !

MUNCE. [*jumping up.*] Oh, don't you ! Don't you then ! We'll soon see about that. I bin treatin' you jolly well, I 'ave. I 'eld my tongue all this time when I might 'ave said things, on'y I didden want to round on a pal. [*To* JANE CLEGG.] 'Ere, ast 'im about 'is fancy woman! . .

HENRY CLEGG. You swine!

MUNCE. Go on, ast 'im about 'er. Ast 'im what's the matter with 'er. Go on, ast 'im that.

HENRY CLEGG. You dirty dog! [*He rushes at* MUNCE, *and they close and struggle together.*] I'll choke the life out of you.

JANE CLEGG. You'll be hanged if you do that, Henry!

HENRY CLEGG. [*snorting with disgust.*] You're not worth killing!

MUNCE. [*gasping.*] You'll 'ear about this, you will! I'll 'ave you put in jail for it, see! If I don't get my money, I'll get somethink. Jus' you wait! I'll py you aht, so 'elp me Gawd, I will!

He stumbles towards the door.

JANE CLEGG. Mr. Munce, would you like your money?

MUNCE. It's no good tryin' to come it over me! . .

JANE CLEGG. It's twenty-five pounds, isn't it?

MUNCE. Yes, that's all! Fancy me bein' stumped for twenty-five quid! Me what never failed yet, an' then to be 'alf-throttled! . .

JANE CLEGG. If you'll sit down for a little while and forget that you've been half throttled, perhaps I'll pay the money to you.

MUNCE. [*incredulously.*] You said you woulden py nothink! [*He comes back to the table, and slaps his hand on it.*] Look 'ere, I ain't goin' to be 'umbugged! . .

JANE CLEGG. Have I tried to humbug you, Mr. Munce?

MUNCE. [*in a puzzled tone.*] No. No, you ain't. That's true enough. But there's no knowin'. . .

JANE CLEGG. Listen, Mr. Munce, I'll pay you the twenty-five pounds on one condition.

MUNCE. What is it?

JANE CLEGG. That you tell me about my husband's fancy woman!

MUNCE. Gimme the money first?

HENRY CLEGG. Blackguard!

MUNCE. Gentleman!

JANE CLEGG. I haven't got the money in the house, Mr. Munce, but I'll give it to you to-morrow.

MUNCE. That's all very fine! . .

JANE CLEGG. You'll have to trust me, Mr. Munce. After all, you've told most of the story to me already, haven't you? I know that there is a fancy woman. . . Henry didn't deny it . . and I understand there will be a . . fancy child! You see, the remainder of the story hardly matters, only I'm curious. . . I'm just curious to know all of it.

MUNCE. I don't know much meself about it, on'y one dy las' week I see 'im an' 'er talkin' in the street! . .

JANE CLEGG. Yes, in the street!

HENRY CLEGG. Look here, I can't stand this. I'll own up. It's true.

MUNCE. I said to 'im when I come 'ere that last time, " That was a fine bit o' skirt you 'ad to-dy!" and then 'e tole me abaht it. She'd on'y jus' been to the doctor! . .

JANE CLEGG. I see!

HENRY CLEGG. I tell you I own up. Isn't that enough?

MUNCE. 'E said if 'e 'ad the money 'e'd clear out of Englan' with the woman! . .

HENRY CLEGG. You're a pal. So help me God, you are!

JANE CLEGG. If he had the money? . .

MUNCE. Yes. Go to Canada or somewhere!

JANE CLEGG. Canada! Canada! Oh! [*Her nerve fails for a moment; but she recovers herself.*] I suppose that was why he took the money. He wanted me to give him money!

HENRY CLEGG. I can't help it. You've never understood me, never tried to. You've always sort of preached at me, and I'm not the sort that can stand being preached at. You're different from me. You're hard and you don't make allowances. Kitty's more my match than you are. I've been happy with her, happier than I've ever been with you, and that's straight.

JANE CLEGG. [*to* MUNCE.] Will you come in the morning, Mr. Munce, for the money, and we can go to the solicitor together, and arrange the matter.

MUNCE. You're not plyin' about with me, are you? You mean it, don't you?

HENRY CLEGG. My wife means everything she says. Don't you insinuate! . .

MUNCE. Awright, awright! You'd be upset if you was me.

JANE CLEGG. Good night, Mr. Munce. Come at eleven o'clock.

MUNCE. Good night, Mrs. Clegg. [*He stands about irresolutely.*] Look 'ere, jus' gimme a little IOU for the money. It 'ud sort of ease my mind.

HENRY CLEGG. [*hustling him.*] Go on, get out of this! Her word's good enough for you.

MUNCE. Oh, she's awright. It's you's the rotter! Don't you shove me, or you see! That's all. See! Don't you shove me! I'll 'ave you up! . .

JANE CLEGG. Mr. Munce, please remember that my children are asleep.

MUNCE. I'm very sorry, Mrs. Clegg. Well, look 'ere, I know you're straight. I'll be easy in my mind awright. I'll pop roun' 'ere to-morrer an' we'll settle it all up. Goo' night, Mrs. Clegg. [*He takes her hand and shakes it warmly.*] You saved me, straight you 'ave. Never failed yet, an' there ain't many bookies can sy that! Give you my word! I woulden 'a' bin nasty! . .

JANE CLEGG. Good night, Mr. Munce.

MUNCE. Good night! Good night! [*He picks up his hat and puts it on.*] I be roun' to-morrer. [*He looks at*

HENRY CLEGG.] You an' me ain't friends, see. I don't want nothink more to do with you. Absolute rotter!

HENRY CLEGG. Go on! Get out!

MUNCE. Serve you right if she'd let you go to quod, an' your fancy woman to the work-'ouse. Tooloo! [*He goes out walking quickly up the passage. He opens the street door. Holding the street door open.*] Absolute rotter! [*He goes out.*]

JANE CLEGG. [*sitting down before the fire.*] That's true, isn't it, Henry?

HENRY CLEGG. What?

JANE CLEGG. You are an absolute rotter.

HENRY CLEGG. I don't know. I'm not a bad chap, really. I'm just weak. I'd be all right if I had a lot of money and a wife that wasn't better than I am . . Oh, I know, Jane! You are better than I am. Any fool can see that! It doesn't do a chap much good to be living with a woman who's his superior, at least not the sort of chap I am. I ought to have married a woman like myself, or a bit worse. That's what Kitty is. She's worse than I am, and that sort of makes me love her. It's different with you. I always feel mean here. Yes, I am mean. I know that; but it makes me meaner than I really am to be living with you. [*He sits down at the table and begins to fill his pipe.*] Do you understand, Jane? Somehow, the mean things I do that don't amount to much, I can't tell 'em to you, or carry 'em off as if they weren't mean, and I do meaner things to cover them up. That's the way of it. I don't act like that with Kitty.

JANE CLEGG. It's funny, isn't it, Henry?

HENRY CLEGG. [*lighting his pipe.*] Yes, I suppose it is. Damned funny!

JANE CLEGG. It's so funny that we married at all. I used to think you were so fine before I married you. You were so jolly and free and light-hearted . . Somehow, I feel as if I'd lost you in the church that day! Do you

VOL. I Q

know ? It's as if I went there to find you, and found some one else.

HENRY CLEGG. And you're not like what I thought you were !

JANE CLEGG. No. [*She picks up her sewing and makes a few stitches.* HENRY CLEGG *gets up from the table and draws a chair up to the fire. He sits for a second or two smoking.*] Henry, have you spent all that money ?

HENRY CLEGG. I haven't spent any of it. I've got . . well, I have spent some of it.

JANE CLEGG. Why didn't you pay Mr. Munce, then ?

HENRY CLEGG. What ! Not likely. I need all of it !

JANE CLEGG. Yes, I suppose you do. When are you going to Canada ?

HENRY CLEGG. Eh ?

JANE CLEGG. You're going with her, aren't you ?

HENRY CLEGG. [*after a short pause.*] Yes.

JANE CLEGG. I suppose the money you spent was on the tickets ?

HENRY CLEGG. Yes.

JANE CLEGG. When are you going ?

HENRY CLEGG. [*with a great effort.*] To-morrow !

JANE CLEGG. To-morrow ! . . [*She puts her sewing down, and looks steadily in front of her.* HENRY CLEGG *gets up and begins to pace the room.*] I suppose that was why you were so anxious that I should pay the money to Mr. Morrison to-night. If he'd gone to Mr. Harper this evening you might have been arrested before you had time to get away ?

HENRY CLEGG. Yes.

JANE CLEGG. You tried to kiss me ! . . Oh ! Oh ! You Judas !

HENRY CLEGG. What could I do ? I had to think of Kitty. She's frightened, Jane, damned frightened. She didn't want to have a child, and she's scared. If I'd been arrested ! . . Oh, it's horrible to think of her sitting somewhere waiting, and me not there !

JANE CLEGG. I used to wait, and you weren't there.

HENRY CLEGG. Yes, but she hasn't any spirit.

JANE CLEGG. You wouldn't have told me, or your mother ? Johnnie and Jenny ! . .

HENRY CLEGG. I wouldn't have liked leaving Jenny. Johnnie's your child.

JANE CLEGG. What's Kitty like, Henry ?

HENRY CLEGG. She's prettier than you.

JANE CLEGG. Yes ?

HENRY CLEGG. Well, it's hard to say. You're a finer woman than she is, but she's my sort, and you're not. [*He pauses in his pacing, and then comes to the fireplace and stands before her.*] You're a rum sort of woman, Jane. There aren't many women would talk about this the way you do.

JANE CLEGG. No ?

HENRY CLEGG. It's just as if we were strangers talking about something that didn't matter.

JANE CLEGG. It is like that, isn't it, only I have two children, and you're their father.

HENRY CLEGG. [*sitting down.*] Well, I don't know! It's a funny sort of a world ; mixed-up like !

JANE CLEGG. Does Kitty live far from here ?

HENRY CLEGG. Other side of the town.

JANE CLEGG. Alone ?

HENRY CLEGG. Lodgings !

JANE CLEGG. What does she do ?

HENRY CLEGG. She's in a shop ! . .

JANE CLEGG. Yes, she must be very frightened . . What train do you catch to-morrow ?

HENRY CLEGG. You speak as if you wanted me to go.

JANE CLEGG. How else would you have me speak ?

HENRY CLEGG. It doesn't seem right somehow. I

mean, I'm your husband and all that. I should have thought you'd want me to stay.

JANE CLEGG. You wouldn't stay, would you?

HENRY CLEGG. Well, no! I promised Kitty!

JANE CLEGG. You keep the promises you make to her. [*He nods his head.*] Why should I wish you to stay with me? You are a different man from the one I married. You don't love me. You've never been loyal to me. There isn't any sense in living with a man if he's not loyal! . .

HENRY CLEGG. I can't make you out. It doesn't seem right, somehow. I don't pretend to be a religious chap! . .

JANE CLEGG. It wouldn't be much good, would it?

HENRY CLEGG. But still I believe in religion. I mean to say, I know I'm not doing the right thing. I'm going away with Kitty, but I know I'm doing wrong. It's religion tells me that. You don't seem to understand that. You talk as if it was just a case of you and me not suiting . . and that was all. It's not right. You ask mother! She wouldn't talk as you're talking. That's because she's religious. If she were you, she wouldn't let me go quietly. She'd tear Kitty to bits.

JANE CLEGG. I suppose so. [*Rising and extending her hand to him.*] Good-bye, Henry!

HENRY CLEGG. How do you mean?

JANE CLEGG. Good-bye, of course. You'll go to Kitty to-night. It . . it'll be more convenient to-morrow.

HENRY CLEGG. [*standing up and gaping at her.*] My God!

JANE CLEGG. You didn't think I'd let you stay here to-night with me! Oh, Henry, it wouldn't be decent! . .

HENRY CLEGG. You mean I'm to go now.

JANE CLEGG. Yes.

HENRY CLEGG. But . .

JANE CLEGG. There can be no argument about it.

You must go now. It would be like committing a sin to let you stay with me to-night!

HENRY CLEGG. I don't understand you. Damn it, you're condoning the offence.

JANE CLEGG. [*again holding out her hand.*] Good night, Henry, and good-bye. I'm very tired.

HENRY CLEGG. You really mean it?

JANE CLEGG. Yes.

HENRY CLEGG. I can't understand you. [*He looks about him irresolutely.*] I can't go off like this without seeing the youngsters and the mater! . .

JANE CLEGG. You'll have to go to-morrow, so it won't make much difference to you if you go to-night!

HENRY CLEGG. You really do mean it?

JANE CLEGG. I do.

HENRY CLEGG. Oh, well! . . I suppose I can go up and look at the kids?

JANE CLEGG. You might wake them, and they'd wonder! . .

HENRY CLEGG. I could have a peep at them!

JANE CLEGG. It would be better not.

HENRY CLEGG. All right! [*He goes into the hall and puts on his hat and coat. He returns to the room.*] How'll you explain?

JANE CLEGG. I'll tell your mother! . .

HENRY CLEGG. You'll look after her, won't you? She's not a bad old soul though she does get on my nerves.

JANE CLEGG. Yes, I'll look after her.

There is silence for a few moments.

HENRY CLEGG. Well! [*He looks at her as if he does not know what to do.*]

JANE CLEGG. Good-bye!

HENRY CLEGG. [*taking her hand.*] Good-bye, Jane. I've not been a good husband . . You're well rid of me. [*He tries to put his arms round her, but she struggles out of his reach.*] You might give me a kiss before I go.

JANE CLEGG. [*covering her face with her hand and speaking like one who is horrified.*] I couldn't, I couldn't.

HENRY CLEGG. [*with an affectation of jauntiness.*] Well, of course, if that's how you look at it. Good-bye, once more!

JANE CLEGG. [*she turns her back to him.*] Good-bye!

HENRY CLEGG. Well, I'm damned! [*He goes into the hall, and puts his hand on the door. He waits for a moment.*] I'm off now.

She does not reply. He opens the door, and then waits a little while. She does not move. He goes out and closes the door after him. She stands for a few moments gazing into the fire. Then she turns down the light and goes upstairs to bed.

CURTAIN

THE VOYSEY INHERITANCE

H. GRANVILLE-BARKER

THE VOYSEY INHERITANCE

was first played at the Court Theatre on the afternoon of November 7, 1905.

MR. VOYSEY	A. E. George.
MRS. VOYSEY	Florence Haydon.
TRENCHARD VOYSEY, K.C.	Eugene Mayeur.
HONOR VOYSEY	Geraldine Olliffe.
MAJOR BOOTH VOYSEY	Charles Fulton.
MRS. BOOTH VOYSEY	Grace Edwin.
CHRISTOPHER	Harry C. Duff.
EDWARD VOYSEY	Thalberg Corbett.
HUGH VOYSEY	Dennis Eadie.
MRS. HUGH VOYSEY	Henrietta Watson.
ETHEL VOYSEY	Alexandra Carlisle.
DENIS TREGONING	Frederick Lloyd.
ALICE MAITLAND	Mabel Hackney.
MR. BOOTH	O. B. Clarence.
THE REV. EVAN COLPUS	Edmund Gwenn.
PEACEY	Trevor Lowe.
PHOEBE	Gwynneth Galton.
MARY	Mrs. Fordyce.

No performance of this play, either as a whole or in part, may be given without the Author's permission. Amateurs should apply to the COLLECTION BUREAU, THE INCORPORATED SOCIETY OF AUTHORS, 11 Gower Street, London, W.C.1; professionals to the Author himself in the care of the publishers.

THE VOYSEY INHERITANCE

THE FIRST ACT

The Office of Voysey and Son is in the best part of Lincoln's Inn. Its panelled rooms give out a sense of grandmotherly comfort and security, very grateful at first to the hesitating investor, the dubious litigant. MR. VOYSEY'S *own room into which he walks about twenty past ten of a morning radiates enterprise besides. There is polish on everything; on the windows, on the mahogany of the tidily packed writing-table that stands between them, on the brasswork of the fireplace in the other wall, on the glass of the firescreen which preserves only the pleasantness of a sparkling fire, even on* MR. VOYSEY'S *hat as he takes it off to place it on the little red curtained shelf behind the door.* MR. VOYSEY *is sixty or more and masterful; would obviously be master anywhere from his own home outwards, or wreck the situation in his attempt. Indeed there is a buccaneering air sometimes in the twist of his glance, not altogether suitable to a family solicitor. On this bright October morning,* PEACEY, *the head clerk, follows just too late to help him off with his coat, but in time to take it and hang it up with a quite unnecessary subservience.* MR. VOYSEY *is evidently not capable enough to like capable men about him.* PEACEY, *not quite removed from Nature, has made some attempts to acquire protective colouring. A very drunken client might mistake him for his master. His voice very easily became a toneless echo of* MR. VOYSEY'S; *later his features caught a line or two from that mirror of all the necessary virtues into which he was so constantly gazing; but how his clothes even when new contrive to look like old ones of* MR. VOYSEY'S *is a mystery, and to his tailor a most annoying one. And* PEACEY *is just a respectful number of years his master's junior. Relieved of his coat,* MR. VOYSEY *carries to his table the bunch of beautiful roses he is accustomed to bring to the office three times a week and places them for a moment only near the bowl of water there ready to receive them while he takes up his letters. These lie ready too, opened mostly, one or two private ones left closed and discreetly separate. By this time the usual salutations have passed,* PEACEY'S *" Good morning, sir";* MR. VOYSEY'S *" Morning, Peacey". Then as he gets to his letters* MR. VOYSEY *starts his day's work.*

MR. VOYSEY. Any news for me?

PEACEY. I hear bad accounts of Alguazils preferred, sir.

MR. VOYSEY. Oh . . who from?

PEACEY. Merrit and James's head clerk in the train this morning.

MR. VOYSEY. They looked all right on . . Give me the "Times". [PEACEY *goes to the fireplace for the "Times"; it is warming there.* MR. VOYSEY *waves a letter, then places it on the table.*] Here, that's for you . . Gerrard's Cross business. Anything else?

PEACEY. [*as he turns the "Times" to its Finance page.*] I've made the usual notes.

MR. VOYSEY. Thank'ee.

PEACEY. Young Benham isn't back yet.

MR. VOYSEY. Mr. Edward must do as he thinks fit about that. Alguazils, Alg—oh, yes.

He is running his eye down the columns. PEACEY *leans over the letters.*

PEACEY. This is from Mr. Leader about the codicil . . You'll answer that ?
MR. VOYSEY. Mr. Leader. Yes. Alguazils. Mr. Edward's here, I suppose.
PEACEY. No, sir.
MR. VOYSEY. [*his eye twisting with some sharpness.*] What !
PEACEY. [*almost alarmed.*] I beg pardon, sir.
MR. VOYSEY. Mr. Edward.
PEACEY. Oh, yes, sir, been in his room some time. I thought you said Headley ; he's not due back till Thursday.
MR. VOYSEY *discards the " Times " and sits to his desk and his letters.*
MR. VOYSEY. Tell Mr. Edward I've come.
PEACEY. Yes, sir. Anything else ?
MR. VOYSEY. Not for the moment. Cold morning, isn't it ?
PEACEY. Quite surprising, sir.
MR. VOYSEY. We had a touch of frost down at Chislehurst.
PEACEY. So early !
MR. VOYSEY. I want it for the celery. All right, I'll call through about the rest of the letters.
PEACEY *goes, having secured a letter or two, and* MR. VOYSEY *having sorted the rest (a proportion into the waste-paper basket) takes up the forgotten roses and starts setting them into a bowl with an artistic hand. Then his son* EDWARD *comes in.* MR. VOYSEY *gives him one glance and goes on arranging the roses but says cheerily . .*
MR. VOYSEY. Good morning, my dear boy.
EDWARD *has little of his father in him and that little is undermost. It is a refined face but self-consciousness takes the place in it of imagination, and in suppressing traits of brutality in his character it looks as if the young man had suppressed his sense of humour*

too. *But whether or no, that would not be much in evidence now, for* EDWARD *is obviously going through some experience which is scaring him (there is no better word). He looks not to have slept for a night or two, and his standing there, clutching and unclutching the bundle of papers he carries, his eyes on his father, half appealingly but half accusingly too, his whole being altogether so unstrung and desperate, makes* MR. VOYSEY'S *uninterrupted arranging of the flowers seem very calculated indeed. At last the little tension of silence is broken.*

EDWARD. Father . .
MR. VOYSEY. Well?
EDWARD. I'm glad to see you.

This is a statement of fact. He doesn't know that the commonplace phrase sounds ridiculous at such a moment.

MR. VOYSEY. I see you've the papers there.
EDWARD. Yes.
MR. VOYSEY. You've been through them?
EDWARD. As you wished me . .
MR. VOYSEY. Well? [EDWARD *doesn't answer. Reference to the papers seems to overwhelm him with shame.* MR. VOYSEY *goes on with cheerful impatience.*] Come, come, my dear boy, don't take it like this. You're puzzled and worried, of course. But why didn't you come down to me on Saturday night? I expected you . . I told you to come. Then your mother was wondering why you weren't with us for dinner yesterday.
EDWARD. I went through all the papers twice. I wanted to make quite sure.
MR. VOYSEY. Sure of what? I told you to come to me.
EDWARD. [*he is very near crying.*] Oh, father.
MR. VOYSEY. Now look here, Edward, I'm going to ring and dispose of these letters. Please pull yourself together. [*He pushes the little button on his table.*]

THE VOYSEY INHERITANCE

EDWARD. I didn't leave my rooms all day yesterday.

MR. VOYSEY. A pleasant Sunday! You must learn, whatever the business may be, to leave it behind you at the Office. Why, life's not worth living else.

PEACEY *comes in to find* MR. VOYSEY *before the fire ostentatiously warming and rubbing his hands.*

Oh, there isn't much else, Peacey. Tell Simmons that if he satisfies you about the details of this lease it'll be all right. Make a note for me of Mr. Grainger's address at Mentone. I shall have several things to dictate to Atkinson. I'll whistle for him.

PEACEY. Mr. Burnett . . Burnett and Marks had just come in, Mr. Edward.

EDWARD. [*without turning.*] It's only fresh instructions. Will you take them?

PEACEY. All right.

PEACEY *goes, lifting his eyebrows at the queerness of* EDWARD'S *manner. This* MR. VOYSEY *sees, returning to his table with a little scowl.*

MR. VOYSEY. Now sit down. I've given you a bad forty-eight hours, have I? Well, I've been anxious about you. Never mind, we'll thresh the thing out now. Go through the two accounts. Mrs. Murberry's first . . how do you find it stands?

EDWARD. [*his feelings choking him.*] I hoped you were playing off some joke on me.

MR. VOYSEY. Come now.

EDWARD *separates the papers precisely and starts to detail them; his voice quite toneless. Now and then his father's sharp comments ring out in contrast.*

EDWARD. We've got the lease of her present house, several agreements . . and here's her will. Here's also a power of attorney expired some time over her securities and her property generally . . it was made out for six months.

MR. VOYSEY. She was in South Africa.

EDWARD. Here's the Sheffield mortgage and the

Henry Smith mortgage with Banker's receipts . . her Banker's to us for the interest up to date . . four and a half and five per cent. Then . . Fretworthy Bonds. There's a note scribbled in your writing that they are at the Bank; but you don't say what Bank.

MR. VOYSEY. My own . . Stukeley's.

EDWARD. [*just dwelling on the words.*] Your own. I queried that. There's eight thousand five hundred in three and a half India stock. And there are her Banker's receipts for cheques on account of those dividends. I presume for those dividends.

MR. VOYSEY. Why not?

EDWARD. [*gravely.*] Because then, father, there are her Banker's half-yearly receipts for other sums amounting to an average of four hundred and twenty pounds a year. But I find no record of any capital to produce this.

MR. VOYSEY. Go on. What do you find?

EDWARD. Till about three years back there seems to have been eleven thousand in Queenslands which would produce—did produce exactly the same sum. But after January of that year I find no record of 'em.

MR. VOYSEY. In fact the Queenslands are missing, vanished?

EDWARD. [*hardly uttering the word.*] Yes.

MR. VOYSEY. From which you conclude?

EDWARD. I supposed at first that you had not handed me all the papers.

MR. VOYSEY. Since Mrs. Murberry evidently still gets that four twenty a year, somehow; lucky woman.

EDWARD. [*in agony.*] Oh!

MR. VOYSEY. Well, we'll return to the good lady later. Now let's take the other.

EDWARD. The Hatherley Trust.

MR. VOYSEY. Quite so.

EDWARD. [*with one accusing glance.*] Trust.

MR. VOYSEY. Go on.

EDWARD. Father .
His grief comes uppermost again and MR. VOYSEY *meets it kindly.*
MR. VOYSEY. I know, my dear boy. I shall have lots to say to you. But let's get quietly through with these details first.
EDWARD. [*bitterly now.*] Oh, this is simple enough. We're young Hatherley's only trustees till his coming of age in about five years' time. The property was eighteen thousand invested in Consols. Certain sums were to be allowed for his education; we seem to be paying them.
MR. VOYSEY. Regularly.
EDWARD. Quite. But where's the capital?
MR. VOYSEY. No record?
EDWARD. Yes . . A note by you on a half sheet . . Refer to the Bletchley Land Scheme.
MR. VOYSEY. That was ten years ago. Haven't I credited him with the interest on his capital?
EDWARD. The balance ought to be re-invested. There's this (*a sheet of figures*) in your hand-writing. You credit him with the Consol interest.
MR. VOYSEY. Quite so.
EDWARD. But I think I've heard you say that the Bletchley scheme paid seven and a half.
MR. VOYSEY. At one time. Have you also taken the trouble to calculate what will be due from us to the lad?
EDWARD. Yes . . even on the Consol basis . . capital and compound interest . . about twenty-six thousand pounds.
MR. VOYSEY. A respectable sum. In five years' time?
EDWARD. When he comes of age.
MR. VOYSEY. That gives us, say, four years and six months in which to think about it.
EDWARD *waits, hopelessly, for his father to speak again: then says* . .

EDWARD. Thank you for showing me these, sir. Shall I put them back in your safe now?

MR. VOYSEY. Yes, you'd better. There's the key. [EDWARD *reaches for the bunch, his face hidden.*] Put them down. Your hand shakes . . why, you might have been drinking . . I'll put them away later. It's no use having hysterics, Edward. Look your trouble in the face.

EDWARD'S *only answer is to go to the fire, as far from his father as the room allows. And there he leans on the mantelpiece, his shoulders heaving.*

MR. VOYSEY. I'm sorry, my dear boy. I wouldn't tell you if I could help it.

EDWARD. I can't believe it. And that you should be telling me . . such a thing.

MR. VOYSEY. Let yourself go . . have your cry out, as the women say. It isn't pleasant, I know. It isn't pleasant to inflict it on you.

EDWARD. How I got through that outer office this morning, I don't know. I came early but some of them were here. Peacey came into my room; he must have seen there was something up.

MR. VOYSEY. That's no matter.

EDWARD. [*able to turn to his father again; won round by the kind voice.*] How long has it been going on? Why didn't you tell me before? Oh, I know you thought you'd pull through; but I'm your partner . . I'm responsible too. Oh, I don't want to shirk that . . don't think I mean to shirk that, father. Perhaps I ought to have discovered, but those affairs were always in your hands. I trusted . . I beg your pardon. Oh, it's us . . not you. Every one has trusted us.

MR. VOYSEY. [*calmly and kindly still.*] You don't seem to notice that I'm not breaking my heart like this.

EDWARD. What's the extent of the mischief? When did it begin? Father, what made you begin it?

MR. VOYSEY. I didn't begin it.

EDWARD. You didn't. Who then?

MR. VOYSEY. My father before me. [EDWARD *stares*.] That calms you a little.

EDWARD. I'm glad . . my dear father! [*and he puts out his hand. Then just a doubt enters his mind*.] But I . . it's amazing.

MR. VOYSEY. [*shaking his head*.] My inheritance, Edward.

EDWARD. My dear father!

MR. VOYSEY. I had hoped it wasn't to be yours.

EDWARD. D'you mean to tell me that this sort of thing has been going on here for years? For more than thirty years!

MR. VOYSEY. Yes.

EDWARD. That's a little hard to understand just at first, sir.

MR. VOYSEY. [*sententiously*.] We do what we must in this world, Edward; I have done what I had to do.

EDWARD. [*his emotion well cooled by now*.] Perhaps I'd better just listen quietly while you explain.

MR. VOYSEY. [*concentrating*.] You know that I'm heavily into Northern Electrics.

EDWARD. Yes.

MR. VOYSEY. But you don't know how heavily. When I got the tip the Municipalities were organising the purchase, I saw of course the stock must be up a hundred and forty-five—a hundred and fifty in no time. Now Leeds will keep up her silly quarrel with the other place . . they won't apply for powers for another ten years. I bought at ninety-five. What are they to-day?

EDWARD. Seventy-two.

MR. VOYSEY. Seventy-one and a half. And in ten years I may be . . I'm getting on for seventy, Edward. That's mainly why you've had to be told.

EDWARD. With whose money are you so heavily into Northern Electrics?

MR. VOYSEY. The firm's money.
EDWARD. Clients' money?
MR. VOYSEY. Yes.
EDWARD. [*coldly.*] Well . . I'm waiting for your explanation, sir.
MR. VOYSEY. You seem to have recovered pretty much.
EDWARD. No, sir, I'm trying to understand, that's all.
MR. VOYSEY. [*with a shrug.*] Children always think the worst of their parents, I suppose. I did of mine. It's a pity.
EDWARD. Go on, sir, go on. Let me know the worst.
MR. VOYSEY. There's no immediate danger. I should think any one could see that from the figures there. There's no real risk at all.
EDWARD. Is that the worst?
MR. VOYSEY. [*his anger rising.*] Have you studied these two accounts or have you not?
EDWARD. Yes, sir.
MR. VOYSEY. Well, where's the deficiency in Mrs. Murberry's income . . has she ever gone without a shilling? · What has young Hatherley lost?
EDWARD. He stands to lose—
MR. VOYSEY. He stands to lose nothing if I'm spared for a little, and you will only bring a little common sense to bear and try to understand the difficulties of my position.
EDWARD. Father, I'm not thinking ill of you . . that is, I'm trying not to. But won't you explain how you're justified . . ?
MR. VOYSEY. In putting our affairs in order?
EDWARD. Are you doing that?
MR. VOYSEY. What else?
EDWARD. [*starting patiently to examine the matter.*] How bad were things when you first came to control them?
MR. VOYSEY. Oh, I forget.
EDWARD. You can't forget.
MR. VOYSEY. Well . . pretty bad.

THE VOYSEY INHERITANCE

EDWARD. Do you know how it was my grandfather began to—

MR. VOYSEY. Muddlement, muddlement! Fooled away hundreds and thousands on safe things . . well, then, what was he to do? He'd no capital, no credit, and was in terror of his life. My dear Edward, if I hadn't found it out in time, he'd have confessed to the first man who came and asked for a balance sheet.

EDWARD. Well, what exact sum was he to the bad then?

MR. VOYSEY. I forget. Several thousands.

EDWARD. But surely it has not taken all these years to pay off—

MR. VOYSEY. Oh, hasn't it!

EDWARD. [*making his point.*] Then how does it happen, sir, that such a comparatively recent trust as young Hatherley's has been broken into?

MR. VOYSEY. Well, what could be safer than to use that money? There's a Consol investment and not a sight wanted of either capital or interest for five years.

EDWARD. [*utterly beaten.*] Father, are you mad?

MR. VOYSEY. On the contrary, when my clients' money is entirely under my control, I sometimes re-invest it. The difference between the income this money was bringing to them and the profits it then actually brings to me, I . . I utilise in my endeavour to fill up the deficit in the firm's accounts . . I use it to put things straight. Doesn't it follow that the more low-interest-bearing capital I can use the better . . the less risky things I have to put it into. Most of young Hatherley's Consol capital . . the Trust gives me full discretion . . is now out on mortgage at four and a half and five . . safe as safe can be.

EDWARD. But he should have the benefit.

MR. VOYSEY. He has the amount of his Consol interest.

EDWARD. Where are the mortgages? Are they in his name?

MR. VOYSEY. Some of them . . some of them. That

really doesn't matter. With regard to Mrs. Murberry .. those Fretworthy Bonds at my bank .. I've raised five thousand on them. But I can release her Bonds to-morrow if she wants them.

EDWARD. Where's the five thousand?

MR. VOYSEY. I'm not sure .. it was paid into my own account. Yes, I do remember. Some of it went to complete a purchase .. that and two thousand more out of the Skipworth fund.

EDWARD. But, my dear father—

MR. VOYSEY. Well?

EDWARD. [*summing it all up very simply.*] It's not right.

MR. VOYSEY *considers his son for a moment with a pitying shake of the head.*

MR. VOYSEY. Why? .. why is it so hard for a man to see beyond the letter of the law! Will you consider, Edward, the position in which I found myself at that moment? Was I to see my father ruined and disgraced without lifting a finger to help him? .. quite apart from the interest of our clients. I paid back to the man who would have lost most by my father's mistakes every penny of his money. And he never knew the danger he'd been in .. never passed an uneasy moment about it. It was I that lay awake. I have now somewhere a letter from that man to my father thanking him effusively for the way in which he'd conducted some matter. It comforted my poor father. Well, Edward, I stepped outside the letter of the law to do that service. Was I right or wrong?

EDWARD. In the result, sir, right.

MR. VOYSEY. Judge me by the result. I took the risk of failure .. I should have suffered. I could have kept clear of the danger if I'd liked.

EDWARD. But that's all past. The thing that concerns me is what you are doing now.

MR. VOYSEY. [*gently reproachful now.*] My boy, can't

you trust me a little ? It's all very well for you to come in at the end of the day and criticise. But I who have done the day's work know how that work had to be done. And here's our firm, prosperous, respected and without a stain on its honour. That's the main point, isn't it ?

EDWARD. [*quite irresponsive to this pathetic appeal.*] Very well, sir. Let's dismiss from our minds all prejudices about speaking the truth . . acting upon one's instructions, behaving as any honest firm of solicitors must behave . .

MR. VOYSEY. Nonsense, I tell no unnecessary lies. If a man of any business ability gives me definite instructions about his property, I follow them.

EDWARD. Father, no unnecessary lies !

MR. VOYSEY. Well, my friend, go and knock it into Mrs. Murberry's head, if you can, that four hundred and twenty pounds of her income hasn't, for the last eight years, come from the place she thinks it's come from, and see how happy you'll make her.

EDWARD. But is that four hundred and twenty a year as safe to come to her as it was before you meddled with the capital ?

MR. VOYSEY. I see no reason why—

EDWARD. What's the security ?

MR. VOYSEY. [*putting his coping stone on the argument.*] My financial ability.

EDWARD. [*really not knowing whether to laugh or cry.*] Why, one 'd think you were satisfied with this state of things.

MR. VOYSEY. Edward, you really are most unsympathetic and unreasonable. I give all I have to the firm's work . . my brain . . my energies . . my whole life. I can't turn my abilities into hard cash at par . . I wish I could. Do you suppose that if I could establish every one of these people with a separate and consistent bank balance to-morrow that I shouldn't do it ?

EDWARD. [*thankfully able to meet anger with anger.*]

Do you mean to tell me that you couldn't somehow have put things right by this?

MR. VOYSEY. Somehow? How?

EDWARD. If thirty years of this sort of thing hasn't brought you hopelessly to grief . . during that time there must have been opportunities . .

MR. VOYSEY. Must there! Well, I hope that when I'm under ground, you may find them.

EDWARD. I!

MR. VOYSEY. Put everything right with a stroke of your pen, if it's so easy!

EDWARD. I!

MR. VOYSEY. You're my partner and my son; you'll inherit the business.

EDWARD. [*realising at last that he has been led to the edge of this abyss.*] Oh no, father.

MR. VOYSEY. Why else have I had to tell you all this?

EDWARD. [*very simply.*] Father, I can't. I can't possibly. I don't think you've any right to ask me.

MR. VOYSEY. Why not, pray?

EDWARD. It's perpetuating the dishonesty.

MR. VOYSEY *hardens at the unpleasant word.*

MR. VOYSEY. You don't believe that I've told you the truth.

EDWARD. I want to believe it.

MR. VOYSEY. It's no proof . . my earning these twenty or thirty people their rightful incomes for the last—how many years?

EDWARD. Whether what you have done and are doing is wrong or right . . I can't meddle in it.

For the moment MR. VOYSEY *looks a little dangerous.*

MR. VOYSEY. Very well. Forget all I've said. Go back to your room. Get back to your own mean drudgery. My life work—my splendid life work—ruined! What does that matter?

EDWARD. Whatever did you expect of me?

MR. VOYSEY. [*making a feint at his papers.*] Oh, nothing, nothing. [*Then he slams them down with great effect.*] Here's a great edifice built up by years of labour and devotion and self-sacrifice . . a great arch you may call it . . a bridge which is to carry our firm to safety with honour. [*This variation of Disraeli passes unnoticed.*] My work! And now, as I near the end of my life, it still lacks the keystone. Perhaps I am to die with my work just incomplete. Then is there nothing that a son might do? Do you think I shouldn't be proud of you, Edward . . that I shouldn't bless you from—wherever I may be, when you completed my life's work . . with perhaps just one kindly thought of your father?

In spite of this oratory, the situation is gradually impressing EDWARD.

EDWARD. What will happen if I . . if I desert you?

MR. VOYSEY. I'll protect you as best I can.

EDWARD. I wasn't thinking of myself, sir.

MR. VOYSEY. [*with great nonchalance.*] Well, I shan't mind the exposure, you know. It won't make me blush in my coffin . . and you're not so quixotic, I hope, as to be thinking of the feelings of your brothers and sisters. Considering how simple it would have been for me to go to my grave in peace and quiet and let you discover the whole thing afterwards, the fact that I didn't, that I have taken thought for the future of all of you might perhaps have convinced you that I . . ! But there . . consult your own safety.

EDWARD *has begun to pace the room; indecision growing upon him.*

EDWARD. This is a queer thing to have to make up one's mind about, isn't it, father?

MR. VOYSEY. [*watching him closely and modulating his voice.*] My dear boy, I understand the shock to your feelings that this disclosure must have been.

EDWARD. Yes, I came this morning thinking that next week would see us in the dock together.

MR. VOYSEY. And I suppose if I'd broken down and begged your pardon for my folly, you'd have done anything for me, gone to prison smiling, eh?

EDWARD. I suppose so.

MR. VOYSEY. Yes, it's easy enough to forgive. I'm sorry I can't go in sack-cloth and ashes to oblige you. [*Now he begins to rally his son; easy in his strength.*] My dear Edward, you've lived a quiet humdrum life up to now, with your poetry and your sociology and your agnosticism and your ethics of this and your ethics of that . . dear me, these are the sort of garden oats which young men seem to sow nowadays ! . . and you've never before been brought face to face with any really vital question. Now don't make a fool of yourself just through inexperience. Try and give your mind without prejudice to the consideration of a very serious matter. I'm not angry at what you've said to me. I'm quite willing to forget it. And it's for your own sake and not for mine, Edward, that I do beg you to—to—to be a man and take a practical common-sense view of the position you find yourself in. It's not a pleasant position, I know, but it's unavoidable.

EDWARD. You should have told me before you took me into partnership. [*Oddly enough it is this last flicker of rebellion which breaks down* MR. VOYSEY'S *caution. Now he lets fly with a vengeance.*]

MR. VOYSEY. Should I be telling you at all if I could possibly help it? Don't I know that you're about as fit for the job as a babe unborn? Haven't I been worrying over that for these last three years? But I'm in a corner . . and am I to see my firm come to smash simply because of your scruples? If you're a son of mine you'll do as I tell you. Hadn't I the same choice to make? . . and it's a safer game for you now than it was for me then. D'you suppose I didn't have scruples? If you run away from this, Edward, you're a coward. My father was a coward and he suffered for it to the end of his days. I was sick-nurse to him here more than partner. Good lord! . . of course it's pleasant and comfortable to keep within the law . . then the law will look after you. Otherwise you have to look pretty sharp after yourself. You have to cultivate your own sense of right and wrong ; deal your own justice. But that makes a bigger man of you, let me tell you. How easily . . how easily could I have walked out of my father's office and left him to his fate ; no one would have blamed me ! But I didn't. I thought it my better duty to stay and . . yes, I say it with all reverence . . to take up my cross. Well, I've carried that cross pretty successfully. And what's more, it's made a happy man of me . . a better, stronger man than skulking about in shame and in fear of his life ever made of my poor dear father. [*Relieved at having let out the truth, but doubtful of his wisdom in doing so, he changes his tone.*] I don't want what I've been saying to influence you, Edward. You are a free agent . . and you must decide upon your own course of action. Now don't let's discuss the matter any more for the moment.

EDWARD *looks at his father with clear eyes.*

EDWARD. Don't forget to put these papers away.

He restores them to their bundles and hands them back: it is his only comment. MR. VOYSEY *takes them and his meaning in silence.*

MR. VOYSEY. Are you coming down to Chislehurst soon ? We've got Hugh and his wife, and Booth and Emily, and Christopher for two or three days, till he goes back to school.

EDWARD. How is Chris ?

MR. VOYSEY. All right again now . . grows more like his father. Booth's very proud of him. So am I.

EDWARD. I think I can't face them all just at present.

MR. VOYSEY. Nonsense.

EDWARD. [*a little wave of emotion going through him.*] I feel as if this thing were written on my face. How I shall get through business I don't know!

MR. VOYSEY. You're weaker than I thought, Edward.

EDWARD. [*a little ironically.*] A disappointment to you, father?

MR. VOYSEY. No, no.

EDWARD. You should have brought one of the others into the firm. . Trenchard or Booth.

MR. VOYSEY. [*hardening.*] Trenchard! [*he dismisses that.*] Well, you're a better man than Booth. Edward, you mustn't imagine that the whole world is standing on its head merely because you've had an unpleasant piece of news. Come down to Chislehurst tonight . . well, say to-morrow night. It'll be good for you . . stop your brooding . . that's your worst vice, Edward. You'll find the household as if nothing had happened. Then you'll remember that nothing really has happened. And presently you'll get to see that nothing need happen, if you keep your head. I remember times, when things have seemed at their worst, what a relief it's been to me . . my romp with you all in the nursery just before your bed time. Do you remember!

EDWARD. Yes. And cutting your head open once with that gun.

MR. VOYSEY. [*in a full glow of fine feeling.*] And, my dear boy, if I knew that you were going to inform the next client you met of what I've just told you . .

EDWARD. [*with a shudder.*] Oh, father!

MR. VOYSEY. . . And that I should find myself in prison to-morrow, I wouldn't wish a single thing I've ever done undone. I have never wilfully harmed man or woman. My life's been a happy one. Your dear mother has been spared to me. You're most of you good children and a credit to what I've done for you.

EDWARD. [*the deadly humour of this too much for him.*] Father!

MR. VOYSEY. Run along now, run along. I must finish my letters and get into the City.

He might be scolding a schoolboy for some trifling fault. EDWARD *turns to have a look at the keen unembarrassed face.* MR. VOYSEY *smiles at him and proceeds to select from the bowl a rose for his buttonhole.*

EDWARD. I'll think it over, sir.

MR. VOYSEY. Of course, you will. And don't brood, Edward, don't brood.

So EDWARD *leaves him ; and having fixed the rose to his satisfaction, he rings his table telephone and calls through it to the listening clerk.*

Send Atkinson to me, please. [*Then he gets up, keys in hand to lock away Mrs. Murberry's and the Hatherley Trust papers.*]

THE SECOND ACT

The VOYSEY *dining-room at Chislehurst, when children and grandchildren are visiting, is dining-table and very little else. And at this moment in the evening when five or six men are sprawling back in their chairs, and the air is clouded with smoke, it is a very typical specimen of the middle-class English domestic temple ; the daily sacrifice consummated, the acolytes dismissed, the women safely in the drawing-room, and the chief priests of it taking their surfeited ease round the dessert-piled altar. It has the usual red-papered walls (like a reflection, they are, of the underdone beef so much consumed within them), the usual varnished woodwork which is known as grained oak ; there is the usual, hot, mahogany furniture ; and, commanding point of the whole room, there is the usual black-marble sarcophagus of a fireplace. Above this hangs one of the two or three oil paintings, which are all that break the red pattern of the walls, the portrait painted in 1880 of an undistinguished looking gentleman aged sixty ; he is shown sitting in a more graceful attitude than it could ever have been comfortable for him to assume.* MR. VOYSEY'S *father it is, and the brass plate at the bottom of the frame tells us that the portrait was a presentation one. On the mantelpiece stands, of course, a clock ; at either end a china vase filled with paper spills. And in front of the fire,—since that is the post of vantage,—stands at this moment* MAJOR BOOTH VOYSEY. *He is the second son, of the age that it is necessary for a Major to be, and of an appearance that many ordinary Majors in ordinary regiments are. He went into the army because he thought it would be like a schoolboy's idea of it; and, being there, he does his little all to keep it so. He stands astride, hands in pockets, coat-tails through his arms, cigar in mouth, moustache bristling. On either side of him sits at the table an old gentleman; the one is* MR. EVAN COLPUS, *the vicar of their parish, the other* MR. GEORGE BOOTH, *a friend of long standing, and the Major's godfather.* MR. COLPUS *is a harmless enough anachronism, except for the waste of £400 a year in which his stipend involves the community. Leaving most of his parochial work to an energetic curate, he devotes his serious attention to the composition of two sermons a week. They deal with the difficulties of living the christian life as experienced by people who have nothing else to do. Published in series from time to time, these form suitable presents for bedridden parishioners.* MR. GEORGE BOOTH, *on the contrary, is as gay an old gentleman as can be found in Chislehurst. An only son, his father left him at the age of twenty-five a fortune of a hundred thousand pounds (a plum, as he called it). At the same time he had the good sense to dispose of his father's business, into which he had been most unwillingly introduced five years earlier, for a like sum before he was able to depreciate its value. It was* MR. VOYSEY'S *invaluable assistance in this transaction which first bound the two together in great friendship. Since that time* MR. BOOTH *has been bent on nothing but enjoying himself. He has even remained a bachelor with that object. Money has given him all he wants, therefore he loves and reverences money; while his imagination may be estimated by the fact that he has now reached the age of sixty-five, still possessing more of it than he knows what to do with. At the head of the table, meditatively crack-*

ing walnuts, sits MR. VOYSEY. *He has his back there to the conservatory door—you know it is the conservatory door because there is a curtain to pull over it, and because half of it is frosted glass with a purple key pattern round the edge. On* MR. VOYSEY'S *left is* DENIS TREGONING, *a nice enough young man. And at the other end of the table sits* EDWARD, *not smoking, not talking, hardly listening, very depressed. Behind him is the ordinary door of the room, which leads out into the dismal draughty hall. The Major's voice is like the sound of a cannon through the tobacco smoke.*

MAJOR BOOTH VOYSEY. Of course I'm hot and strong for conscription . .

MR. GEORGE BOOTH. My dear boy, the country 'd never stand it. No Englishman—

MAJOR BOOTH VOYSEY. [*dropping the phrase heavily upon the poor old gentleman.*] I beg your pardon. If we . . the Army . . say to the country . . upon our honour conscription is necessary for your safety . . what answer has the country? What? [*he pauses defiantly.*] There you are . . none!

TREGONING. Booth will imagine because one doesn't argue that one has nothing to say. You ask the country.

MAJOR BOOTH VOYSEY. Perhaps I will. Perhaps I'll chuck the Service and go into the House. [*then falling into the sing-song of a favourite phrase.*] I'm not a conceited man . . but I believe that if I speak out upon a subject I understand and only upon that subject the House will listen . . and if others followed my example we should be a far more business-like and go-ahead community.

He pauses for breath and MR. BOOTH *seizes the opportunity.*

MR. GEORGE BOOTH. If you think the gentlemen of England will allow themselves to be herded with a lot of low fellers and made to carry guns—!

MAJOR BOOTH VOYSEY. [*obliterating him once more.*] Just one moment. Have you thought of the physical improvement which conscription would bring about in the manhood of the country? What England wants is Chest! [*He generously inflates his own.*] Chest and Discipline. Never mind how it's obtained. Don't we suffer from a lack of it in our homes? The servant question now . .

MR. VOYSEY. [*with the crack of a nut.*] Your godson talks a deal, don't he? You know, when our Major gets into a club, he gets on the committee . . gets on any committee to inquire into anything . . and then goes on at 'em just like this. Don't you, Booth?

BOOTH *knuckles under easily enough to his father's sarcasm.*

MAJOR BOOTH VOYSEY. Well, sir, people tell me I'm a useful man on committees.

MR. VOYSEY. I don't doubt it . . your voice must drown all discussion.

MAJOR BOOTH VOYSEY. You can't say I don't listen to you, sir.

MR. VOYSEY. I don't . . and I'm not blaming you. But I must say I often think what a devil of a time the family will have with you when I'm gone. Fortunately for your poor mother, she's deaf.

MAJOR BOOTH VOYSEY. And wouldn't you wish me, sir, as eldest son . . Trenchard not counting . .

MR. VOYSEY. [*with the crack of another nut.*] Trenchard not counting. By all means, bully them. Never mind whether you're right or wrong . . bully them. I don't manage things that way myself, but I think it's your best chance . . if there weren't other people present I might say your only chance, Booth.

MAJOR BOOTH VOYSEY. [*with some discomfort.*] Ha! If I were a conceited man, sir, I could trust you to take it out of me.

MR. VOYSEY. [*as he taps* MR. BOOTH *with the nut*

crackers.] Help yourself, George, and drink to your godson's health. Long may he keep his chest notes! Never heard him on parade, have you?

MR. TREGONING. I notice military men must display themselves . . that's why Booth acts as a firescreen. I believe that after mess that position is positively rushed.

MAJOR BOOTH VOYSEY. [*cheering to find an opponent he can tackle.*] If you want a bit of fire, say so, you sucking Lord Chancellor. Because I mean to allow you to be my brother-in-law, you think you can be impertinent.

So TREGONING *moves to the fire and that changes the conversation.*

MR. VOYSEY. By the bye, Vicar, you were at Lady Mary's yesterday. Is she giving us anything towards that window?

MR. COLPUS. Five pounds more; she has promised me five pounds.

MR. VOYSEY. Then how will the debt stand?

MR. COLPUS. Thirty-three . . no, thirty-two pounds.

MR. VOYSEY. We're a long time clearing it off.

MR. COLPUS. [*gently querulous.*] Yes, now that the window is up, people don't seem so ready to contribute as they were.

TREGONING. We must mention that to Hugh!

MR. COLPUS. [*tactful at once.*] Not that the work is not universally admired. I have heard Hugh's design praised by quite competent judges. But certainly I feel now it might have been wiser to have delayed the unveiling until the money was forthcoming.

TREGONING. Never deliver goods to the Church on credit.

MR. COLPUS. Eh? [TREGONING *knows he is a little hard of hearing.*]

MR. VOYSEY. Well, as it was my wish that my son should do the design, I suppose in the end I shall have to send you a cheque.

MAJOR BOOTH VOYSEY. Anonymously.

MR. COLPUS. Oh, that would be—

MR. VOYSEY. No, why should I? Here, George Booth, you shall halve it with me.

MR. GEORGE BOOTH. I'm damned if I do.

MR. COLPUS. [*proceeding, conveniently deaf.*] You remember that at the meeting we had of the parents and friends to decide on the positions of the names of the poor fellows and the regiments and coats of arms, and so on . . when Hugh said so violently that he disapproved of the war and made all those remarks about Rand-lords and Bibles and said he thought of putting in a figure of Britannia blushing for shame or something . . I'm beginning to fear that may have created a bad impression.

MAJOR BOOTH VOYSEY. Why should they mind . . what on earth does Hugh know about war? He couldn't tell a battery horse from a bandsman. I don't pretend to criticise art. I think the window 'd be very pretty if it wasn't so broken up into bits.

MR. GEORGE BOOTH. [*fortified by his " damned " and his last glass of port.*] These young men are so ready with their disapproval. When I was young, people weren't always questioning this and questioning that.

MAJOR BOOTH VOYSEY. Lack of discipline.

MR. GEORGE BOOTH. [*hurrying on.*] The way a man now even stops to think what he's eating and drinking . . ! And in religious matters . . Vicar, I put it to you . . there's no uniformity at all.

MR. COLPUS. Ah . . I try to keep myself free from the disturbing influences of modern thought.

MR. GEORGE BOOTH. You know, Edward, you're worse even than Hugh is.

EDWARD. [*glancing up mildly at this sudden attack.*] What have I done, Mr. Booth?

MR. GEORGE BOOTH. [*not the readiest of men.*] Well . . aren't you another of those young men who go about the world making difficulties?

EDWARD. What sort of difficulties?

MR. GEORGE BOOTH. [*triumphantly.*] Just so . . I never can make out. . . Surely when you're young you can ask the advice of your elders and when you grow up you find Laws . . lots of laws divine and human laid down for our guidance. [*Well in possession of the conversation he spreads his little self.*] I look back over a fairly long life and . . perhaps I should say by Heaven's help . . I find nothing that I can honestly reproach myself with. And yet I don't think I ever took more than five minutes to come to a decision upon any important point. One's private life is, I think, one's own affair . . I should allow no one to pry into that. But as to worldly things . . well, I have come into several sums of money and my capital is still intact . . ask your father. [MR. VOYSEY *nods gravely.*] I've never robbed any man. I've never lied over anything that mattered. As a citizen I pay my taxes without grumbling very much. Yes, and I sent conscience money too upon one occasion. I consider that any man who takes the trouble can live the life of a gentleman. [*And he finds that his cigar is out.*]

MAJOR BOOTH VOYSEY. [*not to be outdone by this display of virtue.*] Well, I'm not a conceited man, but—

TREGONING. Are you sure, Booth?

MAJOR BOOTH VOYSEY. Shut up. I was going to say when my young cub of a brother-in-law-to-be interrupted me, that Training, for which we all have to be thankful to you, sir, has much to do with it. [*Suddenly he pulls his trousers against his legs.*] I say, I'm scorching! D'you want another cigar, Denis?

TREGONING. No, thank you.

MAJOR BOOTH VOYSEY. I do.

And he glances round, but TREGONING *sees a box on the table and reaches it. The Vicar gets up.*

MR. COLPUS. M-m-m-must be taking my departure.

MR. VOYSEY. Already!

MAJOR BOOTH VOYSEY. [*frowning upon the cigar box.*] No, not those. Where are the Ramon Allones? What on earth has Honor done with them?

MR. VOYSEY. Spare time for a chat with Mrs. Voysey before you go. She has ideas about a children's tea fight.

MR. COLPUS. Certainly I will.

MAJOR BOOTH VOYSEY. [*scowling helplessly around.*] My goodness! .. one can never find anything in this house.

MR. COLPUS. I won't say good-bye, then.

He is sliding through the half-opened door when ETHEL *meets him flinging it wide. She is the younger daughter, the baby of the family, but twenty-three now.*

MR. VOYSEY. I say, it's cold again to-night! An ass of an architect who built this place .. such a draught between these two doors.

He gets up to draw the curtain. When he turns COLPUS *has disappeared, while* ETHEL *has been followed into the room by* ALICE MAITLAND, *who shuts the door after her.* MISS ALICE MAITLAND *is a young lady of any age to thirty. Nor need her appearance alter for the next fifteen years; since her nature is healthy and well-balanced. She possesses indeed the sort of athletic chastity which is a characteristic charm of Northern spinsterhood. It mayn't be a pretty face, but it has alertness and humour; and the resolute eyes and eyebrows are a more innocent edition of* MR. VOYSEY'S, *who is her uncle.* ETHEL *goes straight to her father (though her glance is on* DENIS *and his on her) and chirps, birdlike, in her spoiled-child way.*

ETHEL. We think you've stayed in here quite long enough.

MR. VOYSEY. That's to say, Ethel thinks Denis has been kept out of her pocket much too long.

ETHEL. Ethel wants billiards .. not proper billiards

. . snooker or something. Oh, papa, what a dessert you've eaten. Greedy pig!

    ALICE *is standing behind* EDWARD, *considering his hair-parting apparently.*

    ALICE. Crack me a filbert, please, Edward . . I had none.

    EDWARD. [*jumping up, rather formally well-mannered.*] I beg your pardon, Alice. Won't you sit down?

    ALICE. No.

    MR. VOYSEY. [*taking* ETHEL *on his knee.*] Come here, puss. Have you made up your mind yet what you want for a wedding present?

    ETHEL. [*rectifying a stray hair in his beard.*] After mature consideration, I decide on a cheque.

    MR. VOYSEY. Do you!

    ETHEL. Yes, I think that a cheque will give most scope to your generosity. If you desire to add any trimmings in the shape of a piano or a Turkey carpet you may . . and Denis and I will be very grateful. But I think I'd let yourself go over a cheque.

    MR. VOYSEY. You're a minx.

    ETHEL. What is the use of having money if you don't spend it on me?

    MAJOR BOOTH VOYSEY. [*giving up the cigar search.*] Here, who's going to play?

    MR. GEORGE BOOTH. [*pathetically as he gets up.*] Well, if my wrist will hold out . .

    MAJOR BOOTH VOYSEY. [*to* TREGONING.] No, don't you bother to look for them. [*He strides from the room, his voice echoing through the hall.*] Honor, where are those Ramon Allones?

    ALICE. [*calling after.*] She's in the drawing-room with Auntie and Mr. Colpus.

    MR. VOYSEY. Now I should suggest that you and Denis go and take off the billiard table cover. You'll find folding it up a very excellent amusement.

He illustrates his meaning with his table napkin and by putting together the tips of his forefingers, roguishly.
ETHEL. I am not going to blush. I do kiss Denis . occasionally . . when he asks me.
MR. GEORGE BOOTH. [*teasing her.*] You are blushing.
ETHEL. I am not. If you think we're ashamed of being in love, we're not, we're very proud of it. We will go and take off the billiard table cover and fold it up . . and then you can come in and play. Denis, my dear, come along solemnly, and if you flinch I'll never forgive you. [*She marches off and reaches the door before her defiant dignity breaks down; then suddenly—*] Denis, I'll race you.
And she flashes out. DENIS, *loyal, but with no histrionic instincts, follows her rather sheepishly.*
DENIS. Ethel, I can't after dinner.
MR. VOYSEY. Women play that game better than men. A man shuffles through courtship with one eye on her relations.
The Major comes stalking back, followed in a fearful flurry by his elder sister, HONOR. *Poor* HONOR (*her female friends are apt to refer to her as Poor* HONOR) *is a phenomenon common to most large families. From her earliest years she has been bottle-washer to her brothers. While they were expensively educated she was grudged schooling; her highest accomplishment was meant to be mending their clothes. Her fate is a curious survival of the intolerance of parents towards her sex until the vanity of their hunger for sons had been satisfied. In a less humane society she would have been exposed at birth. But if a very general though patronising affection, accompanied by no consideration at all, can bestow happiness,* HONOR *is not unhappy in her survival. At this moment, however, her life is a burden.*
MAJOR BOOTH VOYSEY. Honor, they are not in the dining-room.

HONOR. But they must be!—Where else can they be?
She has a habit of accentuating one word in each sentence and often the wrong one.
MAJOR BOOTH VOYSEY. That's what you ought to know.
MR. VOYSEY. [*as he moves towards the door.*] Well . . will you have a game?
MR. GEORGE BOOTH. I'll play you fifty up, not more. I'm getting old.
MR. VOYSEY. [*stopping at a dessert dish.*] Yes, these are good apples of Bearman's. I think six of my trees are spoilt this year.
HONOR. Here you are, Booth.
She triumphantly discovers the discarded box, at which the Major becomes pathetic with indignation.
MAJOR BOOTH VOYSEY. Oh, Honor, don't be such a fool. These are what we've been smoking. I want the Ramon Allones.
HONOR. I don't know the difference.
MAJOR BOOTH VOYSEY. No, you don't, but you might learn.
MR. VOYSEY. [*in a voice like the crack of a very fine whip.*] Booth.
MAJOR BOOTH VOYSEY. [*subduedly.*] What is it, sir?
MR. VOYSEY. Look for your cigars yourself. Honor, go back to your reading or your sewing or whatever you were fiddling at, and fiddle in peace.
MR. VOYSEY *departs, leaving the room rather hushed.*
MR. BOOTH *has not waited for this parental display.*
Then ALICE *insinuates a remark very softly.*
ALICE. Have you looked in the library?
MAJOR BOOTH VOYSEY. [*relapsing to an injured mutter.*] Where's Emily?
HONOR. Upstairs with little Henry, he woke up and cried.
MAJOR BOOTH VOYSEY. Letting her wear herself to rags over the child . . !

HONOR. Well, she won't let me go.

MAJOR BOOTH VOYSEY. Why don't you stop looking for those cigars?

HONOR. If you don't mind, I want a reel of blue silk, now I'm here.

MAJOR BOOTH VOYSEY. I daresay they are in the library. What a house!

He departs.

HONOR. Booth is so trying.

ALICE. Honor, why do you put up with it?

HONOR. Some one has to.

ALICE. [*discreetly nibbling a nut, which* EDWARD *has cracked for her.*] I'm afraid I think Master Major Booth ought to have been taken in hand early . . with a cane.

HONOR. [*as she vaguely burrows into corners.*] Papa did. But it's never prevented him booming at us . . oh, ever since he was a baby. Now he's flustered me so I simply can't think where this blue silk is.

ALICE. All the Pettifers desired to be remembered to you, Edward.

HONOR. I must do without it. [*But she goes on looking.*] I sometimes think, Alice, that we're a very difficult family . . except perhaps Edward.

EDWARD. Why except me?

HONOR. [*who has only excepted out of politeness to present company.*] And you were always difficult . . to yourself. [*Then she starts to go, threading her way through the disarranged chairs.*] Mr. Colpus will shout so loud at mother and she hates people to think she's so very deaf. I thought Mary Pettifer looking old . . [*And she talks herself out of the room.*]

ALICE. [*after her.*] She's getting old.

Now ALICE *does sit down; as if she'd be glad of her tête-à-tête.*

ALICE. I was glad not to spend August abroad for

once. We drove into Cheltenham to a dance . . carpet. I golfed a lot.

EDWARD. How long were you with them?

ALICE. Not a fortnight. It doesn't seem three months since I was here, does it?

EDWARD. I'm down so very little.

ALICE. I'm here a disgraceful deal.

EDWARD. You know they're always pleased.

ALICE. Well, being a homeless person! But what a cart-load to descend all at once . . yesterday and to-day. The Major and Emily . . Emily's not at all well. Hugh and Mrs. Hugh. And me. Are you staying?

EDWARD. No. I must get a word with my father . .

ALICE. Edward, a business life is not healthy for you. You look more like half-baked pie-crust than usual.

EDWARD. [*a little enviously.*] You're very well.

ALICE. I'm always well and nearly always happy.

MAJOR BOOTH *returns. He has the right sort of cigar in his mouth and is considerably mollified.*

ALICE. You found them?

MAJOR BOOTH VOYSEY. Of course, they were there. Thank you very much, Alice. Now I want a knife.

ALICE. I must give you a cigar-cutter for Christmas, Booth.

MAJOR BOOTH VOYSEY. Beastly things, I hate 'em, thank you. [*He eyes the dessert disparagingly.*] Nothing but silver ones.

EDWARD *hands him a carefully opened pocket-knife.* Thank you, Edward. And I must take one of the candles. Something's gone wrong with the library ventilator and you never can see a thing in that room.

ALICE. Is Mrs. Hugh there?

MAJOR BOOTH VOYSEY. Writing letters. Things are neglected, Edward, unless one is constantly on the look out. The Pater only cares for his garden. I must speak seriously to Honor.

He has returned the knife, still open, and now having lit his cigar at the candle he carries this off.

ALICE. Honor has the patience of a . . of an old maid.

EDWARD. Yes, I suppose her mission in life isn't a very pleasant one. [*He gives her a nut, about the fifteenth.*] Here; 'scuse fingers.

ALICE. Thank you. [*Looking at him, with her head on one side and her face more humorous than ever.*] Edward, why have you given up proposing to me?

He starts, flushes; then won't be outdone in humour.

EDWARD. One can't go on proposing for ever.

ALICE. [*reasonably.*] Why not? Have you seen any-one you like better?

EDWARD. No.

ALICE. Well . . I miss it.

EDWARD. What satisfaction did you find in refusing me?

ALICE. [*as she weighs the matter.*] I find satisfaction in feeling that I'm wanted.

EDWARD. Without any intention of giving yourself . . throwing yourself away.

ALICE. [*teasing his sudden earnestness.*] Ah, now you come from mere vanity to serious questions.

EDWARD. Mine was a very serious question to you.

ALICE. But, Edward, all questions are serious to you. I call you a perfect little pocket-guide to life . . all questions and answers; what to eat, drink, and avoid, what to believe and what to say . .

EDWARD. [*sententiously.*] Well . . everything matters.

ALICE. [*making a face.*] D'you plan out every detail of your life . . every step you take . . every mouthful?

EDWARD. That would be waste of thought. One must lay down principles.

ALICE. I prefer my plan, I always do what I know I want to do. Crack me another nut.

EDWARD. Haven't you had enough?

ALICE. I know I want one more.

He cracks another, with a sigh which sounds ridiculous in that connection.

I know it just as I knew I didn't want to marry you . . each time.

EDWARD. Oh, you didn't make a rule of saying no.

ALICE. As you proposed . . on principle? No, I always gave you a fair chance. I'll give you one now if you like. Courage, I might say yes . . all in a flash. Oh, you'd never get over it.

EDWARD. I think we won't run the risk.

ALICE. Edward, how rude you are. [*She eats her nut contentedly.*] There's nothing wrong, is there?

EDWARD. Nothing at all.

They are interrupted by the sudden appearance of MRS. HUGH VOYSEY, *a brisk, bright little woman, in an evening gown, which she has bullied a cheap dressmaker into making look exceedingly smart.* BEATRICE *is as hard as nails and as clever as paint. But if she keeps her feelings buried pretty deep it is because they are precious to her; and if she is impatient with fools it is because her own brains have had to win her everything in the world, so perhaps she does overvalue them a little. She speaks always with great decision and little effort.*

BEATRICE. I believe I could write important business letters upon an island in the middle of Fleet Street. But while Booth is poking at a ventilator with a billiard cue . . no, I can't.

She goes to the fireplace, waving her half-finished letter.

ALICE. [*soothingly.*] Didn't you expect Hugh back to dinner?

BEATRICE. Not specially . . He went to rout out some things from his studio. He'll come back in a filthy mess.

ALICE. Ssh! Now, if you listen . . Booth doesn't

THE VOYSEY INHERITANCE

enjoy making a fuss by himself . . you'll hear him put up Honor.

They listen. But what happens is that BOOTH *appears at the door, billiard cue in hand, and says solemnly* . .

MAJOR BOOTH VOYSEY. Edward, I wish you'd come and have a look at this ventilator, like a good fellow.

Then he turns and goes again, obviously with the weight of an important matter on his shoulders. With the ghost of a smile EDWARD *gets up and follows him.*

ALICE. If I belonged to this family I should hate Booth.

With which comment she joins BEATRICE *at the fireplace.*

BEATRICE. A good day's shopping?

ALICE. 'M. The baby bride and I bought clothes all the morning. Then we had lunch with Denis and bought furniture.

BEATRICE. Nice furniture?

ALICE. Very good and very new. They neither of them know what they want. [*Then suddenly throwing up her chin and exclaiming.*] When it's a question of money I can understand it . . but if one can provide for oneself or is independent why get married! Especially having been brought up on the sheltered life principle . . one may as well make the most of its advantages . . one doesn't go falling in love all over the place as men seem to . . most of them. Of course with Ethel and Denis it's different. They've both been caught young. They're two little birds building their nest and it's all ideal. They'll soon forget they've ever been apart.

Now HONOR *flutters into the room, patient but wild-eyed.*

HONOR. Mother wants last week's " Notes and Queries ". Have you seen it?

BEATRICE. [*exasperated at the interruption.*] No.

HONOR. It ought not to be in here. [*So she proceeds to look for it.*] She's having a long argument with Mr. Colpus over Oliver Cromwell's relations.

ALICE. [*her eyes twinkling.*] I thought Auntie didn't approve of Oliver Cromwell.

HONOR. She doesn't, and she's trying to prove that he was a brewer or something. I suppose some one has taken it away.

So she gives up the search and flutters out again.

ALICE. This is a most unrestful house.

BEATRICE. I once thought of putting the Voyseys into a book of mine. Then I concluded they'd be as dull there as they are anywhere else.

ALICE. They're not duller than most people.

BEATRICE. But how very dull that is!

ALICE. They're a little noisier and perhaps not quite so well-mannered. But I love them.

BEATRICE. I don't. I should have thought love was just what they couldn't inspire.

ALICE. Of course, Hugh is unlike any of the others.

BEATRICE. He has most of their bad points. But I don't love Hugh.

ALICE. [*her eyebrows up, though she smiles.*] Beatrice, you shouldn't say so.

BEATRICE. Sounds affected, doesn't it? Never mind; when he dies I'll wear mourning . . but not weeds; I bargained against that when we were engaged.

ALICE. [*her face growing a little thoughtful.*] Beatrice, I'm going to ask questions. You were in love with Hugh when you married him?

BEATRICE. Well . . I married him for his money . .

ALICE. He hadn't much.

BEATRICE. I had none . . and I wanted to write books. Yes, I loved him.

ALICE. And you thought you'd be happy?

BEATRICE. [*considering carefully.*] No, I didn't. I hoped he'd be happy.

ALICE. [*a little ironical.*] Did you think your writing books would make him so?

BEATRICE. My dear Alice, shouldn't a man . . or a woman feel it a very degrading thing to have their happiness depend upon somebody else?

ALICE. [*after pausing to find her phrase.*] There's a joy of service. Is that very womanly of me?

BEATRICE. [*ironical herself now.*] Ah, but you've four hundred a year.

ALICE. What has that to do with it?

BEATRICE. [*putting her case very precisely.*] Fine feelings, my dear, are as much a luxury as clean gloves. Now, I've had to earn my own living; consequently there isn't one thing in my life that I have ever done quite genuinely for its own sake . . but always with an eye towards bread-and-butter, pandering to the people who were to give me that. I warned Hugh . . he took the risk.

ALICE. What risk?

BEATRICE. That one day I'd be able to get on without him.

ALICE. By the time he'd learnt how not to without you?

BEATRICE. Well, women must have the courage to be brutal.

The conservatory door opens and through it come MR. VOYSEY *and* MR. BOOTH *in the midst of a discussion.*

MR. VOYSEY. My dear man, stick to the shares and risk it.

MR. GEORGE BOOTH. No, of course, if you seriously advise me—

MR. VOYSEY. I never advise greedy children; I let 'em overeat 'emselves and take the consequences—

ALICE. [*shaking a finger.*] Uncle Trench, you've

been in the garden without a hat after playing billiards in that hot room.

MR. GEORGE BOOTH. We had to give up . . my wrist was bad. They've started pool.

BEATRICE. Is Booth going to play?

MR. VOYSEY. We left him instructing Ethel how to hold a cue.

BEATRICE. Ah! I can finish my letter.

Off she goes. ALICE *is idly following with a little paper her hand has fallen on behind the clock.*

MR. VOYSEY. Don't run away, my dear.

ALICE. I'm taking this to Auntie . . "Notes and Queries" . . she wants it.

MR. GEORGE BOOTH. Damn . . this gravel's stuck to my shoe.

MR. VOYSEY. That's a new-made path.

MR. GEORGE BOOTH. Now don't you think it's too early to have put in those plants?

MR. VOYSEY. No, we've had a frost or two already.

MR. GEORGE BOOTH. I should have kept the bed a good ten feet farther from that tree.

MR. VOYSEY. Nonsense, the tree's to the north of it. This room's cold. Why don't they keep the fire up? [*He proceeds to put coals on it.*]

MR. GEORGE BOOTH. You were too hot in that billiard room. You know, Voysey . . about those Alguazils?

MR. VOYSEY. [*through the rattling of the coals.*] What?

MR. GEORGE BOOTH. [*trying to pierce the din.*] Those Alguazils.

MR. VOYSEY *with surprising inconsequence points a finger at the silk handkerchief across* MR. BOOTH'S *shirt front.*

MR. VOYSEY. What d'you put your handkerchief there for?

MR. GEORGE BOOTH. Measure of precau— [*at that*

moment he sneezes.] Damn it . . if you've given me a chill dragging me through your infernal garden . .

MR. VOYSEY. [*slapping him on the back.*] You're an old crock.

MR. GEORGE BOOTH. Well, I'll be glad of this winter in Egypt. [*He returns to his subject.*] And if you think seriously, that I ought to sell out of the Alguazils before I go . .? [*He looks with childlike inquiry at his friend, who is apparently yawning slightly.*] Why can't you take them in charge? . . and I'll give you a power of attorney . . or whatever it is . . and you can sell out if things look bad.

At this moment PHOEBE, *the middle-aged parlourmaid, comes in, tray in hand. Like an expert fisherman,* MR. VOYSEY *once more lets loose the thread of the conversation.*

MR. VOYSEY. D'you want to clear?

PHOEBE. It doesn't matter, sir.

MR. VOYSEY. No, go on . . go on.

So MARY, *the young housemaid, comes in as well, and the two start to clear the table. All of which fidgets poor* MR. BOOTH *considerably. He sits shrivelled up in the armchair by the fire; and now* MR. VOYSEY *attends to him.*

MR. VOYSEY. What d'you want with high interest at all . . you never spend half your income?

MR. GEORGE BOOTH. I like to feel that my money is doing some good in the world. Mines are very useful things and forty-two per cent is pleasing.

MR. VOYSEY. You're an old gambler.

MR. GEORGE BOOTH. [*propitiatingly.*] Ah, but then I've you to advise me. I always do as you tell me in the end, now you can't deny that. . .

MR. VOYSEY. The man who don't know must trust in the man who do! [*He yawns again.*]

MR. GEORGE BOOTH. [*modestly insisting.*] There's

five thousand in Alguazils—what else could we put it into?

MR. VOYSEY. I can get you something at four and a half.

MR. GEORGE BOOTH. Oh, Lord . . that's nothing.

MR. VOYSEY. [*with a sudden serious friendliness.*] I wish, my dear George, you'd invest more on your own account. You know—what with one thing and the other—I've got control of practically all you have in the world. I might be playing old Harry with it for all you know.

MR. GEORGE BOOTH. [*overflowing with confidence.*] My dear feller . . if I'm satisfied! Ah, my friend, what'll happen to your firm when you depart this life! . . not before my time, I hope, though.

MR. VOYSEY. [*with a little frown.*] What d'ye mean?

MR. GEORGE BOOTH. Edward's no use.

MR. VOYSEY. I beg your pardon . . very sound in business.

MR. GEORGE BOOTH. May be . . but I tell you he's no use. Too many principles, as I told him just now. Men have confidence in a personality, not in principles. Where would you be without the confidence of your clients?

MR. VOYSEY. [*candidly.*] True!

MR. GEORGE BOOTH. He'll never gain that.

MR. VOYSEY. I fear you dislike Edward.

MR. GEORGE BOOTH. [*with pleasant frankness.*] Yes, I do.

MR. VOYSEY. That's a pity. That's a very great pity.

MR. GEORGE BOOTH. [*with a flattering smile.*] He's not his father and never will be. What's the time?

MR. VOYSEY. [*with inappropriate thoughtfulness.*] Twenty to ten.

MR. GEORGE BOOTH. I must be trotting.

MR. VOYSEY. It's early.

MR. GEORGE BOOTH. Oh, and I've not said a word to Mrs. Voysey . .

As he goes to the door he meets EDWARD, *who comes*

in apparently looking for his father; at any rate catches his eye immediately, while MR. BOOTH *obliviously continues.*

MR. GEORGE BOOTH. Will you stroll round home with me?

MR. VOYSEY. I can't.

MR. GEORGE BOOTH. [*mildly surprised at the short reply.*] Well, good night. Good night, Edward.

He trots away.

MR. VOYSEY. Leave the rest of the table, Phoebe.

PHOEBE. Yes, sir.

MR. VOYSEY. You can come back in ten minutes.

PHOEBE *and* MARY *depart and the door is closed. Alone with his son* MR. VOYSEY *does not move; his face grows a little keener, that's all.*

MR. VOYSEY. Well, Edward?

EDWARD *starts to move restlessly about, like a cowed animal in a cage; silently for a moment or two. Then when he speaks, his voice is toneless and he doesn't look at his father.*

EDWARD. Would you mind, sir, dropping with me for the future all these protestations about putting the firm's affairs straight . . about all your anxieties and sacrifices. I see now, of course . . a cleverer man than I could have seen it yesterday . . that for some time, ever since, I suppose, you recovered from the first shock and got used to the double dealing, this hasn't been your object at all. You've used your clients' capital to produce your own income . . to bring us up and endow us with. Booth's ten thousand pounds; what you are giving Ethel on her marriage . . It's odd it never struck me yesterday that my own pocket money as a boy must have been quite simply withdrawn from some client's account. You've been very generous to us all, father. I suppose about half the sum you've spent on us first and last would have put things right.

MR. VOYSEY. No, it would not.

EDWARD. [*appealing for the truth.*] Yes, yes . . at some time or other !

MR. VOYSEY. Well, if there have been good times there have been bad times. At present the three hundred a year I'm to allow your sister is going to be rather a pull.

EDWARD. Three hundred a year . . while you don't attempt to make a single client safe. Since it isn't lunacy, sir . . I can only conclude that you enjoy such a position.

MR. VOYSEY. Safe ? Three trusts—two of them big ones—have been wound up within this last eighteen months, and the accounts have been above suspicion. What's the object of all this rodomontade, Edward ?

EDWARD. If I'm to remain in the firm, it had better be with a very clear understanding of things as they are.

MR. VOYSEY. [*firmly, not too anxiously.*] Then you do remain ?

EDWARD. [*in a very low voice.*] I must remain.

MR. VOYSEY. [*quite gravely.*] That's wise of you . . I'm very glad. [*And he is silent for a moment.*] And now we needn't discuss the unpractical side of it any more.

EDWARD. But I want to make one condition. And I want some information.

MR. VOYSEY. [*his sudden cheerfulness relapsing again.*] Well ?

EDWARD. Of course no one has ever discovered . . and no one suspects this state of things ?

MR. VOYSEY. Peacey knows.

EDWARD. Peacey !

MR. VOYSEY. His father found out.

EDWARD. Oh. Does he draw hush money ?

MR. VOYSEY. [*curling a little at the word.*] It is my custom to make him a little present every Christmas. [*He becomes benevolent.*] I don't grudge the money . . Peacey's a devoted fellow.

EDWARD. Certainly this should be a heavily taxed

industry. [*Then he smiles at his vision of the mild old clerk.*] Peacey! There's another thing I want to ask, sir. Have you ever under stress of circumstances done worse than just make this temporary use of a client's capital? You boasted to me yesterday that no one had ever suffered in pocket in the end because of you. Is that absolutely true?

MR. VOYSEY *draws himself up, dignified and magniloquent.*

MR. VOYSEY. My dear Edward, for the future my mind is open to you; you can discover for yourself how matters stand to-day. But I decline to gratify your curiosity as to what is over and done with.

EDWARD. [*with entire comprehension.*] Thank you, sir. The condition of my remaining is that we should really try as unobtrusively as you like and put things straight.

MR. VOYSEY. [*with a little polite shrug.*] I've no doubt you'll prove an abler man of business than I.

EDWARD. We can begin by halving the salary I draw from the firm; that leaves me enough.

MR. VOYSEY. I see . . Retrenchment and Reform.

EDWARD. And it seems to me that you can't give Ethel this five thousand pounds dowry.

MR. VOYSEY. [*shortly, with one of the quick twists of his eye.*] I have given my word to Denis . .

EDWARD. Because the money isn't yours to give.

MR. VOYSEY. [*in an indignant crescendo.*] I should not dream of depriving Ethel of what, as my daughter, she has every right to expect. I am surprised at your suggesting such a thing.

EDWARD. [*pale and firm.*] I'm set on this, father.

MR. VOYSEY. Don't be such a fool, Edward. What would it look like . . suddenly to refuse without rhyme or reason? What would old Tregoning think?

EDWARD. Oh, can't you see it's my duty to prevent this?

MR. VOYSEY. You can prevent it by telling the nearest policeman. It is my duty to pay no more attention to these scruples of yours than a nurse pays to her child's tantrums. Understand, Edward, I don't want to force you to continue my partner. Come with me gladly or don't come at all.

EDWARD. [*dully.*] It is my duty to be of what use I can to you, sir. Father, I want to save you if I can.

He flashes into this exclamation of almost broken-hearted affection. MR. VOYSEY *looks at his son for a moment and his lip quivers. Then he steels himself.*

MR. VOYSEY. Thank you! I have saved myself quite satisfactorily for the last thirty years, and you must please believe that by this time I know my own business best.

EDWARD. [*hopelessly.*] Can't we find the money some other way? How do you manage now about your own income?

MR. VOYSEY. I have a bank balance and a cheque book, haven't I? I spend what I think well to spend. What's the use of earmarking this or that as my own? You say none of it is my own. I might say it's all my own. I think I've earned it.

EDWARD. [*anger coming on him.*] That's what I can't forgive. If you'd lived poor . . if you'd really done all you could for your clients and not thought only of your own aggrandisement . . then, even though things were no better than they are now, I could have been proud of you. But, father, own the truth to me, at least . . that's my due from you, considering how I'm placed by all you've done. Didn't you simply seize this opportunity as a means to your own ends, to your own enriching?

MR. VOYSEY. [*with a sledge-hammer irony.*] Certainly. I sat that morning in my father's office, studying the helmet of the policeman in the street below, and thinking what a glorious path I had happened on to wealth and honour and renown. [*Then he begins to bully* EDWARD *in the kindliest way.*] My dear boy, you evidently haven't begun to grasp the ABC of my position. What has carried me to victory? The confidence of my clients. What has earned that confidence? A decent life, my integrity, my brains? No, my reputation for wealth . . that, and nothing else. Business nowadays is run on the lines of the confidence trick. What makes old George Booth so glad to trust me with every penny he possesses? Not affection . . he's never cared for anything in his life but his collection of prints.

EDWARD. [*stupefied, helpless.*] Is he involved?

MR. VOYSEY. Of course he's involved, and he's always after high interest too . . it's little one makes out of him. But there's a further question here, Edward. Should I have had confidence in myself if I'd remained a poor man? No, I should not. You must either be the master of money or its servant. And if one is not opulent in one's daily life one loses that wonderful . . financier's touch. One must be confident oneself . . and I saw from the first that I must at any cost inspire confidence. My whole public and private life has tended to that. All my surroundings . . you and your brothers and sisters that I have brought into, and up, and put out in the world so worthily . . you in your turn inspire confidence.

EDWARD. Not our worth, not our abilities, nor our virtues, but the fact that we travel first class and take cabs when we want to.

MR. VOYSEY. [*impatiently.*] Well, I haven't organised Society upon a basis of wealth.

EDWARD. I sat down yesterday to make a list of the people who are good enough to trust their money to us. It'll be a pretty long one . . and it's an interesting one, from George Booth with his big income to old Nursie with her savings which she brought you so proudly to invest. But you've let those be, at least.

MR. VOYSEY. I just . . took the money . .

EDWARD. Father!

MR. VOYSEY. Five hundred pounds. Not worth worrying about.

EDWARD. That's damnable.

MR. VOYSEY. Indeed. I give her seventy-five pounds a year for it. Would you like to take charge of that account, Edward? I'll give you five hundred to invest to-morrow.

EDWARD, *hopelessly beaten, falls into an almost comic state of despair.*

EDWARD. My dear father, putting every moral question aside . . it's all very well your playing Robin Hood in this magnificent manner; but have you given a moment's thought to the sort of inheritance you'll be leaving me?

MR. VOYSEY. [*pleased for the first time.*] Ah! That is a question you have every right to ask.

EDWARD. If you died to-morrow could we pay eight shillings in the pound . . or seventeen . . or five? Do you know?

MR. VOYSEY. And the answer is, that by your help I have every intention, when I die, of leaving a will behind me of property to you all running into six figures. D'you think I've given my life and my talents for a less result than that? I'm fond of you all . . and I want you to be proud of me . . and I mean that the name of Voysey shall be carried high in the world by my children and grandchildren. Don't you be afraid, Edward. Ah, you lack experience, my boy . . you're not full grown yet . . your impulses are a bit chaotic. You emotionalise over your work, and you reason about your emotions. You must sort yourself. You must realise that money-making is one thing, and religion another, and family life a third . . and that if we apply our energies whole-heartedly to each of these in turn, and realise that different laws govern each, that there is a different end to be served, a different ideal to be striven for in each . .

His coherence is saved by the sudden appearance of

his wife, who comes round the door smiling benignly. Not in the least put out, in fact a little relieved, he greets her with an affectionate shout, for she is very deaf.

MR. VOYSEY. Hullo, mother!

MRS. VOYSEY. Oh, there you are, Trench. I've been deserted.

MR. VOYSEY. George Booth gone?

MRS. VOYSEY. Are you talking business? Perhaps you don't want me.

MR. VOYSEY. No, no .. no business.

MRS. VOYSEY. [*who has not looked for his answer.*] I suppose the others are in the billiard room.

MR. VOYSEY. [*vociferously.*] We're not talking business, old lady.

EDWARD. I'll be off, sir.

MR. VOYSEY. [*genial as usual.*] Why don't you stay? I'll come up with you in the morning.

EDWARD. No, thank you, sir.

MR. VOYSEY. Then I shall be up about noon to-morrow.

EDWARD. Good night, mother.

MRS. VOYSEY *places a plump kindly hand on his arm and looks up affectionately.*

MRS. VOYSEY. You look tired.

EDWARD. No, I'm not.

MRS. VOYSEY. What did you say?

EDWARD. [*too weary to repeat himself.*] Nothing, mother dear.

He kisses her cheek, while she kisses the air.

MR. VOYSEY. Good night, my boy.

Then he goes. MRS. VOYSEY *is carrying her "Notes and Queries". This is a dear old lady, looking older, too, than probably she is. Placid describes her. She has had a life of little joys and cares, has never measured herself against the world, never even questioned the shape and size of the little corner of it in which she lives. She has loved an indulgent husband*

and borne eight children, six of them surviving, healthy. That is her history.

MRS. VOYSEY. George Booth went some time ago. He said he thought you'd taken a chill walking round the garden.

MR. VOYSEY. I'm all right.

MRS. VOYSEY. D'you think you have?

MR. VOYSEY. [*in her ear.*] No.

MRS. VOYSEY. You should be careful, Trench. What did you put on?

MR. VOYSEY. Nothing.

MRS. VOYSEY. How very foolish! Let me feel your hand. You are quite feverish.

MR. VOYSEY. [*affectionately.*] You're a fuss-box, old lady.

MRS. VOYSEY. [*coquetting with him.*] Don't be rude, Trench.

HONOR *descends upon them. She is well into that nightly turmoil of putting everything and everybody to rights which always precedes her bed-time. She carries a shawl, which she clasps round her mother's shoulders, her mind and gaze already on the next thing to be done.*

HONOR. Mother, you left your shawl in the drawing-room. Can they finish clearing?

MR. VOYSEY. [*arranging the folds of the shawl with real tenderness.*] Now who's careless!

PHOEBE *comes into the room.*

HONOR. Phoebe, finish here and then you must bring in the tray for Mr. Hugh.

MRS. VOYSEY. [*having looked at the shawl and* HONOR, *and connected the matter in her mind.*] Thank you, Honor. You'd better look after your father; he's been walking round the garden without his cape.

HONOR. Papa!

MR. VOYSEY. Phoebe, you get that little kettle and

boil it, and brew me some whisky and water. I shall be all right.

HONOR. [*fluttering more than ever.*] I'll get it. Where's the whisky? And Hugh coming back at ten o'clock with no dinner. No wonder his work goes wrong. Here it is! Papa, you do deserve to be ill.

Clasping the whisky decanter, she is off again. MRS. VOYSEY *sits at the dinner table and adjusts her spectacles. She returns to "Notes and Queries", one elbow firmly planted and her plump hand against her plump cheek. This is her favourite attitude; and she is apt, when reading, to soliloquise in her deaf woman's voice. At least, whether she considers it soliloquy or conversation is not easy to discover.* MR. VOYSEY *stands with his back to the fire, grumbling and pulling faces.*

MRS. VOYSEY. This is a very perplexing correspondence about the Cromwell family. One can't deny the man had good blood in him . . his grandfather Sir Henry, his uncle Sir Oliver . .

MR. VOYSEY. There's a pain in my back.

MRS. VOYSEY. . . and it's difficult to discover where the taint crept in.

MR. VOYSEY. I believe I strained myself putting in all those strawberry plants.

MARY, *the house-parlour maid, carries in a tray of warmed-up dinner for* HUGH *and plants it on the table.*

MRS. VOYSEY. Yes, but then how was it he came to disgrace himself so? I believe the family disappeared. Regicide is a root and branch curse. You must read this letter signed C. W. A. . . it's quite interesting. There's a misprint in mine about the first umbrella maker . . now where was it . . [*And so the dear lady will ramble on indefinitely.*]

THE THIRD ACT

The dining-room looks very different in the white light of a July noon. Moreover, on this particular day, it isn't even its normal self. There is a peculiar luncheon spread on the table. The embroidered cloth is placed cornerwise and on it are decanters of port and sherry; sandwiches, biscuits, and an uncut cake; two little piles of plates and one little pile of napkins. There are no table decorations, and indeed the whole room has been made as bare and as tidy as possible. Such preparations denote one of the recognised English festivities, and the appearance of PHOEBE, *the maid, who has just completed them, the set solemnity of her face and the added touches of black to her dress and cap, suggest that this is probably a funeral. When* MARY *comes in, the fact that she has evidently been crying and that she decorously does not raise her voice above an unpleasant whisper makes it quite certain.*

MARY. Phoebe, they're coming back . . and I forgot one of the blinds in the drawing-room.

PHOEBE. Well, pull it up quick and make yourself scarce. I'll open the door.

MARY *got rid of,* PHOEBE *composes her face still more rigorously into the aspect of formal grief, and, with a touch to her apron as well, goes to admit the funeral party. The first to enter are* MRS. VOYSEY *and* MR. BOOTH, *she on his arm; and the fact that she is in widow's weeds makes the occasion clear. The little old man leads his old friend very tenderly.*

MR. GEORGE BOOTH. Will you come in here?

MRS. VOYSEY. Thank you.
With great solicitude he puts her in a chair; then takes her hand.
MR. GEORGE BOOTH. Now I'll intrude no longer.
MRS. VOYSEY. You'll take some lunch?
MR. GEORGE BOOTH. No.
MRS. VOYSEY. Not a glass of wine?
MR. GEORGE BOOTH. If there's anything I can do just send round.
MRS. VOYSEY. Thank you.
He reaches the door, only to be met by the Major and his wife. He shakes hands with them both.
MR. GEORGE BOOTH. My dear Emily! My dear Booth!
EMILY *is a homely, patient, pale little woman of about thirty-five. She looks smaller than usual in her heavy black dress and is meeker than usual on an occasion of this kind. The Major, on the other hand, though his grief is most sincere, has an irresistible air of being responsible for, and indeed rather proud of, the whole affair.*
BOOTH. I think it all went off as he would have wished.
MR. GEORGE BOOTH. [*feeling that he is called on for praise.*] Great credit . . great credit.
He makes another attempt to escape and is stopped this time by TRENCHARD VOYSEY, *to whom he is extending a hand and beginning his formula. But* TRENCHARD *speaks first.*
TRENCHARD. Have you the right time?
MR. GEORGE BOOTH. [*taken aback and fumbling for his watch.*] I think so . . I make it fourteen minutes to one. [*He seizes the occasion.*] Trenchard, as a very old and dear friend of your father's, you won't mind me saying how glad I was that you were present to-day. Death closes all. Indeed . . it must be a great regret to you that you did not see him before . . before . .

TRENCHARD. [*his cold eye freezing this little gush.*] I don't think he asked for me.

MR. GEORGE BOOTH. [*stoppered.*] No? No! Well .. well. . .

At this third attempt to depart he actually collides with some one in the doorway. It is HUGH VOYSEY.

MR. GEORGE BOOTH. My dear Hugh . . I won't intrude.

Quite determined to escape, he grasps his hand, gasps out his formula and is off. TRENCHARD *and* HUGH, *eldest and youngest sons, are as unlike each other as it is possible for* VOYSEYS *to be, but that isn't very unlike.* TRENCHARD *has in excelsis the cocksure manner of the successful barrister ;* HUGH *the rather sweet though querulous air of diffidence and scepticism belonging to the unsuccessful man of letters or artist. The self-respect of* TRENCHARD'S *appearance is immense, and he cultivates that air of concentration upon any trivial matter, or even upon nothing at all, which will some day make him an impressive figure upon the Bench.* HUGH *is always vague, searching Heaven or the corners of the room for inspiration, and even on this occasion his tie is abominably crooked. The inspissated gloom of this assembly, to which each member of the family as he arrives adds his share, is unbelievable. Instinct apparently leads them to reproduce as nearly as possible the appearance and conduct of the corpse on which their minds are fixed.* HUGH *is depressed partly at the inadequacy of his grief :* TRENCHARD *conscientiously preserves an air of the indifference which he feels ;* BOOTH *stands statuesque at the mantelpiece ; while* EMILY *is by* MRS. VOYSEY, *whose face in its quiet grief is nevertheless a mirror of many happy memories of her husband.*

BOOTH. I wouldn't hang over her, Emily.

EMILY. No, of course not.

Apologetically, she sits by the table.

TRENCHARD. I hope your wife is well, Hugh?

HUGH. Thank you, Trench: I think so. Beatrice is in America . . doing some work there.

TRENCHARD. Really!

There comes in a small, well-groomed, bullet-headed boy in Etons. This is the Major's eldest son. Looking scared and solemn he goes straight to his mother.

EMILY. Now be very quiet, Christopher . .

Then DENIS TREGONING *appears.*

TRENCHARD. Oh, Tregoning, did you bring Honor back?

DENIS. Yes.

BOOTH. [*at the table.*] A glass of wine, mother.

MRS. VOYSEY. What?

BOOTH *hardly knows how to turn his whisper decorously into enough of a shout for his mother to hear. But he manages it.*

BOOTH. Have a glass of wine?

MRS. VOYSEY. Sherry, please.

While he pours it out with an air of its being medicine on this occasion and not wine at all, EDWARD *comes quickly into the room, his face very set, his mind obviously on other matters than the funeral. No one speaks to him for the moment and he has time to observe them all.* TRENCHARD *is continuing his talk to* DENIS.

TRENCHARD. Give my love to Ethel. Is she ill that—

TREGONING. Not exactly, but she couldn't very well be with us. I thought perhaps you might have heard. We're expecting . .

He hesitates with the bashfulness of a young husband. TRENCHARD *helps him out with a citizen's bow of respect for a citizen's duty.*

TRENCHARD. Indeed. I congratulate you. I hope all will be well. Please give my best love to Ethel.

BOOTH. [*in an awful voice.*] Lunch, Emily?

EMILY. [*scared.*] I suppose so, Booth, thank you.

BOOTH. I think the boy had better run away and play . . [*He checks himself on the word.*] Well, take a book and keep quiet; d'ye hear me, Christopher?

CHRISTOPHER, *who looks incapable of a sound, gazes at his father with round eyes.* EMILY *whispers* "*Library*" *to him and adds a kiss in acknowledgement of his good behaviour. After a moment he slips out, thankfully.*

EDWARD. How's Ethel, Denis?

TREGONING. A little smashed, of course, but no harm done . . I hope.

ALICE MAITLAND *comes in, brisk and businesslike; a little impatient of this universal cloud of mourning.*

ALICE. Edward, Honor has gone to her room; I must take her some food and make her eat it. She's very upset.

EDWARD. Make her drink a glass of wine, and say it is necessary she should come down here. And d'you mind not coming back yourself, Alice?

ALICE. [*her eyebrows up.*] Certainly, if you wish.

BOOTH. [*overhearing.*] What's this? What's this?

ALICE *gets her glass of wine and goes. The Major is suddenly full of importance.*

BOOTH. What is this, Edward?

EDWARD. I have something to say to you all.

BOOTH. What?

EDWARD. Well, Booth, you'll hear when I say it.

BOOTH. Is it business? . . because I think this is scarcely the time for business.

EDWARD. Why?

BOOTH. Do you find it easy and reverent to descend from your natural grief to the consideration of money? . . I do not. [*He finds* TRENCHARD *at his elbow.*] I hope you are getting some lunch, Trenchard.

EDWARD. This is business and rather more than business, Booth. I choose now, because it is something I

wish to say to the family, not write to each individually . .
and it will be difficult to get us all together again.

BOOTH. [*determined at any rate to give his sanction.*]
Well, Trenchard, as Edward is in the position of trustee
—executor . . I don't know your terms . . I suppose . .

TRENCHARD. I don't see what your objection is.

BOOTH. [*with some superiority.*] Don't you? I
should not have called myself a sentimental man, but . .

EDWARD. You had better stay, Denis; you represent
Ethel.

TREGONING. [*who has not heard the beginning of this.*]
Why?

HONOR *has obediently come down from her room. She
is pale and thin, shaken with grief and worn out
besides; for needless to say the brunt of her father's
illness, the brunt of everything has been on her. Six
weeks' nursing, part of it hopeless, will exhaust any one.
Her handkerchief is to her eyes and every minute
or two she cascades tears.* EDWARD *goes and affectionately puts his arm round her.*

EDWARD. My dear Honor, I am sorry to be so . .
so merciless. There! . . there! [*He hands her into the
room; then turns and once more surveys the family, who
this time mostly return the compliment. Then he says
shortly.*] I think you might all sit down. [*And then.*]
Shut the door, Booth.

BOOTH. Shut the door!

EDWARD *goes close to his mother and speaks very
distinctly, very kindly.*

EDWARD. Mother, we're all going to have a little
necessary talk over matters . . now, because it's most
convenient. I hope it won't . . I hope you don't mind.
Will you come to the table?

MRS. VOYSEY *looks up as if understanding more than
he says.*

MRS. VOYSEY. Edward . .

VOL. I   U

EDWARD. Yes, mother dear?
BOOTH. [*commandingly.*] You'll sit here, mother, of course.

He places her in her accustomed chair at the foot of the table. One by one the others sit down, EDWARD *apparently last. But then he discovers that* HUGH *has lost himself in a corner of the room and is gazing into vacancy.*

EDWARD. Hugh, would you mind attending?
HUGH. What is it?
EDWARD. There's a chair.

HUGH *takes it. Then for a minute—while* EDWARD *is trying to frame in coherent sentences what he must say to them—for a minute there is silence, broken only by* HONOR'S *sniffs, which culminate at last in a noisy little cascade of tears.*

BOOTH. Honor, control yourself.

And to emphasise his own perfect control he helps himself majestically to a glass of sherry. Then says . .

BOOTH. Well, Edward?
EDWARD. I'll come straight to the point which concerns you. Our father's will gives certain sums to you all . . the gross amount would be something over a hundred thousand pounds. There will be no money.

He can get no further than the bare statement, which is received only with varying looks of bewilderment, until MRS. VOYSEY, *discovering nothing from their faces, breaks this second silence.*

MRS. VOYSEY. I didn't hear.
HUGH. [*in his mother's ear.*] Edward says there's no money.
TRENCHARD. [*precisely.*] I think you said . . " will be ".
BOOTH. [*in a tone of mitigated thunder.*] Why will there be no money?

EDWARD. [*letting himself go.*] Because every penny by right belongs to the clients father spent his life in defrauding. I mean that in its worst sense . . swindling . . thieving. I have been in the swim of it, for the past year . . oh, you don't know the sink of iniquity. And now I must collect every penny, any money that you can give me ; put the firm into bankruptcy ; pay back all we can. I'll stand my trial . . it'll come to that with me . . and as soon as possible. [*He pauses, partly for breath, and glares at them all.*] Are none of you going to speak ? Quite right, what is there to be said ? [*Then with a gentle afterthought.*] I'm sorry to hurt you, mother.

The VOYSEY *family is simply buried deep by this avalanche of horror.* MRS. VOYSEY, *though, who has been watching* EDWARD *closely, says very calmly . .*

MRS. VOYSEY. I can't hear quite all you say, but I guess what it is. You don't hurt me, Edward . . I have known of this for a long time.

EDWARD. [*with almost a cry.*] Oh, mother, did he know you knew ?

MRS. VOYSEY. What do you say ?

TRENCHARD. [*collected and dry.*] I may as well tell you, Edward, I suspected everything wasn't right about the time of my last quarrel with my father. I took care not to pursue my suspicions. Was father aware that you knew, mother ?

MRS. VOYSEY. We never discussed it. There was once a great danger, I believe . . when you were all younger . . of his being found out. But we never discussed it.

EDWARD. [*swallowing a fresh bitterness.*] I'm glad it isn't such a shock to all of you.

HUGH. [*alive to a dramatic aspect of the matter.*] My God . . before the earth has settled on his grave !

EDWARD. I thought it wrong to put off telling you.

HONOR, *the word swindling having spelt itself out in her mind, at last gives way to a burst of piteous grief.*

HONOR. Oh, poor papa ! . . poor papa !

EDWARD. [*comforting her kindly.*] Honor, we shall want your help and advice.

The Major has recovered from the shock, to swell with importance. It being necessary to make an impression he instinctively turns first to his wife.

BOOTH. I think, Emily, there was no need for you to have been present at this exposure, and that now you had better retire.

EMILY. Very well, Booth.

She gets up to go, conscious of her misdemeanour. But as she reaches the door, an awful thought strikes the Major.

BOOTH. Good Heavens . . I hope the servants haven't been listening ! See where they are, Emily . . and keep them away . . distract them. Open the door suddenly. [*She does so, more or less, and there is no one behind it.*] That's all right.

Having watched his wife's departure, he turns with gravity to his brother.

BOOTH. I have said nothing as yet, Edward. I am thinking.

TRENCHARD. [*a little impatient at this exhibition.*] That's the worst of these family practices . . a lot of money knocking around and no audit ever required. The wonder to me is to find an honest solicitor at all.

BOOTH. Really, Trenchard !

TRENCHARD. Well, do think of the temptation.

EDWARD. Why are one's clients such fools ?

TRENCHARD. The world's getting more and more into the hands of its experts, and it certainly does require a particular sort of honesty.

EDWARD. Here were all these funds simply a lucky-bag into which he dipped.

TRENCHARD. Did he keep no accounts of any sort ?

EDWARD. Scraps of paper. Most of the original

investments I can't even trace. The money doesn't exist.

BOOTH. Where's it gone?

EDWARD. [*very directly.*] You've been living on it.

BOOTH. Good God!

TRENCHARD. What can you pay in the pound?

EDWARD. As we stand? . . six or seven shillings, I daresay. But we must do better than that.

To which there is no response.

BOOTH. All this is very dreadful. Does it mean beggary for the whole family?

EDWARD. Yes, it should.

TRENCHARD. [*sharply.*] Nonsense.

EDWARD. [*joining issue at once.*] What right have we to a thing we possess?

TRENCHARD. He didn't make you an allowance, Booth . . your capital's your own, isn't it?

BOOTH. [*awkwardly placed between the two of them.*] Really . . I—I suppose so.

TRENCHARD. Then that's all right.

EDWARD. [*vehemently.*] It was stolen money, most likely.

TRENCHARD. Ah, most likely. But Booth took it in good faith.

BOOTH. I should hope so.

EDWARD. [*dwelling on the words.*] It's stolen money.

BOOTH. [*bubbling with distress.*] I say, what ought I to do?

TRENCHARD. Do . . my dear Booth? Nothing.

EDWARD. [*with great indignation.*] Trenchard, we owe reparation—

TRENCHARD. [*readily.*] Quite so, but to whom? From which client or client's account was Booth's money taken? You say yourself you don't know. Very well then!

EDWARD. [*grieved.*] Trenchard!

TRENCHARD. No, my dear Edward. The law will take anything it has a right to and all it can get; you needn't be afraid. There's no obligation, legal or moral, for any of us to throw our pounds into the wreck that they may become pence.

EDWARD. That's just what he would have said.

TRENCHARD. It's what *I* say. But what about your own position . . can we get you clear?

EDWARD. That doesn't matter.

BOOTH'S *head has been turning incessantly from one to the other and by this he is just a bristle of alarm.*

BOOTH. But I say, you know, this is awful! Will this have to be made public?

TRENCHARD. No help for it.

The Major's jaw drops; he is speechless. MRS. VOYSEY'S *dead voice steals in.*

MRS. VOYSEY. What is all this?

TRENCHARD. Edward suggests that the family should beggar itself in order to pay back to every client to whom father owed a pound perhaps ten shillings instead of seven.

MRS. VOYSEY. He will find that my estate has been kept quite separate.

EDWARD *hides his face in his hands.*

TRENCHARD. I'm very glad to hear it, mother.

MRS. VOYSEY. When Mr. Barnes died, your father agreed to appointing another trustee.

TREGONING. [*diffidently.*] I suppose, Edward, I'm involved?

EDWARD. [*lifting his head quickly.*] Denis, I hope not. I didn't know that anything of yours—

TREGONING. Yes . . all I got under my aunt's will.

EDWARD. See how things are . . I've not found a trace of that yet. We'll hope for the best.

TREGONING. [*setting his teeth.*] It can't be helped.

MAJOR BOOTH *leans over the table and speaks in the loudest of whispers.*

BOOTH. Let me advise you to say nothing of this to Ethel at such a critical time.

TREGONING. Thank you, Booth, naturally I shan't.

HUGH, *by a series of contortions, has lately been giving evidence of a desire or intention to say something.*

EDWARD. Well, what is it, Hugh?

HUGH. I have been wondering . . if he can hear this conversation.

Up to now it has all been meaningless to HONOR, *in her nervous dilapidation, but this remark brings a fresh burst of tears.*

HONOR. Oh, poor papa . . poor papa!

MRS. VOYSEY. I think I'll go to my room. I can't hear what any of you are saying. Edward can tell me afterwards.

EDWARD. Would you like to go too, Honor?

HONOR. [*through her sobs.*] Yes, please, I would.

TREGONING. I'll get out, Edward. Whatever you think fit to do . . Oh, well, I suppose there's only one thing to be done.

EDWARD. Only that.

TREGONING. I wish I were in a better position as to work, for Ethel's sake and—and the child's.

EDWARD. Shall I speak to Trenchard?

TREGONING. No . . he knows I exist in a wig and gown. If I can be useful to him, he'll be useful to me, I daresay. Good-bye, Hugh. Good-bye, Booth.

By this time MRS. VOYSEY *and* HONOR *have been got out of the room:* TREGONING *follows them. So the four brothers are left together.* HUGH *is vacant,* EDWARD *does not speak,* BOOTH *looks at* TRENCHARD, *who settles himself to acquire information.*

TRENCHARD. How long have things been wrong?

EDWARD. He told me the trouble began in his father's time and that he'd been battling with it ever since.

TRENCHARD. [*smiling.*] Oh, come now . . that's impossible.

EDWARD. I believed him! Now I look through the papers, such as they are, I can find only one irregularity that's more than ten years old, and that's only to do with old George Booth's business.

BOOTH. But the Pater never touched his money . . why, he was a personal friend.

EDWARD. Did you hear what Denis said?

TRENCHARD. Very curious his evolving that fiction about his father . . I wonder why. I remember the old man. He was honest as the day.

EDWARD. To get my sympathy, I suppose.

TRENCHARD. I think one can trace the psychology of it deeper than that. It would give a finish to the situation . . his handing on to you an inheritance he had received. You know every criminal has a touch of the artist in him.

HUGH. [*suddenly roused.*] That's true.

TRENCHARD. What position did you take up when he told you?

EDWARD. [*shrugging.*] You know what the Pater was.

TRENCHARD. Well . . what did you attempt to do?

EDWARD. I urged him at least to put some of the smaller people right. He said . . he said that would be penny wise and pound foolish. So I've done what I could myself . . since he's been ill . . Nothing to count . .

TRENCHARD. With your own money?

EDWARD. The little I had. He kept tight hold to the end.

TRENCHARD. Can you prove that you did that?

EDWARD. I suppose I could.

TRENCHARD. It's a good point.

BOOTH. [*not to be quite left out.*] Yes, I must say—

TRENCHARD. You ought to have written him a letter, and left the firm the moment you found out. Even then, legally . . ! But as he was your father . . What was his object in telling you? He didn't think you'd take a hand?

EDWARD. I've thought of every reason . . and now I really believe it was that he might have some one to boast to of his financial exploits.

TRENCHARD. [*appreciatively.*] I daresay.

BOOTH. Scarcely a thing to boast of!

TRENCHARD. Depends on the point of view.

EDWARD. Then, of course, he always protested that things would come right . . that he'd clear the firm and have a hundred thousand to the good. Or that if he were not spared I might do it. But he must have known that was impossible.

TRENCHARD. But there's the gambler all over.

EDWARD. Drawing up this will!

TRENCHARD. Childish!

EDWARD. I'm the sole executor.

TRENCHARD. So I should think! Was I down for anything?

EDWARD. No.

TRENCHARD. [*without resentment.*] How he did hate me!

EDWARD. You're safe from the results of his affection anyway.

TRENCHARD. What on earth made you stay in the firm once you knew?

EDWARD *does not answer for a moment.*

EDWARD. I thought I might prevent things from getting any worse. I think I did . .

TRENCHARD. You knew the personal risk you were running?

EDWARD. [*bowing his head.*] Yes.

TRENCHARD, *the only one of the three who comprehends, looks at his brother for a moment with something that might almost be admiration. Then he stirs himself.*

TRENCHARD. I must be off. Work waiting . . end of term, you know.

BOOTH. Shall I walk to the station with you?

TRENCHARD. I'll spend a few minutes with mother. [*He says, at the door, very respectfully.*] You'll count on my professional assistance, please, Edward.

EDWARD. [*simply.*] Thank you, Trenchard.

So TRENCHARD *goes. And the Major, who has been endeavouring to fathom his final attitude, then comments—*

BOOTH. No heart, y'know! Great brain! If it hadn't been for that distressing quarrel he might have saved our poor father. Don't you think so, Edward?

EDWARD. Perhaps.

HUGH. [*giving vent to his thoughts at last with something of a relish.*] The more I think this out, the more devilishly humorous it gets. Old Booth breaking down by the grave . . Colpus reading the service . .

EDWARD. Yes, the Vicar's badly hit.

HUGH. Oh, the Pater had managed his business for years.

BOOTH. Good God . . how shall we ever look old Booth in the face again?

EDWARD. I don't worry about him; he can die quite comfortably enough on our six shillings in the pound. It's one or two of the smaller fry who will suffer.

BOOTH. Now, just explain to me . . I didn't interrupt while Trenchard was talking . . of what exactly did this defrauding consist?

EDWARD. Speculating with a client's capital . . pocketing the gains . . you cut the losses; and you keep paying the client his ordinary income.

BOOTH. So that he doesn't find it out?

EDWARD. Quite so.

BOOTH. In point of fact, he doesn't suffer?

EDWARD. He doesn't suffer till he finds it out.

BOOTH. And all that's wrong now is that some of the capital is missing.

EDWARD. [*half amused, half amazed at this process of reasoning.*] Yes, that's all that's wrong.

BOOTH. What is the—ah—deficit? [*The word rolls from his tongue.*]

EDWARD. Anything between two and three hundred thousand pounds.

BOOTH. [*very impressed and not unfavourably.*] Dear me . . this is a big affair!

HUGH. [*following his own line of thought.*] Quite apart from the rights and wrongs of this, only a very able man could have kept a straight face to the world all these years, as the Pater did.

BOOTH. I suppose he sometimes made money by these speculations.

EDWARD. Very often. His own expenditure was heavy, as you know.

BOOTH. [*with gratitude for favours received.*] He was a very generous man.

HUGH. Did nobody ever suspect?

EDWARD. You see, Hugh, when there was any pressing danger . . if a big trust had to be wound up . . he'd make a great effort and put the accounts straight.

BOOTH. Then he did put some accounts straight?

EDWARD. Yes, when he couldn't help himself.

BOOTH *looks very inquiring and then squares himself up to the subject.*

BOOTH. Now look here, Edward. You told us that he told you that it was the object of his life to put these accounts straight. Then you laughed at that. Now you tell me that he did put some accounts straight.

EDWARD. [*wearily.*] My dear Booth, you don't understand.

BOOTH. Well, let me understand . . I am anxious to understand.

EDWARD. We can't pay ten shillings in the pound.

BOOTH. That's very dreadful. But do you know that there wasn't a time when we couldn't have paid five?

EDWARD. [*acquiescent.*] Perhaps.

BOOTH. Very well then! If it was true about his father and all that . . and why shouldn't we believe him if we can? . . and he did effect an improvement, that's to his credit, isn't it? Let us at least be just, Edward.

EDWARD. [*patiently polite.*] I am sorry if I seem unjust. But he has left me in a rather unfortunate position.

BOOTH. Yes, his death was a tragedy. It seems to me that if he had been spared he might have succeeded at length in this tremendous task and restored to us our family honour.

EDWARD. Yes, Booth, he spoke very feelingly of that.

BOOTH. [*irony lost upon him.*] I can well believe it. And I can tell you that now . . I may be right or I may be wrong . . I am feeling far less concerned about the clients' money than I am at the terrible blow to the Family which this exposure will strike. Money, after all, can to a certain extent be done without . . but Honour—

This is too much for EDWARD.

EDWARD. Our honour! Does any one of you mean to give me a single penny towards undoing all the wrong that has been done?

BOOTH. I take Trenchard's word for it that that would be illegal.

EDWARD. Well . . don't talk to me of honour.

BOOTH. [*somewhat nettled at this outburst.*] I am speaking of the public exposure. Edward, can't that be prevented?

EDWARD. [*with quick suspicion.*] How?

BOOTH. Well . . how was it being prevented before he died—before we knew anything about it?

EDWARD. [*appealing to the spirits that watch over him.*]

Oh, listen to this! First Trenchard . . and now you! You've the poison in your blood, every one of you. Who am I to talk? I daresay so have I.

BOOTH. [*reprovingly*.] I am beginning to think that you have worked yourself into rather an hysterical state over this unhappy business.

EDWARD. [*rating him*.] Perhaps you'd have been glad . . glad if I'd held my tongue and gone on lying and cheating . . and married and begotten a son to go on lying and cheating after me . . and to pay you your interest in the lie and the cheat.

BOOTH. [*with statesmanlike calm*.] Look here, Edward, this rhetoric is exceedingly out of place. The simple question before us is . . What is the best course to pursue?

EDWARD. There is no question before us. There's only one course to pursue.

BOOTH. [*crushingly*.] You will let me speak, please. In so far as our poor father was dishonest to his clients, I pray that he may be forgiven. In so far as he spent his life honestly endeavouring to right a wrong which he had found already committed . . I forgive him. I admire him, Edward. And I feel it my duty to—er—reprobate most strongly the—er—gusto with which you have been holding him up in memory to us . . ten minutes after we have stood round his grave . . as a monster of wickedness. I think I may say I knew him as well as you . . better. And . . thank God! . . there was not between him and me this—this unhappy business to warp my judgement of him. [*He warms to his subject*.] Did you ever know a more charitable man . . a larger-hearted? He was a faithful husband . . and what a father to all of us, putting us out into the world and fully intending to leave us comfortably settled there. Further . . as I see this matter, Edward . . when as a young man he was told this terrible secret and entrusted with such a frightful task .. did he turn his back on it like a coward? No. He went through it heroically to the end of his life. And as he died I imagine there was no more torturing thought than that he had left his work unfinished. [*He is very satisfied with this peroration.*] And now if all these clients can be kept receiving their natural incomes and if father's plan could be carried out of gradually replacing the capital—

EDWARD *at this raises his head and stares with horror.*

EDWARD. You're asking me to carry on this .. Oh, you don't know what you're talking about!

The Major, having talked himself back to a proper eminence, remains good-tempered.

BOOTH. Well, I'm not a conceited man .. but I do think that I can understand a simple financial problem when it has been explained to me.

EDWARD. You don't know the nerve .. the unscrupulous daring it requires to—

BOOTH. Of course, if you're going to argue round your own incompetence—

EDWARD. [*very straight.*] D'you want your legacy?

BOOTH. [*with dignity.*] In one moment I shall get very angry. Here am I doing my best to help you and your clients .. and there you sit imputing to me the most sordid motives. Do you suppose I should touch, or allow to be touched, the money which father has left us till every client's claim was satisfied?

EDWARD. My dear Booth, I know you mean well—

BOOTH. I'll come down to your office and work with you.

At this cheerful prospect even poor EDWARD *can't help smiling.*

EDWARD. I'm sure you would.

BOOTH. [*feeling that it is a chance lost.*] If the Pater had ever consulted me ..

At this point TRENCHARD *looks round the door to say* . .

TRENCHARD. Are you coming, Booth?

BOOTH. Yes, certainly. I'll talk this over with Trenchard. [*As he gets up and automatically stiffens, he is reminded of the occasion and his voice drops.*] I say . . we've been speaking very loud. You must do nothing rash. I've no doubt he and I can devise something which will obviate . . and then I'm sure I shall convince you . . [*Glancing into the hall he apparently catches* TRENCHARD'S *impatient eye, for he departs abruptly saying* . .] All right, Trenchard, you've eight minutes.

BOOTH'S *departure leaves* HUGH, *at any rate, really at his ease.*

HUGH. This is an experience for you, Edward!

EDWARD. [*bitterly.*] And I feared what the shock might be to you all! Booth has made a good recovery.

HUGH. You wouldn't have him miss such a chance of booming at us.

EDWARD. It's strange that people will believe you can do right by means which they know to be wrong.

HUGH. [*taking great interest in this.*] Come, what do we know about right and wrong? Let's say legal and illegal. You're so down on the governor because he has trespassed against the etiquette of your own profession. But now he's dead . . and if there weren't the scandal to think of . . it's no use the rest of us pretending to feel him a criminal, because we don't. Which just shows that money . . and property—

At this point he becomes conscious that ALICE MAITLAND *is standing behind him, her eyes fixed on his brother. So he interrupts himself to ask* . .

HUGH. D'you want to speak to Edward?

ALICE. Please, Hugh.

HUGH. I'll go.

He goes, a little martyr-like, to conclude the evolution

of his theory in soliloquy ; his usual fate. ALICE *still looks at* EDWARD *with soft eyes, and he at her rather appealingly.*

ALICE. Auntie has told me.

EDWARD. He was fond of you. Don't think worse of him than you can help.

ALICE. I'm thinking of you.

EDWARD. I may just escape.

ALICE. So Trenchard says.

EDWARD. My hands are clean, Alice.

ALICE. [*her voice falling lovingly.*] I know that.

EDWARD. Mother's not very upset.

ALICE. She had expected a smash in his lifetime.

EDWARD. I'm glad that didn't happen.

ALICE. Yes. I've put Honor to bed. It was a mercy to tell her just at this moment. She can grieve for his death and his disgrace at the same time . . and the one grief will soften the other perhaps.

EDWARD. Oh, they're all shocked enough at the disgrace . . but will they open their purses to lessen the disgrace?

ALICE. Will it seem less disgraceful to have stolen ten thousand pounds than twenty?

EDWARD. I should think so.

ALICE. I should think so, but I wonder if that's the Law. If it isn't, Trenchard wouldn't consider the point. I'm sure Public Opinion doesn't say so . . and that's what Booth is considering.

EDWARD. [*with contempt.*] Yes.

ALICE. [*ever so gently ironical.*] Well, he's in the Army . . he's almost in Society . . and he has to get on in both; one mustn't blame him. Of course if the money could have been given back with a flourish of trumpets . . ! But even then I doubt whether the advertisement would bring in what it cost.

EDWARD. [*very serious.*] But when one thinks how the money was obtained!

ALICE. When one thinks how most money is obtained !

EDWARD. They've not earned it!

ALICE. [*her eyes humorous.*] If they had they might have given it you and earned more. Did I ever tell you what my guardian said to me when I came of age ?

EDWARD. I'm thankful your money's out of the mess.

ALICE. It wouldn't have been, but I was made to look after it myself . . much against my will. My guardian was a person of great character and no principles, the best and most lovable man I've ever met . . I'm sorry you never knew him, Edward . . and he said once to me . . You've no particular right to your money. You've not earned it or deserved it in any way. And don't be either surprised or annoyed when any enterprising person tries to get it from you. He has at least as much right to it as you have . . if he can use it better perhaps he has more right. Shocking sentiments, aren't they ? But perhaps that's why I've less patience with some of these clients than you have, Edward.

EDWARD *shakes his head, treating these paradoxes as they deserve.*

EDWARD. Alice . . one or two of them will be beggared.

ALICE. [*sincerely.*] Yes, that is bad. What's to be done ?

EDWARD. There's old nurse . . with her poor little savings gone !

ALICE. Surely that can be helped ?

EDWARD. The Law's no respecter of persons . . that's its boast. Old Booth with more than he wants will keep enough and to spare. My old nurse, with just enough, may starve. But it'll be a relief to clear out this nest of lies, even though one suffers one's self. I've been ashamed to walk into that office, Alice . . I'll hold my head high in prison though.

He shakes himself stiffly erect, his chin high. ALICE *quizzes him.*

VOL. I   X

ALICE. Edward, I'm afraid you're feeling heroic.

EDWARD. I!

ALICE. You looked quite like Booth for the moment. [*This effectually removes the starch.*] Please don't glory in your martyrdom. It would be very stupid to send you to prison and you must do your best to keep out. [*She goes on very practically.*] We were thinking if anything could be done for these people who'll be beggared.

EDWARD. It isn't that I'm not sorry for them all . .

ALICE. Of course not.

EDWARD. I suppose I was feeling heroic. I didn't mean to.

He has become a little like a child with her.

ALICE. It's the worst of acting on principle . . one is so apt to think more of one's attitude than of the use of what one is doing.

EDWARD. Fraud must be exposed.

ALICE. And people must be ruined . . !

EDWARD. What else is there to be done?

ALICE. Well . . have you thought?

EDWARD. There's nothing else to be done.

ALICE. No. When on principle there's nothing to be done I'm afraid I've no use for that principle.

He looks at her; she is smiling, it is true, but smiling quite gravely. EDWARD *is puzzled. Then the yeast of her suggestion begins to work in his mind slowly, perversely at first.*

EDWARD. Unless you expect me to take Booth's advice . . go on with the game . . as an honest cheat . . plunge, I suppose just twice as wildly as my father did on the chance that things might come right . . which he never bothered his head about. Booth offers to come to the office and assist me.

ALICE. There's something attractive about Booth at the right distance.

EDWARD. Oh . . give him the money . . send him to the City or Monte Carlo . . he might bring it off. He's like my father . . believes in himself.

ALICE. These credulous men!

EDWARD. [*ignoring her little joke.*] But don't think I've any talents that way, principles or no. What have I done so far? Sat in the shame of it for a year. I did take a hand . . if you knew what it felt like . . I managed to stop one affair going from bad to worse.

ALICE. If that was the best you could do wasn't it worth doing? Never mind your feelings.

EDWARD. And that may cost me . . at the best I'll be struck off . . one's livelihood gone.

ALICE. The cost is your own affair.

She is watching him, stilly and closely. Suddenly his face lights a little and he turns to her.

EDWARD. I'll tell you what I could do.

ALICE. Yes.

EDWARD. It's just as irregular.

ALICE. That doesn't shock me . . I'm lawless by birthright, being a woman.

EDWARD. There are four or five accounts I believe I could get quite square. Mrs. Travers . . well, she'd never starve, but I'd like to see those two young Lyndhursts safe. There's money to play with, Heaven knows. It'd take a year or more to get it right and cover the tracks. Cover the tracks . . sounds well, doesn't it?

ALICE. Then you'd give yourself up as you'd meant to do now?

EDWARD. Go bankrupt.

ALICE. It'd be worse for you then at the trial?

EDWARD. [*with a touch of another sort of pride.*] You said that was my affair.

ALICE. [*pain in her voice and eyes.*] Oh, Edward!

EDWARD. Shall I do it?

ALICE. [*turning away.*] Why must you ask me?

EDWARD. If you've taken my principles from me, give me advice in exchange.

ALICE. [*after a moment.*] No . . you must decide for yourself.

He jumps up and begins to pace about, doubtful, distressed.

EDWARD. Ah, but . . it means still lying and shuffling! And I'd sworn to be free of that. And . . it wouldn't be easy. I'm no good at that sort of devilment. I should muddle it and fail.

ALICE. Would you?

He catches a look from her.

EDWARD. I might not.

ALICE. And do you need success for a lure . . like a common man?

EDWARD. You want me to try?

For answer, she dares only put out her hand, and he takes it.

ALICE. Oh, my dear . . cousin!

EDWARD. [*excitedly.*] My people must hold their tongues. I needn't have told them.

ALICE. Don't tell them this! They won't understand. *I* shall be jealous if you tell them.

EDWARD. [*looking at her as she at him.*] You'll have the right to be. If I bring it off the glory shall be yours.

ALICE. Thank you. I've always wanted to have something useful to my credit . . and I'd almost given up hoping.

Then suddenly his face changes, his voice changes and he grips the hand he is holding so tightly as to hurt her.

EDWARD. Ah, no, no, no, no, if my father's story were true . . perhaps he began like this. Doing the right thing in the wrong way . . then doing the wrong thing . . then bringing himself to what he was . . and so me to this. [*He flings away from her.*] No, Alice, I won't . . I won't do it. I daren't take that first step down. There's a worse risk than failure . . I might succeed.

    ALICE *stands very still, looking at him.*

    ALICE. Yes, that's the big risk. Well . . I'll take it.

    He turns to her, in wonder.

    EDWARD. You?

    ALICE. I'll risk your becoming a bad man. That's a big risk for me.

    He understands, and is calmed and made happy.

    EDWARD. Then there is no more to be said, is there?

    ALICE. Not now. [*As she drops this gentle hint she hears something—the hall door opening.*] Here's Booth back again.

    EDWARD. [*with a really mischievous grin.*] He'll be so glad he's convinced me.

    ALICE. I must go back to Honor, poor girl. I wonder she has a tear left.

    She leaves him, briskly, brightly; leaves her cousin with his mouth set and a light in his eyes.

THE FOURTH ACT

MR. VOYSEY'S *room at the office is* EDWARD'S *now. It has somehow lost that brilliancy which the old man's occupation seemed to give it. Perhaps it is only because this December morning is dull and depressing, but the fire isn't bright and the panels and windows don't shine as they did. There are no roses on the table either.* EDWARD, *walking in as his father did, hanging his hat and coat where his father's used to hang, is certainly the palest shadow of that other masterful presence. A depressed, drooping shadow too. This may be what* PEACEY *feels, if no more, for he looks very surly as he obeys the old routine of following his chief to this room on his arrival. Nor has* EDWARD *so much as a glance for his clerk. They exchange the formalest of greetings.* EDWARD *sits joylessly to his desk, on which the morning's pile of letters lies, unopened now.*

PEACEY. Good morning, sir.

EDWARD. Good morning, Peacey. Any notes for me?

PEACEY. Well, I've hardly been through the letters yet, sir.

EDWARD. [*his eyebrows meeting.*] Oh . . and I'm half an hour late myself this morning.

PEACEY. I'm very sorry, sir.

EDWARD. If Mr. Bullen calls, you had better show him those papers I gave you. Write to Metcalfe as soon as possible; say I've seen Mr. Vickery myself this morning and the houses will not be proceeded with. Better show me the letter.

PEACEY. Very good, sir.

ACT IV] THE VOYSEY INHERITANCE 311

EDWARD. That's all, thank you.
PEACEY *gets to the door, where he stops, looking not only surly but nervous now.*
PEACEY. May I speak to you a moment, sir?
EDWARD. Certainly.
PEACEY, *after a moment, makes an effort, purses his mouth and begins.*
PEACEY. Bills are beginning to come in upon me as is usual at this season, sir. My son's allowance at Cambridge is now rather a heavy item of my expenditure. I hope that the custom of the firm isn't to be neglected now that you are the head of it, Mr. Edward . . . Two hundred your father always made it at Christmas . . in notes if you please.
Towards the end of this EDWARD *begins to pay great attention. When he answers his voice is harsh.*
EDWARD. Oh, to be sure . . your hush money.
PEACEY. [*bridling.*] That's not a very pleasant word.
EDWARD. This is an unpleasant subject.
PEACEY. Well, it's not one I wish to discuss. Your father always gave me the notes in an envelope when he shook hands with me at Christmas.
EDWARD. Why notes now? Why not a rise in salary?
PEACEY. Mr. Voysey's custom, sir, from before my time . . my father . .
EDWARD. Yes. It's an hereditary pull you have over the firm, isn't it?
PEACEY. I remember my father only saying to me when he retired . . been dead twenty-six years, Mr. Edward . . I have told the governor you know what I know; then Mr. Voysey saying . . I treat you as I did your father, Peacey. We'd never another word with him on the subject.
EDWARD. A decent arrangement . . and the cheapest, no doubt. Of the raising of salaries there might have been no end.

PEACEY. Mr. Edward, that's uncalled for. We have served you and yours most faithfully. I know my father would sooner have cut off his hand than do anything to embarrass the firm.

EDWARD. But business is business, Peacey. Surely he could have had a partnership for the asking.

PEACEY. Ah, that's another matter, sir.

EDWARD. Well . .

PEACEY. A matter of principle, if you'll excuse me. I must not be taken to approve of the firm's conduct. Nor did my dear father approve. And at anything like partnership he would have drawn the line.

EDWARD. I beg your pardon.

PEACEY. Well, that's all right, sir. Always a bit of friction in coming to an understanding about anything, isn't there, sir?

He is going when EDWARD'S *question stops him.*

EDWARD. Why didn't you speak about this last Christmas?

PEACEY. You were so upset at your father's death.

EDWARD. My father died the August before that.

PEACEY. Well . . truthfully, Mr. Edward?

EDWARD. As truthfully as you think suitable.

The irony of this is wasted on PEACEY, *who becomes pleasantly candid.*

PEACEY. Well, I'd always thought there must be a smash when your father died . . but it didn't come. I couldn't make you out. But then again by Christmas you seemed all on edge and I thought anything might happen. So I kept quiet and said nothing.

EDWARD. I see. Your son's at Cambridge?

PEACEY. Yes.

EDWARD. I wonder you didn't bring him into the firm.

PEACEY. [*taking this very kind.*] Thank you. But I hope James may go to the bar. Our only son . . I didn't grudge him my small savings to help him wait for his chance . . ten years if need be.

EDWARD. I hope he'll make his mark before then. I'm glad to have had this talk with you, Peacey. I'm sorry you can't have the money you want.

He returns to his letters, a little steely-eyed. PEACEY, *quite at his ease, makes for the door yet again, saying. .*

PEACEY. Oh, any time will do, sir.

EDWARD. You can't have it at all.

PEACEY. [*brought up short.*] Can't I?

EDWARD. [*very decidedly indeed.*] No . . I made up my mind about this eighteen months ago. My father had warned me, but since his death the trust business of the firm is not conducted as it used to be. We no longer make illicit profits out of our clients. There are none for you to share.

Having thus given the explanation he considers due, he goes on with his work. But PEACEY *has flushed up.*

PEACEY. Look here, Mr. Edward, I'm sorry we began this discussion. You'll give me my two hundred as usual, please, and we'll drop the subject.

EDWARD. You can drop the subject.

PEACEY. [*his voice rising sharply.*] I want the money. I think it is not gentlemanly in you, Mr. Edward, to try like this and get out of paying it me. Your father would never have made such an excuse.

EDWARD. [*flabbergasted.*] Do you think I'm lying to you?

PEACEY. [*with a deprecating swallow.*] I've no wish to criticise your statements or your actions at all, sir. It was no concern of mine how your father treated his clients.

EDWARD. And now it's not to concern you how honest I am. You want your money just the same.

PEACEY. Well, don't be sarcastic . . a man does get used to a state of affairs whatever it may be.

EDWARD. [*with considerable force.*] My friend, if I

drop sarcasm I shall have to tell you very candidly what I think of you.

PEACEY. That I'm a thief because I've taken money from a thief?

EDWARD. Worse than a thief. You're content that others should steal for you.

PEACEY. And who isn't?

EDWARD *is really pleased with the aptness of this. He at once changes his tone, which indeed had become rather bullying.*

EDWARD. What, my dear Peacey, you study sociology? Well, it's too big a question to discuss now. But I'm afraid the application of this bit of it is that I have for the moment, at some inconvenience to myself, ceased to receive stolen goods, so I am in a position to throw a stone at you. I have thrown it.

PEACEY, *who would far sooner be bullied than talked to like this, turns very sulky.*

PEACEY. Then I resign my position here.

EDWARD. Very well.

PEACEY. And I happen to think the secret's worth its price.

EDWARD. Perhaps some one will pay it you.

PEACEY. [*feebly threatening.*] Don't presume upon it's not being worth my while to make use of what I know.

EDWARD. [*not unkindly.*] My good Peacey, it happens to be the truth I told you just now. Well, how on earth do you suppose you can successfully blackmail a man who has so much to gain by exposure and so little to lose as I?

PEACEY. [*peeving.*] I don't want to ruin you, sir, and I have a great regard for the firm . . but you must see that I can't have my income reduced in this way without a struggle.

EDWARD. [*with great cheerfulness.*] Very well, my friend, struggle away.

PEACEY. [*his voice rising high and thin.*] Well, is it

fair dealing on your part to dock the money suddenly like this? I have been counting on it most of the year, and I have been led into heavy expenses. Why couldn't you have warned me?

EDWARD. Yes, that's true, Peacey, it was stupid of me. I'm sorry.

PEACEY *is a little comforted by this quite candid acknowledgement.*

PEACEY. Things may get easier for you by and bye.

EDWARD. I hope so.

PEACEY. Will you reconsider the matter then?

At this gentle insinuation EDWARD *looks up exasperated.*

EDWARD. Then you don't believe what I told you?

PEACEY. Yes, I do.

EDWARD. But you think that the fascination of swindling one's clients will ultimately prove irresistible?

PEACEY. That's what your father found, I suppose you know.

This gives EDWARD *such pause that he drops his masterful tone.*

EDWARD. I didn't.

PEACEY. He got things as right as rain once.

EDWARD. Did he?

PEACEY. So my father told me. But he started again.

EDWARD. Are you sure of this?

PEACEY. [*expanding pleasantly.*] Well, sir, I knew your father pretty well. When I first came into the firm, now, I simply hated him. He was that sour; so snappy with every one . . as if he had a grievance against the whole world.

EDWARD. [*pensively.*] It seems he had in those days.

PEACEY. His dealings with his clients were no business of mine. I speak as I find. After a bit he was very kind to me, thoughtful and considerate. He got to be so pleasant and generous to every one—

EDWARD. That you have great hopes of me yet?

PEACEY. [*who has a simple mind.*] No, Mr. Edward, no. You're different from your father . . one must make up one's mind to that. And you may believe me or not, but I should be very glad to know that the firm was solvent and going straight. I'm getting on in years myself now. I'm not much longer for the business, and there have been times when I have sincerely regretted my connection with it. If you'll let me say so, I think it's very noble of you to have undertaken the work you have. [*Then, as everything seems smooth again.*] And Mr. Edward, if you'll give me enough to cover this year's extra expense I think I may promise you that I shan't expect money again.

EDWARD. [*good-tempered, as he would speak to an importunate child.*] No, Peacey, no!

PEACEY. [*fretful again.*] Well, sir, you make things very difficult for me.

EDWARD. Here's a letter from Mr. Cartwright which you might attend to. If he wants an appointment with me, don't make one till the New Year. His case can't come on before February.

PEACEY. [*taking the letter.*] I show myself anxious to meet you in every way—[*he is handed another.*]

EDWARD. " Perceval Building Estate " . . that's yours too.

PEACEY. [*putting them both down resolutely.*] But I refuse to be ignored. I must consider my whole position. I hope I may not be tempted to make use of the power I possess. But if I am driven to proceed to extremities . .

EDWARD. [*breaking in upon this bunch of tags.*] My dear Peacey, don't talk nonsense . . you couldn't proceed to an extremity to save your life. You've taken this money irresponsibly for all these years. You'll find you're no longer capable even of such a responsible act as tripping up your neighbour.

This does completely upset the gentle blackmailer. He loses one grievance in another.

PEACEY. Really, Mr. Edward, I am a considerably older man than you, and I think that whatever our positions—

EDWARD. Don't let us argue, Peacey. You're quite at liberty to do whatever you think worth your while.

PEACEY. It's not the money, I can do without that, but these personalities—

EDWARD. I apologise for them. Don't forget the letters.

PEACEY. I will not, sir.

He takes them with great dignity and is leaving the room.

PEACEY. Here's Mr. Hugh waiting.

EDWARD. To see me? Ask him in.

PEACEY. Come in, Mr. Hugh, please.

HUGH *comes in,* PEACEY *holding the door for him with a frigid politeness of which he is quite oblivious. At this final slight* PEACEY *goes out in dudgeon.*

EDWARD. How are you, Hugh?

HUGH. Good Lord!

And he throws himself into the chair by the fire.
EDWARD, *quite used to this sort of thing, goes quietly on with his work, adding encouragingly after a moment. .*

EDWARD. How's Beatrice?

HUGH. She's very busy.

He studies his boots with the gloomiest expression. And indeed, they are very dirty and his turned-up trousers are muddy at the edge. They are dark trousers and well cut, but he wears with them a loose coat and waistcoat of a peculiar light brown check. Add to this the roughest of overcoats and a very soft hat. Add also the fact that he doesn't shave well or regularly and that his hair wants cutting, and HUGH'S *appearance this morning is described. As he is quite capable of sitting silently by the fire for a whole morning* EDWARD *asks him at last* . .

EDWARD. What d'you want ?

HUGH. [*with vehemence.*] I want a machine gun planted in Regent Street . . and one in the Haymarket . . and one in Leicester Square and one in the Strand . . and a dozen in the City. An earthquake would be simpler. Or why not a nice clean tidal wave ? It's no good preaching and patching up any longer, Edward. We must begin afresh. Don't you feel, even in your calmer moments, that this whole country is simply hideous ? The other nations must look after themselves. I'm patriotic . . I only ask that we should be destroyed.

EDWARD. It has been promised.

HUGH. I'm sick of waiting. [*Then as* EDWARD *says nothing.*] You say this is the cry of the weak man in despair ! I wouldn't be anything but a weak man in this world. I wouldn't be a king, I wouldn't be rich . . I wouldn't be a Borough Councillor . . I should be so ashamed. I've walked here this morning from Hampstead. I started to curse because the streets were dirty. You'd think that an Empire could keep its streets clean ! But then I saw that the children were dirty too.

EDWARD. That's because of the streets.

HUGH. Yes, it's holiday time. Those that can cross a road safely are doing some work now . . earning some money. You'd think a governing race, grabbing responsibilities, might care for its children.

EDWARD. Come, we educate them now. And I don't think many work in holiday time.

HUGH. [*encouraged by contradiction.*] Education ! What's that ? Joining the great conspiracy which we call our civilisation. But one mustn't. One must stand aside and give the show away. By the bye, that's what I've come for.

EDWARD. [*pleasantly.*] What? I thought you'd only come to talk.

HUGH. Take that money of mine for your clients. You ought to have had it when you asked for it. It has never belonged to me, in any real . . in any spiritual sense, so it has been just a clog to my life.

EDWARD. [*surprised.*] My dear Hugh . . this is very generous of you.

HUGH. Not a bit. I only want to start fresh and free.

EDWARD. [*sitting back from his work.*] Hugh, do you really think our money carries a curse with it?

HUGH. [*with great violence.*] Think! I'm the proof of it! Look at me! I felt I must create or die. I said I'd be an artist. The governor gave me a hundred and fifty a year . . the rent of a studio and the price of a velvet coat he thought it; that was all he knew about art. But my respectable training got me engaged and married. Marriage in a studio puzzled the governor, so he guessed it at two hundred and fifty a year . . and looked for lay-figure babies, I suppose. Ha, ha! Well, I've learnt my job. I work in a sort of way, Edward, though you mightn't think it. Well, what have I really learnt . . about myself . . that's the only learning . . that there's nothing I can do or be but reflects our drawing-room at Chislehurst.

EDWARD. [*considering.*] What do you earn in a year? I doubt if you can afford to give this up.

HUGH. Oh, Edward . . you clank the chain with the best of them. Afford! If I can't get free from these crippling advantages . .! Unless I find out what I'm worth in myself . . whether I even exist or not . .! Am I only a pretence of a man animated by an income?

EDWARD. But you can't return to nature on the London pavements.

HUGH. No. Nor in England at all . . it's nothing but a big back garden. [*Now he collects himself for a final outburst.*] Is there no place on this earth where a man can prove his right to live by some other means than robbing his neighbour? Put me there naked and penniless. Put me to that test. If I can't answer it, then turn down your thumb . . Oh God . . and I won't complain.

EDWARD *waits till the effects of this explosion are over.*

EDWARD. And what does Beatrice say to your emigrating to the backwoods . . if that is exactly what you mean?

HUGH. Now that we're separating—

EDWARD. [*taken aback.*] What?

HUGH. We mean to separate.

EDWARD. The first I've heard of it.

HUGH. Beatrice is making some money by her books, so it has become possible.

EDWARD. [*humorously.*] Have you told any one yet?

HUGH. We must now, I suppose.

EDWARD. Say nothing at home until after Christmas.

HUGH. They'll insist on discussing it solemnly. Ar-r-r. [*Then he whistles.*] Emily knows!

EDWARD. [*having considered.*] I shan't take your money . . there's no need. All the good has been done that I wanted to do. No one will be quite beggared now. So why should you be?

HUGH. [*with clumsy affection.*] We've taken a fine lot of interest in your labours, haven't we, Hercules?

EDWARD. You hold your tongue about the office affairs, don't you? It's not through one of us it should come out, and I've told you more than Booth and the others.

HUGH. When will you be quit of the beastly business?

EDWARD. [*becoming reserved and cold at once.*] Some day.

HUGH. What do you gain by hanging on now?

EDWARD. Occupation.

HUGH. But, Edward, it must be an awfully wearying state of things. I suppose any moment a policeman may knock at the door . . so to speak?

EDWARD. [*appreciating the figure of speech.*] Any moment. I take no precautions. I made up my mind that at least I wouldn't lower myself to that. And perhaps it's why the policeman doesn't come. At first I listened for him, day by day. Then I said to myself . . next week. But a year has gone by and more. I've ceased expecting to hear the knock at all.

HUGH. But look here . . is all this worth while, and have you the right to make a mean thing of your life like this?

EDWARD. Does my life matter?

HUGH. Well . . of course!

EDWARD. It's so much easier to believe not. The world that you kick against is using me up. A little wantonly . . a little needlessly, I do think. But let her. As I sit here now drudging honestly, I declare I begin to understand my father. But no doubt, it's all I'm fit for . . to nurse fool's money.

HUGH. [*responding at once to this vein.*] Nonsense. We all want a lesson in values. We're never taught what is worth having and what isn't. Why should your real happiness be sacrificed to the sham happiness which people have invested in the firm? I've never believed that money was valuable. I remember once giving a crossing-sweeper a sovereign. The sovereign was nothing. But the sensation I gave him was an intrinsically valuable thing.

He is fearfully pleased with his essay in philosophy.

EDWARD. And he could buy other sensations with the sovereign.

HUGH. But none like the first. You mean to stay here till something happens?

EDWARD. I do. This is what I'm brought to. No more good to be done. And I haven't the faith in myself to do wrong. And it's only your incurable optimist who has enterprise enough for suicide . . even business suicide.

HUGH. Ah . . I'm that. But I can't boast. Heaven knows when I shall really get out of it either. [*Then the realities of life overwhelm him again.*] Beatrice won't let me go until we're each certain of two hundred a year. And she's quite right . . I should only get into debt. You know that two fifty a year of mine is a hundred and eighty now.

EDWARD. [*mischievous.*] Why would you invest sensationally?

HUGH. [*with great seriousness.*] I put money into things which I knew ought to succeed . .

The telephone rings. EDWARD *speaks through it.*

EDWARD. Certainly . . bring him in. [*Then to his brother, who sits on the table idly disarranging everything.*] You'll have to go now, Hugh.

HUGH. [*shaking his head gloomily.*] You're one of the few people I can talk to, Edward.

EDWARD. I like listening.

HUGH. [*as much cheered as surprised.*] Do you? I believe talking does stir up the world's atoms a bit.

In comes old MR. GEORGE BOOTH, *older too in looks than he was eighteen months back. Very dandyishly dressed, he still seems by no means so happy as his clothes might be making him.*

MR. BOOTH. 'Ullo, Hugh! I thought I should find you, Edward.

EDWARD. [*formally.*] Good morning, Mr. Booth.

HUGH. [*as he collects his hat, his coat, his various properties.*] Well . . Beatrice and I go down to Chislehurst to-morrow. I say . . d'you know that old Nursie is furious with you about something?

EDWARD. [*shortly.*] Yes, I know. Good-bye.

HUGH. How are you?

He launches this inquiry at MR. BOOTH *with great suddenness just as he leaves the room. The old gentleman jumps; then jumps again at the slam of the door. And then he frowns at* EDWARD *in a frightened sort of way.*

EDWARD. Will you come here . . or will you sit by the fire ?

MR. BOOTH. This'll do. I shan't detain you long.

He takes the chair by the table and occupies the next minute or two carefully disposing of his hat and gloves.

EDWARD. Are you feeling all right again ?

MR. BOOTH. A bit dyspeptic. How are you ?

EDWARD. Quite well, thanks.

MR. BOOTH. I'm glad . . I'm glad. [*he now proceeds to cough a little, hesitating painfully.*] I'm afraid this isn't very pleasant business I've come upon.

EDWARD. D'you want to go to Law with any one ?

MR. BOOTH. No . . oh, no. I'm getting too old to quarrel.

EDWARD. A pleasant symptom.

MR. BOOTH. [*with a final effort.*] I mean to withdraw my securities from the custody of your firm . . [*and he adds apologetically*] with the usual notice, of course.

It would be difficult to describe what EDWARD *feels at this moment. Perhaps something of the shock that the relief of death may be as an end to pain so long endured that it has been half forgotten. He answers very quietly, without a sign of emotion.*

EDWARD. Thank you . . May one ask why ?

MR. BOOTH. [*relieved that the worst is over.*] Certainly . . certainly. I think you must know, Edward, I have never been able to feel that implicit confidence in your ability which I had in your father's. Well, it is hardly to be expected, is it ?

EDWARD. [*with a grim smile.*] No.

MR. BOOTH. I can say that without unduly depreciating you. Men like your father are few and far between. No doubt things go on here as they have always done, but . . since his death I have not been happy about my affairs.

EDWARD. [*speaking as it is his duty to.*] I think you need be under no apprehension . .

MR. BOOTH. I daresay not. But for the first time in my long life to be worried about money affairs . . I don't like the feeling. The possession of money has always been a pleasure to me . . and for what are perhaps my last years I don't wish it to be otherwise. Remember you have practically my entire property unreservedly in your control.

EDWARD. Perhaps we can arrange to hand you over the reins to an extent which will ease your mind, and at the same time not . .

MR. BOOTH. I thought of that. I am very sorry to seem to be slighting your father's son. I have not moved in the matter for eighteen months. Really, one feels a little helpless . . and the transaction of business requires more energy than . . But I saw my doctor yesterday, Edward, and he told me . . well, it was a warning. And so I felt it my duty . . especially as I made up my mind to it some time ago. [*He comes to the end of this havering at last and adds.*] In point of fact, Edward, more than a year before your father died I had quite decided that I could never trust my affairs to you as I had to him.

EDWARD *starts almost out of his chair ; his face pale, his eyes black.*

EDWARD. Did he know that?

MR. BOOTH. [*resenting this new attitude.*] I think I never said it in so many words. But I fancy he guessed.

EDWARD. [*as he relaxes and turns, almost shuddering, from the possibility of dreadful knowledge.*] Don't say so . . he never guessed. [*Then, with a sudden fresh impulse.*] I hope you won't do this, Mr. Booth.

MR. BOOTH. I have quite made up my mind.

EDWARD. Let me persuade you—

MR. BOOTH. [*conciliatory*.] I shall make a point of telling the family that you are in no way to blame. And in the event of any personal legal difficulties I shall always be delighted to come to you. My idea is for the future to employ merely a financial agent—

EDWARD. [*still quite unstrung really, and his nerves betraying him.*] Why didn't you tell my father . . why didn't you?

MR. BOOTH. I did not choose to distress him by—

EDWARD. [*pulling himself together; speaking half to himself.*] Well . . well . . this is one way out. And it's not my fault.

MR. BOOTH. You're making a fearful fuss about a very simple matter, Edward. The loss of one client, however important he may be . . Why, this is one of the best family practices in London. I am surprised at your lack of dignity.

EDWARD *yields smilingly to this assertiveness.*

EDWARD. Yes . . I have no dignity. Will you walk off with your papers now?

MR. BOOTH. What notice is usual?

EDWARD. To a good solicitor, five minutes. Ten to a poor one.

MR. BOOTH. You'll have to explain matters a bit to me.

Now EDWARD *settles to his desk again; really with a certain grim enjoyment of the prospect.*

EDWARD. I will. Mr. Booth, how much do you think you're worth?

MR. BOOTH. [*easily.*] Do you know, I actually couldn't say off-hand.

EDWARD. But you've a rough idea?

MR. BOOTH. To be sure.

EDWARD. You'll get not quite half that out of us.

MR. BOOTH. [*precisely.*] I think I said I had made up my mind to withdraw the whole amount.

EDWARD. You should have made up your mind sooner.

MR. BOOTH. I don't in the least understand you, Edward.

EDWARD. The greater part of your capital doesn't exist.

MR. BOOTH. [*with some irritation.*] Nonsense, it must exist. [*He scans* EDWARD'S *set face in vain.*] You mean that it won't be prudent to realise? You can hand over the securities. I don't want to reinvest simply because—

EDWARD. I can't hand over what I haven't got.

This sentence falls on the old man's ears like a knell.

MR. BOOTH. Is anything . . wrong?

EDWARD. [*grim and patient.*] How many more times am I to say that we have robbed you of half your property?

MR. BOOTH. [*his senses failing him.*] Say that again.

EDWARD. It's quite true.

MR. BOOTH. My money . . gone?

EDWARD. Yes.

MR. BOOTH. [*clutching at a straw of anger.*] You've been the thief . . you . . you . . ?

EDWARD. I wouldn't tell you if I could help it . . my father.

That actually calls the old man back to something like dignity and self-possession. He thumps on EDWARD'S *table furiously.*

MR. BOOTH. I'll make you prove that.

And now EDWARD *buries his face in his arms and just goes off into hysterics.*

EDWARD. Oh, you've fired a mine!

MR. BOOTH. [*scolding him well.*] Slandering your dead father . . and lying to me, revenging yourself by frightening me . . because I detest you.

EDWARD. Why . . haven't I thanked you for putting an end to my troubles? I do . . I promise you I do.

MR. BOOTH. [*shouting, and his sudden courage failing as he shouts.*] Prove it . . prove it to me! You don't frighten me so easily. One can't lose half of all one has and then be told of it in two minutes . . sitting at a table. [*His voice tails off to a piteous whimper.*]

EDWARD. [*quietly now and kindly.*] If my father had told you in plain words you'd have believed him.

MR. BOOTH. [*bowing his head.*] Yes.

EDWARD *looks at the poor old thing with great pity.*

EDWARD. What on earth did you want to do this for? You need never have known . . you could have died happy. Settling with all those charities in your will would certainly have smashed us up. But proving your will is many years off yet, we'll hope.

MR. BOOTH. [*pathetic and bewildered.*] I don't understand. No, I don't understand . . because your father . . But I must understand, Edward.

EDWARD. Don't shock yourself trying to understand my father, for you never will. Pull yourself together, Mr. Booth. After all, this isn't a vital matter to you. It's not even as if you had a family to consider . . like some of the others.

MR. BOOTH. [*vaguely.*] What others?

EDWARD. Don't imagine your money has been specially selected for pilfering.

MR. BOOTH. [*with solemn incredulity.*] One has read of this sort of thing but . . I thought people always got found out.

EDWARD. [*brutally humorous.*] Well . . you've found us out.

MR. BOOTH. [*rising to the full appreciation of his wrongs.*] Oh . . I've been foully cheated!

EDWARD. [*patiently.*] I've told you so.

MR. BOOTH. [*his voice breaks, he appeals pitifully.*] But by you, Edward . . say it's by you.

EDWARD. [*unable to resist his quiet revenge.*] I've not the ability or the personality for such work, Mr. Booth . . nothing but principles, which forbid me even to lie to you.

The old gentleman draws a long breath and then speaks with great awe, blending into grief.

MR. BOOTH. I think your father is in Hell . . I'd have gone there myself to save him from it. I loved him very truly. How he could have had the heart! We were friends for nearly fifty years. Am I to think now he only cared for me to cheat me?

EDWARD. [*venturing the comfort of an explanation.*] No . . he didn't value money quite as you do.

MR. BOOTH. [*with sudden shrill logic.*] But he took it. What d'you mean by that?

EDWARD *leans back in his chair and changes the tenor of their talk.*

EDWARD. Well, you're master of the situation now. What are you going to do?

MR. BOOTH. To get my money back?

EDWARD. No, that's gone.

MR. BOOTH. Then give me what's left and—

EDWARD. Are you going to prosecute?

MR. BOOTH. [*shifting uneasily in his chair.*] Oh, dear . . is that necessary? Can't somebody else do that? I thought the Law . . What'll happen if I don't?

EDWARD. What do you suppose I'm doing here still?

MR. BOOTH. [*as if he were being asked a riddle.*] I don't know.

EDWARD. [*earnestly.*] As soon as my father died, I began of course to try and put things straight . . doing as I thought best . . that is . . as best I could. Then I made up my accounts showing who has lost and who hasn't . . they can criticise those as they please and that's all done with. And now I've set myself to a duller sort of work. I throw penny after penny hardly earned into the half-filled pit of our deficit. But I've been doing that for what it's worth in the time that was left to me . . till this should happen. If you choose to let things alone —which won't hurt you, will it?—and hold your tongue, I can go on with the job till the next smash comes, and I'll beg that off too if I can. This is my duty, and it's my duty to ask you to let me go on with it. [*He searches* MR. BOOTH'S *face and finds there only disbelief and fear. He bursts out.*] Oh, you might at least believe me. It can't hurt you to believe me.

MR. BOOTH. You must admit, Edward, it isn't easy to believe anything in this office . . just for the moment.

EDWARD. [*bowing to the extreme reasonableness of this.*] I suppose not . . I can prove it to you. I'll take you through the books . . you won't understand them . . but I can boast of this much.

MR. BOOTH. I think I'd rather not. D'you think I ought to hold any further communication with you at all? [*And at this he takes his hat.*]

EDWARD. [*with a little explosion of contemptuous anger.*] Certainly not. Prosecute . . prosecute!

MR. BOOTH. [*with dignity.*] Don't lose your temper. You know it's my place to be angry with you.

EDWARD. But . . [*then he is elaborately explanatory.*] I shall be grateful if you'll prosecute.

MR. BOOTH. [*more puzzled than ever.*] There's something in this which I don't understand.

EDWARD. [*with deliberate unconcern.*] Think it over.

MR. BOOTH. [*hesitating, fidgeting.*] Surely I oughtn't to have to make up my mind! There must be a right or a wrong thing to do. Edward, can't you tell me?

EDWARD. I'm prejudiced, you see.

MR. BOOTH. [*angrily.*] I believe you're simply trying to practise upon my goodness of heart. Certainly I ought to prosecute at once . . Oughtn't I? [*Then at the nadir of helplessness.*] Can't I consult another solicitor?

EDWARD. [*his chin in the air.*] You can write to the "Times" about it!

MR. BOOTH. [*shocked and grieved at his attitude.*] Edward, how can you be so cool and heartless?

EDWARD. [*changing his tone.*] D'you think I shan't be glad to sleep at nights?

MR. BOOTH. Perhaps you'll be put in prison?

EDWARD. I am in prison .. a less pleasant one than Wormwood Scrubbs. But we're all prisoners, Mr. Booth.

MR. BOOTH. [*wagging his head.*] Yes, this is what comes of your philosophy. Why aren't you on your knees?

EDWARD. To you?

This was not what MR. BOOTH *meant, but as he gets up from his chair he feels all but mighty.*

MR. BOOTH. And why should you expect me to shrink from vindicating the law?

EDWARD. [*shortly.*] I don't. I've explained you'll be doing me a kindness. When I'm wanted you'll find me here at my desk. [*Then as an afterthought.*] If you take long to decide .. don't alter your behaviour to my family in the meantime. They know the main points of the business and—

MR. BOOTH. [*knocked right off his balance.*] Do they! Good God! .. I'm invited to dinner the day after tomorrow .. that's Christmas Eve. The hypocrites!

EDWARD. [*unmoved.*] I shall be there .. that will have given you two days. Will you tell me then?

MR. BOOTH. [*protesting violently.*] I can't go .. I can't have dinner with them. I must be ill.

EDWARD. [*with a half smile.*] I remember I went to dine at Chislehurst to tell my father of my decision.

MR. BOOTH. [*testily.*] What decision?

EDWARD. To remain in the firm when I first knew what was happening.

MR. BOOTH. [*interested.*] Was I there?

EDWARD. I daresay.

MR. BOOTH *stands there, hat, stick, and gloves in hand, shaken by this experience, helpless, at his wits' end. He falls into a sort of fretful reverie, speaking half to himself but yet as if he hoped that* EDWARD, *who is wrapped in his own thoughts, would have the decency to answer, or at least listen, to what he is saying.*

MR. BOOTH. Yes, how often I dined with him. Oh, it was monstrous! [*His eyes fall on the clock.*] It's nearly lunch time now. Do you know I still can hardly believe it all? I wish I hadn't found it out. If he hadn't died I should never have found it out. I hate to have to be vindictive . . it's not my nature. Indeed I'm sure I'm more grieved than angry. But it isn't as if it were a small sum. And I don't see that one is called upon to forgive crimes . . or why does the Law exist? I feel that this will go near to killing me. I'm too old to have such troubles . . it isn't right. And now if I have to prosecute—

EDWARD. [*at last throwing in a word.*] Well . . you need not.

MR. BOOTH. [*thankful for the provocation.*] Don't you attempt to influence me, sir.

He turns to go.

EDWARD. And what's more, with the money you have left . .

EDWARD *follows him politely.* MR. BOOTH *flings the door open.*

MR. BOOTH. You'll make out a cheque for that at once, sir, and send it me.

EDWARD. You might . .

MR. BOOTH. [*clapping his hat on, stamping his stick.*] I shall do the right thing, sir, never fear.

So he marches off in fine style, having, he thinks, had the last word and all. But EDWARD, *closing the door after him, mutters . .*

EDWARD. . . Save your soul! . . I'm afraid I was going to say.

THE FIFTH ACT

Naturally it is the dining-room—consecrated as it is to the distinguishing orgy of the season—which bears the brunt of what an English household knows as Christmas decorations. They consist chiefly of the branches of holly (that unyielding tree), stuck cock-eyed behind the top edges of the pictures. The one picture conspicuously not decorated is that which now hangs over the fireplace, a portrait of MR. VOYSEY, *with its new gilt frame and its brassplate marking it also as a presentation.* HONOR, *hastily and at some bodily peril, pulled down the large bunch of mistletoe which a callous housemaid had suspended above it, in time to obviate the shock to family feelings which such impropriety would cause. Otherwise the only difference between the dining-room's appearance at half-past nine on Christmas Eve and on any other evening in the year is that little piles of queer-shaped envelopes seem to be lying about, while there is quite a lot of tissue paper and string to be seen peeping from odd corners. The electric light is reduced to one bulb, but when the maid opens the door showing in* MR. GEORGE BOOTH *she switches on the rest.*

PHOEBE. This room is empty, sir. I'll tell Mr. Edward.

She leaves him to fidget towards the fireplace and back, not removing his comforter or his coat, scarcely turning down the collar, screwing his cap in his hands. In a very short time EDWARD *comes in, shutting the door and taking stock of the visitor before he speaks.*

ACT V] THE VOYSEY INHERITANCE

EDWARD. Well?

MR. GEORGE BOOTH. [*feebly.*] I hope my excuse for not coming to dinner was acceptable. I did have . . I have a very bad headache.

EDWARD. I daresay they believed it.

MR. GEORGE BOOTH. I have come immediately to tell you my decision . . perhaps this trouble will then be a little more off my mind.

EDWARD. What is it?

MR GEORGE BOOTH. I couldn't think the matter out alone. I went this afternoon to talk it over with my old friend Colpus. [*At this news* EDWARD'S *eyebrows contract and then rise.*] What a terrible shock to him!

EDWARD. Oh, nearly three of his four thousand pounds are quite safe.

MR. GEORGE BOOTH. That you and your father . . you, whom he baptized . . should have robbed him! I never saw a man so utterly prostrate with grief. That it should have been your father! And his poor wife! . . though she never got on with your father.

EDWARD. [*with cheerful irony.*] Oh, Mrs. Colpus knows too, does she?

MR. GEORGE BOOTH. Of course he told Mrs. Colpus. This is an unfortunate time for the storm to break on him. What with Christmas Day and Sunday following so close they're as busy as can be. He has resolved that during this season of peace and goodwill he must put the matter from him if he can. But once Christmas is over . . ! [*He envisages the Christian old vicar giving* EDWARD *a hell of a time then.*]

EDWARD. [*coolly.*] So you mean to prosecute. If you don't, you've inflicted on the Colpuses a lot of unnecessary pain and a certain amount of loss by telling them.

MR. GEORGE BOOTH. [*naïvely.*] I never thought of that. No, Edward, I have decided not to prosecute.

EDWARD *hides his face for a moment.*

EDWARD. And I've been hoping to escape! Well . . it can't be helped [*and he sets his teeth.*]

MR. GEORGE BOOTH. [*with touching solemnity.*] I think I could not bear to see the family I have loved brought to such disgrace. And I want to ask your pardon, Edward, for some of the hard thoughts I have had of you. I consider this effort of yours to restore to the firm the credit which your father lost a very striking one. You sacrifice your profits, I understand, to replacing the capital that has been misappropriated. Very proper . . more than proper.

EDWARD. No. No. To pay interest on money that doesn't exist but ought to . . and the profits don't cover that or anything like it.

MR. GEORGE BOOTH. Patience . . I shouldn't be surprised if you worked up the business very well.

EDWARD. [*again laying the case before* MR. BOOTH, *leaning forward to him.*] Mr. Booth, you were fond of my father. You see the help you could give us, don't you?

MR. GEORGE BOOTH. By not prosecuting?

EDWARD. [*earnestly.*] Beyond that. If you'd cut your losses . . for the moment, and take only what's yours by right . . why, that would relieve me of four thousand three hundred a year . . and I could do so much with it. There are one or two bad cases still. One woman—I believe you know her—it's not that she's so poor . . and perhaps I'm not justified now in doing anything special . . but she's got children . . and if you'd help . .

MR. GEORGE BOOTH. Stop, Edward . . stop at once. If you attempt to confuse me I must take professional advice. Colpus and I have discussed this and quite made up our minds. And I've made a note or two. [*He produces a bit of paper and a pencil.* EDWARD *stiffens.*] May we understand that in straightening affairs you can show a proper preference for one client over another?

EDWARD. [*pulled up, draws back in his chair.*] No . . you had better not understand that.

MR. GEORGE BOOTH. Why can't you?

EDWARD. Well . . suppose if I want to, I can?

MR. GEORGE BOOTH. Edward, do please be straightforward.

EDWARD. Why should I?

MR. GEORGE BOOTH. You certainly should. Do you mean to compare your father's ordinary business transactions—the hundreds of them—with his black treachery to . . to the Vicar?

EDWARD. Or to you?

MR. GEORGE BOOTH. Or to me.

EDWARD. Besides that, holding your tongue should be worth something extra now, shouldn't it?

MR. GEORGE BOOTH. I don't want to argue. My own position morally — and otherwise — is a strong one . . so Colpus impresses on me . . and he has some head for business.

EDWARD. Well, what are your terms?

MR. GEORGE BOOTH. This is my note of them. [*He takes refuge in his slip of paper.*] I make these conditions, if you please, Edward, on the Vicar's behalf and my own. They are . . [*now the pencil comes into play, ticking off each item*] that you at once return us the balance of any capital there is left . .

EDWARD. [*cold again.*] I am providing for that.

MR. GEORGE BOOTH. Good. That you should continue, of course, to pay us the usual interest upon the rest of our capital, which ought to exist and does not. And that you should, year by year, pay us back by degrees out of the earnings of the firm as much of that capital as you can afford. We will agree upon the sum . . say a thousand a year. I doubt if you can ever restore us all we have lost, but do your best and I shan't complain. There, I think that is fair dealing!

EDWARD *does not take his eyes off* MR. BOOTH *until the whole meaning of this proposition has settled in his brain. Then, without warning, he goes off into peals of laughter, much to the alarm of* MR. BOOTH, *who has never thought him over-sane.*

EDWARD. How funny! How very funny!

MR. GEORGE BOOTH. Edward, don't laugh.

EDWARD. I never heard anything quite so funny!

MR. GEORGE BOOTH. Edward, stop laughing.

EDWARD. Oh, you Christian gentlemen!

MR. GEORGE BOOTH. Don't be hysterical. The money's ours.

EDWARD'S *laughter gives way to the deepest anger of which he is capable.*

EDWARD. I'm giving my soul and body to restoring you and the rest of you to your precious money bags .. and you'll wring me dry. Won't you? Won't you?

MR. GEORGE BOOTH. Now be reasonable. Argue the point quietly.

EDWARD. Go to the devil, sir.

And with that he turns away from the flabbergasted old gentleman.

MR. GEORGE BOOTH. Don't be rude.

EDWARD. [*his anger vanishing.*] I beg your pardon.

MR. GEORGE BOOTH. You're just excited. If you take time to think of it, I'm reasonable.

EDWARD. [*his sense of humour returning.*] Most! Most! [*There is a knock at the door.*] Come in. Come in.

HONOR *intrudes an apologetic head.*

HONOR. Am I interrupting business? I'm so sorry.

EDWARD. [*crowing in a mirthless enjoyment of his joke.*] No! Business is over .. quite over. Come in, Honor.

HONOR *puts on the table a market basket bulging with little paper parcels, and, oblivious of* MR. BOOTH'S *distracted face, tries to fix his attention.*

HONOR. I thought, dear Mr. Booth, perhaps you wouldn't mind carrying round this basket of things yourself. It's so very damp underfoot that I don't want to send one of the maids out to-night if I can possibly avoid it . . and if one doesn't get Christmas presents the very first thing on Christmas morning quite half the pleasure in them is lost, don't you think?

MR. GEORGE BOOTH. Yes . . yes.

HONOR. [*fishing out the parcels one by one.*] This is a bell for Mrs. Williams . . something she said she wanted so that you can ring for her, which saves the maids : cap and apron for Mary : cap and apron for Ellen : shawl for Davis when she goes out to the larder—all useful presents —and that's something for you, but you're not to look at it till the morning.

Having shaken each of these at the old gentleman, she proceeds to re-pack them. He is now trembling with anxiety to escape before any more of the family find him there.

MR. GEORGE BOOTH. Thank you . . thank you! I hope my lot has arrived. I left instructions . .

HONOR. Quite safely . . and I have hidden them. Presents are put on the breakfast table to-morrow.

EDWARD. [*with an inconsequence that still further alarms* MR. BOOTH.] When we were all children our Christmas breakfast was mostly made off chocolates.

Before the basket is packed, MRS. VOYSEY *sails slowly into the room, as smiling and as deaf as ever.* MR. BOOTH *does his best not to scowl at her.*

MRS. VOYSEY. Are you feeling better, George Booth?

MR. GEORGE BOOTH. No. [*Then he elevates his voice with a show of politeness.*] No, thank you . . I can't say I am.

MRS. VOYSEY. You don't look better.

MR. GEORGE BOOTH. I still have my headache. [*With a distracted shout.*] Headache.

MRS. VOYSEY. Bilious, perhaps! I quite understood you didn't care to dine. But why not have taken your coat off? How foolish in this warm room!

MR. GEORGE BOOTH. Thank you. I'm—er—just off.

He seizes the market basket. At that moment MRS. HUGH *appears.*

BEATRICE. Your shawl, mother. [*And she clasps it round* MRS. VOYSEY'S *shoulders.*]

MRS. VOYSEY. Thank you, Beatrice. I thought I had it on. [*Then to* MR. BOOTH, *who is now entangled in his comforter.*] A merry Christmas to you.

BEATRICE. Good evening, Mr. Booth.

MR. GEORGE BOOTH. I beg your pardon. Good evening, Mrs. Hugh.

HONOR. [*with sudden inspiration, to the company in general.*] Why shouldn't I write in here .. now the table's cleared!

MR. GEORGE BOOTH. [*sternly, now he is safe by the door.*] Will you see me out, Edward?

EDWARD. Yes.

He follows the old man and his basket, leaving the others to distribute themselves about the room. It is a custom of the female members of the VOYSEY *family, especially about Christmas time, to return to the dining-room, when the table has been cleared, and occupy themselves in various ways which require space and untidiness. Sometimes as the evening wears on they partake of cocoa, sometimes they abstain.*
BEATRICE *has a little work-basket, containing a buttonless glove and such things, which she is rectifying.* HONOR'S *writing is done with the aid of an enormous blotting book, which bulges with apparently a year's correspondence. She sheds its contents upon the end of the dining table and spreads them abroad.*
MRS. VOYSEY *settles to the fire, opens the "Nineteenth Century" and is instantly absorbed in it.*

BEATRICE. Where's Emily?

HONOR. [*mysteriously*.] Well, Beatrice, she's in the library talking to Booth.

BEATRICE. Talking to her husband; good Heavens! I know she has taken my scissors.

HONOR. I think she's telling him about you.

BEATRICE. What about me?

HONOR. You and Hugh.

BEATRICE. [*with a little movement of annoyance.*] I suppose this is Hugh's fault. It was carefully arranged no one was to be told till after Christmas.

HONOR. Emily told me . . and Edward knows . . and Mother knows . .

BEATRICE. I warned Mother a year ago.

HONOR. Every one seems to know but Booth . . so I thought he'd better be told. I suggested one night so that he might have time to think over it . . but Emily said that'd wake Alfred. Besides she's nearly always asleep herself when he comes to bed.

BEATRICE. Why do they still have that baby in their room?

HONOR. Emily thinks it her duty.

At this moment EMILY *comes in, looking rather trodden upon.* HONOR *concludes in the most audible of whispers . .*

HONOR. Don't say anything . . it's my fault.

BEATRICE. [*fixing her with a severe forefinger.*] Emily . . have you taken my best scissors?

EMILY. [*timidly.*] No, Beatrice.

HONOR. [*who is diving into the recesses of the blotting book.*] Oh, here they are! I must have taken them. I do apologise!

EMILY. [*more timidly still.*] I'm afraid Booth's rather cross . . he's gone to look for Hugh.

BEATRICE. [*with a shake of her head.*] Honor . . I've a good mind to make you do this sewing for me.

In comes the Major, strepitant. He takes, so to speak, just time enough to train himself on BEATRICE *and then fires.*

BOOTH. Beatrice, what on earth is this Emily has been telling me?

BEATRICE. [*with elaborate calm.*] Emily, what have you been telling Booth?

BOOTH. Please . . please do not prevaricate. Where is Hugh?

MRS. VOYSEY. [*looking over her spectacles.*] What did you say, Booth?

BOOTH. I want Hugh, Mother.

MRS. VOYSEY. I thought you were playing billiards together.

EDWARD *strolls back from despatching* MR. BOOTH, *his face thoughtful.*

BOOTH. [*insistently.*] Edward, where is Hugh?

EDWARD. [*with complete indifference.*] I don't know.

BOOTH. [*in trumpet tones.*] Honor, will you oblige me by finding Hugh and saying I wish to speak to him, here, immediately?

HONOR, *who has leapt at the sound of her name, flies from the room without a word.*

BEATRICE. I know quite well what you want to talk about, Booth. Discuss the matter by all means if it amuses you . . but don't shout.

BOOTH. I use the voice Nature has gifted me with, Beatrice.

BEATRICE. [*as she searches for a glove button.*] Certainly Nature did let herself go over your lungs.

BOOTH. [*glaring round with indignation.*] This is a family matter, otherwise I should not feel it my duty to interfere . . as I do. Any member of the family has a right to express an opinion. I want Mother's. Mother, what do you think?

MRS. VOYSEY. [*amicably.*] What about?

BOOTH. Hugh and Beatrice separating.
MRS. VOYSEY. They haven't separated.
BOOTH. But they mean to.
MRS. VOYSEY. Fiddle-de-dee!
BOOTH. I quite agree with you.
BEATRICE. [*with a charming smile.*] Such reasoning would convert a stone.
BOOTH. Why have I not been told?
BEATRICE. You have just been told.
BOOTH. [*thunderously.*] Before.
BEATRICE. The truth is, dear Booth, we're all so afraid of you.
BOOTH. [*a little mollified.*] Ha . . I should be glad to think that.
BEATRICE. [*sweetly.*] Don't you?
BOOTH. [*intensely serious.*] Beatrice, your callousness shocks me! That you can dream of deserting Hugh . . a man of all others who requires constant care and attention.
BEATRICE. May I remark that the separation is as much Hugh's wish as mine?
BOOTH. I don't believe that.
BEATRICE. [*her eyebrows up.*] Really!
BOOTH. I don't imply that you're lying. But you must know that it's Hugh nature to wish to do anything that he thinks anybody wishes him to do. All my life I've had to stand up for him . . and by Jove, I'll continue to do so.
EDWARD. [*from the depths of his armchair.*] If you'd taught him to stand up for himself—
    The door is flung almost off its hinges by HUGH, *who then stands stamping and pale green with rage.*
HUGH. Look here, Booth . . I will not have you interfering with my private affairs. Is one never to be free from your bullying?
BOOTH. You ought to be grateful.

HUGH. Well, I'm not.
BOOTH. This is a family affair.
HUGH. It is not!
BOOTH. [*at the top of his voice.*] If all you can do is to contradict me, you'd better listen to what I've got to say . . quietly.

HUGH, *quite shouted down, flings himself petulantly into a chair. A hush falls.*

EMILY. [*in a still small voice.*] Would you like me to go, Booth?
BOOTH. [*severely.*] No, Emily. Unless anything has been going on which cannot be discussed before you . . [*then more severely still*] and I hope that is not so.
HUGH. [*muttering rebelliously.*] Oh, you have the mind of a . . an official flunkey!
BOOTH. Why do you wish to separate?
HUGH. What's the use of telling you? You won't understand.
BEATRICE. [*who sews on undisturbed.*] We don't get on well together.
BOOTH. [*amazedly.*] Is that all?
HUGH. [*snapping at him.*] Yes, that's all. Can you find a better reason?
BOOTH. [*with brotherly contempt.*] I have given up expecting common sense from you. But Beatrice—! [*His tone implores her to be reasonable.*]
BEATRICE. It doesn't seem to me any sort of sense that people should live together for purposes of mutual irritation.
BOOTH. [*protesting.*] My dear girl! . . that sounds like a quotation from your last book.
BEATRICE. It isn't. I do think, Booth, you might read that book . . for the honour of the Family.
BOOTH. [*successfully side-tracked . .*] I have bought it, Beatrice, and—
BEATRICE. That's the principal thing, of course—

BOOTH. [. . *and discovering it.*] But do let us keep to the subject.

BEATRICE. [*with flattering sincerity.*] Certainly, Booth. And there is hardly any subject that I wouldn't ask your advice about. But upon this . . please let me know better. Hugh and I will be happier apart.

BOOTH. [*obstinately.*] Why?

BEATRICE. [*with resolute patience, having vented a little sigh.*] Hugh finds that my opinions distress him. And I have at last lost patience with Hugh.

MRS. VOYSEY. [*who has been trying to follow this through her spectacles.*] What does Beatrice say?

BOOTH. [*translating into a loud sing-song.*] That she wishes to leave her husband because she has lost patience!

MRS. VOYSEY. [*with considerable acrimony.*] Then you must be a very ill-tempered woman. Hugh has a sweet nature.

HUGH. [*shouting self-consciously.*] Nonsense, Mother.

BEATRICE. [*shouting good-humouredly.*] I quite agree with you, Mother. [*She continues to her husband in an even just tone.*] You have a sweet nature, Hugh, and it is most difficult to get angry with you. I have been seven years working up to it. But now that I am angry, I shall never get pleased again.

The Major returns to his subject, refreshed by a moment's repose.

BOOTH. How has he failed in his duty? Tell us. I'm not bigoted in his favour. I know your faults, Hugh.

He wags his head at HUGH, *who writhes with irritation.*

HUGH. Why can't you leave them alone . . leave us alone?

BEATRICE. I'd state my case against Hugh, if I thought he'd retaliate.

HUGH. [*desperately rounding on his brother.*] If I tell

you, you won't understand. You understand nothing! Beatrice is angry with me because I won't prostitute my art to make money.

BOOTH. [*glancing at his wife.*] Please don't use metaphors of that sort.

BEATRICE. [*reasonably.*] Yes, I think Hugh ought to earn more money.

BOOTH. [*quite pleased to be getting along at last.*] Well, why doesn't he?

HUGH. I don't want money.

BOOTH. You can't say you don't want money any more than you can say you don't want bread.

BEATRICE. [*as she breaks off her cotton.*] It's when one has known what it is to be a little short of both . .

Now the Major spreads himself and begins to be very wise, while HUGH, *to whom this is more intolerable than all, can only clutch his hair.*

BOOTH. You know I never considered Art a very good profession for you, Hugh. And you won't even stick to one department of it. It's a profession that gets people into very bad habits, I consider. Couldn't you take up something else? You could still do those wood-cuts in your spare time to amuse yourself.

HUGH. [*commenting on this with two deliberate shouts of simulated mirth.*] Ha! Ha!

BOOTH. [*sublimely superior.*] Well, it wouldn't much matter if you didn't do them at all!

BEATRICE. [*subtly.*] Booth, there speaks the true critic.

BOOTH. [*deprecating any title to omniscience.*] Well, I don't pretend to know much about Art but—

HUGH. It would matter to me. There speaks the artist.

BEATRICE. The arrogance of the artist!

HUGH. We have a right to be arrogant.

BEATRICE. Good workmen are humble.

HUGH. And look to their wages.

BEATRICE. Well, I'm only a workman.
With that she breaks the contact of this quiet deadly hopeless little quarrel by turning her head away. The Major, who has given it most friendly attention, comments . .
BOOTH. Of course! Quite so! I'm sure all that is a very interesting difference of opinion. But it's nothing to separate about.
MRS. VOYSEY leaves her armchair for her favourite station at the dining table.
MRS. VOYSEY. Booth is the only one of you that I can hear at all distinctly. But if you two foolish young people think you want to separate . . try it. You'll soon come back to each other and be glad to. People can't fight against Nature for long. And marriage is a natural state . . once you're married.
BOOTH. [*with intense approval.*] Quite right, Mother.
MRS. VOYSEY. I know.
She resumes the "Nineteenth Century". The Major, to the despair of everybody, makes yet another start; trying oratory this time.
BOOTH. My own opinion is, Beatrice and Hugh, that you don't realise the meaning of the word marriage. I don't call myself a religious man . . but dash it all, you were married in Church! And you then entered upon an awful compact! Surely, as a woman, Beatrice, the religious point of it ought to appeal to you. Good Lord, suppose everybody were to carry on like this! And have you considered, Beatrice, that . . whether you're right or whether you're wrong . . if you desert Hugh, you cut yourself off from the Family?
BEATRICE. [*with the sweetest of smiles.*] That will distress me terribly.
BOOTH. [*not doubting her for a moment.*] Of course.
HUGH flings up his head and finds relief at last in many words.

HUGH. I wish to Heaven I'd ever been able to cut myself off from the Family! Look at Trenchard.

BOOTH. [*gobbling a little at this unexpected attack.*] I do not forgive Trenchard for quarrelling with and deserting our father.

HUGH. Trenchard quarrelled because that was his only way of escape.

BOOTH. Escape from what?

HUGH. From tyranny! . . from hypocrisy! . . from boredom! . . from his Happy English Home!

BEATRICE. [*kindly.*] Hugh . . Hugh . . it's no use.

BOOTH. [*attempting sarcasm.*] Speak so that Mother can hear you!

But HUGH *isn't to be stopped now.*

HUGH. Why are we all dull, cubbish, uneducated . . that is, hopelessly middle-class?

BOOTH. [*taking this as very personal.*] Cubbish!

HUGH. . . Because it's the middle-class ideal that you should respect your parents . . live with them . . think with them . . grow like them. Natural affection and gratitude! That's what's expected, isn't it?

BOOTH. [*not to be obliterated.*] Certainly.

HUGH. Keep your children ignorant of all that you don't know, penniless except for your good pleasure, dependent on you for permission to breathe freely . . and be sure that their gratitude will be most disinterested, and their affection very natural. If your father's a drunkard or poor, then perhaps you get free and can form an opinion of your own . . and can love him or hate him as he deserves. But our father and mother were models. They did their duty by us . . and taught us ours. Trenchard escaped, as I say. You took to the Army . . so of course you've never discovered how behind the times you are. [*The Major is stupent.*] I tried to express myself in art . . and found there was nothing to express . . I'd been so well brought up. D'you blame me if I wander about in search of a soul of some sort ? And Honor—

BOOTH. [*disputing savagely.*] Honor is very happy at home. Every one loves her.

HUGH. [*with fierce sarcasm.*] Yes . . what do we call her ? Mother's right hand ! I wonder they bothered to give her a name. By the time little Ethel came they were tired of training children . . [*his voice loses its sting ; he doesn't complete this sentence.*]

BEATRICE. Poor little Ethel . .

BOOTH. Poor Ethel !

They speak as one speaks of the dead, and so the wrangling stops. Then EDWARD *interposes quietly.*

EDWARD. Ah, my dear Hugh . .

HUGH. I haven't spoken of your fate, Edward. That's too shameful.

EDWARD. Not at all. I sit at my desk daily as the servant of men whose ideal of life is to have a thousand a year . . or two thousand . . or three . .

BOOTH. Well ?

EDWARD. That's all.

BOOTH. What's the point ? One must live.

HUGH. And if Booth can be said to think, he honestly thinks that's living.

BOOTH. We will return, if you please, to the original subject of discussion. Hugh, this question of a separation—

Past all patience, HUGH *jumps up and flings his chair back to its place.*

HUGH. Beatrice and I mean to separate. And nothing you may say will prevent us. The only difficulty in the way is money. Can we command enough to live apart comfortably ?

BOOTH. Well ?

HUGH. Well . . we can't.

BOOTH. Well ?

HUGH. So we can't separate.

BOOTH. [*speaking with bewilderment.*] Then what in Heaven's name have we been discussing it for?

HUGH. I haven't discussed it! I don't want to discuss it! Mind—can't you mind your own business? Now I'll go back to the billiard-room and my book.

He is gone before the poor Major can recover his lost breath.

BOOTH. [*as he does recover it.*] I am not an impatient man . . but really . . [*and then words fail him.*]

BEATRICE. [*commenting calmly.*] Hugh, I am told, was a spoilt child. They grow to hate their parents sooner than others. You taught him to cry for what he wanted. Now that he's older and doesn't get it, that makes him a wearisome companion.

BOOTH. [*very sulky now.*] You married him with your eyes open, I suppose?

BEATRICE. How few women marry with their eyes open!

BOOTH. You have never made the best of Hugh.

BEATRICE. I have spared him that indignity.

BOOTH. [*vindictively.*] I am very glad that you can't separate.

BEATRICE. As soon as I'm reasonably sure of earning an income I shall walk off from him.

The Major revives.

BOOTH. You will do nothing of the sort, Beatrice.

BEATRICE. [*unruffled.*] How will you stop me, Booth?

BOOTH. I shall tell Hugh he must command you to stay.

BEATRICE. [*with a little smile.*] I wonder would that still make a difference. It was one of the illusions of my girlhood that I should love a man who would master me.

BOOTH. Hugh must assert himself.

He begins to walk about, giving some indication of how it should be done. BEATRICE'S *smile has vanished.*

BEATRICE. Don't think I've enjoyed taking the lead in everything throughout my married life. But some one had to plan and scheme and be foreseeing . . we weren't sparrows or lilies of the field . . some one had to get up and do something, if not for money, at least for the honour of it. [*She becomes conscious of his strutting and smiles rather mischievously.*] Ah . . if I'd married you, Booth!

BOOTH'S *face grows beatific.*

BOOTH. Well, I must own to thinking that I am a masterful man . . that it's the duty of every man to be so. [*He adds forgivingly.*] Poor old Hugh!

BEATRICE. [*unable to resist temptation.*] If I'd tried to leave you, Booth, you'd have whipped me . . wouldn't you?

BOOTH. [*ecstatically complacent.*] Ha . . well . . !

BEATRICE. Do say yes. Think how it'll frighten Emily.

The Major strokes his moustache and is most friendly.

BOOTH. Hugh's been a worry to me all my life. And now as Head of the Family . . Well, I suppose I'd better go and give the dear chap another talking to. I quite see your point of view, Beatrice.

BEATRICE. Why disturb him at his book?

MAJOR BOOTH *leaves them, squaring his shoulders as becomes a lord of creation. The two sisters-in-law go on with their work silently for a moment; then* BEATRICE *adds . .*

BEATRICE. Do you find Booth difficult to manage, Emily?

EMILY. [*putting down her knitting to consider the matter.*] No. It's best to allow him to talk himself out. When he's done that he'll often come to me for advice. I let him get his own way as much as possible . . or think he's getting it. Otherwise he becomes so depressed.

BEATRICE. [*quietly amused.*] Edward shouldn't hear this. What has he to do with women's secrets?

EDWARD. I won't tell . . and I'm a bachelor.

EMILY. [*solemnly as she takes up her knitting again.*] Do you really mean to leave Hugh?

BEATRICE. [*slightly impatient.*] Emily, I've said so.

They are joined by ALICE MAITLAND, *who comes in gaily.*

ALICE. What's Booth shouting about in the billiard-room?

EMILY. [*pained.*] Oh .. on Christmas Eve, too!

BEATRICE. Don't you take any interest in my matrimonial affairs?

MRS. VOYSEY *shuts up the "Nineteenth Century" and removes her spectacles.*

MRS. VOYSEY. That's a very interesting article. The Chinese Empire must be in a shocking state! Is it ten o'clock yet?

EDWARD. Past.

MRS. VOYSEY. [*as* EDWARD *is behind her.*] Can any one see the clock?

ALICE. It's past ten, Auntie.

MRS. VOYSEY. Then I think I'll go to my room.

EMILY. Shall I come and look after you, Mother?

MRS. VOYSEY. If you'd find Honor for me, Emily.

EMILY *goes in search of the harmless necessary* HONOR *and* MRS. VOYSEY *begins her nightly chant of departure.*

MRS. VOYSEY. Good night, Alice. Good night, Edward.

EDWARD. Good night, Mother.

MRS. VOYSEY. [*with sudden severity.*] I'm not pleased with you, Beatrice.

BEATRICE. I'm sorry, Mother.

But without waiting to be answered the old lady has sailed out of the room. BEATRICE, EDWARD, *and* ALICE *are attuned to each other enough to be able to talk with ease.*

BEATRICE. Hugh is right about his family. It'll never make any new life for itself.

EDWARD. There are Booth's children.

BEATRICE. Poor little devils!

ALICE. [*judiciously*.] Emily is an excellent mother.

BEATRICE. Yes . . they'll grow up good men and women. And one will go into the Army and one into the Navy and one into the Church . . and perhaps one to the Devil and the Colonies. They'll serve their country and govern it and help to keep it like themselves . . dull and respectable . . hopelessly middle-class. [*She puts down her work now and elevates an oratorical fist.*] Genius and Poverty may exist in England, if they'll hide their heads. For show days we've our aristocracy. But never let us forget, gentlemen, that it is the plain solid middle-class man who has made us . . what we are.

EDWARD. [*in sympathetic derision.*] Hear, hear . . ! and cries of bravo!

BEATRICE. Now, that is out of my book . . the next one. [*She takes up her work again.*] You know, Edward . . however scandalous it was, your father left you a man's work to do.

EDWARD. [*his face cloudy.*] An outlaw's!

BEATRICE. [*whimsical after a moment.*] I mean that. At all events you've not had to be your father's right arm . . or the instrument of justice . . or a representative of the people . . or anything second-hand of that sort, have you?

EDWARD. [*with sudden excitement.*] Do you know what I found out the other day about [*he nods at the portrait.*] . . him?

BEATRICE. [*inquiring calmly.*] What?

EDWARD. He saved his firm once. That was true. A pretty capable piece of heroism. Then, fifteen years afterwards . . he started again.

BEATRICE. [*greatly interested.*] Did he now?

EDWARD. It can't have been merely through weakness . .

BEATRICE. [*with artistic enthusiasm.*] Of course not.

He was a man of imagination and a great financier. He had to find scope for his abilities or die. He despised these fat little clients living so snugly on their fattening little incomes . . and put them and their money to the best use he could.

EDWARD. [*shaking his head solemnly.*] Fine phrases for robbery.

BEATRICE *turns her clever face to him and begins to follow up her subject keenly.*

BEATRICE. But didn't Hugh tell me that your golden deed has been robbing your rich clients for the benefit of the poor ones ?

ALICE. [*who hasn't missed a word.*] That's true.

EDWARD. [*gently.*] Well . . we're all a bit in debt to the poor, aren't we ?

BEATRICE. Quite so. And you don't possess and your father didn't possess that innate sense of the sacredness of property . . [*she enjoys that phrase*] which mostly makes your merely honest man. Nor did the man possess it who picked my pocket last Friday week . . nor does the tax-gatherer . . nor do I. And whether we can boast of our opinions depends on such a silly lot of prejudices and cowardices that—

EDWARD. [*a little pained by as much of this as he takes to be serious.*] Why wouldn't he own the truth to me about himself ?

BEATRICE. He was a bit of a genius. Perhaps he took care not to know it. Would you have understood ?

EDWARD. Perhaps not. But I loved him.

BEATRICE *looks again at the gentle, earnest face.*

BEATRICE. Through it all ?

EDWARD. Yes. And not from mere force of habit either.

BEATRICE. [*with reverence in her voice now.*] That might silence a bench of judges. Well . . well . .

Her sewing finished, she stuffs the things into her

basket, gets up in her abrupt unconventional way and goes without another word. Her brain is busy with the Voysey Inheritance. EDWARD *and* ALICE *are left in chairs by the fire, facing each other like an old domestic couple.*

EDWARD. Stay and talk with me.

ALICE. I want to. Something has happened .. since dinner.

EDWARD. Can you see that?

ALICE. What is it?

EDWARD. [*with sudden exultation.*] The smash has come .. and not by my fault. Old George Booth—

ALICE. Has he been here?

EDWARD. Can you imagine it? He got at the truth. I told him to take his money .. what there was of it .. and prosecute. He won't prosecute, but he bargains to take the money .. and then to bleed us, sovereign by sovereign, as I earn sovereign by sovereign with the sweat of my soul. I'll see him in his Christian Heaven first .. the Jew!

ALICE. [*keeping her head.*] You can't reason with him?

EDWARD. No. He thinks he has the whip hand, and the Vicar has been told .. who has told his wife. She knows how not to keep a secret. It has come at last.

ALICE. So you're glad?

EDWARD. So thankful—my conscience is clear. I've done my best. [*Then as usual with him, his fervour collapses.*] And oh, Alice .. has it been worth doing?

ALICE. [*encouragingly.*] Half-a-dozen poor devils pulled safe out of the fire.

EDWARD. But I'm wondering now if that won't be found out, or if I shan't just confess to the pious fraud when the time comes. Somehow I don't seem to have the conviction to carry any job through. A weak nature, my father said. He knew.

ALICE. You have a religious nature.

EDWARD. [*surprised.*] Oh, no!

ALICE. [*proceeding to explain.*] Which means, of course, that you don't cling to creeds and ceremonies. And the good things and the well-done jobs of this worldly world don't satisfy you . . so you shirk contact with it all you can.

EDWARD. [*his eyes far away.*] Yes. Do you never feel that there aren't enough windows in a house?

ALICE. [*prosaically.*] In this weather . . too many.

EDWARD. In my office then—I feel it when I'm at work—one is out of all hearing of all the music of the world. And when one does get back to Nature, instead of being curves to her roundness, one is all corners.

ALICE. [*smiling at him.*] And you love to think prettily, don't you . . just as Hugh does. You do it quite well, too. [*Then briskly.*] But, Edward, may I scold you?

EDWARD. For that?

ALICE. Why have you grown to be more of a sloven than ever lately? Yes, a spiritual sloven, I call it—deliberately letting yourself be unhappy.

EDWARD. Is happiness under one's control?

ALICE. My friend, you shouldn't neglect your happiness any more than you neglect to wash your face. I was desperate about you . . so I came down to your office.

EDWARD. Yes, you did.

ALICE. But I found you master there, and I thanked God. Because with us, Edward, for these last eighteen months you've been more like a moral portent than a man—without a smile to throw to a friend . . or an opinion upon any subject. Why did you throw up your boys' club? Why didn't you vote last November?—too out of keeping with your unhappy fate?

EDWARD. [*contrite at this.*] I was wrong not to vote.

ALICE. You don't even eat properly.

With that she completes the accusation and EDWARD *searches round for a defence.*

EDWARD. But, Alice, it was always an effort to do all these things . . and lately every effort has had to go to my work, hasn't it?

ALICE. Oh . . if you only did them on principle . . I retract . . far better not do them at all.

EDWARD. Don't laugh at me.

ALICE. Edward, is there nothing you want from life . . want for its own sake? That's the only test.

EDWARD. I daren't ask.

ALICE. Yes, you dare. It's all so long past that awful time when you were . . more than a bit of a prig.

EDWARD. [*with enough sense of humour to whisper back.*] Was I?

ALICE. I'm afraid so! He still stalks through my dreams sometimes . . and I wake in a sweat. But I think he's nearly done with. [*Then her voice rises stirringly.*] Oh, don't you see what a blessing this cursed burden of disgrace and work was meant to be to you?

EDWARD. [*without a smile now.*] But lately, Alice, I've hardly known myself. Sometimes I've lost my temper . . I've been brutal.

ALICE. I knew it. I knew that would happen. It's your own wicked nature coming out at last. That's what we've been waiting for . . that's what we want. That's you.

EDWARD. [*still serious.*] I'm sorry for it.

ALICE. Oh, Edward, be a little proud of poor humanity . . take your own share in it gladly. It so discourages the rest of us if you don't.

Suddenly he breaks down completely.

EDWARD. I can't let myself be glad and live. There's the future to think of, and I'm so afraid of that. I must pretend I don't care . . even to myself . . even to you.

ALICE. [*her mocking at an end.*] What is it you fear

most about the future . . not just the obviously unpleasant things ?

EDWARD. They'll put me in prison.

ALICE. Even then ?

EDWARD. Who'll be the man who comes out ?

ALICE. Yourself, and more than ever yourself.

EDWARD. No, no ! I'm a coward. I can't stand alone, and after that I shall have to. I need affection . . I need friends. I cling to people that I don't care for deeply . . just for the comfort of it. I've no real home of my own. Every house that welcomes me now I like to think of as something of a home. And this disgrace in store will leave me . . homeless.

There he sits shaken. ALICE *waits a moment, not taking her eyes from him ; then speaks.*

ALICE. Edward, there's something else I want to scold you for. You've still given up proposing to me. Certainly that shows a lack of courage . . and of perseverance. Or is it the loss of what I always considered a very laudable ambition ?

EDWARD *is hardly able to trust his ears. Then he looks into her face and his thankfulness frames itself into a single sentence.*

EDWARD. Will you marry me ?

ALICE. Yes, Edward.

For a minute he just holds his breath with happiness. But he shakes himself free of it, almost savagely.

EDWARD. No, no, no, we mustn't be stupid. I'm sorry I asked you that.

ALICE. [*with serene strength.*] I'm glad that you want me. While I live . . where I am will be Home.

EDWARD. [*struggling with himself.*] No, it's too late. And if you'd said Yes before I came into my inheritance . . perhaps I shouldn't have given myself to the work. So be glad that it's too late. I am.

ALICE. [*happily.*] Marry you when you were only a

well-principled prig. . . Thanks! I didn't want you . . and I don't believe you really wanted me. But now you do, and you must always take what you want.

EDWARD. [*turning to her again.*] My dear, what have we to start life upon . . to build our house upon? Poverty . . and prison.

ALICE. [*mischievous.*] Edward, you seem to think that all the money in the world was invested in your precious firm. I have four hundred a year of my own. At least let that tempt you.

EDWARD *catches her in his arms with a momentary little burst of passion.*

EDWARD. You're tempting me.

She did not resist, but nevertheless he breaks away from her, disappointed with himself. She goes on, quietly, serenely.

ALICE. Am I? Unworthily? Oh, my dear, don't be afraid of wanting me. Shall we be less than friends by being more? If I thought that, should I ever have let it come to this? But now you must . . look at me and make your choice . . to refuse me my work and happiness in life and to cripple your own nature . . or to take my hand.

She puts out her hand frankly, as a friend should. With only a second's thought he, happy too now, takes it as frankly. Then she sits beside him and quite cheerfully changes the subject.

ALICE. Now, about old Mr. George Booth. What will he do?

EDWARD. [*responsive though impatient.*] Nothing. I shall be before him.

ALICE. Can we bargain with him to keep the firm going somehow? . . for if we can, I'm afraid we must.

At this EDWARD *makes a last attempt to abandon himself to his troubles.*

EDWARD. No, no . . let it end here, it'll be so useless.

They'll all be round in a day or two after their money like wasps after honey. And now they know I won't lift a finger in my own defence . . what sort of mercy will they have?

ALICE. [*triumphantly completing her case.*] Edward, I have a faith by which I hope to live, not humbly, but defying the world to be my master. Dare to surrender yourself entirely, and you'll find them powerless against you. You see, you had something to hope or fear from Mr. Booth, for you hoped in your heart he'd end your trouble. But conquer that last little atom of fear which we call selfishness, and you'll find you are doing what you wish with selfish men. [*And she adds fervently.*] Yes, the man who is able, and cares deeply, and yet has nothing to hope or fear is all-powerful . . even in little things.

EDWARD. But will nothing ever happen to set me free? Shall I never be able to rest for a moment . . turn round and say I've succeeded or I've failed?

ALICE. That's asking too much, and it isn't what matters . . one must have faith to go on.

EDWARD. Suppose they all meet and agree and syndicate themselves and keep me at it for life.

ALICE. Yes, I daresay they will, but what else could you wish for?

EDWARD. Than that dreary round!

ALICE. But the world must be put tidy. And it's the work which splendid criminals leave for poor commonplace people to do.

EDWARD. [*with a little laugh.*] And I don't believe in Heaven either.

ALICE. [*close to him.*] But there's to be our life. What's wrong with that?

EDWARD. My dear, when they put me in prison for swindling— [*He makes the word sound its worst.*]

ALICE. I think they won't, for it wouldn't pay them. But if they are so stupid . . I must be very careful.

EDWARD. Of what?

ALICE. To avoid false pride. I shall be foolishly proud of you.

EDWARD. It's good to be praised sometimes . . by you.

ALICE. My heart praises you. Good night.

EDWARD. Good night.

She kisses his forehead. But he puts up his face like a child, so she bends down and for the first time their lips meet. Then she steps back from him, adding happily, with perhaps just a touch of shyness.

ALICE. Till to-morrow.

EDWARD. [*echoing in gratitude the hope and promise in her voice.*] Till to-morrow.

She leaves him to sit there by the table for a few moments longer, looking into his future, streaked as it is to be with trouble and joy. As whose is not? From above . . from above the mantelpiece, that is to say . . the face of the late MR. VOYSEY *seems to look down upon his son not unkindly, though with that curious buccaneering twist of the eyebrows which distinguished his countenance in life.*

HINDLE WAKES

STANLEY HOUGHTON

HINDLE WAKES

was first produced by Miss Horniman's Repertory Company from the Gaiety Theatre, Manchester, before the Incorporated Stage Society, at the Aldwych Theatre, on Sunday, June 16, 1912, with the following cast:

MRS. HAWTHORN	Ada King.
CHRISTOPHER HAWTHORN	Charles Bibby.
FANNY HAWTHORN	Edyth Goodall.
MRS. JEFFCOTE	Daisy England.
NATHANIEL JEFFCOTE	Herbert Lomas.
ALAN JEFFCOTE	J. V. Bryant.
SIR TIMOTHY FARRAR	Edward Landor.
BEATRICE FARRAR	Sybil Thorndike.
ADA	Hilda Davies.

The Play produced by LEWIS CASSON.

Applications for permission to perform this play should be made: for professional production, to THE INTERNATIONAL COPYRIGHT BUREAU, LTD., Dewar House, Haymarket, London, S.W.1; for amateur performances, to SAMUEL FRENCH, LTD., Southampton Street, Strand, London, W.C.2.

HINDLE WAKES

ACT I

SCENE I

The scene is triangular, representing a corner of the living-room kitchen of No. 137, Burnley Road, Hindle, a house rented at about 7s. 6d. a week. In the left-hand wall, low down, there is a door leading to the scullery. In the same wall, but farther away from the spectator, is a window looking on to the backyard. A dresser stands in front of the window. About half-way up the right-hand wall is the door leading to the hall or passage. Nearer, against the same wall, a high cupboard for china and crockery. The fireplace is not visible, being in one of the walls not represented. However, down in the L. corner of the stage is an arm-chair, which stands by the hearth. In the middle of the room is a square table, with chairs on each side. The room is cheerful and comfortable. It is nine o'clock on a warm August evening. Through the window can be seen the darkening sky, as the blind is not drawn. Against the sky an outline of roof-tops and mill chimneys. The only light is the dim twilight from the open window. Thunder is in the air. When the curtain rises CHRISTOPHER HAWTHORN, *a decent, white-bearded man of nearly sixty, is sitting in the arm-chair smoking a pipe.* MRS. HAWTHORN, *a keen, sharp-faced woman of fifty-five, is standing gazing out of the window. There is a flash of lightning and a rumble of thunder far away.*

MRS. HAWTHORN. It's passing over. There'll be no rain.

CHRISTOPHER. Ay! We could do with some rain.

There is a flash of lightning.

CHRISTOPHER. Pull down the blind and light the gas.

MRS. HAWTHORN. What for?

CHRISTOPHER. It's more cosy-like with the gas.

MRS. HAWTHORN. You're not afraid of the lightning?

CHRISTOPHER. I want to look at that railway guide.

MRS. HAWTHORN. What's the good? We've looked at it twice already. There's no train from Blackpool till five past ten, and it's only just on nine now.

CHRISTOPHER. Happen we've made a mistake.

MRS. HAWTHORN. Happen we've not. Besides, what's the good of a railway guide? You know trains run as they like on Bank Holiday.

CHRISTOPHER. Ay! Perhaps you're right. You don't think she'll come round by Manchester?

MRS. HAWTHORN. What would she be doing coming round by Manchester?

CHRISTOPHER. You can get that road from Blackpool.

MRS. HAWTHORN. Yes. If she's coming from Blackpool.

CHRISTOPHER. Have you thought she may not come at all?

MRS. HAWTHORN. [*grimly.*] What do you take me for?

CHRISTOPHER. You never hinted.

MRS. HAWTHORN. No use putting them sort of ideas into your head.

Another flash and a peal of thunder.

CHRISTOPHER. Well, well, those are lucky who haven't to travel at all on Bank Holiday.

MRS. HAWTHORN. Unless they've got a motor-car, like Nat Jeffcote's lad.

CHRISTOPHER. Nay. He's not got one.

MRS. HAWTHORN. What? Why, I saw him with my own eyes setting out in it last Saturday week after the mill shut.

CHRISTOPHER. Ay! He's gone off these Wakes with his pal George Ramsbottom. A couple of thick beggars, those two!

MRS. HAWTHORN. Then what do you mean telling me he's not got a motor-car?

CHRISTOPHER. I said he hadn't got one of his own. It's his father's. You don't catch Nat Jeffcote parting with owt before his time. That's how he holds his lad in check, as you might say.

MRS. HAWTHORN. Alan Jeffcote's seldom short of cash. He spends plenty.

CHRISTOPHER. Ay! Nat gives him what he asks for, and doesn't want to know how he spends it either. But he's got to ask for it first. Nat can stop supplies any time if he's a mind.

MRS. HAWTHORN. That's likely, isn't it?

CHRISTOPHER. Queerer things have happened. You don't know Nat like I do. He's a bad one to get across with.

Another flash and gentle peal. MRS. HAWTHORN *gets up.*

MRS. HAWTHORN. I'll light the gas.

She pulls down the blind and lights the gas.

CHRISTOPHER. When I met Nat this morning he told me that Alan had telegraphed from Llandudno on Saturday asking for twenty pounds.

MRS. HAWTHORN. From Llandudno?

CHRISTOPHER. Ay! Reckon he's been stopping there. Run short of brass.

MRS. HAWTHORN. And did he send it?

CHRISTOPHER. Of course he sent it. Nat doesn't stint the lad. [*He laughs quietly.*] Eh, but he can get through it, though!

MRS. HAWTHORN. Look here. What are you going to say to Fanny when she comes?

CHRISTOPHER. Ask her where she's been.

MRS. HAWTHORN. Ask her where she's been! Of course we'll do that. But suppose she won't tell us?

CHRISTOPHER. She's always been a good girl.

MRS. HAWTHORN. She's always gone her own road. Suppose she tells us to mind our own business?

CHRISTOPHER. I reckon it is my business to know what she's been up to.

MRS. HAWTHORN. Don't you forget it. And don't let her forget it either. If you do, I promise you I won't!

CHRISTOPHER. All right. Where's that post card?

MRS. HAWTHORN. Little good taking heed of that.

CHRISTOPHER *rises and gets a picture post card from the dresser.*

CHRISTOPHER. [*reading.*] " Shall be home before late on Monday. Lovely weather." [*Looking at the picture.*] North Pier, Blackpool. Very like, too.

MRS. HAWTHORN. [*suddenly.*] Let's have a look. When was it posted?

CHRISTOPHER. It's dated Sunday.

MRS. HAWTHORN. That's nowt to go by. Any one can put the wrong date. What's the post-mark? [*She scrutinises it.*] " August 5th, summat P.M." I can't make out the time.

CHRISTOPHER. August 5th. That was yesterday, all right. There'd only be one post on Sunday.

MRS. HAWTHORN. Then she was in Blackpool up to yesterday, that's certain.

CHRISTOPHER. Ay!

MRS. HAWTHORN. Well, it's a mystery.

CHRISTOPHER. [*shaking his head.*] Or summat worse.

MRS. HAWTHORN. Eh? You don't think that, eh?

CHRISTOPHER. I don't know what to think.

MRS. HAWTHORN. Nor me neither.

They sit silent for a time. There is a rumble of thunder, far away. After it has died away a knock is heard at the front door. They turn and look at each other. MRS. HAWTHORN *rises and goes out in silence. In a few moments* FANNY HAWTHORN *comes in, followed by* MRS. HAWTHORN. FANNY *is a sturdy, determined, dark little girl, with thick lips, a broad, short nose and big black eyes. She is dressed rather smartly, but not very tastefully. She stands by the table unpinning her hat and talking cheerfully.* MRS. HAWTHORN *stands by the door and* CHRISTOPHER *remains in his chair. Both look at* FANNY *queerly.*

FANNY. Well, you didn't expect me as soon as this, I'll bet. I came round by Manchester. They said the trains would run better that way to-night. Bank Holiday, you know. I always think they let the Manchester trains through before any of the others, don't you?

MRS. HAWTHORN. We didn't see how you were to get here till past ten if you came direct. We've been looking up in the Guide.

FANNY. No. I wasn't for coming direct at any price. Mary wanted to.

CHRISTOPHER. Mary!

CHRISTOPHER *is about to rise in astonishment, but* MRS. HAWTHORN *makes signs to him behind* FANNY'S *back.*

MRS. HAWTHORN. Oh! So Mary Hollins wanted to come back the other way, did she?

FANNY. Yes. But I wasn't having any. They said the Manchester trains would be—oh! I've told you all that already.

MRS. HAWTHORN. So you've had a good time, Fanny?

FANNY. Rather! A fair treat. What do you think?

MRS. HAWTHORN. Was Mary Hollins with you all the time?

FANNY. Of course she was.

VOL. I 2 B

She steals a puzzled glance at MRS. HAWTHORN.

MRS. HAWTHORN. And she came back with you to-night?

FANNY. Yes.

MRS. HAWTHORN. And where's she gone now?

FANNY. She's gone home, of course. Where else should she go?

There is a short pause.

CHRISTOPHER. [*quietly.*] You're telling lies, my girl.

FANNY. What, father?

CHRISTOPHER. That's not the truth you've just been saying.

FANNY. What's not the truth?

CHRISTOPHER. You didn't spend the week-end in Blackpool with Mary Hollins.

FANNY. Who says I didn't?

CHRISTOPHER. I say so.

FANNY. Why do you think I didn't, father?

CHRISTOPHER. Well, did you?

FANNY. Yes, I did.

CHRISTOPHER *turns helplessly to his wife.*

MRS. HAWTHORN. All right, Chris, wait a minute. Look here, Fanny, it's no use trying to make us believe you've been away with Mary.

FANNY. What? I can bring you any number of folk out of Hindle who saw us in Blackpool last week.

MRS. HAWTHORN. Last week, happen. Not this week-end?

FANNY. Yes.

MRS. HAWTHORN. Bring them, then.

FANNY. How can I bring them to-night? They've most of them not come back yet.

MRS. HAWTHORN. Tell us who to ask, then.

FANNY [*thinking.*] Ask Polly Britwistle. Or Ethel Slater.

MRS. HAWTHORN. Yes. After you've got at them and given them a hint what to say.

FANNY. Of course if you'll believe that it's no use asking Mary. You'd only say she was telling lies as well.
There is a pause.
FANNY. Will you go round and see Mary?
CHRISTOPHER. No.
MRS. HAWTHORN. Fanny, it's no use seeing Mary. You may as well own up and tell us where you've been.
FANNY. I've been to Blackpool with Mary Hollins.
MRS. HAWTHORN. You've not. You weren't there this week-end.
FANNY. Why, I sent you a picture post card on Sunday.
MRS. HAWTHORN. Yes, we got that. Who posted it?
FANNY. I posted it myself at the pillar-box on the Central Pier.
There is a pause. They do not believe her.
FANNY. [*flaring up*.] I tell you I've been all week-end at Blackpool with Mary Hollins.
CHRISTOPHER. [*quietly*.] No, you've not.
FANNY. [*pertly*.] Well, that's settled then. There's no need to talk about it any more.
A pause. FANNY *nervously twists her handkerchief.*
FANNY. Look here. Who's been saying I didn't?
CHRISTOPHER. We know you didn't.
FANNY. But you can't know.
MRS. HAWTHORN. As certain as there's a God in Heaven we know it.
FANNY. Well, that's not so certain after all.
CHRISTOPHER. Fanny! Take heed what you're saying.
FANNY. Why can't you speak out? What do you know? Tell me that.
MRS. HAWTHORN. It's not for us to tell you anything. It's for you to tell us where you've been.
FANNY. [*mutinously*.] I've told you.
They do not speak. FANNY *rises quickly.*

MRS. HAWTHORN. Where are you going?

FANNY. Are you trying to hinder me from going out when I please, now? I'm going to see Mary Hollins.

MRS. HAWTHORN. What for?

FANNY. To fetch her here. You shall see her whether you like it or not.

CHRISTOPHER. Fanny, I've already seen Mary Hollins.

FANNY *turns and stares at him in surprise.*

FANNY. When?

CHRISTOPHER. This morning.

FANNY. She was at Blackpool this morning.

CHRISTOPHER. So was I.

FANNY. [*amazed.*] What were you doing there?

CHRISTOPHER. I went there with Jim Hollins. We went on purpose to see Mary.

FANNY. So it's Mary as has given me away, is it?

CHRISTOPHER. [*nodding, slowly.*] Yes. You might say so.

FANNY. [*angrily.*] I'll talk to her.

CHRISTOPHER. It wasn't her fault. She couldn't help it.

MRS. HAWTHORN. Now will you tell us where you've been?

FANNY. No, I won't. I'll see Mary first. What did she say to you?

CHRISTOPHER. When I told thee I went with Jim Hollins to Blackpool, I didn't tell thee quite everything, lass. [*Gently.*] Mary Hollins was drowned yesterday afternoon.

FANNY. What! [*She stares at* CHRISTOPHER *in horror.*]

CHRISTOPHER. It was one of them sailing boats. Run down by an excursion steamer. There was over twenty people on board. Seven of them was drowned.

FANNY. Oh! My poor Mary!

FANNY *sinks down into her chair and stares dully at* CHRISTOPHER.

MRS. HAWTHORN. You didn't know that?
FANNY. [*shaking her head.*] No, no. [*She buries her head in her arms on the table and begins to sob.*]
MRS. HAWTHORN. Now then, Fanny. [*She is about to resume her inquisition.*]
CHRISTOPHER. Hold on, mother. Wait a bit. Give her a chance.
MRS. HAWTHORN. [*waving him aside.*] Now then, Fanny. You see you've been telling lies all the time.
FANNY *sobs*.
MRS. HAWTHORN. Listen to me. You weren't at Blackpool this week-end.
FANNY. [*to herself.*] Poor, poor Mary!
MRS. HAWTHORN. [*patiently.*] You weren't at Blackpool this week-end.
FANNY *sobs*.
MRS. HAWTHORN. Were you?
FANNY. [*sobbing.*] N—no. [*She shakes her head without raising it.*]
MRS. HAWTHORN. Where were you?
FANNY. Shan't tell you.
MRS. HAWTHORN. You went away for the week-end? [*No answer.*] Did you go alone? [*No answer.*] You didn't go alone, of course. [*No answer.*] Who did you go with?
FANNY. Leave me alone, mother.
MRS. HAWTHORN. Who did you go with? Did you go with a fellow?
FANNY *stops sobbing. She raises her head the tiniest bit so that she can see her mother without seeming to do so. Her eyes are just visible above her arm.* MRS. HAWTHORN *marks the movement, nevertheless.*
MRS. HAWTHORN. [*nodding.*] Yes. You went with a chap?
FANNY. [*quickly dropping her head again.*] No, I didn't.

MRS. HAWTHORN. [*roughly.*] You little liar, you did! You know you did! Who was he?

    MRS. HAWTHORN seizes FANNY by the shoulder and shakes her in exasperation. FANNY sobs.

MRS. HAWTHORN. Will you tell us who he was?

FANNY. [*sharply.*] No, I won't.

There is a slight pause.

CHRISTOPHER. This is what happens to many a lass, but I never thought to have it happen to a lass of mine!

MRS. HAWTHORN. Why didn't you get wed if you were so curious? There's plenty would have had you.

FANNY. Chance is a fine thing. Happen I wouldn't have had them!

MRS. HAWTHORN. Happen you'll be sorry for it before long. There's not so many will have you now, if this gets about.

CHRISTOPHER. He ought to wed her.

MRS. HAWTHORN. Of course he ought to wed her, and shall too, or I'll know the reason why! Come now, who's the chap?

FANNY. Shan't tell you.

MRS. HAWTHORN. Look here.

    She places her hand on FANNY'S arm. FANNY turns round fiercely and flings it off.

FANNY. Leave me alone, can't you? You ought to be thankful he did take me away. It saved my life, anyhow.

MRS. HAWTHORN. How do you make that out?

FANNY. I'd have been drowned with Mary if I hadn't gone to Llandudno.

MRS. HAWTHORN. Llandudno? Did you say—? [*She stops short.*]

CHRISTOPHER. Why, mother, that's—

MRS. HAWTHORN. [*cutting him short.*] Be quiet, can't you?

    She reflects for a moment, and then sits down at the other side of the table, opposite FANNY.

MRS. HAWTHORN. [*with meaning.*] When you were in Llandudno did you happen to run across Alan Jeffcote?

FANNY *looks up and they stare hard at each other.*

FANNY. [*at length.*] How did you know?

MRS. HAWTHORN. [*smiling grimly.*] I didn't. You've just told me.

FANNY. [*gives a low moan.*] Oh! [*She buries her head and sobs.*]

MRS. HAWTHORN. [*to* CHRISTOPHER.] Well? What do you think of her now?

CHRISTOPHER. [*dazed.*] Nat Jeffcote's lad!

MRS. HAWTHORN. Ay! Nat Jeffcote's lad. But what does that matter? If it hadn't been him it would have been some other lad.

CHRISTOPHER. Nat and me were lads together. We were pals.

MRS. HAWTHORN. Well, now thy girl and Nat's lad are pals. Pull thyself together, man. What art going to do about it?

CHRISTOPHER. I don't know, rightly.

MRS. HAWTHORN. Aren't you going to give her a talking-to?

CHRISTOPHER. What's the good?

MRS. HAWTHORN. What's the good? Well, I like that! My father would have got a stick to me. [*She turns to* FANNY.] Did he promise to wed you?

FANNY. [*in a low voice.*] No.

MRS. HAWTHORN. Why not?

FANNY. Never asked him.

MRS. HAWTHORN. You little fool! Have you no common sense at all? What did you do it for if you didn't make him promise to wed you?

FANNY *does not reply.*

MRS. HAWTHORN. Do you hear me? What made you do it?

FANNY *sobs.*

CHRISTOPHER. Let her be, mother.

MRS. HAWTHORN. She's turned stupid. [*To* FANNY.] When did you go? [*No answer.*] Did you go in his motor-car? [*No answer.*] Where did you stay?

There is no answer, so she shakes FANNY.

Will you take heed of what I'm saying? Haven't you got a tongue in your head? Tell us exactly what took place.

FANNY. I won't tell you anything more.

MRS. HAWTHORN. We'll see about that.

CHRISTOPHER [*rising.*] That's enough, mother. We'll leave her alone to-night. [*He touches* FANNY *on the shoulder.*] Now then, lass, no one's going to harm thee. Stop thy crying. Thou'd better get upstairs to bed. Happen thou's fagged out.

MRS. HAWTHORN. You are soft. You're never going to let her off so easy?

CHRISTOPHER. There's plenty of time to tackle her in the morning. Come, lass.

FANNY *rises and stands by the table, wiping her eyes.*

Get to bed and have some sleep, if thou can.

Without a word FANNY *slowly goes to the door and out of the room. She does not look at either of them.*

MRS. HAWTHORN. Now then. What's to be done?

CHRISTOPHER. Ay! That's it.

MRS. HAWTHORN. You'll have to waken up a bit if we're to make the most of this. I can tell you what's the first job. You'll have to go and see Nathaniel Jeffcote.

CHRISTOPHER. I'll see him at the mill to-morrow.

MRS. HAWTHORN. To-morrow! You'll go and see him to-night. Go up to the house at Bank Top. If Alan's come home with Fanny he'll be there as well, and you can kill two birds with one stone.

CHRISTOPHER. It's a nasty job.

MRS. HAWTHORN. It's got to be done, and the sooner the better. How would it be if I come with you?

CHRISTOPHER. [*hastily.*] Nay. I'll go alone.

MRS. HAWTHORN. I'm afraid you'll be too soft. It's a fine chance, and don't you forget it.

CHRISTOPHER. A fine chance?

MRS. HAWTHORN. To get her wed, thou great stupid. We're not going to be content with less. We'll show them up if they turn nasty.

CHRISTOPHER. He ought to wed her. I don't know what Nat'll say.

MRS. HAWTHORN. Look here, if you're not going to stand out for your rights I'll come myself. I'm not afraid of Nat Jeffcote, not if he owned twenty mills like Daisy Bank.

CHRISTOPHER. I'm not afraid of him, neither, though he's a bad man to tackle. [*He rises.*] Where's my hat?

MRS. HAWTHORN *gives him his hat and stick, and he goes to the door.*

MRS. HAWTHORN. I say. I wonder if she's done this on purpose, after all. Plenty of girls have made good matches that way.

CHRISTOPHER. She said they never mentioned marriage. You heard her.

MRS. HAWTHORN. Well, he mightn't have gone with her if she had. Happen she's cleverer than we think!

CHRISTOPHER. She always was a deep one.

MRS. HAWTHORN. That's how Bamber's lass got hold of young Greenwood.

CHRISTOPHER. But there was a— He couldn't help it, so well.

MRS. HAWTHORN. Yes. [*She reflects.*] Ah, well. You never know what may happen.

CHRISTOPHER *goes out followed by* MRS. HAWTHORN *as the curtain falls.*

Scene II

The breakfast-room at Nathaniel Jeffcote's house, Bank Top, Hindle Vale, is almost vast, for the house is one of those great old-fashioned places standing in ample grounds that are to be found on the outskirts of the smaller Lancashire manufacturing towns. They are inhabited by wealthy manufacturers who have resisted the temptation to live at St. Anne's-on-the-Sea, or Blackpool. In the wall facing the spectator is the door from the hall, which when the door is open can be seen distinctly, a big square place. The fireplace is in the right-hand wall, and a bow window in the left-hand one. The furniture is solid and costly, but the room is comfortable and looks as if it is intended to be lived in. A table stands in the middle, a sideboard near the door, arm-chairs near the hearth, whilst other chairs and furniture (including a bookcase filled with standard works) complete the rather ponderous interior. The Jeffcotes use the breakfast-room for all meals except ceremonious ones, when the dining-room is requisitioned and an elaborate dinner is substituted for the high tea which Nathaniel persists in regarding as an essential of comfort and homeliness. It is about 10.30 on the same Bank Holiday evening. The room is well lighted by gas, not electricity, but of course there is no fire.

NATHANIEL JEFFCOTE *and his wife are sitting alone in the room. He is a tall, thin, gaunt, withered domineering man of sixty. When excited or angry he drops into dialect, but otherwise his speech, though flat, is fairly accurate.* MRS. JEFFCOTE *has even more fully adapted herself to the responsibilities and duties imposed by the possession of wealth. She is a plump, mild, and good-natured woman. She sits under the chandelier embroidering, whilst her husband sits in an arm-chair by the empty hearth working calculations in a small shiny black notebook, which he carries about with him everywhere, in a side pocket.*

MRS. JEFFCOTE. I asked Mrs. Plews to let me have a look through Hindle Lodge to-day.

JEFFCOTE. [*looking up.*] Eh? What's that?

MRS. JEFFCOTE. Mrs. Plews is leaving Hindle Lodge at Christmas.

JEFFCOTE. What of it?

MRS. JEFFCOTE. I was thinking it would do very well for Alan when he gets married.

JEFFCOTE. Is Alan talking about getting married?

MRS. JEFFCOTE. Beatrice was mentioning it last week.

JEFFCOTE. How long have they been engaged? A year?

MRS. JEFFCOTE. Eleven months. I remember it was on September the 5th that it happened.

JEFFCOTE. How on earth can you remember that?

MRS. JEFFCOTE. Because September the 5th is your birthday.

JEFFCOTE. Is it? [*He grunts.*] Well, eleven months isn't so long after all. Let 'em wait a bit longer.

MRS. JEFFCOTE. I thought we might be speaking for the Lodge.

JEFFCOTE. What do they want with a house like the Lodge? Isn't there plenty of room here? We've got four living-rooms and fourteen bedrooms in this house, and there's never more than three of them going at the same time.

MRS. JEFFCOTE. Really, Nat! They'll want a house of their own, no matter how many bedrooms we've got empty, and it's only natural.

JEFFCOTE. There's no hurry as far as I can see. Alan won't be twenty-five till next March, will he?

MRS. JEFFCOTE. You were only twenty-two when you married me.

JEFFCOTE. I didn't marry a girl who'd been brought

up like Beatrice Farrar. I married a girl who could help me to make money. Beatrice won't do that. She'll help to spend it, likely.

MRS. JEFFCOTE. Well, he'll have it to spend. What's money for?

JEFFCOTE. Money's power. That's why I like money. Not for what it can buy.

MRS. JEFFCOTE. All the same, you've always done yourself pretty well, Nat.

JEFFCOTE. Because it pays in the long run. And it's an outward sign. Why did I buy a motor-car? Not because I wanted to go motoring. I hate it. I bought it so that people could see Alan driving about in it, and say, " There's Jeffcote's lad in his new car. It cost five hundred quid." Tim Farrar was so keen on getting his knighthood for the same reason. Every one knows that him and me started life in a weaving shed. That's why we like to have something to show 'em how well we've done. That's why we put some of our brass into houses and motors and knighthoods and fancy articles of the kind. I've put a deal of brass into our Alan, and Tim Farrar's put a deal into his Beatrice, with just the same object in view.

There is a short pause. JEFFCOTE *goes on with his reckoning and* MRS. JEFFCOTE *with her sewing. Then she speaks quietly.*

MRS. JEFFCOTE. I was wondering what you intend to do for Alan when he gets married.

JEFFCOTE. Do for him? What do you mean?

MRS. JEFFCOTE. He doesn't get a regular salary, does he?

JEFFCOTE. [*suspiciously.*] Has Alan been putting you up to talk to me about this?

MRS. JEFFCOTE. Well, Nat, if he has—?

JEFFCOTE. Why can't he talk to me himself?

MRS. JEFFCOTE. [*placidly continuing.*] You're not

such a good one to tackle. I daresay he thought I should do it better than he would.

JEFFCOTE. I don't keep him short, do I?

MRS. JEFFCOTE. No. But Sir Timothy will expect him to show something more definite before the wedding.

JEFFCOTE. Tim Farrar don't need to be afraid. I hope he'll leave his lass as much as I shall leave Alan. That lad'll be the richest man in Hindle some day.

MRS. JEFFCOTE. I daresay. Some day! That's not much good to set up house on. Why don't you take him into partnership?

JEFFCOTE. Partnership?

MRS. JEFFCOTE. You always say he works hard enough.

JEFFCOTE. [*grudgingly*.] Well enough.

MRS. JEFFCOTE. I suppose it comes to this. You don't want to take him into partnership because it would mean parting with some of that power you're so fond of.

JEFFCOTE. He mightn't work so well if he was his own master.

MRS. JEFFCOTE. But if you gave him a junior partnership he wouldn't be his own master. You'd see to that.

JEFFCOTE. [*jocularly dropping into dialect*.] Eh, lass! thou'd better come and manage mill thyself.

MRS. JEFFCOTE. I shouldn't make such a bad job of it, neither! Remember that if you take him in you'll have less work to do yourself. He'll share the responsibility.

JEFFCOTE. Hold on a bit. The owd cock's not done with yet.

MRS. JEFFCOTE. If Beatrice starts talking about the date—

JEFFCOTE. Oh, if you'll stop your worritting I daresay I'll take the lad into partnership on his wedding-day.

MRS. JEFFCOTE. Can I tell Sir Timothy that?

JEFFCOTE. If you like. I told him myself six months ago.

MRS. JEFFCOTE. You are a caution, Nat, indeed you

are! Why couldn't you tell me so at once, instead of making a fool of me like this?

JEFFCOTE. I like to hear thee talking, lass.

Having brought off this characteristic stroke of humour, JEFFCOTE *resumes his work. The door opens and* ADA *comes in.*

ADA. If you please, sir, there's some one to see you.

JEFFCOTE. [*absorbed.*] Eh?

MRS. JEFFCOTE. Who is it, Ada?

ADA. His name's Hawthorn, ma'am.

MRS. JEFFCOTE. It'll be Christopher Hawthorn, Nat.

JEFFCOTE. What does he want coming so late as this? Fetch him in here.

ADA *goes out.* Can't be owt wrong at the mill, seeing it's Bank Holiday.

ADA *shows in* CHRISTOPHER, *who stands near the door.*

MRS. JEFFCOTE. Good evening, Mr. Hawthorn.

CHRISTOPHER. Good evening, Mrs. Jeffcote.

JEFFCOTE. [*rising.*] Well, Chris!

CHRISTOPHER. Well, Nat!

These two old comrades address each other by their first names, although master and man.

JEFFCOTE. Sit down. The rain's held off.

CHRISTOPHER. Ay! [*He is obviously ill at ease.*]

MRS. JEFFCOTE. Where have you been these Wakes?

CHRISTOPHER. Nowhere.

MRS. JEFFCOTE. What? Stopped at home?

CHRISTOPHER. Ay! Somehow we don't seem quite as keen on Blackpool as we used to be. And the missus was badly last week with her leg, and what with one thing and another we let it drift this time round. You've not been away, either?

MRS. JEFFCOTE. No, we went to Norway in June, you know.

CHRISTOPHER. Ay! so you did. That must be a fine place—from the pictures.

MRS. JEFFCOTE. Alan is away, though. He is motoring in North Wales. We expect him back to-night.

JEFFCOTE. Business is too bad to go away, Chris. I was down in Manchester Tuesday and Friday. It isn't Wakes in Manchester, thou knows!

CHRISTOPHER. Anything doing?

JEFFCOTE. I landed ten sets of those brown jacconets on Friday. Five for October and five for November.

CHRISTOPHER. For the forty-four inch looms?

JEFFCOTE. Ay! And hark you, Chris! they're complaining about the tint. Not bright enough, they say in India. They've sent a pattern over this mail. You'd better have a look at it to-morrow. We've got to give them what they want, I reckon.

CHRISTOPHER. I don't think they do know what they want in India, Nat.

JEFFCOTE. You're about right there, Chris.

A pause. CHRISTOPHER *looks uncomfortably at* MRS. JEFFCOTE.

JEFFCOTE. [*at length.*] When are you going to bed, mother?

MRS. JEFFCOTE. [*taking the hint.*] Any time now.

JEFFCOTE. That's right. Just reach me the whisky before you go.

MRS. JEFFCOTE *gets a bottle of whisky, a syphon, and glasses from the sideboard cupboard.*

MRS. JEFFCOTE. Are you going to sit up for Alan?

JEFFCOTE. Why? Hasn't he got his latchkey?

MRS. JEFFCOTE. I expect so.

JEFFCOTE. Then I reckon he'll be able to find the keyhole, and if he can't he won't thank me for sitting up to welcome him.

MRS. JEFFCOTE. [*smiling.*] You do talk some nonsense, Nat. Good night, Mr. Hawthorn.

CHRISTOPHER. [*rising.*] Good night, Mrs. Jeffcote.
MRS. JEFFCOTE *goes out of the room.*
JEFFCOTE. Have a drink, Chris?
CHRISTOPHER. No thanks, Nat.
JEFFCOTE. [*incredulously.*] Get away!
CHRISTOPHER. Well—just a small one, then.
JEFFCOTE *pours out two drinks.*
JEFFCOTE. Light your pipe, Chris.
CHRISTOPHER. Ay! Thanks. [*He does so.*]
JEFFCOTE. It's a long while since we had a quiet chat together. We don't see so much of each other as we did thirty years ago?
CHRISTOPHER. No. You've other fish to fry, I reckon.
JEFFCOTE. I'm always right glad to see you. How long have you been taping for me, Chris?
CHRISTOPHER. I came to you in '95. I remember because Joe Walmesley's shed was burnt down the same year.
JEFFCOTE. Ay! That was during the General Election, when Tories knocked out Mark Smethurst in Hindle. Joe was speaking at one of Mark's meetings when they come and told him his mill was afire. That was the only time I ever saw Joe Walmesley cry.
CHRISTOPHER. He was fond of them looms, was Joe!
JEFFCOTE. You missed your way, Chris, you did indeed, when you wouldn't come in with me and put your savings into Trafalgar Mill.
CHRISTOPHER. That's what the missus is never tired of telling me.
JEFFCOTE. You might have been my partner these fifteen years instead of only my slasher.
CHRISTOPHER. You'd never have got on with a partner, Nat. You're too fond of your own way.
JEFFCOTE. You're right there. I've been used to it for a good while now.

CHRISTOPHER. You don't remember Daisy Bank being built, Nat?

JEFFCOTE. No. I was living over Blackburn way then.

CHRISTOPHER. I was only a lad at the time. I used to come along the river bank on Sundays with the other lads. There were no weaving sheds in Hindle Vale in those days; nothing but fields all the way to Harwood Bridge. Daisy Bank was the first shed put up outside Hindle proper. They called it Daisy Bank because of the daisies in the meadows. All the side of the brow falling away towards the river was thick with them. Thick dotted it was, like the stars in the sky of a clear night.

JEFFCOTE Look here, old lad, thou didn't come up here at this time of night just to talk about daisies.

CHRISTOPHER. Eh?

JEFFCOTE. You've come up here with a purpose, haven't you?

CHRISTOPHER. That's so, Nat.

JEFFCOTE. I could see that. That's why I sent the missus to bed. I know you of old. What is it that's troubling you? Get it off your chest!

CHRISTOPHER. It's about my lass.

JEFFCOTE. Hullo!

CHRISTOPHER. I'm worried about her.

JEFFCOTE. What's she been doing?

CHRISTOPHER. Getting into trouble.

JEFFCOTE. What sort of trouble?

CHRISTOPHER. [*troubled.*] Well, thou knows—there's only one sort of trouble—

JEFFCOTE. Ay—ay! With a lad?

CHRISTOPHER. Ay!

There is a slight pause.

CHRISTOPHER. It's only by chance we found it out. The missus is in a fine way about it, I can tell you!

JEFFCOTE. Then it's proper serious, like?

CHRISTOPHER. They've been away together, these Wakes.

JEFFCOTE. [*whistling*.] Humph! She's a cool customer. What art going to do in the matter?

CHRISTOPHER. That's what I've come up to see thee about. I wasn't for coming to-night, but missus, she was set on it.

JEFFCOTE. Quite right, too. I'll help thee any road I can. But you mustn't take it too much to heart. It's not the first time a job like this has happened in Hindle, and it won't be the last!

CHRISTOPHER. That's true. But it's poor comfort when it's your own lass that's got into trouble.

JEFFCOTE. There's many a couple living happy to-day as first come together in that fashion.

CHRISTOPHER. Wedded, you mean?

JEFFCOTE. Ay! Wedded, of course. What else do you think I meant? Does the lad live in Hindle?

CHRISTOPHER. Ay! [*He does not know how to break it to* JEFFCOTE.]

JEFFCOTE. Whose shed does he work at?

CHRISTOPHER. Well, since you put it that way, he works at yours.

JEFFCOTE. At Daisy Bank? Do I know him?

CHRISTOPHER. Ay! You know him well.

JEFFCOTE. Then by Gad! I'll have it out with him to-morrow. If he doesn't promise to wed thy Fanny I'll give him the sack!

CHRISTOPHER. [*dazed*.] Give him the sack!

JEFFCOTE. And I'll go further. If he'll be a decent lad and make it right with her at once, I'll see that he's well looked after at the mill. We're old pals, Chris, and I can't do no fairer than that, can I?

CHRISTOPHER. No.

JEFFCOTE. Now, then, who's the chap?

CHRISTOPHER. Thou'll be a bit surprised-like, I reckon.

JEFFCOTE. Spit it out!
CHRISTOPHER. It's thy lad, Alan.
JEFFCOTE. [*sharply.*] What? [*A slight pause.*] Say that again.
CHRISTOPHER. Thy lad, Alan.
JEFFCOTE. My lad?
CHRISTOPHER. Ay!

After a short pause, JEFFCOTE *springs up in a blazing rage.*

JEFFCOTE. Damn you, Chris Hawthorn! why the devil couldn't you tell me so before?
CHRISTOPHER. I were trying to tell thee, Nat—
JEFFCOTE. Trying to tell me! Hasn't thou got a tongue in thy head that thou mun sit there like a bundle of grey-cloth while I'm making a fool of myself this road? [*He paces up and down in his agitation.*] Here! How do you know it's Alan? Who says it's Alan?
CHRISTOPHER. Fanny.
JEFFCOTE. Fanny, eh? How do you know she's not lying?
CHRISTOPHER. [*stoutly.*] You can settle it soon enough by asking Alan. I thought to have found him here to-night.
JEFFCOTE. He's not come home yet.
CHRISTOPHER. No.
JEFFCOTE. And a good job for him, too!
CHRISTOPHER. Wouldn't he fetch Fanny back, think you?
JEFFCOTE. Would he, the dickens! He's not altogether without sense. Do you think he'd run her in the car through Hindle market-place and up Burnley Road and set her down at your house for all the folk to see?
CHRISTOPHER. No.
JEFFCOTE. [*suddenly flaring up again.*] The bally young fool! I'd like to break his silly neck for him! And that lass of thine is just as much to blame as he is! I've marked her—the hot-blooded little wench!

CHRISTOPHER. I can't defend her. She's always been a bit of a mystery to her mother and me. There's that in her veins as keeps her restless and uneasy. If she sees you want her to do one thing she'll go right away and do t'other out of pure cussedness. She won't be driven, not any road. I had a dog just like her once.

JEFFCOTE. Eh, old lad, it's a good job you never had any boys if you don't know how to manage a girl!

CHRISTOPHER. Happen I could have managed lads better. I never could clout a girl properly.

JEFFCOTE. I can manage my lad without clouting. Always could.

CHRISTOPHER. Folk are different, you see. Happen you couldn't have managed our Fanny.

JEFFCOTE. I'd have had a damn good try! Where is she now?

CHRISTOPHER. At the house. She was overdone, and I sent her to bed to get her out of range of the missus's tongue. She was talking rather bitter, like.

JEFFCOTE. She had a sharp way with her when she was Sarah Riley, had your missus, and I reckon it won't have improved with the passing of years! I shouldn't wonder if it was your missus who got the truth out of Fanny.

CHRISTOPHER. So it was.

JEFFCOTE. And what did she get out of her? Let's be knowing just what took place.

CHRISTOPHER. I can tell you nowt save that they stayed in Llandudno. You'll have to go to your lad for the rest of the story.

JEFFCOTE. All right. I'll see you to-morrow at the mill. There's nowt more to be done to-night.

CHRISTOPHER. Maybe it's a queer fancy, but I'd like to have seen him to-night. There's no chance of him coming in shortly, think you?

JEFFCOTE. He may come in the next five minutes,

or he may not come home at all. There's no telling what may happen on Bank Holiday.

CHRISTOPHER. Then it's no use me waiting a while?

JEFFCOTE. Nay, you can't wait here. I'm going to bed. I'm not going to let this business spoil a night's rest. I'd advise you to look on it in the same light.

CHRISTOPHER. Ah, Nat, but it's not so hard on you as it is on me!

JEFFCOTE. Is it not? How do you know what plans of mine will come to naught through this job? [*More kindly.*] Come, old lad, thou mun clear out. Thou can do nowt here.

CHRISTOPHER. Well, I've not said all that my missus told me to say, and I doubt she'll be on my track, but I reckon it's a bit too previous afore we've seen the lad.

JEFFCOTE. If your wife wants to say anything to me, she's welcome. You'd better fetch her up here to-morrow night, and bring Fanny along as well. I'll be ready for you by then.

CHRISTOPHER. To-morrow night?

JEFFCOTE. About nine o'clock. Do you understand?

CHRISTOPHER. Ay! [*He goes to the door, and* JEFFCOTE *rises.*] My wife said—

JEFFCOTE. [*curtly.*] I can guess all that thy wife said. You can tell her this from me. I'll see you're treated right. Do you hear?

JEFFCOTE *opens the door.*

CHRISTOPHER. I can't ask for more than that.

JEFFCOTE. I'll see you're treated right.

They go into the hall out of sight. ADA *comes into the room with a tray, which she places on the table. The tray holds bread, cheese, butter, a bottle of beer and a tumbler.*

JEFFCOTE. [*out of sight in the hall.*] I'm not afraid of thy wife, if you are.

The front door bangs. JEFFCOTE *returns into the room and sees the tray, which he examines irritably.*

JEFFCOTE. What's this for?

ADA. Mr. Alan's tray, sir. We always leave it when he's out late.

JEFFCOTE. [*flaring up.*] Take it away!

ADA. Take it away, sir?

JEFFCOTE. Yes. Do you hear? Take the damned thing away!

ADA. What about Mr. Alan's supper, sir?

JEFFCOTE. Let him do without.

ADA. Yes, sir.

ADA *takes the tray out.* JEFFCOTE *watches her, and then goes to the window to see if it is fastened.* MRS. JEFFCOTE, *mostly undressed and attired in a dressing wrap, appears in the hall.*

MRS. JEFFCOTE. Nat?

JEFFCOTE. What do you want?

MRS. JEFFCOTE. Is anything the matter?

JEFFCOTE. Why?

MRS. JEFFCOTE. I thought I heard you swearing, that's all.

JEFFCOTE. Happen I was.

MRS. JEFFCOTE. You've not quarrelled with Christopher Hawthorn?

JEFFCOTE. No, we're the best of friends. He only wanted my opinion about summat.

MRS. JEFFCOTE. What had you got to swear about, then?

JEFFCOTE. I was giving him my opinion.

MRS. JEFFCOTE. Well, but—

JEFFCOTE. That's enough. Get along to bed with you. Maybe I'll tell you all about it to-morrow. Maybe I won't!

MRS. JEFFCOTE. Well, I'm glad it's no worse. I thought you were coming to blows.

MRS. JEFFCOTE *goes out and upstairs.* JEFFCOTE *sees the two glasses of whisky and soda which neither of the men has remembered to touch. He takes his own and drinks it.* ADA *appears.*

ADA. Please, sir, do you want anything else?

JEFFCOTE. No. Get to bed. [*She is going.*] Have the other girls gone upstairs yet?

ADA. Yes, sir.

JEFFCOTE. And you've fastened the back door?

ADA. Yes, sir.

JEFFCOTE. Good night.

ADA. Good night, sir.

ADA *goes upstairs.* JEFFCOTE *slowly drinks the second glass of whisky and soda. He puts both the empty glasses on the sideboard and looks round the room. He turns out all the gases except one, which he leaves very low. He goes out into the hall, leaving the breakfast-room door open, and is seen to go out of sight to the front door, as if to assure himself that it is on the latch. Then he turns the hall gas very low indeed, and goes upstairs.*

THE CURTAIN FALLS

SCENE III

The curtain rises again immediately. The scene is the same room about two hours later, that is to say at about one o'clock in the morning. Everything looks just the same. At first there is silence. Then is heard the scratching noise of a latchkey being inserted into the front door. The process takes some time. At last the door is heard to open, and some one stumbles in, making rather too much noise. The door is closed very quietly. A match is struck in the hall, out of sight. It goes out at once. Then a figure is dimly seen to appear in the doorway of the breakfast-room, lean against the jamb and look round. It is ALAN JEFFCOTE, *who if he could be seen distinctly would be found a well-made, plump, easy-going young fellow, with a weak but healthy and attractive face and fair hair. He is of the type that runs to stoutness after thirty, unless diet and exercise are carefully attended to. At present he is too fond of luxury and good living to leave any doubt that this pleasant fellow of twenty-five will be a gross, fleshly man at forty. He is dressed by a good Manchester tailor, and everything he has is of the best. He does not stint his father's money. He has been to the Manchester Grammar School and Manchester University, but he has not lost the characteristic Hindle burr in his accent, though he speaks correctly as a rule. He does not ever speak affectedly, so that his speech harmonises with that of the other characters. This is important, for though he has had a far better education than any of the other characters except* BEATRICE, *he is essentially one of them, a Hindle man. He has no feeling that he is provincial, or that the provinces are not the principal asset of England. London he looks upon as a place where rich Lancashire men go for a spree, if they have not time to go to Monte Carlo or Paris. Manchester he looks upon as the centre or headquarters for Lancashire manufacturers, and therefore more important than London. But after all he thinks that Manchester is merely the office for Hindle and the other Lancashire towns, which are the actual source of wealth. Therefore Hindle, Blackburn, Bolton, Oldham, and the rest are far more important in his eyes than London or Manchester, and perhaps he is right. Anyhow, the feeling gives him sufficient assurance to stroll into the most fashionable hotels and restaurants, conscious that he can afford to pay for whatever he fancies, that he can behave himself, that he can treat the waiters with the confidence of an aristocrat born—and yet be patently a Lancashire man. He would never dream of trying to conceal the fact, nor indeed could he understand why anybody should wish to try and conceal such a thing. He is now slightly intoxicated, not seriously drunk, only what he would himself describe as " a bit tight ". He strikes another match and lurches towards the gas, only to find that it is already lighted. He blows out the match and tries to turn up the gas. As he reaches up he knocks a small bronze vase off the end of the mantel-piece. It falls into the fire-irons with an appalling crash.*

ALAN. Curse it!

He turns up the gas and clumsily picks up and replaces the vase. He sees on the mantel-piece a couple of letters addressed to him. He tears them open, stares at them, and crams them unread into his pocket. Then he gazes at the table as if in search of something.

ALAN. Where's that tray? Where the devil's that tray?

He shakes his head and proceeds to look in the sideboard cupboard for food. He can find none, so he turns to the whisky and soda, and fills one of the empty glasses. This he puts on the mantel-piece, and then he sits in the arm-chair by the hearth, sinks back and holds his head in his hands. He seems to be going to sleep. In the hall is observed a flickering light, coming nearer by degrees. Old NATHANIEL JEFFCOTE *appears, a lean picturesque figure in pyjamas and dressing-gown, carrying in one hand a lighted bedroom candle and in the other a poker. He comes to the door of the room, stands at the threshold and contemplates his son. At length* ALAN *seems to feel that he is not alone, for he slowly steals a glance round to the door, and encounters his father's stern gaze.*

ALAN. Hello! [*He smiles amiably.*] Thought you were in bed.

JEFFCOTE. So it's you, is it? What are you making all this din about?

ALAN. 'S not my fault. You don't s'pose I did it on purpose, do you?

JEFFCOTE. I'll not have you coming in and raising Cain at this time of night. It's enough to waken the dead!

ALAN. I can't help it. They go and stick that beastly thing up there! [*He points to the vase.*] Can't blame me for knocking it over. 'S not my fault. [*He hiccoughs.*] I can't help it.

JEFFCOTE. Are you drunk?

ALAN [*rising and standing with his back to the hearth in a dignified way.*] You've never seen me drunk yet! [*He hiccoughs.*]

JEFFCOTE *approaches him and scrutinises him by the light of the candle.*

JEFFCOTE. I've never seen thee nearer drunk, anyhow. Thou didn't drive the car home in this state, surely?

ALAN. No fear!

JEFFCOTE. Where have you left it?

ALAN. At "George and Dragon", in Hindle.

JEFFCOTE. I see. You've been at "George and Dragon"? Didn't they chuck you out at eleven?

ALAN. Ay! Then we went round to the Liberal Club.

JEFFCOTE. Who's "we"?

ALAN. Me and George Ramsbottom.

JEFFCOTE. Has George Ramsbottom been with you this week-end?

ALAN. No. I met him at the "Midland" at Manchester. We had a bit of dinner together.

JEFFCOTE. Ah! Where's George Ramsbottom been during the week-end?

ALAN. After his own devices.

JEFFCOTE. Humph! Like thyself, no doubt?

ALAN. Happen!

JEFFCOTE. What's thou been up to these Wakes?

ALAN. Nothing. Why?

JEFFCOTE. [*holding the candle up to* ALAN'S *face.*] Hast been with a girl?

ALAN. [*flinching slightly.*] No.

JEFFCOTE. Thou hardened young liar!

ALAN. [*staggered.*] Why?

JEFFCOTE. [*looking hard at him.*] Chris Hawthorn's been here to-night.

ALAN. [*vaguely.*] Chris Hawthorn?

JEFFCOTE. Ay!

ALAN *cannot bear his father's gaze. He is not able to keep up the pretence of coolness any longer. He turns towards the arm-chair and stumbles into it, his attitude of collapse denoting surrender.*

JEFFCOTE. Thou cursed young fool! I could find it in my heart to take a strap to thee, so I could. Why hadn't thou the sense to pay for thy pleasures, instead of getting mixed up with a straight girl? I've never kept thee short of brass. And if thou must have a straight girl, thou might have kept off one from the mill. Let alone her father's one of my oldest friends.

ALAN. What does he say?

JEFFCOTE. Say? What dost thou think he said? Does thou think as he come up here to return thanks?

ALAN. But—but, how did he know?

JEFFCOTE. The lass has told them, so it appears.

ALAN. She promised not to.

JEFFCOTE. Happen she did. And what then?

ALAN. What's going to be done?

JEFFCOTE. I said I'd see him treated right.

ALAN. [*brightening.*] What'll they take?

JEFFCOTE. [*dangerously.*] I said I'd see them treated

right. If thou expects I'm going to square it with a cheque, and that thou's going to slip away scot-free, thou's sadly mistaken.

ALAN. What do you want me to do?

JEFFCOTE. I know what thou's going to do. Thou's going to wed the lass.

ALAN. What do you say?

JEFFCOTE. Thou's heard me all right.

ALAN. Wed her? Fanny Hawthorn!

JEFFCOTE. Ay! Fanny Hawthorn.

ALAN. But I cannot.

JEFFCOTE. Why not?

ALAN. You know—Beatrice—I can't!

JEFFCOTE. Thou mun tell Beatrice it's off.

ALAN. How can I do that?

JEFFCOTE. That's thy look-out.

ALAN. [*rising and holding on to the mantel-piece.*] Look here. I can't do it. It isn't fair to Beatrice.

JEFFCOTE. It's a pity thou didn't think of that before thou went to Llandudno!

ALAN. But what can I tell her?

JEFFCOTE. Thou mun tell her the truth if thou can't find owt better to say.

ALAN. The truth!

ALAN *again collapses in the chair. A pause.*

JEFFCOTE. What's done is done. We've got to stand by it.

ALAN. Father! I don't want to wed Fanny. I want to wed Beatrice.

JEFFCOTE. Dost thou love Beatrice?

ALAN. Yes.

JEFFCOTE. I'm glad of it. It's right that thou should suffer as well as her.

ALAN *is overcome, and drops into dialect as he pleads.*

ALAN. Father, thou'll not make me do it! Thou'll

not make me do it! I cannot. I'd have all the folk in Hindle laughing at me.

ALAN *breaks down, excitement and drink combined being too much for him.*

JEFFCOTE. [*brusquely.*] Come now, pull thyself together.

ALAN. Ay! It's easy talking that road.

JEFFCOTE. Thou art a man, now. Not a kid!

ALAN. It's me that's got to go through it. It doesn't hurt thee if I wed Fanny Hawthorn.

JEFFCOTE. Does it not?

ALAN. No.

JEFFCOTE. So thou thinks it easy for me to see thee wed Fanny Hawthorn? Hearken! Dost know how I began life? Dost know that I started as tenter in Walmesley's shed when I were eight years of age, and that when the time comes I shall leave the biggest fortune ever made in the cotton trade in Hindle? Dost know what my thought has been when labouring these thirty years to get all that brass together? Not what pleasure I could get out of spending, but what power and influence I were piling up the while. I was set on founding a great firm that would be famous not only all over Lancashire but all over the world, like Horrockses or Calverts or Hornbys of Blackburn. Dost think as I weren't right glad when thou goes and gets engaged to Tim Farrar's lass? Tim Farrar as were Mayor of Hindle and got knighted when the King come to open the new Town Hall. Tim Farrar that owns Lane End Shed, next biggest place to Daisy Bank in Hindle. Why, it were the dearest wish of my heart to see thee wed Tim Farrar's lass; and, happen, to see thee running both mills afore I died. And now what falls out? Lad as I'd looked to to keep on the tradition and build the business bigger still, goes and weds one of my own weavers! Dost think that's no disappointment to me? Hearken! I'd put down ten thousand quid if thou could honestly wed

Beatrice Farrar. But thou can't honestly wed her, not if I put down a million. There's only one lass thou can honestly wed now, and that's Fanny Hawthorn, and by God I'm going to see that thou does it!

> JEFFCOTE *stalks out of the room with his candle and his poker, which he has never put down, and* ALAN *remains huddled up and motionless in a corner of the arm-chair.*

THE CURTAIN FALLS

ACT II

The scene is again the breakfast-room at the JEFFCOTES' *house. It is shortly after 8* P.M. *on the day following that on which the First Act took place. The evening meal, tea, is just over. Only* MR. *and* MRS. JEFFCOTE *have partaken of it.* ADA *has almost finished clearing away, there is a loaded tray on the sideboard and the coloured cloth is not yet spread, although the white cloth has been removed.* MRS. JEFFCOTE *is sitting by the hearth, and* JEFFCOTE *is standing with his back to the empty fireplace filling his pipe. It is not yet dark, but the light is fading.*

JEFFCOTE. [*to* ADA.] Come now, lass, be sharp with your siding away.

ADA *is about to spread the coloured cloth.* MRS. JEFFCOTE *rises and assists her.*

MRS. JEFFCOTE. Give me that end, Ada.

They spread the cloth whilst JEFFCOTE *lights his pipe, and then* ADA *hurries out with the tray.*

JEFFCOTE. That girl wants wakening up.

MRS. JEFFCOTE. What are you in such a hurry about, Nat?

JEFFCOTE. I've got summat to say to you.

MRS. JEFFCOTE. Something to say to me. Why couldn't you say it whilst we were having tea?

JEFFCOTE. It's not quite the sort of thing to say before the servant.

MRS. JEFFCOTE. [*surprised.*] Why, Nat, what is it?

JEFFCOTE. Last night you were talking of taking Hindle Lodge for Alan?

MRS. JEFFCOTE. Yes. I was going to call on Mrs. Plews this afternoon, only it came on wet.

JEFFCOTE. [*briefly.*] Don't go.

MRS. JEFFCOTE. Why not?

JEFFCOTE. There's no need.

MRS. JEFFCOTE. Surely, Nat, you've not changed your mind again?

JEFFCOTE. Alan won't want to live in a place like Hindle Lodge.

MRS. JEFFCOTE. His wife will.

JEFFCOTE. How do you know that?

MRS. JEFFCOTE. I've asked her.

JEFFCOTE. Nay, you've not.

MRS. JEFFCOTE. Why, Nat, I mentioned it to Beatrice only a week ago.

JEFFCOTE. Happen you did. Alan's not going to marry Beatrice.

MRS. JEFFCOTE. [*dumbfoundered.*] Not going to marry— [*She stops.*]

JEFFCOTE. That's what I said.

MRS. JEFFCOTE. Why? Have they quarrelled?

JEFFCOTE. No.

MRS. JEFFCOTE. Then, what's the matter? What has happened? When did you get to know about it?

JEFFCOTE. I first got to know about it last night.

MRS. JEFFCOTE. That was what you were talking to Alan about when you went downstairs last night?

JEFFCOTE. Ay!

MRS. JEFFCOTE. And you said you were lecturing him on coming home so late. Why didn't you tell me the truth?

JEFFCOTE. I knew you'd learn it soon enough, and I didn't want to spoil your night's rest.

MRS. JEFFCOTE. Why didn't you tell me to-day, then?

JEFFCOTE. I've been at the Mill all day.

MRS. JEFFCOTE. You could have told me as soon as you came home.

JEFFCOTE. I didn't want to spoil your tea for you.

MRS. JEFFCOTE. [*wiping her eyes.*] As if that mattered!

JEFFCOTE. Well, then, I didn't want to spoil my tea.

MRS. JEFFCOTE. Oh! Nat, what is it that's happened?

JEFFCOTE. To put it in a nutshell, Alan's not going to marry Beatrice because another girl has a better right to him.

MRS. JEFFCOTE. But how can that be? He's been engaged to Beatrice for nearly a year.

JEFFCOTE. [*grimly.*] He's only been engaged to Beatrice. With the other girl he's gone a step further.

MRS. JEFFCOTE. He's not gone and got wed already?

JEFFCOTE. No. He's not got wed. He dispensed with the ceremony.

MRS. JEFFCOTE. Dispensed with it?

JEFFCOTE. Did without.

MRS. JEFFCOTE. [*shocked.*] Oh, Nat!

JEFFCOTE. Ay. He spent last week-end with a girl at Llandudno.

MRS. JEFFCOTE. The creature!

JEFFCOTE. Eh?

MRS. JEFFCOTE. [*indignantly.*] Why are such women allowed to exist?

JEFFCOTE. [*scratching his head.*] Thou mun ask me another. I never looked on it in that light before.

MRS. JEFFCOTE. And at Llandudno, too, of all places! Why, I've been there many a time.

JEFFCOTE. What's that got to do with it?

MRS. JEFFCOTE. I shall never be able to fancy it again! And I'm so fond of the place.

JEFFCOTE. That's a pity. Happen you'll get over the feeling when they're married.

MRS. JEFFCOTE. But, Nat, it's impossible! Alan can't marry a woman of that sort!

JEFFCOTE. She's not a woman of that sort. She's a straight girl.

MRS. JEFFCOTE. How can you call her that?

JEFFCOTE. Well, you know what I mean. It's not been a matter of business with her.

MRS. JEFFCOTE. I don't see that that makes things any better. There might have been some excuse for her if it had been a matter of business. Really, Nat, you must see that the woman is not fit to marry Alan!

JEFFCOTE. Not quite so fast. You don't even know who she is yet.

MRS. JEFFCOTE. Whoever she is, if she's not above going away for the week-end with a man she can't be fit to marry our son.

JEFFCOTE. Not even when our son's the man she's been away with?

MRS. JEFFCOTE. That has nothing to do with the case. It is evident that she is a girl with absolutely no principles.

JEFFCOTE. Dash it all! at that rate some folk might say that Alan's not fit to marry her because of what he's done.

MRS. JEFFCOTE. Well, if you can't see the difference—
He does not choose to. She shrugs her shoulders and continues.
I'm surprised at you, Nat, I really am. You seem to take a delight in being perverse and making difficulties.

JEFFCOTE. Upon my soul, mother, I'd no idea thou were such an unscrupulous one before. Don't you want to do what's right?

MRS. JEFFCOTE. Can't you offer the girl some money?

JEFFCOTE. Would you think that right treatment?

MRS. JEFFCOTE. She wouldn't object. She'd jump at it.

JEFFCOTE. Shall I tell you who she is?

MRS. JEFFCOTE. Of course you'll tell me who she is.

Though that won't make me much wiser, for I don't suppose I've ever heard her name before.

JEFFCOTE. What makes you think that?

MRS. JEFFCOTE. I'm sure nobody I know would do a thing like that.

JEFFCOTE. She's not exactly a friend of yours, but her father is a very old friend of mine. His name's Christopher Hawthorn.

MRS. JEFFCOTE. [*open-mouthed.*] What!

JEFFCOTE. And the lass is his daughter Fanny.

MRS. JEFFCOTE. Fanny Hawthorn! Do you mean to tell me that the lad's going to marry one of our own weavers? Why, Nat, you must be out of your senses!

JEFFCOTE. [*stubbornly.*] Think so?

MRS. JEFFCOTE. Why, all the folk in Hindle will be laughing at us.

JEFFCOTE. Anything else?

MRS. JEFFCOTE. I should just think I have got something else. What about Timothy Farrar, for instance? Have you thought what he'll say?

JEFFCOTE. What does it matter what Tim Farrar says?

MRS. JEFFCOTE. There's Beatrice.

JEFFCOTE. Ay! there's Beatrice. I'm right sorry for that girl. But there's the other girl to be considered, mind you.

MRS. JEFFCOTE. Does Beatrice know yet?

JEFFCOTE. No. I told Alan we'd go up to Farrar's to-night and have it out with them.

MRS. JEFFCOTE. Perhaps he's there now.

JEFFCOTE. Nay. He'll not be back from Manchester yet. He was stopping later because Raleigh's had got a cable in from India, and it wasn't translated when I left. Business before pleasure, mother!

MRS. JEFFCOTE. Then, thank goodness, it's not too late.

JEFFCOTE. What do you mean by that?

MRS. JEFFCOTE. This affair has got to be stopped.

JEFFCOTE. Now, old lass, don't thou start meddling with what doesn't concern thee.

MRS. JEFFCOTE. That a nice thing! It concerns me as much as you. I've a right to have my say when it comes to a wife for Alan, and I'll not give way without a struggle to a girl like Fanny Hawthorn.

JEFFCOTE. Come, now, what's wrong with her, after all?

MRS. JEFFCOTE. She's a girl without any character.

JEFFCOTE. Now, I should say she's a girl with a good deal of character.

MRS. JEFFCOTE. The wrong sort.

JEFFCOTE. How do you know that? We don't know what made her go away with Alan.

MRS. JEFFCOTE. I do. It was one of two things. Either she's thoroughly wicked, or else she was simply trying to make him marry her, and whichever it was it's evident she's no fit wife for Alan.

JEFFCOTE. Alan should have thought of that earlier.

MRS. JEFFCOTE. You are taking much too serious a view of this affair, Nat; you are, indeed. Mind you, I'm not defending what Alan's done. I'm as shocked as any one. I know it's a sin, and a grievous one too. What puzzles me is how he could do it. I wonder what made him. I don't know where he got it from. I'm sure he didn't get it from my side of the family!

JEFFCOTE. Happen he got it from Adam.

MRS. JEFFCOTE. Very well, then, all the more reason why you should overlook it.

JEFFCOTE. We can't overlook them sort of things in Lancashire same as we could in the Garden of Eden.

MRS. JEFFCOTE. If you can't overlook it altogether, there's no reason why you should want to punish the lad like this. It's just cruelty, that's what it is, to make him marry a girl out of the mill.

JEFFCOTE. You mean she's beneath him ?

MRS. JEFFCOTE. Of course she's beneath him.

JEFFCOTE. It's queer what short memories some folks have ! What was my father, I should like to know ? And thine, too, if it comes to that ? Why, I wore clogs myself until I was past twenty.

MRS. JEFFCOTE. Yes, and if you don't look out your grandson will wear them again. Don't forget the old saying : " There's three generations from clogs to clogs ".

JEFFCOTE. A man may wear worse things than clogs. They're grand tackle for keeping the feet out of the wet.

MRS. JEFFCOTE. Don't talk so foolishly, Nat ! I know as well as you do that before you die you're hoping to see Alan a big man. Member for Hindle, perhaps. You know whether a wife like Fanny Hawthorn would be a hindrance to him or not.

JEFFCOTE. If a man's wife gets in the road of his career, then his career will have to suffer.

MRS. JEFFCOTE. And every one knows what that means. He'll be blaming her all the time for standing in his light, and so his home life will be ruined as well.

JEFFCOTE. Marriage is a ticklish business anyhow. There's always the chance of a bust-up.

MRS. JEFFCOTE. Chance indeed ! It's as sure as Fate if Alan marries Fanny, and you know that. They'll be separated in five years. We've seen cases like that before.

JEFFCOTE. And shall again, I've little doubt.

MRS. JEFFCOTE. Well, Alan's shan't be one of them if I can help it.

JEFFCOTE. But you can't, old lass. I wear the breeches in this house.

MRS. JEFFCOTE. I'll be no party to it, anyhow ! It shan't be said that I didn't lift my voice against the wedding.

MRS. JEFFCOTE *is nearly sobbing by this time. The room is in semi-darkness.* JEFFCOTE *listens.*

JEFFCOTE. There's the front door. It'll be Alan. Come now, mother, don't make a scene.

MRS. JEFFCOTE *wipes her eyes.* ADA *comes in.*

ADA. If you please, ma'am, Sir Timothy Farrar and Miss Beatrice.

MRS. JEFFCOTE. Oh! [*A pause.*] Mr. Alan hasn't come in yet?

ADA. No, ma'am.

MRS. JEFFCOTE. Are they in the drawing-room?

ADA. Yes, ma'am.

MRS. JEFFCOTE. Very well.

ADA *withdraws.*

MRS. JEFFCOTE. Dear me, Nat, this is very awkward. Why doesn't Alan come home? It's too bad of him, it is indeed.

JEFFCOTE. He's ashamed to face his mother, happen?

MRS. JEFFCOTE. He should know his mother better than that.

JEFFCOTE. Then he's trying to drive it too late to go up to Farrar's to-night.

MRS. JEFFCOTE. That's more likely.

JEFFCOTE. Very well. He's reckoned without his dad. If he's too much of a coward to face the music himself, I'll do it for him.

MRS. JEFFCOTE. What are you going to do?

JEFFCOTE. Just go and send Tim Farrar in here, while you keep Beatrice company in the other room.

MRS. JEFFCOTE. Are you going to tell him?

JEFFCOTE. Ay!

MRS. JEFFCOTE. But what shall I say to Beatrice?

JEFFCOTE. Say nowt.

MRS. JEFFCOTE. But I can't talk to her just as if nothing has happened. It would be like deceiving her. I'm not cut out for a hypocrite.

JEFFCOTE. All right. Tell her everything. She'll have to know some time.

MRS. JEFFCOTE. [*pleading*.] Need she ever know?

JEFFCOTE. Whatever falls out, it's not going to be hushed up.

MRS. JEFFCOTE. Strike a light, Nat.

He lights the gas.

Do I look as if I'd been crying?

JEFFCOTE. Why? Have you been crying?

MRS. JEFFCOTE. No.

JEFFCOTE. It doesn't show. Nothing to speak of.

MRS. JEFFCOTE *goes out, and* JEFFCOTE *lights the other gas-jets, until the room is brightly illuminated. He gets out the whisky and soda.* SIR TIMOTHY FARRAR, *a portly, red-faced, rough Lancashire man of fifty-nine or so, with a scrubby growth of hair under his chin, appears in the doorway. He is much the coarsest and commonest person in the play.*

JEFFCOTE. [*curtly*.] How do, Tim.

SIR TIMOTHY. How do, Nat.

JEFFCOTE. [*nodding to a chair*.] Sit you down.

SIR TIMOTHY. [*choosing the best chair*.] Ay—ay!

JEFFCOTE. [*holding out a cigar-box*.] The old brand.

SIR TIMOTHY. [*choosing the best cigar with deliberation*.] I'll have a drop of whisky, too, Nat.

JEFFCOTE. Help yourself.

JEFFCOTE *places the whisky handy, and then closes the door.*

So they've made you Chairman of Hindle Education Committee, Tim?

SIR TIMOTHY. Ay! Why not? Thou knows I were reet mon for the job.

JEFFCOTE. Thou's not done much studying since thou were eight year of age.

SIR TIMOTHY. Happen I haven't. But I'm going to take damn good care that Hindle new Technical School is the finest in Lancashire. Or Yorkshire either, if it comes to that!

JEFFCOTE. Why not finest in England whilst you are about it?

SIR TIMOTHY. If it's finest in Lancashire and Yorkshire it goes without saying it's finest in England. They don't know how to spend money on them in the South. Besides, what should they want with Technical Schools in them parts? They don't make anything to speak of.

JEFFCOTE. They're a poor lot, it's true.

SIR TIMOTHY. I were in London all last week.

JEFFCOTE. Corporation business?

SIR TIMOTHY. Ay!

JEFFCOTE. Expenses paid?

SIR TIMOTHY. Ay!

JEFFCOTE. That's the style.

SIR TIMOTHY. Where's the lad?

JEFFCOTE. Not got home yet.

SIR TIMOTHY. Beatrice were expecting him to telephone all day, but he didn't. So as soon as we'd done eating she were on pins and needles to look him up.

JEFFCOTE. He was coming round to your place to-night.

SIR TIMOTHY. I told the lass he'd be sure to. She hasn't seen him for ten days, thou knows, and that seems a long time when it's before the wedding. It doesn't seem so long afterwards. That reminds me! Have you seen "The Winning Post" this week?

JEFFCOTE. Nay. I rarely look at it.

SIR TIMOTHY. There's a tale in this week—it'll suit thee down to the ground.

JEFFCOTE. Hold on a bit. There's something I've a mind to tell you.

SIR TIMOTHY. Let me get mine off my chest first. It's about a fellow who took a girl away for the week-end—

JEFFCOTE. So's mine.

SIR TIMOTHY. Oh! It's the same one. [*He is disappointed.*]

JEFFCOTE. Nay, it isn't.

SIR TIMOTHY. How do you know?

JEFFCOTE. Mine's true.

SIR TIMOTHY. True, is it? [*He considers.*] Well, let's hear it. Who's the fellow?

JEFFCOTE. Chap out of Hindle.

SIR TIMOTHY. [*looking him in the face.*] Here! Who's been giving me away?

JEFFCOTE. Eh?

SIR TIMOTHY. I say who's been giving me away?

JEFFCOTE. Thee? [*He stares at* SIR TIMOTHY *and then breaks into a roar of laughter.*] Thou's given thyself away, Tim Farrar. I wasn't talking about thee at all.

SIR TIMOTHY. [*wiping his brow.*] Eh! I thought as some one had seen us at Brighton. I don't mind thee knowing, but if the wrong person gets hold of that sort of thing all Hindle is apt to hear about it. Well, who's the chap?

JEFFCOTE. Our Alan.

SIR TIMOTHY. What! The young devil! I'd like to give him a reet good hiding.

JEFFCOTE. Come. Thou'rt a nice man to talk, after what I've just learned.

SIR TIMOTHY. Hang it all, it's different with me! I'm not engaged to be wed. Why, I haven't even got a wife living. [*Fuming.*] The young beggar!

JEFFCOTE. I thought I'd better tell thee first.

SIR TIMOTHY. Ay—ay! I'll talk pretty straight to him.

JEFFCOTE. Perhaps you'll choose to tell Beatrice yourself.

SIR TIMOTHY. Tell who?

JEFFCOTE. Beatrice.

SIR TIMOTHY. Why? What's it got to do with her?

JEFFCOTE. Some one will have to tell her. She'll have to know sooner or later.

SIR TIMOTHY. God bless my soul, Nat Jeffcote! hast thou told thy missus everything thou did before thou got wed?

JEFFCOTE. I'd nowt to tell her.

SIR TIMOTHY. I always thought there was summat queer about thee, Nat. [*He shakes his head.*] Well, I'm not going to have Bee told of this affair, and that's flat. It's all over and done with.

JEFFCOTE. It's not all over. You don't understand. This girl is a decent girl, thou knows. Daughter of Chris Hawthorn.

SIR TIMOTHY. What! Him as slashes for thee?

JEFFCOTE. Ay!

SIR TIMOTHY. I've seen her. A sulky-looking wench. Well, I cannot see what difference it makes who the girl was. I reckon Alan's not going to marry her.

JEFFCOTE. That's just what he is going to do.

SIR TIMOTHY. What!

JEFFCOTE. You heard what I said.

SIR TIMOTHY. But he's going to marry my Beatrice.

JEFFCOTE. If he does he'll be had up for bigamy.

SIR TIMOTHY. Do you mean to say he's going to throw her over?

JEFFCOTE. There's no need to put it that way.

SIR TIMOTHY. There's no other way to put it if he weds Fanny Hawthorn.

JEFFCOTE. What else can he do?

SIR TIMOTHY. There's ways and means.

JEFFCOTE. For instance—

SIR TIMOTHY. It's only a question of money.

JEFFCOTE. Have you forgotten who she is?

SIR TIMOTHY. She's one of thy weavers. That'll cost thee a trifle more.

JEFFCOTE. She's daughter of one of my oldest friends.

SIR TIMOTHY. I'm one of thy oldest friends, likewise. What about my lass? Have you thought what a fool she'll look?

JEFFCOTE. I'm sorry. But t'other girl must come first. I think well enough of Beatrice to know she'll see it in that light when it's put to her.

SIR TIMOTHY. And who's going to put it to her, I should like to know?

JEFFCOTE. You can put it to her yourself, if you've a mind.

SIR TIMOTHY. Dang it! It's a nice awkward thing to talk to a lass about. Here! before I go any further with this job I want to see Alan, and know for certain what he's going to do.

JEFFCOTE. He'll do what I tell him.

SIR TIMOTHY. I doubt it! I know he's a fool, but I don't think he's such a fool as all that.

The door opens and ALAN *looks in.*

SIR TIMOTHY. Why—talk of the devil—

ALAN. Hello, Sir Timothy! Has Bee come with you?

JEFFCOTE. She's with your mother in the drawing-room.

ALAN. Right.

ALAN *is withdrawing when* JEFFCOTE *calls him back.*

JEFFCOTE. Here! I say! Just wait awhile. We've summat to say to you.

ALAN *comes in reluctantly.*

JEFFCOTE. Anything fresh in Manchester?

ALAN. No.

JEFFCOTE. Nowt for us in that cable?

ALAN. No.

JEFFCOTE. You're very late.

ALAN. I got something to eat in Manchester.

He is for withdrawing again.

JEFFCOTE. Hold on a bit. You'd better shut the door and sit down.

SIR TIMOTHY. Now then, what's all this I hear tell about thee?

ALAN. [*to* JEFFCOTE.] Have you been telling him?

JEFFCOTE. Ay!

ALAN. You'd no right to!

JEFFCOTE. Hello!

ALAN. It was my business.

JEFFCOTE. It was your business right enough, but if I'd left it to you it wouldn't have been done. I can see that you weren't for going up to Farrar's to-night.

ALAN. No, I wasn't.

JEFFCOTE. [*grimly*.] I knew it.

ALAN. And that's just why you hadn't any right to tell Sir Timothy.

JEFFCOTE. You young fool! What was the good of hanging back? Sir Timothy had got to be told some time, I reckon.

ALAN. Why?

JEFFCOTE. Why? You don't suppose he's going to see you throw his Beatrice over without knowing why?

ALAN. Who says I'm going to throw his Beatrice over?

JEFFCOTE. [*looking hard at him*.] I say so.

ALAN. Happen it would be better if you'd stick to what concerns you in future.

JEFFCOTE. [*rising*.] What the deuce dost thou mean by talking to me that road?

SIR TIMOTHY. [*rising*.] Here! hold on a bit. Don't go shouting the lad down, Nat Jeffcote. I want to hear what he's got to say.

ALAN. If father hadn't opened his mouth there'd have been no call to say anything. It wasn't me who started to make difficulties.

SIR TIMOTHY. I'll bet it wasn't. You'd have let the thing slide?

ALAN. I'd have tried to settle it.

SIR TIMOTHY. Then I take it thou's no desire to wed Fanny Hawthorn?

ALAN. I don't think it's necessary.

SIR TIMOTHY. No more do I.

JEFFCOTE. [*to* ALAN]. I thought we had this out last night. Were you so drunk that you couldn't take in what I said?

ALAN. No.

JEFFCOTE. Why did you not speak out then?

ALAN. You never gave me a chance. You did all the talking yourself.

SIR TIMOTHY. I'd be ashamed to say that. I'd like to see the man as could shut my mouth when I'd had too much drink. Thou couldn't do it, Nat, fond of shouting as thou art!

ALAN. He's not your father.

SIR TIMOTHY. Art afraid of him?

ALAN. No.

SIR TIMOTHY. Then stand up to him. I'll back thee up.

ALAN. I've told him I'm not going to wed Fanny. What more does he want?

JEFFCOTE. You've made up your mind?

ALAN. Yes.

JEFFCOTE. Very well. I've rarely been beat up to now, and I'm not going to be beat by my own lad!

SIR TIMOTHY. Hang it all, Nat, thou cannot take him by the scruff of the neck and force him to wed where he doesn't want to!

JEFFCOTE. No, that's true. And no one can force me to leave my brass where I don't want to.

SIR TIMOTHY. Thou's not serious?

JEFFCOTE. I am that.

SIR TIMOTHY. Thou wouldn't care to leave Daisy Bank outside the family.

JEFFCOTE. It wouldn't go outside the family if I left it to his cousin Travis.

SIR TIMOTHY. [*grimacing.*] Thou art a queer chap, Nat!

ALAN. So it comes to this. If I don't marry Fanny you'll leave your brass to Travis?

JEFFCOTE. That's it.

ALAN. I see. [*He thinks a moment.*] And would Travis be expected to take Fanny over along with the mill?

JEFFCOTE *winces, and makes as if to reply angrily, but he thinks better of it and remains grimly silent. A pause.*

ALAN. Very well. Leave it to Travis. I'm going to stick to Beatrice.

JEFFCOTE. Right. You haven't thought what you and Beatrice are going to live on, have you?

ALAN. I'm not such a fool that I can't earn my own living.

JEFFCOTE. What you'll earn won't go very far if you have to keep a girl like Beatrice.

ALAN. Beatrice and I can manage like you and mother did.

JEFFCOTE. No, you can't. You haven't been brought up to it.

ALAN. Then Sir Timothy will help us.

JEFFCOTE. Sir Timothy? Oh, ay! [*He laughs sardonically.*] I'd like to hear what Tim Farrar thinks of the situation now.

SIR TIMOTHY. [*scratching his head.*] It's not straight of thee, Nat. Thou's not acting right.

JEFFCOTE. I've put thee in a bit of a hole, like?

SIR TIMOTHY. Thou's made it very awkward for me.

ALAN. I like that! It was you who told me to stand up to father. You said you'd back me up.

SIR TIMOTHY. Oh, ay! I'll back thee up all right. But there's no good in losing our tempers over this job, thou knows. I don't want to see a split 'twixt thee and thy father.

ALAN. If I don't mind, I don't see why you should.

SIR TIMOTHY. Lord bless thee! if thou art bent on a row, have it thy own way. But thy father's one of my oldest friends, think on, and I'm not going to part from him for thy sake. Thou can quarrel with him if thou's a mind to, but don't expect me to do the same.

ALAN. You're trying to draw out, now.

SIR TIMOTHY. I'll stand in at anything in reason, but I'll be no party to a bust-up. Besides, now I come to think of it, I'm not sure thou's treated my Beatrice right.

ALAN. Hello!

SIR TIMOTHY. No, I'm not. When a chap's engaged he ought to behave himself. From the way thou's been carrying on thou might be married already.

ALAN. Look here! You knew all this five minutes ago, when you told me to stand up to my father. What's happened to change you?

SIR TIMOTHY. Thou's very much mistaken if thou thinks I've changed my mind because thy father's leaving the mill to thy cousin Travis. I'm not the man to do that sort of thing. Besides, what do I care about thy father's brass? I'm worth as much as he is.

JEFFCOTE. [*pleasantly*.] That's a lie, Tim Farrar.

SIR TIMOTHY. Lie or not, I'm worth enough to be able to snap my fingers at thy brass. I'll not see my lass insulted by thy lad, not if thou were ten times as rich as thou makes out!

ALAN. [*exasperated*.] But don't you see—

SIR TIMOTHY. No, I don't.

JEFFCOTE. Yes, you do. You're only trying to draw a red-herring across the track.

SIR TIMOTHY. Be damned to that for a tale!

JEFFCOTE. It's right.

SIR TIMOTHY. Dost take me for a mean beggar?

JEFFCOTE. No. I take thee for a business man. I never think of thee as owt else.

SIR TIMOTHY. [*with heat.*] Dost tell me thou can believe I don't wish Alan to marry Bee just because of what thou's said about leaving thy brass?

JEFFCOTE. I do.

A pause. SIR TIMOTHY *looks hard at* JEFFCOTE.

SIR TIMOTHY. Well! And why not?

JEFFCOTE. Don't ask me. I don't object.

ALAN. Aren't you ashamed to say that?

SIR TIMOTHY. No. And if thou'd been in weaving as long as I have, thou wouldn't either. Thou's got to keep an eye on the main chance.

ALAN. But you've got plenty of money yourself. Quite enough for the two of us.

SIR TIMOTHY. [*whimsically.*] Well, blow me if thou aren't the best business man of the lot! Thou comes along and asks me for my daughter and my money. And what does thou offer in exchange? Nowt but thyself! It isn't good enough, my lad.

ALAN. Good enough or not, it's the best I can do.

SIR TIMOTHY. It won't do for me.

ALAN. I shan't bother about you.

SIR TIMOTHY. Eh? What's that?

ALAN. I don't want to marry you. I shall leave it to Beatrice.

SIR TIMOTHY. Bee'll do what I tell her. Thou can take that from me.

ALAN. No thanks. I'll ask her myself. I don't care a hang for the pair of you. I'm going to stick to Beatrice if she'll have me. You can cut us off with a shilling if you've a mind to, both of you.

SIR TIMOTHY. [*worried.*] Hang it! Thou knows I cannot do that with my Bee. I call it taking a mean advantage of me, that I do!

JEFFCOTE. Why cannot you cut off your lass?

SIR TIMOTHY. Thou knows well enough that I cannot.

JEFFCOTE. I could.

SIR TIMOTHY. I don't doubt it. But, thank God, I'm not like thee, Nat Jeffcote. I sometimes think thou'st got a stone where thy heart should be by rights.

JEFFCOTE. Happen, I've got a pair of scales.

SIR TIMOTHY. That's nowt to boast of. I'd as soon have the stone.

The door opens and MRS. JEFFCOTE *looks in.*

MRS. JEFFCOTE. [*seeing* ALAN.] Beatrice wants to speak to you, Alan.

MRS. JEFFCOTE *enters, followed by* BEATRICE FARRAR, *a determined straightforward girl of about twenty-three.*

SIR TIMOTHY. [*to* BEATRICE.] Now my lass—

BEATRICE. Father, I want to speak to Alan.

SIR TIMOTHY. I'd like to have a word with thee first, Bee.

BEATRICE. Afterwards, father.

SIR TIMOTHY. Ay! but it'll be too late afterwards, happen!

JEFFCOTE. Come, Tim, thou can't meddle with this job.

SIR TIMOTHY. [*worried.*] I call it a bit thick!

BEATRICE. Please, father.

MRS. JEFFCOTE. Come into the drawing-room, Sir Timothy. You can smoke there, you know.

SIR TIMOTHY. [*grumbling.*] A bit thick!

He is led out by MRS. JEFFCOTE. JEFFCOTE *is following, when he turns in the doorway.*

JEFFCOTE. I'll overlook all you've said to-night if you'll be guided by me. But it's your last chance, mind.

ALAN. All right.

JEFFCOTE. [*half to himself.*] I never fancied thy cousin Travis.

SIR TIMOTHY *returns to the doorway.*

SIR TIMOTHY. [*indignantly.*] Here! What's all this? Thou wouldn't let me stop behind! What's thou been saying to Alan?

VOL. I 2 E

JEFFCOTE. Telling him not to make a fool of himself.
SIR TIMOTHY. I don't call it fair—
JEFFCOTE. Come along. Don't thee make a fool of thyself, either.

JEFFCOTE *draws* SIR TIMOTHY *out of the room.*
After they have gone ALAN *closes the door, and then turns slowly to* BEATRICE. *They do not speak at first. At last* BEATRICE *almost whispers.*

BEATRICE. Alan!
ALAN. So they've told you?
BEATRICE. Yes.
ALAN. Perhaps it's as well. I should have hated telling you.
BEATRICE. Alan, why did you—?
ALAN. I don't know. It was her lips.
BEATRICE. Her lips?
ALAN. I suppose so.
BEATRICE. I—I see.
ALAN. I'm not a proper cad, Bee. I haven't been telling her one tale and you another. It was all an accident, like.
BEATRICE. You mean it wasn't arranged?
ALAN. No, indeed, it wasn't. I shouldn't like you to think that, Bee. I ran across her at Blackpool.
BEATRICE. You didn't go to Blackpool to meet her?
ALAN. On my oath I didn't! I went there in the car with George Ramsbottom.
BEATRICE. What became of him?
ALAN. Him! Oh! George is a pal. He made himself scarce.
BEATRICE. Just as you would have done, I suppose, if he had been in your place?
ALAN. Of course! What else can a fellow do? Two's company, you know. But old George would be all right. I daresay he picked up something himself.

BEATRICE. You knew her before you met her at Blackpool?

ALAN. Of course. There's not so many pretty girls in Hindle that you can miss one like Fanny Hawthorn. I knew her well enough, but on the straight, mind you. I thought she looked gay, that was all. I'd hardly spoken to her before I ran into her at the Tower at Blackpool.

BEATRICE. So you met her at the Tower?

ALAN. Yes. We'd just had dinner at the Metropole Grill-room, George and I, and I daresay we had drunk about as much champagne as was good for us. We looked in at the Tower for a lark, and we ran into Fanny in the Ball-room. She had a girl with her—Mary—Mary—something or other. I forget. Anyhow, George took Mary on, and I went with Fanny.

BEATRICE. Yes?

ALAN. Next day I got her to come with me in the car. We went to Llandudno.

BEATRICE. Yes?

ALAN. There's not much more to say.

BEATRICE. And I've got to be satisfied with that?

ALAN. What else do you want me to tell you?

BEATRICE. Didn't you ever think of me?

ALAN. Yes, Bee, I suppose I did. But you weren't there, you see, and she was. That was what did it. Being near her and looking at her lips. Then I forgot everything else. Oh! I know. I'm a beast. I couldn't help it. I suppose you can never understand. It's too much to expect you to see the difference.

BEATRICE. Between me and Fanny?

ALAN. Yes. Fanny was just an amusement—a lark. I thought of her as a girl to have a bit of fun with. Going off with her was like going off and getting tight for once in a way. You wouldn't care for me to do that, but if I did you wouldn't think very seriously about it. You wouldn't want to break off our engagement for that. I wonder if you can look on this affair of Fanny's as something like getting tight—only worse. I'm ashamed of myself, just as I should be if you caught me drunk. I can't defend myself. I feel just an utter swine. What I felt for Fanny was simply—base—horrible—

BEATRICE. And how had you always thought of me?

ALAN. Oh, Bee, what I felt for you was something—higher—finer—

BEATRICE. Was it? Or are you only trying to make yourself believe that?

ALAN. No. I respected you.

BEATRICE. [*thinking*.] I wonder which feeling a woman would rather arouse. And I wonder which is most like love?

ALAN. All the time, Bee, I have never loved any one else but you.

BEATRICE. You say so now. But, forgive me, dear, how am I to know? You have given Fanny the greater proof.

ALAN. I'm trying to show you that Fanny was one thing, you were another. Can't you understand that a fellow may love one girl and amuse himself with another? [*Despondently*.] No, I don't suppose you ever can.

BEATRICE. I think I can. We were different kinds of women. On separate planes. It didn't matter to the one how you treated the other.

ALAN. That's it. Going away with Fanny was just a fancy—a sort of freak.

BEATRICE. But you have never given me any proof half so great as that.

ALAN. Haven't I? I'll give it you now. You know that father says I am to marry Fanny?

BEATRICE. Your mother told me he wished it.

ALAN. Wished it! He's set his mind on it. He won't leave me a farthing unless I marry her.

BEATRICE. What did you tell him?

ALAN. If you can't guess that you haven't much confidence in me.

BEATRICE. That's hardly my fault, is it?

ALAN. No. Well, I told him I'd see him damned first—or words to that effect.

BEATRICE. [*with a movement of pleasure.*] You did?

ALAN. Yes. Is that good enough for you, Bee? You wanted proof that it is you I love. I've chucked away everything I had to expect in the world rather than give you up. Isn't that good enough for you?

BEATRICE. Alan!

ALAN. [*quickly clasping her.*] Bee, in a way I've been faithful to you all the time. I tried hard enough to forget all about you, but I couldn't. Often and often I thought about you. Sometimes I thought about you when I was kissing Fanny. I tried to pretend she was you. She never guessed, of course. She thought it was her I was kissing. But it wasn't. It was you. Oh, the awfulness of having another girl in my arms and wanting you!

BEATRICE *does not answer. She closes her eyes, overcome.*

Bee, you'll stick to me, although I shan't have a penny? I'll get to work, though. I'll work for you. You won't have any cause to reproach me. If only you'll stick to me. If only you'll tell me you forgive me!

BEATRICE. [*at length.*] Could you have forgiven me if I had done the same as you?

ALAN. [*surprised.*] But—you—you couldn't do it!

BEATRICE. Fanny Hawthorn did.

ALAN. She's not your class.

BEATRICE. She's a woman.

ALAN. That's just it. It's different with a woman.

BEATRICE. Yet you expect me to forgive you. It doesn't seem fair!

ALAN. It isn't fair. But it's usual.

BEATRICE. It's what everybody agrees to.

ALAN. You always say that you aren't one of these advanced women. You ought to agree to it as well.

BEATRICE. I do. I can see that there is a difference between men and women in cases of this sort.

ALAN. You can?

BEATRICE. Men haven't so much self-control.

ALAN. Don't be cruel, Bee. There's no need to rub it in!

BEATRICE. I'm not being personal, Alan. I'm old-fashioned enough to really believe there is that difference. You see, men have never had to exercise self-control like women have. And so I'm old-fashioned enough to be able to forgive you.

ALAN. To forgive me, and marry me, in spite of what has happened, and in spite of your father and mine?

BEATRICE. I care nothing for my father or yours. I care a good deal for what has happened, but it shows, I think, that you need me even more than I need you. For I do need you, Alan. So much that nothing on earth could make me break off our engagement, if I felt that it was at all possible to let it go on. But it isn't. It's impossible.

ALAN. Impossible? Why do you say that? Of course it's not impossible.

BEATRICE. Yes, it is. Because to all intents and purposes you are already married.

ALAN. No, Bee!

BEATRICE. You say I'm old-fashioned. Old-fashioned people used to think that when a man treated a girl as you have treated Fanny it was his duty to marry her.

ALAN. You aren't going to talk to me like father, Bee?

BEATRICE. Yes. But with your father it is only a fad. You know it isn't that with me. I love you, and I believe that you love me. And yet I am asking you to give me up for Fanny. You may be sure that only the very strongest reasons could make me do that.

ALAN. Reasons! Reasons! Don't talk about reasons, when you are doing a thing like this!

BEATRICE. You may not be able to understand my reasons. You have always laughed at me because I go to church and believe things that you don't believe.

ALAN. I may have laughed, but I've never tried to interfere with you.

BEATRICE. Nor I with you. We mustn't begin it now, either of us.

ALAN. Is this what your religion leads you to? Do you call it a Christian thing to leave me in the lurch with Fanny Hawthorn? When I need you so much more than I've ever done before?

BEATRICE. I don't know. It's not what I can argue about. I was born to look at things just in the way I do, and I can't help believing what I do.

ALAN. And what you believe comes before me?

BEATRICE. It comes before everything. [*A pause.*] Alan, promise that you'll do what I wish.

ALAN. You love me?

BEATRICE. If I love anything on earth I love you.

ALAN. And you want me to marry Fanny?

BEATRICE. Yes. Oh, Alan! can't you see what a splendid sacrifice you have it in your power to make? Not only to do the right thing, but to give up so much in order to do it. [*A pause.*] Alan, promise me.

ALAN. [*nodding sullenly.*] Very well.

BEATRICE. [*gladly.*] You have sufficient courage and strength?

ALAN. I'll do what you ask, but only because I can see that your talk is all humbug. You don't love me. You are shocked by what I did, and you're glad to find a good excuse for getting rid of me. All right. I understand.

BEATRICE. [*in agony*.] You don't—you don't understand.

ALAN. Faugh! You might have spared me all that goody-goody business.

BEATRICE. [*faintly*.] Please—

ALAN. You don't care for me a bit.

BEATRICE. [*passionately*.] Alan! You don't know what it's costing me.

ALAN *looks at her keenly, and then seizes her violently and kisses her several times. She yields to him and returns his embrace.*

ALAN. [*speaking quickly and excitedly*.] Bee, you're talking nonsense. You can't give me up—you can't give me up, however much you try.

BEATRICE *tears herself away from him.*

BEATRICE. You don't know me. I can. I will. I shall never be your wife.

ALAN. I won't take that for an answer—Bee—

BEATRICE. No, no, no! Never, never! whilst Fanny Hawthorn has a better right to you than I have.

There is a long pause. At length comes a knock at the door.

ALAN. Hello!

JEFFCOTE *puts his head inside.*

JEFFCOTE. Nine o'clock.

ALAN. What of it?

JEFFCOTE. Hawthorns are due up here at nine.

ALAN. [*shortly*.] Oh!

BEATRICE. Is my father there?

JEFFCOTE. Ay! [*Calling*.] Tim!

SIR TIMOTHY *appears in the doorway.*

SIR TIMOTHY. Well? Fixed it up, eh?

BEATRICE. Alan and I are not going to be married, father.

There is a pause.

JEFFCOTE. Ah!

SIR TIMOTHY. I'm sure it's all for the best, lass.
BEATRICE. Are you quite ready, father? I want you to take me home.
SIR TIMOTHY. Ay—ay! Shall I get thee a cab, Bee?
BEATRICE. I'd rather walk, please. [BEATRICE *goes to the door.*] I'll write to you, Alan.
She goes out, followed by SIR TIMOTHY.
JEFFCOTE. So you've thought better of it?
ALAN. Seems so.
JEFFCOTE. And you'll wed Fanny Hawthorn, I take it?
ALAN. [*laconically.*] Ay!
JEFFCOTE. Thou'rt a good lad, Alan. I'm right pleased with thee.
ALAN *bursts into a loud peal of mirthless laughter.*
JEFFCOTE *stares at* ALAN *in surprise.*
JEFFCOTE. What's the matter?
ALAN. Nothing, father.
He flings himself listlessly into an arm-chair.
JEFFCOTE, *after another look at him, scratches his head and goes out.*

THE CURTAIN FALLS

ACT III

The scene is the same as in the previous Act, the time a few minutes later. The room is empty. ADA *opens the door and shows in* MRS. HAWTHORN, CHRISTOPHER, *and* FANNY, *who file in silently and awkwardly. Instead of a hat,* FANNY *is wearing the shawl that Lancashire weavers commonly wear when going to the Mill.*

ADA. [*glancing back at them from the door.*] Will you take a seat, please?

ADA *goes out.* CHRISTOPHER *and* MRS. HAWTHORN *sit on chairs placed against the back wall.* FANNY *remains standing.*

MRS. HAWTHORN. Fanny, sit you down.

FANNY *silently seats herself. They are all three in a row along the back wall, very stiff and awkward. Presently* JEFFCOTE *enters. The* HAWTHORNS *all rise. He greets the three drily.*

JEFFCOTE. [*nodding.*] Evening, Chris. [*To* MRS. HAWTHORN.] Good evening. [*He stops in front of* FANNY.] Good evening, lass.

He eyes her from tip to toe with a searching stare. She returns it quite simply and boldly.

JEFFCOTE. [*satisfied.*] Ay!

He turns away to the hearth, where he takes his stand just as MRS. JEFFCOTE *comes in. She is stiff and ill at ease.*

MRS. JEFFCOTE. [*to them all without looking at them.*] Good evening.

MRS. HAWTHORN *and* CHRISTOPHER *murmur a*

greeting, and MRS. JEFFCOTE *passes on to the fire, having cut them as nearly as she dared.* ALAN *lounges in sheepishly. He does not say anything, but nods to the three in a subdued way, and sits down sullenly on the left, far away from his father and mother.*

JEFFCOTE. [*to the* HAWTHORNS.] Sit down.

They are about to sit against the wall as before, but he stops them.

JEFFCOTE. Not there. Draw up to the table.

They seat themselves round the table. The disposition of the characters is as follows. On the extreme left is ALAN, *in a big arm-chair. Sitting on the left of the table is* FANNY. *Behind the table,* MRS. HAWTHORN. *On the right of the table,* CHRISTOPHER. *Further to the right, in an arm-chair near the hearth, is* MRS. JEFFCOTE. *As for* JEFFCOTE, *he stands up with his back to the empty fireplace. Thus he can dominate the scene and walk about if he feels inclined.*

JEFFCOTE. Well, here we are, all of us. We know what's brought us together. It's not a nice job, but it's got to be gone through, so we may as well get to business right away.

CHRISTOPHER. Ay!

JEFFCOTE. We don't need to say owt about what's happened, do we?

MRS. HAWTHORN. No, I don't see as we need.

MRS. JEFFCOTE. Excuse me. I think we do. I know hardly anything of what has happened.

MRS. HAWTHORN. It's admitted by them both.

MRS. JEFFCOTE. But what is admitted by them both? It's rather important to know that.

MRS. HAWTHORN. You're hoping that we won't be able to prove owt against Alan. You think that happen he'll be able to wriggle out of it.

JEFFCOTE. There'll be no wriggling out. Alan has got to pay what he owes, and I don't think there's any doubt what that is. It's true I've only heard his version. What's Fanny told you?

CHRISTOPHER. Nowt.

JEFFCOTE. Nowt?

CHRISTOPHER. Nowt.

JEFFCOTE. How's that?

MRS. HAWTHORN. She's turned stupid, that's why.

JEFFCOTE. I'll have to have a go at her, then. [*To* FANNY.] It seems my lad met you one night in Blackpool and asked you to go to Llandudno with him?

FANNY. Yes. What then?

JEFFCOTE. He was drunk?

FANNY. No. He wasn't what you'd call drunk.

JEFFCOTE. As near as makes no matter, I'll bet.

FANNY. Anyhow, he was sober enough next morning when we went away.

JEFFCOTE. And where did you stay at Llandudno? Did he take you to an hotel?

FANNY *does not reply*.

MRS. HAWTHORN. [*sharply*.] Now then, Fanny.

JEFFCOTE. Come, lass, open thy mouth.

ALAN. All right, father. I'll answer for Fanny. We stopped at St. Elvies Hotel, Saturday till Monday.

JEFFCOTE. What did you stop as?

ALAN. Man and wife.

MRS. HAWTHORN. [*gratified*.] Ah!

ALAN. You'll find it in the register if you go there and look it up.

JEFFCOTE. [*to* MRS. JEFFCOTE.] There. Are you satisfied?

MRS. JEFFCOTE. Quite, thank you, Nat. That was all I wanted to know. I didn't want there to be any mistake.

CHRISTOPHER. There's one thing bothering me. That postcard. It was posted in Blackpool on Sunday. I don't see how you managed it if you left on Saturday.

FANNY. I wrote it beforehand and left it for Mary to post on Sunday morning.

MRS. HAWTHORN. So Mary was in at all this!

FANNY. If Mary hadn't been drowned you'd never have found out about it. I'd never have opened my mouth, and Alan knows that.

MRS. HAWTHORN. Well, Mary's got her reward, poor lass!

CHRISTOPHER. There's more in this than chance, it seems to me.

MRS. HAWTHORN. The ways of the Lord are mysterious and wonderful. We can't pretend to understand them. He used Mary as an instrument for His purpose.

JEFFCOTE. Happen. But if He did it seems cruel hard on Mary, like. However, it's all over and done with, and can't be mended now, worse luck! These two young ones have made fools of themselves. That don't matter so much. The worst feature of it is they've made a fool of me. We've got to decide what's to be done. [*To* MRS. HAWTHORN.] I gave Chris a message for you last night.

MRS. HAWTHORN. Yes, you said as how you'd see us treated right.

JEFFCOTE. That's it. That's what I'm going to do. Now what do you reckon is the right way to settle this job?

MRS. HAWTHORN. He ought to marry her. I'll never be satisfied with owt less.

JEFFCOTE. That's your idea, too, Chris?

CHRISTOPHER. Ay!

JEFFCOTE. It's mine as well. [MRS. HAWTHORN *nods eagerly*.] Before I knew who the chap was I said he should wed her, and I'm not going back on that now I find he's my own son. The missus there doesn't see it in the same light, but she'll have to make the best of it. She's in a minority of one, as they say.

MRS. HAWTHORN. Then we may take it that Alan's agreeable?

JEFFCOTE. Whether he's agreeable or not I cannot say. He's willing, and that'll have to be enough for you.

MRS. HAWTHORN. You'll excuse me mentioning it, but what about the other girl?

JEFFCOTE. What other girl? Has he been carrying on with another one as well?

MRS. JEFFCOTE. She means Beatrice. Alan was engaged to Miss Farrar.

MRS. HAWTHORN. Yes, that's it. What about her?

JEFFCOTE. That's off now. No need to talk of that.

CHRISTOPHER. The lad's no longer engaged to her?

MRS. JEFFCOTE. No.

MRS. HAWTHORN. And he's quite free to wed our Fanny?

JEFFCOTE. He is so far as we know.

MRS. HAWTHORN. Then the sooner it's done the better.

JEFFCOTE. We've only to get the licence.

CHRISTOPHER. [*brokenly.*] I'm sure—I'm sure—we're very grateful.

MRS. HAWTHORN. [*wiping her eyes.*] Yes, we are indeed. Though, of course, it's only what we'd a right to expect.

CHRISTOPHER. I'm sure, Mrs. Jeffcote, that you'll try and look on Fanny more kindly in time.

MRS. JEFFCOTE. I hope I shall, Mr. Hawthorn. Perhaps it's all for the best. More unlikely matches have turned out all right in the end.

MRS. HAWTHORN. I'm sure there's nothing can be said against Fanny save that she's got a will of her own. And after all, there's a many of us have that.

CHRISTOPHER. She's always been a good girl up to now. You can put trust in her, Alan.

JEFFCOTE. It's evidently high time Alan got wed,

that's all I can say, and it may as well be to Fanny as to any one else. She's had to work at the loom for her living, and that does no woman any harm. My missus has worked at the loom in her time, though you'd never think it to look at her now, and if Fanny turns out half as good as her, Alan won't have done so badly. Now we've got to settle when the wedding's to be.

MRS. JEFFCOTE. What sort of wedding is it to be?

JEFFCOTE. You women had better fix that up.

MRS. JEFFCOTE. It ought to be quiet.

JEFFCOTE. It'll be quiet, you may lay your shirt on that! We shan't hold a reception at the Town Hall this journey.

MRS. JEFFCOTE. I should prefer it to take place at the Registrar's.

MRS. HAWTHORN. No. I'll never agree to that. Not on any account.

MRS. JEFFCOTE. Why not?

MRS. HAWTHORN. No. In church, if you please, with the banns and everything. There's been enough irregular work about this job already. We'll have it done properly this time.

ALAN. I should like to hear what Fanny says.

MRS. HAWTHORN. Fanny'll do what's thought best for her.

ALAN. Anyhow, we'll hear what she thinks about it, if you please.

FANNY. I was just wondering where I come in.

MRS. HAWTHORN. Where you come in? You're a nice one to talk! You'd have been in a fine mess, happen, if you hadn't had us to look after you. You ought to be very thankful to us all, instead of sitting there hard like.

JEFFCOTE. You'd better leave it to us, lass. We'll settle this job for you.

FANNY. It's very good of you. You'll hire the parson and get the licence and make all the arrangements on your own without consulting me, and I shall have nothing to do save turn up meek as a lamb at the church or registry office or whatever it is.

JEFFCOTE. That's about all you'll be required to do.

FANNY. You'll look rather foolish if that's just what I won't do.

MRS. HAWTHORN. Don't talk silly, Fanny.

JEFFCOTE. What does she mean by that?

MRS. HAWTHORN. Nothing. She's only showing off, like. Don't heed her.

MRS. JEFFCOTE. I beg your pardon. We will heed her, if you please. We'll see what it is she means by that.

JEFFCOTE. Hark you, lass. I'm having no hanky-panky work now. You'll have to do what you're bid, or maybe you'll find yourself in the cart.

CHRISTOPHER. Fanny, you'll not turn stupid now?

FANNY. It doesn't suit me to let you settle my affairs without so much as consulting me.

MRS. HAWTHORN. Consulting you! What is there to consult you about, I'd like to know? You want to marry Alan, I suppose, and all we're talking about is the best way to bring it about.

FANNY. That's just where you make the mistake. I don't want to marry Alan.

JEFFCOTE. Eh?

FANNY. And what's more, I haven't the least intention of marrying him.

MRS. HAWTHORN. She's taken leave of her senses!

They are all surprised. ALAN *is puzzled.* MRS. JEFFCOTE *visibly brightens.*

JEFFCOTE. Now then, what the devil do you mean by that?

FANNY. I mean what I say, and I'll trouble you to talk to me without swearing at me. I'm not one of the family yet.

JEFFCOTE. Well, I'm hanged!

He is much more polite to FANNY *after this, for she has impressed him. But now he rubs his head and looks round queerly at the others.*

CHRISTOPHER. Why won't you wed him? Have you got summat against him?

FANNY. That's my affair.

MRS. HAWTHORN. But you must give us a reason.

FANNY *remains obstinately silent.*

CHRISTOPHER. It's no good talking to her when she's in this mood. I know her better than you do. She won't open her mouth, no, not if she was going to be hung.

JEFFCOTE. Dost thou mean to tell me that all us folk are to stand here and let this girl beat us?

CHRISTOPHER. Fanny'll get her own way.

JEFFCOTE. We'll see.

MRS. JEFFCOTE. Why shouldn't she have her own way? I don't think we have any right to press her; I don't really.

MRS. HAWTHORN. All you're after is to get Alan out of the hole he's in. You don't care about Fanny.

MRS. JEFFCOTE. I'm sorry for Fanny, but of course I care more about my own child.

MRS. HAWTHORN. Well, and so do we.

MRS. JEFFCOTE. After all, she knows better than we do whether she wants to marry Alan.

JEFFCOTE. Now then, Alan, what's the meaning of this?

ALAN. I don't know, father.

JEFFCOTE. You've not been getting at her to-day and wheedling her into this?

ALAN. Good Lord, no! What would have been the good of that? Besides, I never thought of it.

JEFFCOTE. Well, *I* can't account for it!

ALAN. Look here, father, just let me have a talk to her alone. It's not likely she'll care to speak with all you folk sitting round.

JEFFCOTE. Do you reckon she'll open her mouth to you?

ALAN. I can but try, though it's true she never takes much notice of what I say.

JEFFCOTE. We'll give you fifteen minutes. [*He looks at his watch.*] If thou cannot talk a lass round in that time thou ought to be jolly well ashamed of thyself. I know I could have done it when I was thy age. Mother, you'd better show Chris and his missus into t'other room for a bit.

MRS. JEFFCOTE *goes to the door*.

MRS. JEFFCOTE. Will you come this way, please?

MRS. JEFFCOTE *goes out, followed by* CHRISTOPHER.

MRS. HAWTHORN. Now, Fanny, think on what you're doing. For God's sake, have a bit of common sense!

FANNY *is silent*. MRS. HAWTHORN *goes out*.

JEFFCOTE. Fifteen minutes. And if you're not done then we shall come in whether or not.

JEFFCOTE *goes out*.

ALAN. Look here, Fanny, what's all this nonsense about?

FANNY. What nonsense?

ALAN. Why won't you marry me? My father's serious enough. He means it when he says he wants you to. He's as stupid as a mule when he once gets an idea into his head.

FANNY. As if I didn't know that. He's like you, for that matter!

ALAN. Well, then, what are you afraid of?

FANNY. Afraid? Who says I am afraid?

ALAN. I don't see what else it can be.

FANNY. You can't understand a girl not jumping at you when she gets the chance, can you?

ALAN. I can't understand you not taking me when you get the chance.

FANNY. How is it you aren't going to marry Beatrice Farrar?

ALAN. I can't marry both of you.

FANNY. Weren't you fond of her?

ALAN. Very.

FANNY. But you were fonder of me—Eh?

ALAN. Well—

FANNY. Come now, you must have been or you wouldn't have given her up for me.

ALAN. I gave her up because my father made me.

FANNY. Made you? Good Lord, a chap of your age!

ALAN. My father's a man who will have his own way.

FANNY. You can tell him to go and hang himself. He hasn't got any hold over you.

ALAN. That's just what he has. He can keep me short of brass.

FANNY. Earn some brass.

ALAN. Ay! I can earn some brass, but it'll mean hard work and it'll take time. And, after all, I shan't earn anything like what I get now.

FANNY. Then all you want to wed me for is what you'll get with me? I'm to be given away with a pound of tea, as it were?

ALAN. No. You know I like you, Fanny—I'm fond of you.

FANNY. You didn't give up Beatrice Farrar because of me, but because of the money.

ALAN. If it comes to that, I didn't really give her up at all. I may as well be straight with you. It was she that gave me up.

FANNY. What did she do that for? Her father's plenty of money, and she can get round him, I'll bet, if you can't get round yours.

ALAN. She gave me up because she thought it was her duty to.

FANNY. You mean because she didn't fancy my leavings.

ALAN. No. Because she thought you had the right to marry me.

FANNY. Glory! She must be queer!

ALAN. It was jolly fine of her. You ought to be the first to see that.

FANNY. Fine to give you up? [*She shrugs her shoulders, and then admits grudgingly.*] Well, I reckon it was a sacrifice of a sort. That is, if she loves you. If I loved a chap I wouldn't do that.

ALAN. You would. You're doing it now.

FANNY. Eh?

ALAN. Women are more unselfish than men and no mistake!

FANNY. What are you getting at?

ALAN. I know why you won't marry me.

FANNY. Do you? [*She smiles.*] Well, spit it out, lad!

ALAN. You're doing it for my sake.

FANNY. How do you make that out?

ALAN. You don't want to spoil my life.

FANNY. Thanks! Much obliged for the compliment.

ALAN. I'm not intending to say anything unkind, but of course it's as clear as daylight that you'd damage my prospects, and all that sort of thing. You can see that, can't you?

FANNY. Ay! I can see it now you point it out. I hadn't thought of it before.

ALAN. Then, that isn't why you refused me?

FANNY. Sorry to disappoint you, but it's not.

ALAN. I didn't see what else it could be.

FANNY. Don't you kid yourself, my lad! It isn't because I'm afraid of spoiling your life that I'm refusing you, but because I'm afraid of spoiling mine! That didn't occur to you?

ALAN. It didn't.

FANNY. You never thought that anybody else could be as selfish as yourself.

ALAN. I may be very conceited, but I don't see how you can hurt yourself by wedding me. You'd come in for plenty of brass, anyhow.

FANNY. I don't know as money's much to go by when it comes to a job of this sort. It's more important to get the right chap.

ALAN. You like me well enough?

FANNY. Suppose it didn't last? Weddings brought about this road have a knack of turning out badly. Would you ever forget it was your father bade you marry me? No fear! You'd bear me a grudge all my life for that.

ALAN. Hang it! I'm not such a cad as you make out.

FANNY. You wouldn't be able to help it. It mostly happens that road. Look at old Mrs. Eastwood—hers was a case like ours. Old Joe Eastwood's father made them wed. And she's been separated from him these thirty years, living all alone in that big house at Valley Edge. Got any amount of brass, she has, but she's so lonesome-like she does her own housework for the sake of something to occupy her time. The tradesfolk catch her washing the front steps. You don't find me making a mess of my life like that.

ALAN. Look here, Fanny, I promise you I'll treat you fair all the time. You don't need to fear that folk'll look down on you. We shall have too much money for that.

FANNY. I can manage all right on twenty-five bob a week.

ALAN. Happen you can. It's not the brass altogether. You do like me, as well, don't you?

FANNY. Have you only just thought of that part of the bargain?

ALAN. Don't be silly. I thought of it long ago. You do like me? You wouldn't have gone to Llandudno with me if you hadn't liked me?

FANNY. Oh! yes, I liked you.

ALAN. And don't you like me now?

FANNY. You're a nice, clean, well-made lad. Oh, ay! I like you right enough.

ALAN. Then, Fanny, for God's sake, marry me, and let's get this job settled.

FANNY. Not me!

ALAN. But you must. Don't you see it's your duty to?

FANNY. Oh! come now, you aren't going to start preaching to me?

ALAN. No. I don't mean duty in the way Beatrice did. I mean your duty to me. You've got me into a hole, and it's only fair you should get me out.

FANNY. I like your cheek!

ALAN. But just look here. I'm going to fall between two stools. It's all up with Beatrice, of course. And if you won't have me I shall have parted from her to no purpose; besides getting kicked out of the house by my father, more than likely!

FANNY. Nay, nay! He'll not punish you for this. He doesn't know it's your fault I'm not willing to wed you.

ALAN. He may. It's not fair, but it would be father all over to do that.

FANNY. He'll be only too pleased to get shut of me without eating his own words. He'll forgive you on the spot, and you can make it up with Beatrice to-morrow.

ALAN. I can never make it up with Bee.

FANNY. Get away!

ALAN. You won't understand a girl like Bee. I couldn't think of even trying for months, and then it may be too late. I'm not the only pebble on the beach. And I'm a damaged one, at that!

FANNY. She's fond of you, you said?

ALAN. Yes. I think she's very fond of me.

FANNY. Then she'll make it up in a fortnight.

ALAN. [*moodily.*] You said you were fond of me once, but it hasn't taken you long to alter.

FANNY. All women aren't built alike. Beatrice is religious. She'll be sorry for you. I was fond of you in a way.

ALAN. But you didn't ever really love me?

FANNY. Love you? Good heavens, of course not! Why on earth should I love you? You were just some one to have a bit of fun with. You were an amusement—a lark.

ALAN. [*shocked.*] Fanny! Is that all you cared for me?

FANNY. How much more did you care for me?

ALAN. But it's not the same. I'm a man.

FANNY. You're a man, and I was your little fancy. Well, I'm a woman, and you were my little fancy. You wouldn't prevent a woman enjoying herself as well as a man, if she takes it into her head?

ALAN. But do you mean to say that you didn't care any more for me than a fellow cares for any girl he happens to pick up?

FANNY. Yes. Are you shocked?

ALAN. It's a bit thick; it is really!

FANNY. You're a beauty to talk!

ALAN. It sounds so jolly immoral. I never thought of a girl looking on a chap just like that! I made sure you wanted to marry me if you got the chance.

FANNY. No fear! You're not good enough for me. The chap Fanny Hawthorn weds has got to be made of different stuff from you, my lad. My husband, if ever I have one, will be a man, not a fellow who'll throw over his girl at his father's bidding! Strikes me the sons of these rich manufacturers are all much alike. They seem a bit weak in the upper storey. It's their fathers' brass that's too much for them, happen! They don't know how to spend it properly. They're like chaps who can't carry their drink because they aren't used to it. The brass gets into their heads, like!

ALAN. Hang it, Fanny, I'm not quite a fool.

FANNY. No. You're not a fool altogether. But there's summat lacking. You're not man enough for me. You're a nice lad, and I'm fond of you. But I couldn't ever marry you. We've had a right good time together, I'll never forget that. It has been a right good time, and no mistake! We've enjoyed ourselves proper! But all good times have to come to an end, and ours is over now. Come along, now, and bid me farewell.

ALAN. I can't make you out rightly, Fanny, but you're a damn good sort, and I wish there were more like you!

FANNY. [*holding out her hand.*] Good-bye, old lad.

ALAN. [*grasping her hand.*] Good-bye, Fanny! And good luck!

A slight pause.

FANNY. And now call them in again.

ALAN. [*looking at his watch.*] Time's not up yet.

FANNY. Never heed! Let's get it over.

ALAN *goes out, and* FANNY *returns to her chair and sits down. Presently* ALAN *comes in and stands by the door, whilst* MRS. JEFFCOTE, MRS. HAWTHORN, *and* CHRISTOPHER *file in and resume their original positions. Last of all comes* JEFFCOTE, *and* ALAN *leaves the door and goes back to his chair.* JEFFCOTE *comes straight behind the table.*

JEFFCOTE. Well? What's it to be?

ALAN *and* FANNY *look at each other.* Come. What's it to be? You, Fanny, have you come to your senses?

FANNY. I've never left them, so far as I know.

JEFFCOTE. Are you going to wed our Alan or are you not?

FANNY. I'm not.

JEFFCOTE. Ah!

MRS. HAWTHORN. Well!

ALAN. It's no good, father. I can't help it. I've done all I can. She won't have me.

JEFFCOTE. I'm beat this time! I wash my hands of it! There's no fathoming a woman. And these are the creatures that want us to give them votes!

After this JEFFCOTE *does not attempt to influence the discussion.*

MRS. HAWTHORN. [*in a shrill voice.*] Do you tell us you're throwing away a chance like this?

FANNY. You've heard.

MRS. HAWTHORN. I call it wicked, I do, indeed! I can see you are downright bad, through and through! There's one thing I tell you straight. Our house is no place for thee after this.

FANNY. You're not really angry with me because of what I've done. It's because I'm not going to have any of Mr. Jeffcote's money that you want to turn me out of the house.

MRS. HAWTHORN. It's not! It's because you choose to be a girl who's lost her reputation, instead of letting Alan make you into an honest woman.

FANNY. How can he do that?

MRS. HAWTHORN. By wedding you, of course.

FANNY. You called him a blackguard this morning.

MRS. HAWTHORN. So he is a blackguard.

FANNY. I don't see how marrying a blackguard is going to turn me into an honest woman!

MRS. HAWTHORN. If he marries you he won't be a blackguard any longer.

FANNY. Then it looks as if I'm asked to wed him to turn him into an honest man?

ALAN. It's no use bandying words about what's over and done with. I want to know what's all this talk of turning Fanny out of doors?

CHRISTOPHER. Take no heed of it! My missus don't rightly know what she's saying just now.

MRS. HAWTHORN. Don't she? You're making a big mistake if you think that. Fanny can go home and fetch her things, and after that she may pack off!

CHRISTOPHER. That she'll not!

MRS. HAWTHORN. Then I'll make it so hot for her in the house, and for thee, too, that thou'll be glad to see the back of her!

FANNY. This hasn't got anything to do with Mr. and Mrs. Jeffcote, has it?

FANNY *rises.*

ALAN. It's got something to do with me, though! I'm not going to see you without a home.

FANNY. [*smiling.*] It's right good of you, Alan, but I shan't starve. I'm not without a trade at my finger tips, thou knows. I'm a Lancashire lass, and so long as there's weaving sheds in Lancashire I shall earn enough brass to keep me going. I wouldn't live at home again after this, not anyhow! I'm going to be on my own in future. [*To* CHRISTOPHER.] You've no call to be afraid. I'm not going to disgrace you. But so long as I've to live my own life I don't see why I shouldn't choose what it's to be.

CHRISTOPHER. [*rising.*] We're in the road here! Come, Sarah!

JEFFCOTE. I'm sorry, Chris. I've done my best for thee.

CHRISTOPHER. Ay! I know. I'm grateful to thee, Nat. [*To* MRS. JEFFCOTE.] Good night, ma'am.

MRS. JEFFCOTE. Good night.

MRS. HAWTHORN *and* CHRISTOPHER *go out, the former seething with suppressed resentment. Neither says anything to* ALAN. JEFFCOTE *opens the door for them and follows them into the hall. As* FANNY *is going out* MRS. JEFFCOTE *speaks.*

MRS. JEFFCOTE. Good-bye, Fanny Hawthorn. If ever you want help, come to me.

FANNY. Ah! You didn't want us to wed?

MRS. JEFFCOTE. No.
FANNY. You were straight enough.
MRS. JEFFCOTE. I'm sure this is the best way out. I couldn't see any hope the other way.
FANNY. Good-bye.

MRS. JEFFCOTE *holds out her hand, and they shake hands. Then* FANNY *goes out with* ALAN. *There is a slight pause.* MRS. JEFFCOTE *goes to the door and looks into the hall, and then returns to her chair. Soon* JEFFCOTE *comes in.*

MRS. JEFFCOTE. Have they gone?
JEFFCOTE. Ay!

JEFFCOTE *sits down in an arm-chair and fills his pipe.*

MRS. JEFFCOTE. Where's Alan?
JEFFCOTE. Don't know.
MRS. JEFFCOTE. What are you going to do about him?
JEFFCOTE. Don't know.

ALAN *opens the door and looks in. He is wearing a light burberry mackintosh and a soft felt hat.*

MRS. JEFFCOTE. Where are you going to, Alan?
ALAN. I'm just running round to Farrar's.
JEFFCOTE. [*surprised.*] To Farrar's?
ALAN. To see Beatrice.
MRS. JEFFCOTE. [*not surprised.*] You're going to ask her to marry you?
ALAN. [*laconically.*] Happen I am!
JEFFCOTE. Well, I'm damned! Dost thou reckon she'll have thee?
ALAN. That remains to be seen.
JEFFCOTE. Aren't you reckoning without me?
ALAN. Can't help that.

JEFFCOTE *grunts.*

ALAN. Hang it! be fair. I've done my best. It's not my fault that Fanny won't have me.
JEFFCOTE. Well, if Beatrice Farrar can fancy thee, it's not for me to be too particular.

ALAN. Thank you, father.

JEFFCOTE. Get along! I'm disgusted with thee!

ALAN *slips out of the door.*

MRS. JEFFCOTE. Beatrice will have him.

JEFFCOTE. How do you know that?

MRS. JEFFCOTE. She loves him; she told me.

JEFFCOTE. There's no accounting for tastes! [*He ruminates.*] So Beatrice loves him, does she? Eh! but women are queer folk! Who'd have thought that Fanny would refuse to wed him?

MRS. JEFFCOTE. It is strange. It makes you feel there is something in Providence after all.

THE CURTAIN FALLS

END OF VOL. I